Rereading Paul
Together

Rereading Paul
Together

Protestant and Catholic
Perspectives on Justification

Edited by David E. Aune

𝕭
Baker Academic
Grand Rapids, Michigan

© 2006 by David E. Aune

Published by Baker Academic
a division of Baker Publishing Group
P.O. Box 6287, Grand Rapids, MI 49516-6287
www.bakeracademic.com

Printed in the United States of America

Library of Congress Cataloging-in-Publication Data
Rereading Paul together : Protestant and Catholic perspectives on justification / edited by David E. Aune.
    p.   cm.
Includes bibliographical references and indexes.
ISBN 10: 0-8010-2840-X (pbk.)
ISBN 978-0-8010-2840-3 (pbk.)
    1. Justification (Christian theology) 2. Protestant churches—Doctrines. 3. Catholic Church—Doctrines. 4. Bible. N.T. Epistles of Paul—Criticism, interpretation. etc. I. Aune, David Edward.
BT764.3.R47 2006
234′.7—dc22   2006020599

Except in chapters 4, 6, and 7, Scripture quotations, unless otherwise indicated, are from the New Revised Standard Version of the Bible [NRSV], copyright 1989, Division of Christian Education of the National Council of the Churches of Christ in the United States of America. Used by permission. All rights reserved.

In Memoriam

David G. Truemper

(1939–2004)

Contents

Preface

This collection of essays is, for the most part, based on a colloquium held February 1–2, 2002, at the University of Notre Dame titled "Rereading Paul Together: A Colloquium on the Modern Critical Study and Teaching of Pauline Theology in Educational and Ecumenical Context." This colloquium was sponsored jointly by the University of Notre Dame and Valparaiso University. The special focus of the colloquium was the Joint Declaration on the Doctrine of Justification,[1] a document ratified by the Lutheran World Federation and representatives of the Roman Catholic Church on October 31, 1999, in Augsburg, Germany. Since by all accounts this was an ecumenical event of great historical significance, culminating in an important agreement that was the fruit of more than thirty years of Lutheran-Catholic dialogue, it seemed appropriate to organize a colloquium centering on this significant document. It also seemed appropriate to expand the discussion from a more restricted Lutheran–Roman Catholic dialogue to a broader Protestant–Roman Catholic discussion, since the doctrine of justification remains a central concern for modern Protestant churches that trace their heritage back to both the magisterial as well as the radical wings of the Reformation. The Joint Declaration was made possible by a common reading of the Pauline letters, hence the title of the present work, *Rereading Paul Together*.

Not all the papers originally presented at this colloquium have been included in this collection, and those that are have been subject to revision. Two essays not part of the original colloquium are those by Susan K.

1. The Lutheran World Federation and the Roman Catholic Church, *Joint Declaration on the Doctrine of Justification* (Grand Rapids: Eerdmans, 2000).

9

Wood and David E. Aune; both were added to fill significant lacunae in the original program of the colloquium, which was restricted to the better part of two days. In the fall of 2000, during the initial planning stages of this colloquium, I approached the late David Truemper (to whom this book is dedicated; see the acknowledgments), chair of the Department of Theology at Valparaiso University, to ask if he, members of his department, and Valparaiso University would consider becoming joint sponsors of the proposed colloquium. This proposal was met with great enthusiasm by David and his colleague Richard DeMaris and subsequently by the Department of Theology at Valparaiso. We decided to begin with an overview of the document of the Joint Declaration (to be presented by David Truemper), followed by papers on the interpretation of Paul in the early church (David Rylaarsdam) and medieval and Reformation readings of Paul (Randall Zachman). Thereafter we thought it important to ask two veteran participants in the American Lutheran-Catholic dialogue to present papers on justification by faith in Pauline thought from a Catholic perspective (Joseph Fitzmyer), and a Lutheran perspective (John Reumann), with responses to each. Then we thought it important to provide theological perspectives on the Joint Declaration by a Roman Catholic theologian (Franz Josef van Beeck, S.J.), and a Lutheran theologian (Michael Root). During the afternoon of February 2 we held three breakout group discussions: "Perspectives on Paul in Church History" (led by Randall Zachman), "The Center(s) of Pauline Thought" (led by Richard DeMaris), and "Understanding the Joint Declaration" (led by David Truemper). Finally, in a concluding plenary session a number of issues raised by the colloquium were discussed, followed by an ecumenical prayer service planned and led by Maxwell Johnson and Michael Driscoll.

In the first chapter, "Introduction to the Joint Declaration on the Doctrine of Justification," David Truemper focuses on three general matters: (1) he summarizes the process that led up to the signing of the Joint Declaration on October 31, 1999 (i.e., How did we get here?); (2) he discusses aspects of the content of the Joint Declaration and its consequences for the work of teaching and scholarship by Roman Catholic and Lutheran institutions of higher learning (i.e., What is this place really like?); and (3) he describes those necessary habits of mind and heart that might lead to further progress in ecumenical dialogue (i.e., How shall we go on from here?).

From the perspective of a Roman Catholic systematic theologian, Susan Wood, professor of theology, Marquette University, then discusses the "Catholic Reception of the Joint Declaration on the Doctrine of Justification." After recounting the process leading up to the Joint Declaration, Professor Wood summarizes the issues raised in the Official Catholic Response to the draft of the Joint Declaration on June 25, 1998, which centered on five matters: (1) the meaning of *simul iustus et peccator*; (2) the question of merit; (3) the doctrine of justification as the sole criterion; (4) whether human beings are passive or whether they cooperate with grace; and (5) the authority of the consensus reached by the Lutheran World Federation. By signing the Official Common Statement,[2] the two dialogue partners have not only reached a high level of consensus on the doctrine of justification but also have nullified the mutual condemnations that have divided the two traditions for centuries. The Catholic doctrine of justification originated from a theology of baptism, while the Reformation doctrine originated in a theology of penance. Thus Catholics emphasize the renewal of the inner person through grace (a metaphysical, anthropological perspective), while Lutherans emphasize justification as forgiving love (an existential, christological perspective). Wood goes on to discuss such issues as the teaching on merit, the theology of *simul iustus et peccator*, baptism and justification, justification as a criterion that norms all other criteria (a traditional Lutheran view that Catholics question), and the effect on church identity (the tendency for both traditions to define themselves contrastively). The consensus is a great step forward, even though there is not yet agreement on the role of justification in social ethics, authority in the church, ministry, the sacraments, or the relationship between the word of God and doctrine.

Responding from the perspective of a Lutheran systematic theologian, Michael Root, dean and professor of theology, Lutheran Theological Southern Seminary, asks how the Joint Declaration affects the self-understanding and tasks of "Lutheran systematic theology," not just theology done by Lutherans. Root first addresses the question of whether there should be such a thing as "Lutheran systematic theology," a theology shaped by distinctively Lutheran commitments. This task is called into question by the Joint Declaration, in which Lutherans and Catholics agree on basic truths of the doctrine of justification, though it should not be understood that Lutherans and Catholics are really saying the same thing about justification. Lutheran theology has traditionally been "contrastive," i.e., formulated in terms of analogous dichotomies considered definitive for the right understanding of Christian faith (law/gospel, letter/spirit, human action/divine action, works/faith). Unlike these contrastive formulations, the mediating character of the Joint Declaration must be anthema. A noncontrastive Lutheran systematic theology (such as those by Robert Jenson and Wolfhart Pannenberg), how-

2. *Joint Declaration on the Doctrine of Justification*, 41–42.

ever, would take up Reformation insights but not make them determinative for its structure and would be open to insights from other traditions. A distinctly Lutheran systematic theology will avoid being sectarian only if it systematically contradicts the contradiction of Christian division. Root then turns to the issue of justification as a criterion, an issue that lacks conceptual clarity among Lutherans; distinctions are rarely made between a necessary criterion, a sufficient criterion, and a necessary and sufficient criterion, or between justification as a criterion and as a hermeneutical key (confused in the Joint Declaration). Eberhard Jüngel is a Lutheran theologian who uses justification with inconsistent meanings and functions and his claim that it is the one and only criterion of all theological statements is implausible. Extreme versions of the criteriological and hermeneutical role of justification raise the question of the normative role of the Bible in Lutheran systematic theology. Root concludes his essay by bringing up two substantive issues: (1) the necessity of a renewed discussion of the *simul iustus et peccator*, and (2) the role of human action in justification.

Turning to the Biblical evidence, Joseph A. Fitzmyer, S.J., professor of New Testament emeritus, The Catholic University of America, discusses justification by faith in Pauline thought from a Roman Catholic perspective. Fitzmyer first summarizes the Old Testament and Palestinian Jewish background of Pauline righteousness and justification as a background for discussing the Christ-event (the passion, death, and resurrection; also the burial, exaltation, and heavenly intercession) and its effects. Paul sums up the effects of the Christ-event under ten different images for conceiving the basic mystery of Christ and his role: justification, salvation, reconciliation, expiation, redemption, freedom, sanctification, transformation, new creation, and glorification, each expressing a distinctive aspect of christocentric soteriology. The most frequently occurring image of the ten, however, is that of justification. Fitzmyer then turns to the theme of Pauline justification in Romans and Galatians where justification, emphasized as an effect of the Christ-event, is an image drawn from an Old Testament and Jewish background. The verb *dikaioō* in the Septuagint means "to acquit, vindicate, declare innocent, justify," a meaning not found in pagan Greek. When Paul speaks of Christ justifying the sinner, he means that because of the Christ-event the sinner hears God's verdict of "not guilty," for God who is "righteous" is the one who justifies the sinner. But does Paul's use of *dikaioō* mean "declare righteous" (the normal Septuagint meaning) or "make righteous" (the effective meaning normally expected with the -oō class of causative verbs)? Since patristic times, the effective sense of "make righteous" dominated (in Chrysostom and Augustine), though in Reformation times Melanchthon maintained both meanings (*Apology* 4.72). No matter how the verb is construed, for Paul sinners are justified by God's grace through faith (Rom. 3:21–26). The phrase "deeds of the law" in Galatians 2:15–16 means "concrete acts demanded by the [Mosaic] law," and therefore Fitzmyer disagrees with J. D. G. Dunn, who construes the phrase to mean "boundary markers." After commenting on Romans 4:1–8 and 10:3, Fitzmyer then discusses other Pauline texts including Philippians 2:12–13; Ephesians 2:8–10; and Acts 13:38–39. He concludes that while justification by grace through faith is an important Pauline tenet, Paul describes the effects of the Christ-event in other ways, so that the gospel cannot be limited to justification by faith.

Richard DeMaris, a Presbyterian professor of theology on the Valparaiso faculty, responds to Joseph Fitzmyer's essay from a Protestant perspective in "Can We Reread Paul Together Any Longer? Joseph A. Fitzmyer's View of Pauline Justification in Context." DeMaris begins by emphasizing the problems that the historical-critical method has presented for the theological understanding of the Bible. While some scholars (e.g., Raymond Brown) maintain that the historical-critical method has led to important ecumenical dialogue, others have called attention to the limits of that method. The problem with a distinctive Catholic or Protestant approach to the Bible is that it opens the door to the provincialization of biblical studies and endangers ecumenical dialogue. The author argues that historical criticism in the dialogue between Catholic and Lutheran biblical scholars that eventuated in the Joint Declaration has actually facilitated the convergence of the two traditions. Fitzmyer's essay, according to DeMaris, is an example of this convergence of Roman Catholic and Protestant thought. Fitzmyer's essay begins like a typical historical-critical study of the Old Testament and Jewish background of righteousness or justification in Paul, though Catholic shading appears in his treatment of the Pauline evidence. He concludes that justification, while the most important, is nevertheless one among many soteriological terms. Among the great changes in Pauline scholarship beginning in the 1970s and 1980s, when the Lutheran-Catholic dialogue on justification was nearing an end, DeMaris mentions many Protestant voices that have questioned the theological centrality of the doctrine of justification and suggests that this has become a new consensus. The author calls attention to the New Perspective on Paul that arose through the work of Stendahl, Sanders, and Dunn. The wide acceptance of many aspects of the New Perspective threatens to diminish the significance of the agreement represented by the Joint Declaration. DeMaris suggests that other clouds on the horizon of Pauline scholarship make it doubtful that the consensus that was foundational for the Joint Declaration can be achieved again in the near future. For example, recent work has thrown doubt on the coherence of Pauline theology. Turning to prospects for the future, the author makes several suggestions centering on the very positive connotation that the noun *dikaiosynē* had in pagan Greek discourse and how that could contribute to a more adequate understanding of righteousness or justification in Paul.

John Reumann, emeritus professor of New Testament at Lutheran Theological Seminary at Philadelphia and a veteran participant in American Lutheran-Catholic dialogue, deals with a Lutheran view of justification by faith in Pauline thought. After briefly summarizing some of the work that went into the production of the Joint Declaration, Reumann focuses on Lutheran tradition, nicely distinguishing his own perspective within it. The author is conscious of serving two masters: academic biblical scholarship (i.e., sound scriptural interpretation) and confessional commitment (i.e., the *Augsburg Confession, Apology, Smalcald Articles*, and the *Formula of Concord*). As a Lutheran, Reumann prefers a wider view of justification (as in the *Augsburg Confession*), not the narrower one as a step in the *ordo salutis* (*Formula of Concord*). Complicating the author's task is the fact that American Lutherans have not been united in emphasizing the centrality of justification. In general, Lutherans expect justification to be forensic, involving an understanding of themselves as sinners until the final eschatological transformation. At the same time justification means that unrighteous people are made righteous. The author then turns to the issue of the biblical data in the Joint Declaration, responding to several criticisms often with helpful insider information: (1) The criticism that the Joint Declaration used too little Scripture has ignored the publications leading up to that document, such as the volume edited by Reumann, *"Righteousness" in the New Testament* (1982). (2) The objection that the section "Biblical Message of Justification" (Joint Declaration, §§8–12) is confusing reflects an unawareness of the problematic drafting history of those paragraphs. (3) The criticism that the Joint Declaration does not reflect the current trends in Pauline studies may be unaware of the decades of work involved and may overestimate the payoff of new methods and approaches for ecumenical discussion. Turning to the issue of righteousness or justification in Philippians, Reumann focuses on a detailed discussion of Philippians 3:4–11.

Margaret Mitchell, Roman Catholic layperson and professor of New Testament at the University of Chicago, offers the essay "A Conversation among Friends" in response to Reumann, emphasizing the important role that personal friendships have in ecumenical cooperation. She maintains that hers is *a* Roman Catholic response, not necessarily representative of all

Roman Catholicism. Turning to methodological considerations, Mitchell focuses on four issues: (1) In the interplay between exegetical and confessional aspects of ecumenical dialogue, the author wonders why Reumann so cautiously approaches the more recent "state of the art" approaches to Pauline studies, since any post-Enlightenment approaches could be seen as problematic. (2) What is the relationship between "the doctrine" and "the experience" of justification by faith for Reumann and for Paul? Do we really have access to Paul's experience of justification from Philippians 3? (3) Reumann emphasizes that Galatians 2:16 is not new with Paul but is a consensus statement of Antiochene theology, a view that Mitchell finds unconvincing. But, given the Lutheran criterion of *sola scriptura*, why does Reumann even need to bolster a biblical statement such as that found in Galatians 2:16 by arguing that it was held by others and not just Paul? (4) Mitchell then raises the question of the extent to which Reumann's interpretation of Philippians 3 is dependent on the Lukan portrait of Paul. Finally, the author turns from methodological issues to a brief comparison between John Chrysostom and John Reumann on the exegesis of Philippians 3. Her own view of the place of justification in Paul's thought is in partial agreement with Fitzmyer's decahedron of ten salvific effects of the Christ-event, though she prefers to use the metaphor of different transparencies that can overlay one another in viewing of the single central Christ-event.

David Rylaarsdam, associate professor of historical theology at Calvin Theological Seminary, provides an overview of early church interpretations of Paul. The author begins by dispelling three untenable theories: (1) Paul was received smoothly and linearly into the theology of the early church; (2) Paul was unimportant, suppressed, or even rejected by the mainstream church until the second century; and (3) the Greek Christian understanding of Pauline soteriology was fundamentally deficient. Rylaarsdam then investigates some Pauline soteriological themes in Origen, Chrysostom, and Augustine.

The author discusses Origen's thought in three stages: (1) the divine economy, (2) divinization, and (3) the soteriological themes of grace, faith, and works. In the divine economy God creates all souls with the possibility that free will may lead them astray. As a result of a premundane fall, each soul is enfleshed according to its degree of sin. In the penal and therapeutic state of corporeality, each soul struggles with good and evil to be morally purified to return to the spiritual world. God's providential goodness uses human freedom and its abuse to move the cosmos toward the restoration of all things. Divinization, not justification, is Origen's primary image of salvation. Human beings are created in the image of God, the Logos, who works in the believer to purify the soul and restore in it the image of God. The soul moves through stages of knowledge, ultimately progressing to a face-to-face knowledge of God, attaining the likeness of God, and so receives the gift of divinity. While grace and faith are necessary for salvation, grace is more essential and logically is prior to faith. Faith is both a gift of God and a work of human beings, though Origin's emphasis on one or the other oscillates. Works are important for salvation, for true faith cannot exist without works; yet faith automatically includes the adoption of Christ's virtues. Perfection is not immediate; believers are guided in growth by moral precepts such as those found in Paul.

Turning to Chrysostom, Rylaarsdam emphasizes the importance of the person of Paul for his Pauline exegesis. For Chrysostom, Paul had reached a higher degree of divinity than any other human and is the outstanding model for imitation, so that imitating Paul is imitating Christ. Chrysostom also emphasized Paul as a zealous teacher, the consummate guide of souls. Chrysostom's most important image of soteriology is union with God made possible by the incarnation, the unity of divinity and flesh making our renewed association with God possible. Grace plays a more important role than human effort in the process of salvation, though the latter is not eliminated. Good works are the fruit of faith because faith brings about a change of the "inclination" or "ruling purpose."

Augustine's interpretation of Paul evolved during his lifetime, moving through Manichaeism to Neoplatonism. After 397 CE he argued that election is not based on faith, as if a reward for merit; in a judgment made before time, God graciously elects some sinners from humanity and not others. Augustine's views on human freedom, grace, faith, and justification evolved further many years later as a result of his struggle with the Pelagians. Fallen humans are responsible agents because they enjoy free choice, but they do not possess the freedom necessary to use the power of free choice appropriately. From fallen humanity God chooses some for salvation, securing a voluntary response of faith by divine mercy alone. Against the Pelagians he asserts that faith is a completely divine gift. By dwelling in us, God moves us to love him, loving himself through us. Nevertheless the believer remains divided between self-love and love for God, interpreting Romans 7:14–25 autobiographically as Paul's own experience of a believer under grace. A Christian can accomplish the good only by great effort, and cooperating with God's grace acquires merit that is itself a gift given only to the elect and not to every believer. Augustine understood *iustificare* to mean "to make just or righteous" and thought that a person is made just by the justice given by God in Christ and by faith in Christ, both gifts of God.

Faith is Christ's saving work in the soul leading it toward the proper love of God and neighbor. Rylaarsdam concludes his essay by comparing Origen, Chrysostom, and Augustine, emphasizing how modern ecumenical dialogue can profit from the colorful palette of early Pauline interpretations.

In "Medieval and Reformation Readings of Paul," Randall Zachman, associate professor of theology at the University of Notre Dame, emphasizes the importance of the theological legacy of Augustine for both the Middle Ages and the Reformation. The central concern dominating the reading of Paul after Augustine was how to love God, others, and ourselves in a rightly ordered way. In the Latin West this reading was challenged by the Reformation; the central issue became how we as sinners can know with certainty that God loves us. These two ways of reading Paul, the Augustinian and the Lutheran, remain to this day. Zachman's essay falls into two main parts: first the Augustinian and Latin reading of Paul, illustrated by a selection of Pauline texts read from this perspective; and second, the Lutheran and Evangelical reading of Paul, similarly illustrated by a selection of Pauline texts read from that perspective.

The Augustinian reading of Paul centered on Jesus' admonition to love the Lord our God with all our mind, soul, and strength, and to love our neighbors as ourselves. Using Neoplatonic ontology, Augustine regarded God as the highest good, with human beings created in his image and likeness so that they might participate in God by loving him, which would be their true and eternal happiness. God must be loved, however, not to make us happy but for the sake of God—and that will result in our happiness. Sin is the perversion of the order of love in which God is not loved for his own sake. Human attempts to find happiness by loving themselves or others will fail, ultimately leading to temporal and eternal death. If sin is misdirected love, grace is God's gift that rightly orders love within us, enabling us to love God for the sake of God, freeing us to love ourselves and others for their own sake. Since we have the ability to love God by grace, we have hope, but because we are tempted to love ourselves or others in the place of God, we have reason to fear. Zachman then describes how various Pauline texts were read from the Augustinian perspective. Passages discussed include, in order, Romans 5:12 (centering on original sin and baptism); 1:24 (those choosing sin are passed over by God); 1:20–21 (Augustine: the impact of sin on the will); 7:7 (the law cannot give us what it commands of us); 8:2 (only grace, given by the Spirit, frees from sin); 5:5 (the grace of God means that the Spirit infuses us with love for God); 7:22–23 (our desires war against this love for God, though desire itself is not sin); Philippians 2:12–13 (the work of salvation is entirely due to the work of God in us); Galatians 6:8 (the grace of God sets the believer on the path of salvation, but it is up to the believer to sow according to the Spirit to reap eternal life from the Spirit); 1 Corinthians 4:7 (we are crowned at the end of the race only because the grace of God is at work in us); Ephesians 1:4 (all striving for eternal life by the grace at work within us is due to the eternal election of God).

Turning to the Lutheran and Evangelical reading of Paul, Zachman argues that the Evangelical reading represented a sharp break with the Augustinian reading of Paul as a whole. Luther provided the catalyst for many readers to turn their attention from the grace of God as work *within* believers, to the grace of God manifested in what God has done *for* us in Jesus Christ. Luther's reading centered on the problem of concupiscence in the baptized. His experience of a terrified conscience moved him to a new understanding of the wrath of God, that is, the active will of God to punish sinners. Luther regarded concupiscence in believers as mortal sin, even if they do not consent to it, and deserving of punishment. After 1519, Luther concluded that the infusion of grace did not reveal sin but rather it was the law of God that did so. Believers are led to despair entirely of all they might do to avoid wrath and attain eternal life. They must turn to Jesus Christ, to the gospel that proclaims that our sin is forgiven not by the gift of God within us but by the cross of Christ. The shift from understanding grace as the work of God within us by the Holy Spirit to the grace of God as the work of God for us in Jesus Christ created a new narrative reading of Paul. Zachman then discusses a series of Pauline texts as read by Lutherans and Evangelicals, often neglected by the Augustinian perspective, including Romans 3:20 (attempting to remove sin and avoid wrath by doing the works of the law is doomed to failure, since the role of the law is to reveal sin); 8:3 (once the law has revealed sin, only Christ has the power to remove this burden from the conscience by taking our sin upon himself and giving us righteousness and life); 5:8 (the Evangelical reading presupposes the terrified conscience: how can I, a sinner, know that God loves me?); 5:1 (only faith in Christ can bring peace to the terrified conscience); 4:23 (since righteousness and eternal life are the free gift of God, one cannot merit these divine blessings); 1 Corinthians 7:7 (not celibacy or monasticism, but the mutual subjection found in marriage and family are the stations to which God has called us); Galatians 1:8 (the Church of Rome was guilty of preaching a gospel contrary to the one preached by Paul).

In the final chapter, David E. Aune, professor of New Testament at the University of Notre Dame, focuses on the nearly impenetrable jungle of readings of Paul relating to justification found throughout the twentieth and early twenty-first centuries. Aune begins by maintaining that from a historical perspective, a religion of works-righteousness is just one way among many of conceptualizing the relations thought to exist between human beings and the divine. The essay focuses on seven issues relating to ways in which modern scholars read Paul, the first of which is the question of Jewish versus Hellenistic influence on Paul. Early in the twentieth century, Paul, though Jewish, was often contrasted with Judaism. The Göttingen-centered history of religions school tended to emphasize Paul's Hellenistic background, though conservatives then tended to trace all features of Paul's thought back to the influence of the Septuagint. Next Aune considers the connection between Paul's Damascus experience and his understanding of justification by faith. While Paul's experience has been labeled either a "conversion" or a "prophetic call," most agree that this experience was linked with his drive to evangelize Gentiles. Many go further and argue that as a result of his Damascus experience, Paul recognized that Jesus was indeed the Messiah and/or that the salvific function of the law was null and void. Some (e.g., Seyoon Kim) have gone so far as to argue that all the basic features of Paul's theology are found in nuce in his conversion/prophetic call. Turning to the issues of particularism and universalism, Aune calls attention to a number of scholars, from F. C. Baur to Boyarin and Dunn, who have maintained that Paul saw Judaism as particularistic and Christianity as universalistic; the chief problem with the law is simply its religious and cultural particularism.

In treating the New Perspective on Paul, the author summarizes the work of several seminal figures, including Krister Stendahl, E. P. Sanders, James D. G. Dunn, and Tom Wright, as well as many who have criticized one or another of their views. Following Sanders, the New Perspective rejected as both false and malevolent the portrait of Judaism formerly gained through reading Paul, a portrait of a decadent, legalistic religion characterized by works-righteousness. Sanders proposed that the basic character of Judaism was "covenantal nomism," by which he meant that Jews were in the covenant because they had been chosen by a gracious God. Provision for sin was made by repentance and atonement, while obedience to the law was how one remained in the covenant, not the means by which one entered the covenant. When Paul became a follower of Jesus, he recognized that salvation is available only through Christ (the solution), and from that position deduced the plight (all other ways of salvation are wrong). Dunn, who gave the New Perspective its name, accepted many aspects of Sanders's reading of Paul but rejected his way of arguing that Paul moved from "solution" to "plight." Dunn argued that "the works of the law" (Gal. 2:16 and elsewhere) did not refer to the ethical demands of the law, obedience to which produced salvation, but rather to the ritual practices of Judaism such as circumcision, food laws, and Sabbath observance—all badges of membership in the Jewish people. Dunn later expanded this understanding by construing "works of the law" to mean practices that distinguish "us" (Jews) from "them" (Gentiles). Tom Wright, who agrees with many of the views of Sanders and Dunn, developed some of these views quite independently of them at about the same period. The essay then turns to summarize some of the many criticisms of the New Perspective, including leveling all varieties of early Judaism to the "covenantal nomism" model, the penchant for overinterpreting Jewish texts that fit this model and underinterpreting those that do not, and the attack on the "Lutheran" interpretation of Paul.

The author then reviews the "new view" of Paul, associated with such Pauline scholars as Lloyd Gaston, Stanley Stowers, John Lodge, and John Gager, as well as Mark Nanos. According to this "new view," which thus far has had little impact on subsequent Pauline scholarship, Paul held to the validity of two covenants, the law for Judaism and Christ for the Gentiles. Jews need not believe in Christ, and Gentiles need not obey the Torah.

Aune then discusses justification by faith, by treating aspects of the Lutheran-Catholic debate (with a particular focus on the work of John Reumann and Joseph Fitzmyer, S.J.); the role that justification plays in the New Perspective (it is denied a central position in Pauline thought, and has social as well as individual dimensions); the Evangelical debate on the imputation of righteousness; the role of justification as a candidate for the center of Paul's thought; and the debate regarding whether *pistis [Iēsou] Christou* constitutes an objective genitive (faith in Christ, the traditional view) or a subjective genitive (Christ's faith, the more recent view). The essay concludes with several reflections, including the striking exegetical agreement on the part of both Lutheran and Roman Catholic Pauline scholars and the meager positive influence of the New Perspective on the Joint Declaration.

David E. Aune

Acknowledgments

The 2002 colloquium on which this collection of essays is based would not have happened were it not for the support and generosity of the Institute for Scholarship in the Liberal Arts at the University of Notre Dame and the theology departments of the University of Notre Dame and Valparaiso University, particularly the chairpersons of each department, John Cavadini of Notre Dame and the late David G. Truemper of Valparaiso. In addition, I want to thank a number of faculty members from both universities who chaired the eight sessions and the breakout group discussions: John Cavadini, Blake Leyerle, Richard DeMaris, David Truemper, Larry Cunningham, Randall Zachman, and Jean Porter. The editor is particularly grateful to Harriet Baldwin, the conference coordinator at the Center for Continuing Education at the University of Notre Dame, for competently superintending all the physical arrangements necessary for holding such a colloquium. The president of the University of Notre Dame, Rev. Edward A. Malloy, C.S.C., graciously opened the colloquium with an official welcome from the university. Finally, I want to express my gratitude to the Rev. Maxwell Johnson and the Rev. Michael Driscoll, both from the Liturgical Studies program in the Department of Theology at the University of Notre Dame, for preparing and presiding at an ecumenical prayer service at the conclusion of the colloquium.

This collection of essays is dedicated to the memory of the Rev. Dr. David G. Truemper (1939–2004). David joined the faculty of the Department of Theology at Valparaiso in 1967 and served as chair from 1993 to 2004. Originally ordained in the Lutheran Church–Missouri Synod, he eventually transferred his clergy status to the Evangelical Lutheran Church of America. David died on October 30, 2004, after a two-year struggle with cancer. The funeral sermon was preached by the Rev. Dr. Frederick A. Niedner, professor and acting chair of the Department of Theology, in the Chapel of the Resurrection on campus on November 3, 2004.[1] At the time of his death David had served as the executive director of the Institute of Liturgical Studies at Valparaiso for twenty-five years, and had also served for nearly thirteen years (1992–2004) as the executive director of the Council of Societies for the Study of Religion, which had executive offices at Valparaiso. He served as secretary of the North American Academy of Liturgy from 1984 to 1996 and was a key figure in its incorporation in 1992. David had a strong ecumenical orientation and was a participant in Lutheran (ELCA)–Mennonite dialogue and the Lutheran (ELCA)–Church of Christ (Disciples of Christ) dialogue initiated in recent years. The Rereading Paul Together colloquium would not have become a reality had it not been for David's enthusiasm, cooperation, and participation, and I am grateful that I got to know him, even though for such a short time. He was indeed a man of the church and of the academy and, as he once was quoted as saying, "[W]hen faith and learning mesh, the result is genuinely thrilling!"

David E. Aune

---

1. Frederick A. Niedner, "Sermon at the Funeral of David G. Truemper," CurTM 32 (2005): 5–9.

Contributors

David E. Aune, professor of New Testament and Christian origins, University of Notre Dame (Notre Dame, Indiana)

Richard E. DeMaris, professor of New Testament, Valparaiso University (Valparaiso, Indiana)

Joseph A. Fitzmyer, S.J., professor of New Testament, emeritus, The Catholic University of America (Washington, DC)

Margaret M. Mitchell, professor of New Testament and early Christian literature, University of Chicago

John Reumann, Ministerium of Pennsylvania Professor of the New Testament and Greek, emeritus, Lutheran Theological Seminary at Philadelphia (Philadelphia, Pennsylvania)

Michael Root, dean and professor of theology, Lutheran Theological Southern Seminary (Columbia, South Carolina); visiting research professor, Institute for Ecumenical Research (Strasbourg, France)

David M. Rylaarsdam, associate professor of historical theology, Calvin Theological Seminary (Grand Rapids, Michigan)

David G. Truemper, late professor of theology, Valparaiso University (Valparaiso, Indiana)

Susan K. Wood, professor of theology, Marquette University (Milwaukee, Wisconsin)

Randall C. Zachman, associate professor of Reformation studies; director, MTS program in theology, University of Notre Dame (Notre Dame, Indiana)

Abbreviations

4QMMT	Miqsat Maʻase ha-Torah
AB	Anchor Bible
ABD	*Anchor Bible Dictionary*. Edited by D. N. Freedman. 6 vols. New York: Doubleday, 1992.
ABR	*Australian Biblical Review*
AnBib	Analecta Biblica
ANRW	*Aufstieg und Niedergang der römischen Welt: Geschichte und Kultur Roms im Spiegel der neueren Forschung*. Edited by H. Temporini and W. Haase. Berlin: Walter de Gruyter, 1972–.
BBR	*Bulletin for Biblical Research*
BDAG	Bauer, W., ed. *Greek-English Lexicon of the New Testament and Other Early Christian Literature*. 3d ed. Chicago: University of Chicago, 1999.
BETL	Bibliotheca Ephemeridum Theologicarum Lovadiensium
BJRL	*Bulletin of the John Rylands University Library of Manchester*
BTB	*Biblical Theology Bulletin*
CBQ	*Catholic Biblical Quarterly*
CCS	Corpus Christianorum: Series Latina. Turnhout: Brepols, 1953–.
CNT	Commentaire du Nouveau Testament
CSEL	Corpus Scriptorum Ecclesiasticorum Latinorum
CurTM	*Currents in Theology and Mission*
DJD	Discoveries in the Judaean Desert
EDNT	*Exegetical Dictionary of the New Testament*. Edited by H. Balz and G. Schneider. ET, Grand Rapids: Eerdmans, 1990–1993.

ER   *The Encyclopedia of Religion.* Edited by M. Eliade. 16 vols. New
          York: Macmillan,1987.
EstBíb   *Estudios Bíblicos*
ET   English translation
EWNT   *Exegetisches Wörterbuch zum Neuen Testament.* Edited by H. Balz
          and G. Scheider. Stuttgart: Kohlhammer, 1990–1993.
FRLANT   Forschungen zur Religion und Literatur des Alten und Neuen
          Testaments
FS   Festschrift
HBD   *HarperCollins Bible Dictionary.* Edited by P. J. Achtemeier et al. 2nd
          ed. San Francisco: HarperSanFrancisco, 1996.
HBT   *Horizons in Biblical Theology*
HTR   *Harvard Theological Review*
ICC   International Critical Commentary
IDBSup   *Interpreter's Dictionary of the Bible: Supplementary Volume.* Edited by
          K. Crim. Nashville: Abingdon, 1976.
Int   *Interpretation*
JAAR   *Journal of the American Academy of Religion*
JBL   *Journal of Biblical Literature*
JES   *Journal of Ecumenical Studies*
JETS   *Journal of the Evangelical Theological Society*
JQR   *Jewish Quarterly Review*
JSNT   *Journal for the Study of the New Testament*
JSNTSup   Journal for the Study of the New Testament: Supplement Series
LSJ   Liddell, H. G., R. Scott, H. S. Jones, *A Greek-English Lexicon.* 9th
          ed. with revised supplement. Oxford: Clarendon, 1996.
LTK^2 Josef Höfer and Karl Rahner, eds. *Lexikon für Theologie und Kirche.*
          2nd ed. Freiburg, Herder, 1957–1965.
LW   Luther's Works
LW   *Lutheran World*
MBS   Message of Biblical Spirituality
NICNT   New International Commentary on the New Testament
NJBC   *The New Jerome Biblical Commentary.* Edited by R. E. Brown, J. A.
          Fitzmyer, and R. E. Murphy. Englewood Cliffs, NJ: Prentice Hall,
          1990.
NovT   *Novum Testamentum*
NovTSup   Supplements to Novum Testamentum
NRSV   New Revised Standard Version
NPNF^1 *Nicene and Post-Nicene Fathers,* Series 1
ns   new series

NTAbh	Neutestamentliche Abhandlungen
NTS	*New Testament Studies*
OBT	Overtures to Biblical Theology
PG	Patrologia Graeca [= Patrologiae Cursus Completus: Series Graeca]. Edited by J.-P. Migne. 162 vols. Paris, 1857–1886.
PL	Patrologia Latina [= Patrologiae Cursus Completus: Series Latina]. Edited by J.-P. Migne. 217 vols. Paris, 1844–1864.
QD	Quaestiones Disputatae
RBL	*Review of Biblical Literature*
SBL	Society of Biblical Literature
SBLSP	Society of Biblical Literature Seminar Papers
SBLSymS	Society of Biblical Literature Symposium Series
SBLMS	Society of Biblical Literature Monograph Series
SBT	Studies in Biblical Theology
SE	*Studia Evangelica*
SNTSMS	Society for New Testament Studies Monograph Series
SubBib	Subsidia Biblica
TDNT	*Theological Dictionary of the New Testament.* Edited by G. Kittel and G. Friedrich. Translated by G. W. Bromiley. 10 vols. Grand Rapids: Eerdmans, 1964–1976
TLZ	*Theologische Literaturzeitung*
TU	Texte und Untersuchungen
TynBul	*Tyndale Bulletin*
VDom	*Verbum Domini*
VTSup	Supplements to Vetus Testamentum
WA	Weimarer Ausgabe (Weimar Edition) = *D. Martin Luthers Werke, Kritische Gesamtausgabe.* 65 vols. Weimar: H. Böhlau, 1883–.
WBC	Word Biblical Commentary
WMANT	Wissenschaftliche Monographien zum Alten und Neuen Testament
WTJ	*Westminster Theological Journal*
WUNT	Wissenschaftliche Untersuchungen zum Alten und Neuen Testament
ZNW	*Zeitschrift für die neutestamentliche Wissenschaft und die Kunde der älteren Kirche*
ZRGG	*Zeitschrift für Religions- und Geistesgeschichte*
ZTK	*Zeitschrift für Theologie und Kirche*

1

Introduction to the Joint Declaration on the Doctrine of Justification

DAVID G. TRUEMPER

The conference that gave rise to this book sought to take seriously for our common work as teachers and students of theology the historic agreement signed at Augsburg, Germany, on October 31, 1999, by representatives of the Roman Catholic Church and of the Lutheran World Federation. Taking that agreement seriously means that these two Christian traditions have reached the point in ecumenical conversation at which they can say to each other that the vitriolic mutual condemnations exchanged in the sixteenth century no longer apply to those Lutheran and Roman Catholic conversation partners engaged in formal dialogue for over thirty years.

Taking that agreement seriously would mean that Roman Catholics and Lutherans would from now on teach their students in such a way as not to condemn one another, and would so interpret their Roman Catholicism and their Lutheranism without feeling the need to demonize the other in order to teach the gospel and the heart and life of Christian theology. It would mean that Roman Catholics and Lutherans would from now on teach their students what is emerging as a common reading of crucial parts of the letters of St. Paul, in particular Romans and Galatians, the two epistles most frequently cited in the Joint Declaration. And further, it would mean that Roman Catholics and Lutherans would hereafter teach their students that the Lutheran or Roman "other" is not an enemy of the cross of Christ, not one whose confession of the ecumenical creeds should be dismissed as a mockery of the Christian faith. Imagine what it would mean for teachers to teach in that climate, within that framework of meaning, and for students to learn from their teachers in that climate, within that framework of meaning!

My intention in this opening chapter is threefold: (1) to rehearse the process that led to the momentous signing in Augsburg in October two years ago; (2) to make some orienting judgments and observations about the content of the Joint Declaration and about its consequences for relationships between the churches and so for the work of teaching and scholarship that is carried on by members of those churches; and (3) to discern and describe those habits of the mind and heart that both made it possible to reach this point and also might open the door to further progress in the work of ecumenical dialogue. In other words: How did we get here? What is this place really like? And how shall we go on from here?

How Did We Get Here?

It wasn't easy. The closer we came, the more bizarre and daunting became the obstacles. Never mind that folks had been at something like serious conversation for over thirty years. Never mind that those conversations, particularly in North America and in Germany, had been carried on in a spirit of excitement and hopefulness. Never mind that each step of the way was marked by amazing degrees of consensus. Even before the date for the signing of the agreement was set, both sides made rather public withdrawals from the process; there were more than 150 (later, the number reached 240) German Lutheran theologians who published their objections to the proposed agreement's alleged capitulation to Roman Catholic theology. At the same time, Roman Catholic leaders published a statement indicating why it would not be possible for their church to commit to the agreement. The rest of Christianity watched and wondered and waited to see what the two churches most responsible for the fracture of Western Christianity would do, some of their members reserving the right to object, should something come of all this, because they had not been invited to the party. In fact, two of the most remarkable and scurrilous objections to the Joint Declaration, after its signing, came from church bodies that had played no part at all in this ecumenical dialogue. One trumpeted to its adherents that liberal Lutherans and Roman Catholics have agreed to "abandon the gospel." The other took out advertisements in a dozen and a half newspapers to say that the participants had lied to one another and to the rest of the churches. Perhaps it is time to say to those who declined to participate in the dialogue, "Be quiet! It is not your place to comment on these proceedings!"

To be sure, ecumenical activity had begun around the turn of the twentieth century. Faith and Order, and Life and Work had begun their operations in the early decades of the twentieth century; these movements would eventually coalesce to create the World Council of Churches. For most of Christianity outside the Roman Catholic Church, those conversations were accelerated just after World War II. Of great importance was the commitment from Eastern Christian leaders to participate in the conversation. Still Rome abstained, claiming to be exclusively the church catholic; all the rest were heretics at worst, or at best "separated brethren." That changed with the work of the Second Vatican Council. Both the commitment to some kind of reconciliation with the Eastern churches and the readiness to speak of non–Roman Catholic Christianity as in some sense deserving the label of "ecclesial communities" (though nevertheless allegedly deficient in matters of orders, authority, and sacramentality) opened the door to the participation of the Roman Catholic communion in what had previously been only a Protestant, and then a Protestant-Eastern, ecumenical movement. The consequences would be staggering, as Rome took the risk of sitting down at the dialogue table without specifying in advance the nature of its role or the shape of the table. To be sure, Rome's position was clear: we are the church, and we'll decide what criteria will be used to grant that title to the rest of you. Of course, that is precisely the position that all the rest had assumed as well. For that is the nature of the question faced in every genuinely ecumenical dialogue: "By *our* criteria, can *you* be regarded as the church of Jesus Christ?"

Indeed, that is the essence of the ecumenical question; once the church had been fractured, every piece of the Christian church has had to assume that it (perhaps even it alone) was the surviving, authentic church. The ecumenical movement is a voyage of discovery in the quest to recover unity. Any participation in ecumenical conversation has meant a willingness on the part of the participating church (body) to put its exclusiveness on the line and to declare its readiness to discover that the "other" might also, in fact and in truth, be the church as well.

It should come as no surprise, then, that the recognition of Joint Declaration has raised profoundly churchly questions and hopes.

From Vatican II to Joint Declaration

By my reading there are three distinguishable strands or processes that led to the Augsburg Accord of 1999. I shall sketch these briefly, only to try to convey the sense both of momentum and of its inevitable counterpart—inertia—in ecumenical conversation.

First, in the United States formal dialogue began in 1965 between the United States Bishops' Commission and the North American Lutherans affiliated with the Lutheran World Federation; the Lutheran Church–Missouri Synod did not officially participate but sent observers. These dialogues are a story in their own right, as they have continued steadily into the present, and in their tenth round of conversations the participants have moved toward a joint publication.[1] From 1979 until 1983 the subject was justification by faith, culminating in a report published in 1985 after round seven of these exemplary conversations.[2] For our purposes it is significant that these conversations resulted in a common statement that contained these telling words: "The entire hope of justification and salvation rests on Christ Jesus and on the gospel whereby the good news of God's merciful action in Christ is made known; we do not place our ultimate trust in anything other than God's promise and saving work in Christ."[3] Given four and a half centuries of contrary statements from both the dialogue partners, that single formula is a stunning accomplishment! A significant feature of these North American conversations is the recurring theme, as voiced by participants from both churches, that the participants had been working to clear out the underbrush of four and a half centuries of mutual suspicion, and had been making a fresh attempt to read both the New Testament and the sixteenth-century texts together—and in such a way that each side could understand the other's reading and intentions.

Second, international Lutheran–Roman Catholic dialogues began in 1967 leading to the so-called Malta Report issued in 1972, titled "The Gospel and the Church." Key there was the observation that a far-reaching consensus was seen to be developing in the interpretation of justification.

Third, a quite different process was begun in late 1980 in Germany.[4] At a meeting of Pope John Paul II with representatives of the Lutheran and Reformed churches in Mainz, the Lutheran bishop, Eduard Lohse, speaking

---

1. Randall Lee and Jeffrey Gros, eds., *The Church as Koinonia of Salvation: Its Structures and Ministries* (Washington, DC: U.S. Conference of Catholic Bishops, 2005).

2. H. George Anderson, T. Austin Murphy, and Joseph A. Burgess, eds., *Justification by Faith*, Lutherans and Catholics in Dialogue 7 (Minneapolis: Augsburg, 1985).

3. Ibid., 16.

4. The following section makes use of information contained in a news release from the Lutheran World Federation, now archived at http://www.lutheranworld.org.

in his capacity as chair of the Council of the Evangelical Church in Germany, expressed the need for better cooperation among the churches with regard to mixed marriages, participation in Sunday worship, and eucharistic fellowship. Six months later Bishop Lohse and Cardinal Ratzinger chaired a Joint Ecumenical Commission, where Lohse called for the churches "to establish in an official, binding way that the condemnations formulated in the Lutheran confessional writings of the sixteenth century 'about the doctrine, form, and practice of the Roman Catholic Church are no longer applicable to today's partner.'" And Cardinal Ratzinger observed that "a corresponding reexamination of the doctrinal decisions of the Council of Trent was also necessary" because "new realities have come into being, and . . . the old massive dissensus to all intents and purposes no longer exists."[5] Subsequent meetings added a concern for the formulation of a common understanding of justification as a basis on which to declare that the mutual condemnations do not apply in the present situation.

These three threads began to be woven together during the 1990s. By 1994 the initial draft of the Joint Declaration was prepared; the operative words read, "We are in a position to declare that mutual doctrinal condemnations regarding the doctrine of justification no longer apply to the partner today."[6] A second draft began to be circulated at the end of January 1995, with a third draft appearing in June 1996. Nearly two years of negotiations, both among the Lutheran World Federation member churches and between the Lutheran World Federation and the Roman Catholic Church, issued in the unanimous affirmation of the Joint Declaration by the Council of the Lutheran World Federation in mid-June 1998. It was a bitter irony that on June 25 of that year, the anniversary of the presentation of the *Augsburg Confession* at the Imperial Diet in 1530, the response of the Roman Catholic Church was published, calling for "further clarification" before the sixteenth-century condemnations could be removed. In particular, this response pointed out the divergences that still remained, and it raised the trenchant criticism that §4.4, in speaking of "the justified as sinner," was especially problematic: "Even taking into account the differences, legitimate in themselves, that come from different theological approaches to the content of faith, from a Catholic point of view the title is already a cause of perplexity."[7] This chilly response, coupled with the significant minority

5. See the Lutheran World Federation news release of October 23, 1999, at http://www.lutheranworld.org/News/LW1/EN/693.EN.html.
6. Ibid.
7. "Response of the Roman Catholic Church to the Joint Declaration," *L'Osservatore Romano*, July 8, 1998.

of objections from among the member churches of the Lutheran World Federation, brought the process to a sudden halt. Then the suggestion was made and agreed to that the parties would formulate a short document making clear their mutual acceptance of the concluding paragraphs of the Joint Declaration without reservations. Cardinal Cassidy affirmed the Roman Catholic Church's readiness to proceed in that fashion at the end of July that year. The Official Common Statement was made public in June 1999 and was signed in Augsburg on October 31, 1999. Along with its Annex, this statement clarifies how the consensus was reached and how in particular §41 of the Joint Declaration could be jointly confirmed.

These delays and concluding negotiations presented an opportunity for objections to surface and gather some momentum—and press coverage. Each side worried publicly about the commitment of the other to the process. In the spring of 1999 about 150 German Lutheran theologians signed a news release objecting to the forthcoming accord, and about 45 of them wrote individual opinions objecting to one or another feature or failure of the Joint Declaration. American Lutherans wondered about the commitment of Cardinals Ratzinger and Cassidy to the process.

Nevertheless, the Official Common Statement was prepared and the ceremony was readied for the joint signing in Augsburg on October 31, 1999. The official Lutheran World Federation press release credits Cardinal Ratzinger and Lutheran Bishop Hanselmann (since deceased) with achieving this breakthrough. And the subsequent remark of the Holy Father to the effect that, once having shaken hands with each other, we must not let go, suggests the possibility that the pope himself may well have intervened to assure the successful conclusion to the process.

Key Features of the Joint Declaration

The structure of the Joint Declaration is straightforward: a preamble, a section on the biblical materials (especially Paul's letters to the Romans and to the Galatians), a section on the doctrine of justification as ecumenical problem, two sections stating and then explicating the common understanding of justification, and a concluding section on the significance and scope of the consensus. Then, of course, there follows the Annex/Appendix, which provides the sources in documents authoritative to each of the churches and in documents from the threads of ecumenical dialogue summarized above.

Paragraph 13 states the achievement of these conversations:

By appropriating insights of recent biblical studies and drawing on modern investigations of the history of theology and dogma, the post-Vatican II ecumenical dialogue has led to a notable convergence concerning justification, with the result that this joint declaration is able to formulate a consensus on basic truths concerning the doctrine of justification. In light of this consensus, the corresponding doctrinal condemnations of the 16th century do not apply to today's partner.

The key statement of convergence/consensus is in §15: "Together we confess: By grace alone, in faith in Christ's saving work and not because of any merit on our part, we are accepted by God and receive the Holy Spirit, who renews our hearts while equipping and calling us to good works."

Also significant is the statement from §18, regarding the unique role of the doctrine of justification: "more than just one part of Christian doctrine, [i]t stands in an essential relation to all truths of faith, which are to be seen as internally related to each other. It is an indispensable criterion which constantly serves to orient all the teaching and practice of our churches to Christ."

Section 4 of the declaration summarizes the common understanding of justification under seven points. Each of the seven subsections makes a common, joint assertion and then adds statements on how each side has come to understand the classic formulations and concerns of the other side. The model is this: (a) we say this together; (b) when Lutherans/Roman Catholics have traditionally said X, we and they understand this to mean XX and so to conform with the statement above. What I take to be significant—and will comment on later—is that this pattern commits the partners to be open to fresh understandings in the light of the contemporary situation rather than holding to an insistence on the stolid reaffirmation of aged language and formula.

The seven topics taken up in this crucial section produce the following careful assertions, each designed and intended to address a facet of the four-century-long controversy between the churches:

1. "We confess together that all persons depend completely on the saving grace of God for their salvation."
2. "We confess together that God forgives sin by grace and at the same time frees human beings from sin's enslaving power and imparts the gift of new life in Christ."
3. "We confess together that sinners are justified by faith in the saving action of God in Christ."

4. "We confess together that in baptism the Holy Spirit unites one with Christ, justifies and truly renews the person. But the justified must all through life constantly look to God's unconditional justifying grace."

5. "We confess together that persons are justified by faith in the Gospel 'apart from works prescribed by the law.'"

6. "We confess together that the faithful can rely on the mercy and promises of God."

7. "We confess together that good works—a Christian life lived in faith, hope and love—follow justification and are its fruits."

The conclusion is then articulated in section 5, §40: "Therefore the Lutheran and the Catholic explications of justification are in their difference open to one another and do not destroy the consensus regarding basic truths." On that basis the next paragraph (41) concludes that the teaching of the Lutheran churches as here presented does not fall under the condemnations of the Council of Trent, and the condemnations in the Lutheran confessions do not apply to the Roman Catholic teaching as here presented. It is to this concluding affirmation that the Official Common Statement signed at Augsburg on October 31, 1999, commits us.

Reception and Repudiation—and a Personal Assessment

I find it noteworthy that, in the wake of the signing of the Augsburg Accord, rejections from traditionally minded Roman Catholics have been based on the assertion that the Joint Declaration sells out to the Lutherans, and that traditionally minded Lutherans reject the Joint Declaration on the alleged grounds that it sells out to the Roman Catholics. But the most remarkable headline I've seen, alluded to earlier, comes from a group calling itself the Way of Life Fundamental Baptist Information Service. Their take is clear from the web site's headline, "Liberal Lutherans and Roman Catholics Agree to Deny the Gospel."

Three issues or questions seem to me to be most significant as one seeks to come to an assessment of the achievement of the Augsburg Accord. One is procedural/ecumenical-political and two are theological. All three are nontrivial, in that one's reaction to these will probably be decisive for one's overall assessment of the Joint Declaration. All three are germane, since they are related to the assertion that the Joint Declaration represents the achievement of "differentiated consensus."

As to procedure, it is important to note that neither partner wishes to dictate the terms of the debate. Nevertheless, voices on both sides have held to the absolute necessity of certain of their own understandings and formulae. In an interview in the summer of 1999, between the issuing of the Official Common Statement and the October 31 signing, Cardinal Ratzinger explained the situation in these words: "Only if the Lutheran doctrine of justification is explained in a way that complies with this measure [i.e., so as to uphold the truth and value of the anathemata of Trent], it is not affected by these excommunications. For he who opposes the doctrine of the Council of Trent opposes the doctrine and faith of the Church."[8] Similarly, the 240 German Lutheran theologians who railed against the Official Common Statement at about the same time complained that the Lutheran side accepted the teachings of the Council of Trent even more frankly in the Annex than in the Joint Declaration itself. Gottfried Martens comments, "A Roman doctrine of justification was taught in this document by using Lutheran expressions."[9] Voices on both sides continue to insist on formulae and meanings that amount to "comfort food," despite the fact that already the North American dialogues had demonstrated the necessity and the sanity of preferring substance over form, of not insisting on pet formulae when new or revised language could convey new insight and consensus.

The first theological issue to which I wish to point is the following. Traditionally, Lutherans have asserted a criteriological role for the doctrine of justification by faith alone. In the seventeenth century, justification by faith alone came to be called the *articulus stantis et cadentis ecclesiae* (article by which the church stands or falls). It is disputed among the Joint Declaration's critics whether that criteriological role is affirmed or denied in the Joint Declaration. The language of the document is simple; whether it means what it seems to mean is debated by the critics. The Annex states, "The doctrine of justification is measure or touchstone for the Christian faith. No teaching may contradict this criterion. In this sense, the doctrine of justification is an indispensable criterion that constantly serves to orient all the teaching and practice of our churches to Christ" (partially quoted from Joint Declaration 18). Now, the critics debate the meaning of the absence of a definite article before "measure or touchstone." In the German version one reads, "ist Maßstab oder Prüfstein." Now, the absence of an article before a predicate noun in German often implies the definite article or, at a minimum,

8. I have only second-hand evidence for this quotation, which I have not been able to verify independently.

9. Gottfried Martens, "Agreement and Disagreement on Justification by Faith Alone," *Concordia Theological Quarterly* 65:3 (July 2001): 208.

the essential connection between the subject and the predicate; German would normally add *ein* if the intent were to suggest that the predicate is one among many possibilities—although the language is equally capable of using a definite article when the intent is to stress the singular or sole nature of the predicate. Lutherans traditionally speak of *the* criterion; Roman Catholics traditionally choose to speak of *multiple* criteria.

The other theological issue about which questions are raised and argument-volleys are hurled by the howitzer-wielding theologians has to do with the congeries of ideas and comments around the two terms *concupiscentia* (concupiscence) and *simul iustus et peccator* (at the same time righteous and sinner). Is concupiscence sin, or only the capacity or propensity to sin—the sort of "soft underbelly" of the baptized believer that leaves one vulnerable to sin? Many Lutherans insist that concupiscence is and remains sin;[10] traditionally minded (and Ratzinger-minded) Roman Catholics prefer a milder understanding of the term. The division surfaces also around the phrase dear to Lutheran ears, *simul iustus et peccator*. Roman Catholic theology has tended to resist that notion, which Lutherans have (uncritically, for the most part) held dear. Is the baptized believer still also a sinner *always*, or only in the event of a lapse of faith and fall into sin?

Around these issues the warmest debates rage. One hopes that the work here offered will contribute light, not heat, in this regard.

Comments from two significantly moderate voices from the participating churches are instructive and worth noting. Avery Dulles, S.J., in a commentary published in *First Things*, observes that there remain two traditional languages about justification: the Roman Catholic language that is scholastic and metaphysical, and the Lutheran language that is existential and relational. As a result, he thinks, more mutual work may and should be done. He observes, "It is necessary to establish that Lutheran proclamation and Catholic speculation are both legitimate derivatives of the same gospel, and therefore compatible. Performative language cannot be unrelated to informative; the law of prayer must harmonize with the law of belief."[11] *Pace* Father Dulles, but that expectation stands the principle of St. Prosper of Aquitaine on its head, which in its original asserts that it is the law of prayer that ought to establish the law of belief: *legem credendi lex statuat supplicandi.*[12]

10. Article II of the *Augsburg Confession* calls "inherited/original sin . . . truly sin," but it does not there use the term *concupiscentia*.
11. "Two Languages of Salvation: The Lutheran-Catholic Joint Declaration," *First Things* 98 (December 1999): 25–30.
12. As quoted in G. Lathrop, *Holy Things* (Minneapolis: Fortress, 1993), 9.

The second commentator is Paul Hinlicky, writing in *The Cresset*, a journal published by Valparaiso University.[13] Hinlicky praises the Joint Declaration on two grounds. First, it does not dismiss the ancient anathemas as simply wrong; they pointed to dangers that had to be identified and rejected—but, of course, neither side finds such errors espoused by today's dialogue partners. Second, Hinlicky finds the Joint Declaration's reformulations to be open to the revisionist Luther studies of such Finnish theologians as Tuomo Mannermaa and their insistence that justifying faith is never *fides abstracta* but always *fides concreta* or *fides incarnata*. He also finds the Joint Declaration's formulations to be an improvement on some of the sixteenth-century language in that they are more christocentric and less anthropocentric. That has a marvelous echo in the remarkable book on justification by Eberhard Jüngel, *Das Evangelium von der Rechtfertigung des Gottlosen als Zentrum des christlichen Glaubens* (ET: *Justification: The Heart of the Christian Faith*).[14]

I wish to conclude this section with four points by way of personal assessment of the Joint Declaration and its achievements.

First, ecumenical dialogue, especially as evidenced in the Lutheran–Roman Catholic conversations that have produced the Joint Declaration, is not about compromise on what might be called least common denominators, but about confessional commitments to the truth—all the while following the simple hermeneutical rule: you may not condemn another's position unless and until you have stated the opposing position in language that the opponent/partner affirms and approves. At every step of the way, Lutherans and Roman Catholics have made progress when they have followed that rule. Or to put the matter a bit differently, the dialogue that has culminated in the Joint Declaration has found a common purchase on catholic and apostolic Christian truth, while being less ready to absolutize the phrases and terms and slogans that have arisen in the meantime. Consider this illustration: catholic and apostolic Christian truth is represented by what we might call "A" statements. Along comes an Arius who makes plausible claims that are judged finally to have abandoned that truth; call these "B" statements. In order to preserve and keep available catholic and apostolic truth for the church in this or another age, the church develops "C" statements. Now the problem with much of our mutual history is that we have insisted on the eternal validity and necessity of our respective "C"

13. Paul Hinlicky, "Process, Convergence, Declaration: Reflections on Doctrinal Dialogue," *The Cresset* (Pentecost 2001): 13–18.

14. 3rd ed.; Tübingen: Mohr Siebeck, 1999; ET, Edinburgh: T & T Clark, 2001.

statements. The dialogue process of the last one-third century has made clear a consensus on "A" statements of the catholic and apostolic truth. Clearing away the underbrush, we have mutually learned that the other's "B" statements are no longer held dear—or at least no longer bear the same meaning as our respective forebears may have intended or understood. We may, then, safely abandon our insistence on the "C" statements, remembering that their purpose was to preserve the essential elements of the "A" statements. What we learn from these dialogues is to suspend the "C" statement when the "B" statements are not in circulation, and to consent together on "A" statements. The trouble is that folks who have not participated in the dialogue process have turned their dearly held "C" statements into idols and fetishes instead of working at the task of understanding the faith and articulating the faith afresh for the contemporary church.[15]

Second, the Joint Declaration succeeds in suspending the anathemas of the sixteenth century on the basis of a fresh and common reading of both the relevant New Testament texts and also the sixteenth-century theological and polemical documents. This reading has been made possible by the more than thirty years of sustained conversation between them, and also by the revisionist readings of the Pauline letters to which they appeal (even though, in the final analysis, the Paul that emerges here is decidedly not the Paul of the revisionists).[16]

Third, the Joint Declaration does not make joint celebration and reception of sacraments possible, at least not in normally foreseen circumstances. Though Lutherans may well find it possible to welcome Roman Catholic communicants, Roman Catholics will continue to face the difficult question of the validity of Lutheran orders since the United States dialogues on *Eucharist and Ministry*[17] have not been "received" by the churches.

Fourth, Lutherans may take the Joint Declaration as a strong encouragement to continue the conversation. In any case, we are committed to do so by the *Augsburg Confession*: "We shall not, on our part, omit doing anything, so far as God and conscience allow, that may serve the cause of Christian

15. I am indebted to my teacher, the long-time and influential participant in the American Lutheran–Roman Catholic dialogues during their first decade, Arthur Carl Piepkorn (of blessed memory). I have not found these remarks of his, once made in personal conversation about the "Eucharist and Sacrifice" stages of the dialogues, to have been published. Nevertheless, I wish to honor his work and his legacy by acknowledging my debt to him for this analysis.

16. Cf. Peter Stuhlmacher, *Revisiting Paul's Doctrine of Justification: A Challenge to the New Perspective* (Downers Grove, IL: InterVarsity, 2001), as well as the aforementioned work by Jüngel.

17. *Eucharist and Ministry*, Lutherans and Catholics in Dialogue 7 (Washington, DC: Published jointly by representatives of the USA National Committee of the Lutheran World Federation and the Bishops' Committee for Ecumenical and Interreligious Affairs, 1970).

unity."[18] To be members of the church of the *Augsburg Confession* is to find ourselves in the posture of offering that very confession to the Roman Catholic Church with the implicit inquiry, "This is the catholic faith, is it not?" In this connection, I am happy to report that, back in the good old days when our respective departments of theology held regular, twice-a-year conversations, Father Edward Kilmartin, S.J. (of blessed memory), responded to my paper on the catholicity of the *Augsburg Confession* by saying that the net result of Vatican II was to answer that Lutheran dialogical question in the affirmative, for Vatican II had, in Kilmartin's view, essentially agreed with the agenda of the reform articles in part two of the *Augsburg Confession*.[19] My sense is that in 1999 the Joint Declaration also answered in the affirmative with regard to articles IV and VI of the *Augsburg Confession*. And, as the Holy Father has said, "we dare not lose the momentum."

Principles for Ecumenical Conversation

In closing, I would like to summarize and comment on what I take to be seven "golden rules" of ecumenical conversation. To some extent these are patently obvious in present process, and to some extent they are extrapolations from conversations with participants whose views have shaped my understanding of these matters. In part, I judge, these principles are evident in the thirty-seven years of Lutheran–Roman Catholic dialogue; in part, I propose them as at least implicit and/or promising.

1. One may disagree with and/or condemn another's position only after one has demonstrated the ability to state the other's position in such a way that the other agrees with that formulation.
2. Since even very simple formulae have great power to create meaning, one must handle theological and doctrinal formulae with great care. One must ask whether this or that formula is an essential expression of the truth as we have come to understand it, or is it (merely) a way people at one time and place chose to articulate essential truth?
3. The truth that is sought in ecumenical conversation resides beneath the surface of venerable and traditional formulae and not necessarily in the formulae per se.

---

18. *Augsburg Confession*, preface, 13. Robert Kolb and Timothy J. Wengert, eds., *The Book of Concord: The Confessions of the Evangelical Lutheran Church* (Minneapolis: Fortress, 2000), 32.

19. Unpublished paper, in the author's possession; the joint meeting in question was held in the fall of 1980.

4. Language and terminology are cultural artifacts and therefore are susceptible to change; thus merely asserting an ancient or traditional formula does not necessarily assert the same thing as the formula originally intended and conveyed.
5. Given the increasingly evident pluralism of the global village we now inhabit, spokespersons for the faith will do well to observe Luther's advice, made in another connection, "Es gehört Bescheidenheit dazu" (modesty required here).[20]
6. Since God's communication with human beings in various cultural settings and cultural circumstances must be held to be in a funda-mental sense "effective," we must conclude that there will be diverse appropriations of even central truths of the Christian faith. Accord-ingly, the goal of ecumenical conversation is mutual understanding and what the Joint Declaration calls "differentiated consensus," not uniformity of formula or of emphasis.
7. Ecumenical conversation is a profoundly churchly action, under-taken not with the goal of defending the fortress of doctrine, but with the awareness that the gospel defends and protects the church, against whose mission not even the gates of Hades will ultimately prevail.[21]

These comments will, I hope, be of some modest use in getting us oriented to the situation in which we find ourselves as we "reread Paul together" in the light of almost four decades of Lutheran–Roman Catholic ecumenical conversation.

20. *Luthers Werke, Tischreden* 5, Nr 5245 (1540).
21. Matt. 16:18. Jesus' words about the confession of Peter are usually taken to mean that the powers of Hades will not successfully attack the church. However, I take them to mean that the pow-ers/gates of Hades will not finally stand against the assault constituted by the church's confession of the gospel of Jesus the Christ.

2

Catholic Reception of the Joint Declaration on the Doctrine of Justification

Susan K. Wood

The Joint Declaration on the Doctrine of Justification was signed in Augsburg, Germany, on Reformation Day, October 31, 1999, by representatives of the Lutheran World Federation and the Roman Catholic Church. This action was the culmination of over thirty years of dialogue between these two bodies. This text is the first joint declaration that the Roman Catholic Church has made with any church of the Reformation and represents official ecclesial reception of the results of dialogue on justification with member churches of the Lutheran World Federation.

Historical Perspective of the Significance of This Action

The doctrine of justification was a central issue in the dispute between Martin Luther and authorities of the Roman Catholic Church in the sixteenth century. The contrasting positions on this doctrine became the subject of condemnations both on the part of the Council of Trent and in the Lutheran confessions. For several hundred years the two communions

44   Susan K. Wood

existed in a relationship of polemical separation and mutual condemnation.
The first U.S. national dialogue took place in July 1965. A Roman Catholic–Lutheran working group was established by the Vatican and the Lutheran
World Federation in 1965. International dialogue between the two groups
began in 1967, soon after the close of the Second Vatican Council. The
first phase of this dialogue showed that there was an emerging agreement
on the doctrine of justification. Thus in 1972 the "Malta Report," titled
"The Gospel and the Church," stated, "Today . . . a far-reaching consensus
is developing in the interpretation of justification (§26)."[1] Subsequent
dialogue statements (All Under One Christ, 1980, §4; The Ministry in the
Church, 1981, §9)[2] repeated this affirmation of the consensus reached.
The United States national dialogues addressed the topic of justification
in the American study, Justification by Faith (1983).[3] In Germany the Joint
Ecumenical Commission and Ecumenical Study Group of Protestant Lutherans and Catholic Theologians studied the condemnations by Catholics
and Lutherans in the sixteenth century on justification and related topics
between 1982 and 1985, publishing the results in The Condemnations of
the Reformation Era: Do They Still Divide? (1988).[4] The whole third phase
of dialogue examined this doctrine more at length and in reference to the
church (Church and Justification: Understanding the Church in the Light of the
Doctrine of Justification [1994]).[5] In 1994 a group of theologians appointed
by the Pontifical Council for Promoting Christian Unity and the Lutheran
World Federation produced a first draft of a joint declaration on the doctrine of justification. That version underwent two revisions in 1996 and
in 1997 before being officially submitted to the Holy See and members of
the Lutheran World Federation for approval.

   On the basis of responses from its member churches, the Lutheran World
Federation Council affirmed the Joint Declaration on June 16, 1998. At
that time the Lutheran World Federation had 124 member churches in 69

1. In Harding Meyer and Lukas Vischer, eds., Growth in Agreement: Reports and Agreed Statements
of Ecumenical Conversations on a World Level, Faith and Order Paper 108 (New York: Paulist Press;
Geneva: World Council of Churches, 1984), 168–89.
   2. Ibid., 241–47, 248–75.
   3. H. George Anderson, T. Austin Murphy, and Joseph A. Burgess, eds., Justification by Faith. Lutherans and Catholics in Dialogue 7 (Minneapolis: Augsburg, 1985).
   4. Karl Lehmann and Wolfhart Pannenberg, eds., The Condemnations of the Reformation Era: Do
They Still Divide? (Minneapolis: Fortress Press, 1990); trans. of Lehrverurteilungen—kirchentrennend?
(Freiburg im Breisgau: Herder, 1988). This is the only one of five volumes of a German study translated
into English.
   5. Lutheran–Roman Catholic Joint Commission, The Church and Justification: The Understanding of
the Church in Light of the Doctrine of Justification (Geneva: Lutheran World Federation; Rome: Pontifical
Council for Promoting Christian Unity, 1994).

countries representing 58 million of the world's 61.5 million Lutherans. The Lutheran World Federation heard from 89 of the 124 churches. Of those responding, eighty affirmed the declaration and five did not. Four answers seemed difficult to interpret, according to the Institute for Ecumenical Research, Strasbourg, France, which analyzed the responses. Of these, one seemed to affirm it, and three seemed not to affirm it. The affirmations came from 91 percent of the churches responding, which represents 54.7 million Lutherans (95 percent of the Lutherans in Lutheran World Federation member churches).[6]

On June 25, 1998, the Roman Catholic Church gave its response to the same declaration.[7] This response mentions "a consensus on basic truths of the doctrine of justification." There is no mention of the nonapplicability of condemnations, even though Cardinal Edward Cassidy, president of the Pontifical Council for Promoting Christian Unity, stated in his press conference that it "shows that the remaining differences in its [the doctrine of justification's] explication are no longer the occasion for doctrinal condemnations (§6)."[8] In fact, the Catholic response seemed to express uncertainty about this nonapplicability: "If, moreover, it is true that in those truths on which a consensus has been reached the condemnations of the Council of Trent no longer apply, the divergences on other points must, on the contrary, be overcome before we can affirm, as is done generically in No. 41, that these points no longer incur the condemnations of the Council of Trent."[9] One must note, however, that this sentence is located in the "Clarifications" section of the response rather than in the "Declaration" section. Cardinal Ratzinger, in a letter to the *Frankfürter Allgemeine Zeitung* (July 11, 1998), pointed out that only the "Declaration" is to be considered strictly as a response to the questions raised in the Joint Declaration.

The primary issues raised by the Official Catholic Response included: (1) the meaning of *simul iustus et peccator*; (2) the question of merit; (3) the doctrine of justification as the sole criterion; (4) whether human beings are passive or whether they cooperate with grace; and (5) the authority of the consensus reached by the Lutheran World Federation.

At that time it was clear that the two dialogue partners had not affirmed the Joint Declaration in the same way. An action of joint signing could take place only if the two parties involved had the same understanding

6. Data from Lutheran World Federation Press Release No. 7/98, http://www.lutheranworld.org/news/counce5.html.
7. "Official Catholic Response to Joint Declaration," *Origins* 28/8 (July 16, 1998): 130–32.
8. Cardinal Edward Cassidy, "Press Conference Statement" *Origins* 28/8 (July 16, 1998): 128–30.
9. Official Catholic Response, §5.

of the significance of such a signing. Consultations between the Roman Catholic Church and the Lutheran World Federation then took place to clarify the basis for a joint signing, leading to an Official Common Statement that could be jointly signed, and a short explanatory Annex to this statement. The Annex did not require ratification of the member churches of the Lutheran World Federation because it is essentially a compilation of quotations from Scripture and confessional documents. Announcement of an official signing was made on June 11, 1999, and the Joint Declaration was signed on October 21, 1999.

By signing the Official Common Statement the two partners in dialogue confirm two points: they have reached a high level of consensus on basic truths regarding the doctrine of justification, and they declare that the mutual condemnations from the time of the Reformation concerning the doctrine of justification do not apply to the teaching on justification as set forth by Lutherans and Roman Catholics in the Joint Declaration. This is not simply one dialogue document among many but the first time the Roman Catholic Church and the Lutheran churches of the world "declare in a binding manner that an understanding has been reached on a question of faith and doctrine which has been divisive for centuries." This declaration constitutes official ecclesial reception of decades of dialogue on this topic.

To realize the significance of this event we have only to remember that a doctrinal condemnation is the highest degree of escalation in theological controversy within a church or between churches. It is the authoritative declaration that a difference with regard to a particular teaching is so grievous as to divide the church. Doctrinal condemnations are the confirmation and seal of church division. On the contrary, the declaration of nonapplicability of a doctrinal condemnation means that the ecumenical dialogue has concluded that the condemnations of a previous era no longer apply to the teaching of a dialogue partner today. Dialogue has reached a point where differences with regard to a particular teaching are no longer church-dividing.

This inapplicability of condemnations does not mean that the two traditions erase their past history or change the doctrinal definitions of the Council of Trent or the Lutheran Confessions. It does mean that the two faith communities do not today hold the positions that are condemned in the way that they were condemned in the sixteenth century. Historical research and present dialogue have exposed misunderstandings of the past and allowed the faith communities to deepen their present understandings so that the remaining differences can be transcended by a common confession of belief.

The heart of the Joint Declaration on the Doctrine of Justification consists of seven affirmations of what Lutherans and Catholics confess together regarding justification. Each positive statement of common confession is followed by a paragraph clarifying the Catholic understanding and another clarifying the Lutheran understanding. These two paragraphs allow the differences within the two traditions to stand, but they are subsumed under a broader agreement. These differences do not destroy the consensus regarding basic truths.[10] This document represents a differentiated consensus rather than uniformity in concept and expression.

The differences between the two traditions are not only differences of emphasis and language, but are also differences in perspective. The Roman Catholic doctrine originated out of a theology of baptism while the Reformation doctrine originated in a theology of penance.[11] Thus where Lutherans emphasize justification as forgiving love, Catholics emphasize the renewal of the interior person through the reception of grace, the new life brought through God's forgiving grace. Within a framework of St. Thomas Aquinas's theology of grace, this was seen as an elevation to a new form of living, an elevation from nature to the supernatural. Lutheran theology, however, did not speak in terms of two states of being, in an ontological sense, but was grounded existentially in the experience of sin and the corresponding experience of forgiveness in spite of that sin. The Roman Catholic view was more metaphysical, the Lutheran more existential. The Roman Catholic position might even be called more anthropological in the sense that it emphasized the change wrought in a person through the activity of grace. The Lutheran position was more christocentric in that it emphasized the activity of Christ toward the sinner. The question is not simply whether these differences are substantial but whether, as expressed in the Joint Declaration, they are church-dividing. The Joint Statement includes both emphases in the common statement: "We confess together that God forgives sin by grace and at the same time frees human beings from sin's enslaving power and imparts the gift of new life in Christ."[12] Together we confess that justification both forgives sins and makes righteous.

The Joint Declaration represents a high level of consensus on the doctrine of justification, but it does not eliminate every difference between Lutherans and Roman Catholics regarding this doctrine. These differences must be

10. Harding Meyer, "Consensus in the Doctrine of Justification," *Ecumenical Trends* 26/11 (1997): 5/165.

11. Lehmann and Pannenberg, eds., *The Condemnations of the Reformation Era*, 33.

12. The Lutheran World Federation and the Roman Catholic Church, *Joint Declaration on the Doctrine of Justification* (Grand Rapids: Eerdmans, 2000), §22.

evaluated. Lutherans and Roman Catholics view many topics through different lenses. If we are to be truly reconciled, we need to be able to view the doctrine through the lens of our dialogue partner. At least one commentator has noted that the main methodological innovation of the Joint Declaration may be the acknowledgment that the unity of faith can be expressed in different languages and in various theological forms with particular emphases.[13] The strangeness of the other worldview poses particular challenges to the reception of this document by both our communions. This essay will develop a few concepts that pose a particular challenge: the concept of merit, the Lutheran understanding of justified and sinner, the importance of justification as criterion of other doctrines, and the issue of church identity.

The Teaching on Merit

The teaching on merit is related to the necessity of good works and rewards for good works. The Joint Declaration states:

> We confess together that good works—a Christian life lived in faith, hope, and love—follow justification and are its fruits. When the justified live in Christ and act in the grace they receive, they bring forth, in biblical terms, good fruit. Since Christians struggle against sin their entire lives, this consequence of justification is also for them an obligation they must fulfill. Thus both Jesus and the apostolic Scriptures admonish Christians to bring forth the works of love. (§37)

Lutherans view the good works of Christians as the fruits and signs of justification and not as one's own "merits." However, they also understand eternal life in accordance with the New Testament as unmerited "reward" in the sense of the fulfillment of God's promise to the believer.[14] According to the Joint Declaration, when Roman Catholics affirm the "meritorious" character of good works, they wish to say that, according to the biblical witness, a reward in heaven is promised for these works (Matt. 5:12; 10:42). Their intention is to emphasize the responsibility of persons for their actions, not to question the character of those works as gifts, and far less to deny that justification always remains the unmerited gift of grace.[15]

13. Hervé Legrand, O.P., "Le consensus différencié sur la doctrine de la Justification (Augsbourg 1999)," Nouvelle revue théologique 124 (2002): 30–56.
14. Joint Declaration, §39.
15. Ibid., §38.

Thus Roman Catholics still affirm the possibility of merit, but justification remains unmerited because the good works are themselves possible only through grace. This recalls Augustine's statement: "What then is the merit of man before grace by which merit he should receive grace? Since only grace makes every good merit of ours, and when God crowns our merits, He crowns nothing else but His own gifts."[16] The Catholic doctrine addresses Christian responsibility, but the primary issue is not what we do but what Christ does for us.

From the Lutheran side, indulgences in the Roman Catholic Church frequently look like a system in which Catholics merit grace. The Roman Catholic position on merit is highly nuanced. Catholics teach cooperation between God's grace and human freedom. Justification has been merited for us by the Passion of Christ.[17] No one can merit the initial grace of forgiveness and justification.[18] However, after this initial grace, again through the grace of the Holy Spirit, Catholics hold that "we can then merit for ourselves and for others the graces needed for our sanctification, for the increase of grace and charity, and for the attainment of eternal life."[19] Human merit is itself a grace and is due to God,[20] and with regard to God, there is no strict right to any merit on the part of human beings.

The gratuity of merit is supported by the scholastics, who identified three different degrees or kinds of merit: de condigno, de congruo, and de digno. In merit de condigno, reward is totally and exclusively proportional to the goodness of an act and is owed according to distributive justice. In merit de congruo, there is no such exact proportion between an act the reward given for it. No obligation exists for the reward in justice, and the conferral of the reward is done only by virtue of the generosity of the benefactor. In merit de digno, the reward raises a recipient to a higher level of worth and effects a transformation in that person. This reward is entirely a gift. The unanimous consensus of the scholastics was that the merit of a good action is only de congruo. It becomes de condigno only by virtue of the unmerited benevolence of God bestowed upon those who are in sanctifying grace, endowed with baptismal faith, and free from grievous sin. Consequently, because they are themselves gratuitous gifts from God,

---

16. Augustine, Ep. 154.5.6: "Quod est ergo meritum hominis ante gratiam, quo merito percipiat gratiam, cum omne bonum meritum nostrum non in nobis faciat nisi gratia et cum Deus coronat merita nostra, nihil aliud coronet quam munera sua?"
17. Catechism of the Catholic Church, §1992.
18. Ibid., §2010.
19. Ibid., §2010.
20. Council of Trent, DS 1545.

neither merit nor reward detract form the total sovereignty of God and the gratuity of grace.[21]

The topic of merit invariably raises questions about indulgences.[22] An indulgence is "a remission before God of the temporal punishment due to sins whose guilt has already been forgiven, which the faithful Christian who is duly disposed gains under certain defined conditions through the Church's help when, as minister of redemption, she dispenses and applies with authority the treasury of the satisfaction won by Christ and the saints."[23] Indulgences do not forgive sin, and they do not justify. They are for persons "who, although reconciled with God, are still marked by those 'remains' of sin which do not leave them totally open to grace."[24] Even in the justified there remain consequences of sin, effects from which we must be purified. The "punishments" and "remains of sin" refer to these negative effects or consequences of sin. The "merit" or "satisfaction" applied to an individual in an indulgence is the merit of Christ. The "treasury of the Church" is none other than "the infinite value, which can never be exhausted, which Christ's merits have before God."[25] It also includes the prayer and good work of the communion of saints.[26]

Three points deserve emphasis. First, the teaching on indulgences underscores the fact that any good we achieve is the work of Christ. Indulgences are an expression of the mercy of God, not a reward merited by our work through our own powers.[27] Healing comes from the work of Christ, not our own efforts. Second, the work of Christ creates a community, a "communion of saints." In the words of Paul VI's Apostolic Constitution on the Revision

21. George H. Tavard, "Merit as an Ecumenical Problem," *Ecumenical Trends* 26/9 (October 1997): 2/130. Tavard notes that merit *de digno* is Bonaventure's distinction (*Breviloquium*, part. 5, ch. 2, n. 3, 4) and that Thomas Aquinas does not recognize merit *de digno* as a category distinct form *de condigno*. Note 2.

22. For current Roman Catholic teaching on indulgences see Pope Paul VI, *Indulgentiarum Doctrina* (Apostolic Constitution on Indulgences), January 2, 1967; Catechism, §§1471–79; *Code of Canon Law* (1983) cc. 992–97. For a discussion of indulgences and ecumenical discussions of justification, see Michael Root, "The Jubilee Indulgence and the *Joint Declaration on the Doctrine of Justification*," *Pro Ecclesia* 9 (Fall 2000): 460–75.

23. See Pope Paul VI, *Indulgentiarum Doctrina* (Apostolic Constitution on Indulgences), January 2, 1967, Norm 1, repeated in *Code of Canon Law* (canon 992), the Catechism (§1471), and *Enchiridion Indulgentiarum: Normae et Concessiones*, 4th ed. (Vatican City: Libreria Editrice Vaticana, 1999), Norms, 1.

24. John Paul II, "Indulgences Are Expression of God's Mercy," §3, *L'Osservatore Romano* (Weekly English Edition), October 6, 1999, cited in Root, "The Jubilee Indulgence and the *Joint Declaration on the Doctrine of Justification*," 462. (This article transcribes the Holy Father's General Audience Address of September 29, 1999.)

25. Catechism, §1476.

26. Ibid., §1477.

27. Paul VI, *Indulgentiarum Doctrina* (1967), §9.

of Indulgences, "The life of each individual son of God is joined in Christ and through Christ by a wonderful link to the life of all his other Christian brethren. Together they form the supernatural unity of Christ's Mystical Body so that, as it were, a single mystical person is formed."[28] Justification creates a community of all those saved in Christ, what we call the "mystical body of Christ." Neither tradition, Catholic or Lutheran, has sufficiently reflected on the implications of Christian community in the process of justification. Finally, even though a Reformation understanding of indulgences may find the theology and practice of indulgences objectionable, these do not contradict a Reformation understanding of justification since they do not bear on how a person is made righteous before God.

Since both justification and indulgences are neuralgic issues for Lutherans, the timing of the teaching on indulgences with respect to the work on the Joint Declaration was unfortunate. On November 29, 1998, the papal bull *Incarnationis Mysterium* was promulgated, proclaiming a special indulgence in connection with the Jubilee Year 2000. Furthermore, a new edition of the *Enchiridion Indulgentiarum*, the handbook on indulgences, was released the month before the Joint Declaration was signed. Consequently, the issue of indulgences has clouded the reception of the Joint Declaration.

The Theology of "Justified and Sinner"

Probably the most significant reservation in the Joint Declaration for Catholics, causing a year's delay in the signing, concerned the section on the justified person as sinner.[29] The question was whether the Lutheran understanding of the justified person as sinful can be compatible with the Catholic doctrine of personal renewal through the sacraments of baptism and penance in which all that can properly be called sin is taken away. The pertinent issues are (1) whether a person is truly renewed by grace, (2) the definition of sin for Lutherans and Catholics, and (3) the nature of concupiscence.

The common confession asserts: "in baptism the Holy Spirit unites one with Christ, justifies and truly renews the person."[30] Lutherans further confess that in Christ sinners are made just before God and are born anew. In

---

28. Ibid., §5.
29. Much of the material in this section of this chapter is from Susan K. Wood, "Observations on Official Catholic Response to Joint Declaration," in "A Symposium on the Vatican's Official Response to the Joint Declaration on Justification," *Pro Ecclesia* 7/4 (1998): 421–24.
30. Joint Declaration, §28.

section 29, which describes the Lutheran understanding of the condition of being "at the same time righteous and sinner," the Joint Declaration uses both imputation and transformation language to describe the change effected by grace. Catholics need to take Lutherans at their word here that a true renewal takes place. This is an instance where Lutherans tend to use both/and language and Catholics either/or language.

The Joint Declaration does not actually use the word "concupiscence" in section 29, leading to some ambiguity in the text: "Sin still lives in them (1 John 1:8; Rom. 7:17, 20), for they repeatedly turn to false gods and do not love God with that undivided love which God requires as their Creator (Deut. 6:5; Matt. 22:36–40 and parallels)." The text continues, "This contradiction to God is as such truly sin. Nevertheless, the enslaving power of sin is broken on the basis of the merit of Christ. It is no longer a sin that 'rules' the Christian." What seems conflated here are repeated sins (in the first sentence) and concupiscence (the sin that no longer "rules"). Perhaps repeated sins do not rule either, but it is difficult to determine this from the text. If so, a distinction between the two types of sin, repeated sins and concupiscence, is not made. At any rate, sin is forgiven daily, and a person is renewed daily in a return to baptism so that this sin no longer brings damnation and eternal death. This seems to suggest a repetition of forgiveness that parallels a repetition of sin.

One problem is that the word "sin" is used equivocally by Lutherans and Catholics. Both confessions would agree that sin is a voluntary disobedience to the divine will. Between the two confessions we can speak of mortal or deadly sin, venial sin, and concupiscence. In the most proper sense sin is the first—mortal or deadly sin—which alienates a person from God so as to result in damnation. This is where Catholics speak of being in a "state of sin" that is incompatible with justification.

Venial sin, however, does not deprive a person of "sanctifying grace, friendship with God, charity and consequently eternal happiness."[31] In this limited sense, even for Catholics, a person can be a sinner and justified at the same time, for such sins do not put persons in a "state of sin." Sin that is not deadly is sin only in some kind of analogous sense. It is "truly" sin, for even venial sins are "voluntary disobedience of the divine will," but not sin in the same way as that kind of sin that deprives a person of justification.

Catholics and Lutherans disagree on whether concupiscence is sin. Concupiscence, although considered truly sinful by Lutherans because it cannot

31. Catechism, §1863.

be said to be a graced love of God, is not the same kind of sin as that which is a voluntary act of disobedience to divine will. Lutherans must therefore consider concupiscence (like venial sin) to be sin only in an analogous sense. It is no longer a sin that "rules" the Christian and does not result in damnation because of the renewal of the Christian in the return to baptism.

Another test question in this regard is whether for Lutherans there can be sin that deprives a person of justification. In the section on good works, *The Book of Concord* names the possibility of sin that precludes justification: "We also reject and condemn the teaching that faith and the indwelling of the Holy Spirit are not lost through malicious sin, but that the holy ones and the elect retain the Holy Spirit even though they fall into adultery and other sins and persist in them."[32] A person can also lose justifying faith.

However, the question here is posed from a Catholic perspective inquiring about the possibility of driving a wedge between *iustus* and *peccator*. Such a question does violence to the original intent of the text, which was not to refute *simul iustus et peccator*. From a Lutheran perspective, it is the wrong question because it is asked from the perspective of the sinner rather than from the perspective of God's gracious mercy in Christ. It is a question asked in the mode of third-person reflection rather than in terms of the direct address with which the promise of justification is stated. For Lutherans the condition of the sinner is left to the hidden will of God. Similarly Catholics teach that existentially we do not know with certainty our salvation although there is a lot of third-person reflection in the abstract about what would constitute the loss of sanctifying grace.

In Lutheran teaching the person with justifying faith does not keep sinning because the promise of justification creates faith, and where faith is present only good works can follow. Good works are the fruit of justifying faith. Lutherans understand justifying faith as placing one's trust wholly in one's Creator and Redeemer and thus living in communion with God.[33] This affects all dimensions of the person and leads to a life in hope and love. The Lutheran approach is to believe in the promise of mercy and leave the condition of the sinner in some kind of apophatic silence.

The churches move toward this point from two different conceptual backgrounds. On the one hand, Roman Catholics affirm the true renewal achieved through grace. The point of departure is the renewal accomplished in baptism. However, this is conceived within the terms of a metaphysics that maintains

32. Theodore G. Tappert, ed. and trans., *The Book of Concord: The Confessions of the Lutheran Church* (Philadelphia: Fortress, 1959), 477. The quotation is from the Epitome of Article IV, which is headed Good Works, False Antitheses, 3.

33. Joint Declaration, §26.

that a person cannot be in two states simultaneously. Either a person is in a state of alienation from God, or that person is in a state of grace and is justified. On the other hand, the Lutheran position seems to be more of a dialectic that departs from an experiential starting point. There is the experience of repeated sins. Justification or salvation takes its meaning from the need to be justified or saved, that is, the experience of sin. The experience of sin speaks to the incapacity of the sinner of achieving his or her salvation on his or her own efforts. The experience of receiving God's promise of justification through faith and the experience of being a sinner incapable of achieving one's own justification coincide. The result is a doctrine of *simul iustus et peccator*.

Here is one example where the differences in the two traditions are neither a matter of linguistics nor emphasis, but are conceptual. In order to ascertain whether the different assertions are compatible one must view them within their own conceptual framework and not superimpose a different framework on one's dialogue partner. The condemnations do not apply here for Lutherans, for they do not pose the question in the categories that Trent condemns, and there is agreement on the qualitative difference between concupiscence and the sin that "rules" or puts one in a state of profound alienation from God.

From a Catholic perspective, it is helpful to note that the scholastic approach to the impossibility of two simultaneous opposite states (the state of sin and the state of grace) is not our only heritage. We also have the witness of the liturgy in which "the law of praying" also constitutes "the law of belief" in the principle *lex orandi, lex credendi*. Before Catholics receive the Eucharist they pray, "O Lord, I am not worthy to receive you, say but the word and my soul will be healed."[34] Since Catholics are supposed to be in the state of grace as they approach the table, this affirmation of unworthiness constitutes a sort of confession of *simul iustus et peccator*. Some might argue that unworthiness is not always an affirmation of sin and might, for example, simply be a demonstration of the distance between creature and creator, or a confession of venial sin rather than moral sin, but the affirmation of unworthiness seems to carry a stronger meaning. Even if, technically, venial sin is sin only analogously, Catholics still consider it to be sin.

The Annex expresses the concept of *simul iustus et peccator* in two paragraphs. The first expresses the state of being justified:

"We confess together that God forgives sin by grace and at the same time frees human beings from sin's enslaving power (. . .)" (JD 22). Justification

34. Luke 7:6–7.

is forgiveness of sins and being made righteous, through which God "imparts the gift of new life in Christ" (JD 22). "Since we are justified by faith, we have peace with God" (Rom. 5:1). We are "called children of God; and that is what we are" (1 John 3:1). We are truly and inwardly renewed by the action of the Holy Spirit, remaining always dependent on his work in us. "So if anyone is in Christ, there is a new creation: everything old has passed away; see, everything has become new!" (2 Cor. 5:17). The justified do not remain sinners in this sense (2.A).

In a second paragraph the Annex expresses the condition of being a sinner:

> Yet we would be wrong were we to say that we are without sin (1 John 1:8–10, cf. JD 28). "(A)ll of us make many mistakes" (Jas 3:2). "Who is aware of his unwitting sins? Cleanse me of many secret faults" (Ps. 19:12). And when we pray, we can only say, like the tax collector, "God, be merciful to me, a sinner" (Luke 18:13).

This is expressed in a variety of ways in our liturgies. Together we hear the exhortation, "Therefore do not let sin exercise dominion in your mortal bodies, to make you obey their passions" (Rom. 6:12). This recalls to us the persisting danger that comes from the power of sin and its action in Christians. To this extent, Lutherans and Catholics can together understand the Christian as *simul iustus et peccator*, despite their different approaches to this subject as expressed in the Join Declaration (§§29–30).

Baptism and Justification

One of the curiosities of history is that Catholics were out of communion with Lutherans for five hundred years on the doctrine of justification, while being in communion on the doctrine and practice of baptism.[35] Baptism has been called by both traditions a sacrament of justification, yet theological treatments of justification remain all too often uninformed by a theology of baptism. The positive reception of the Joint Declaration on the Doctrine of

35. Lutheran–Roman Catholic unity on baptism was confirmed in the United States Joint Statement, "One Baptism for the Remission of Sins" (1966): "We were reasonably certain that the teachings of our respective traditions regarding baptism are in substantial agreement, and this opinion has been confirmed at this meeting": in *Building Unity: Ecumenical Dialogues with Roman Catholic Participation in the United States*, Ecumenical Documents IV, edited by Joseph A. Burgess and Brother Jeffrey Gros, FSC (New York: Paulist Press, 1989), 90.

Justification seems eminently reasonable when remembering this common baptismal foundation of both traditions.

The Joint Declaration on the Doctrine of Justification mentions baptism in six paragraphs. Three of these are in statements representing joint agreement,[36] two in statements referring to Catholic understanding,[37] and one within a Lutheran understanding of the justified as sinner.[38] Roman Catholic and Lutheran confessional teaching on baptism as a sacrament of justification is consonant with the consensus statements in the Joint Declaration on the Doctrine of Justification. Concerning the biblical message of justification, we find:

> 11. [Justification] occurs in the reception of the Holy Spirit in baptism and incorporation into the one body (Rom 8:1f, 9f; 1 Cor 12:12f).

Concerning justification by faith and through grace . . . :

> 25. By the action of the Holy Spirit in baptism, they are granted the gift of salvation, which lays the basis for the whole Christian life.

Concerning the justified as sinner:

> 28. We confess together that in baptism the Holy Spirit unites one with Christ, justifies and truly renews the person.

The statement explicitly asserts that justification occurs in the reception of the Holy Spirit in baptism and that baptism justifies and truly renews. This affirms that baptism and justification are God's action rather than a human work of the church or the recipient of the sacrament.[39] The renewal of the person in justification occurs in Christ through the agency and reception of the Holy Spirit.

These statements are faithful to the tradition of both Lutherans and Catholics, but it perhaps raises the Lutheran teaching on the effects of baptism to a new visibility or emphasis by connecting it more explicitly with a theology of justification.

The Joint Declaration brings together the ideas of justification as transformation and the teaching on being justified and yet a sinner, the

36. Joint Declaration, §§11, 25, 28.
37. Ibid., §§27, 30.
38. Ibid., §29.
39. Large Catechism, 6.10.35.

traditional Catholic claim of being "made" righteous and the traditional Lutheran claim of being "declared" righteous. It says, "We confess together that God forgives sin by grace and at the same time frees human beings from sin's enslaving power and imparts the gift of new life in Christ."[40] The Joint Declaration avoids the traditional impasse by situating jus-tification within the context of interpersonal relationship with Christ through the power of the Spirit, a relationship established in baptism. The interior change in the justified occurs as a result of their new iden-tity as Christians, defined as those who live by being united to Christ and who are called to a life of Christian discipleship.[41] Thus the change in state is ultimately relational; Christians are renewed because they are now related to Christ.

A Criterion That Norms All Other Criteria

For Lutherans the doctrine of justification by faith alone is a criterion that provides the norm for all other criteria. This doctrine stands in an essential relation to all truths of faith and serves to orient all the church's teaching and practice to Christ. Roman Catholics wonder whether it can be seen as *the* criterion. The final draft of the proposed declaration ad-dresses this concern in §18, significantly noting that "When Catholics see themselves bound by several criteria they do not deny the special function of the message of justification." Likewise, Lutherans emphasize the unique significance of this criterion but do not deny the interrelation and signifi-cance of all truths of faith.

The core of the doctrine is the confession of "Christ . . . who alone is to be trusted above all things as the one Mediator (1 Tim 2:5f) through whom God in the Holy Spirit gives himself and pours out his renewing gifts." While Lutherans and Catholics may dispute whether justification by faith is the sole criterion or one criterion among several, both hold unquestioningly that all salvation is the salvation of Christ. Justification is by Christ alone. The uniqueness and salvific universality of Jesus Christ was emphasized by the Congregation for the Doctrine and the Faith in its declaration, *Dominus Jesus*.[42]

40. Joint Declaration, §22.

41. John J. McDonnell, "The Agreed Statement on Justification: A Roman Catholic Perspective," *Ecumenical Trends* 28/4 (May 1999): 11/75.

42. Congregation for the Doctrine and the Faith, "'*Dominus Jesus*': On the Unicity and Salvific Universality of Jesus Christ and the Church," *Origins* 30/14 (September 14, 2000): 209, 211–19. The

Effect on Church Identity

Another challenge to the catechesis of this document lies not so much in the theology it contains but in the question of the effect of this proposed agreement on our concept of church identity. Although perhaps more of an issue for Lutherans, it is not entirely foreign to Roman Catholics. In the 1950s Henri de Lubac wrote: "It is a pity to have to learn your catechism against someone else." Unfortunately, in the past this has been all too true. Different faith traditions tend to define themselves contrastively by what someone else is not. There is a fear that if the differences between churches are overcome, we will lose our ecclesial identity and cease to be either Catholics or Lutherans. This fear has the potential to evoke powerful existential anxieties concerning not only ecclesial identity but also ecclesial survival.

Although Lutherans and Catholics are separated Christian churches, their common belief in Christ and the gospel far outweighs their differences. Christians have become so accustomed to separation that people sometimes wonder why the division among Christian churches is considered scandalous. The Lutheran and Catholic traditions have had different histories since the sixteenth century. They hear different emphases within the one gospel. Ecumenical convergence asks them not to give up their identity or forget their particular histories but to transcend the particularities of their historical differences in order to affirm a substantial unity in which they can declare themselves to be in full, visible communion.

A different threat to church identity is posed when ecumenical agreements are viewed as "lowest common denominator Catholicism." Dialogue is not a negotiating process seeking a lowest common denominator of agreement. Nor is it simply a revisiting of our historical past to clear up misunderstandings, although that is also an ecumenical task. In dialogue, faith traditions must always remain faithful to their deepest identity. In situations where dialogue partners must take account of "binding positions" that explicitly condemn the other, it can be helpful to clarify exactly what the "binding position" of the church is and in what ways it sought to preserve

---

document's teaching in sections 16–18 on the uniqueness and unity of the church is more problematic from an ecumenical perspective, although arguably it is simply a repetition of traditional Roman Catholic teaching. Many ecclesial communities issuing from the Reformation consider themselves to be churches, and some believe themselves to be in historic apostolic succession. Even without historic apostolic succession, some of these groups believe in the real presence in their Eucharist. In reality all Christian groups have their own definition of what constitutes a church and these definitions do not coincide.

the integrity of the gospel in a particular context. Ecumenical consensus is consensus on the gospel and the means of salvation.

This consensus leaves many questions unanswered. For example, it does not give the consequences of an agreement on justification for social ethics, authority in the church, ministry, the sacraments, or the relationship between the word of God and church doctrine. However it does provide a common basis for examining these issues.[43] Ratification of this document does not bring Lutherans and Romans into full communion with each other, but it is an important and historic event in the lives of these communities with far-reaching implications for ongoing catechesis.

43. For example, the tenth round of the U.S. Lutheran–Roman Catholic dialogue built on this consensus in its document, Randall Lee and Jeffrey Gros, FSC, eds., *The Church as Koinonia of Salvation: Its Structures and Ministries*, Lutherans and Catholics in Dialogue 10 (Washington, DC: U.S. Conference of Catholic Bishops, 2004).

3

The Joint Declaration
on the Doctrine of Justification

A Lutheran Systematic Theological Perspective

MICHAEL ROOT

In our postmodern times, the perspective from which a subject is viewed has moved from the unthematized background into the foreground of attention. What is seen and how it is seen is shaped by the angle of sight. Such attention to the subject and the subject's perspective can itself be interpreted as yet another expression of the narcissism of our time. Nevertheless, such a shift need not imply the abandonment of all claims to objectivity, but rather might permit a more careful testing of the way our perspectives not only shape but also limit and distort our judgments and perceptions.

This chapter both proceeds from a particular perspective and attempts to bring that perspective under analysis. We will not look at the Joint Declaration on the Doctrine of Justification from the perspective of a generic Protestant theology (if there is such a thing) but rather from the specific viewpoint of a Lutheran understanding of the content and shape of theology. For Lutherans the doctrine of justification plays a more central and defining role than it does for most, perhaps all, other strands of Protestantism. In addition, while the differences between the specific Lutheran understand-ings of various details of the doctrine of justification and those of, say, the Reformed or Methodist traditions are by no means church-dividing, they matter when the different Protestant traditions discuss justification and related topics with Catholics. The Methodist theologian Geoffrey Wain-wright has noted how, on specifically Methodist grounds, he finds himself agreeing with the Lutheran outlook at some points in the Joint Declaration, with the Catholic outlook at other points, and with neither at still other points.[1] This essay will take up an explicitly Lutheran viewpoint.

This perspective will not be simply presupposed, however. As the perspec-tive shapes what is seen, so what is seen can transform the perspective. This raises the question of how the Joint Declaration affects the self-understand-ing and tasks of Lutheran systematic theology. Should Lutheran systematic theology think of itself in a different way because of the Joint Declaration? Does the Joint Declaration highlight certain issues that Lutheran systematic theology should now take up with increased vigor?

Should There Be Such a Thing as "Lutheran Systematic Theology"?

The Joint Declaration raises a disturbing question: should there continue to be such a thing as "Lutheran systematic theology," that is, systematic theology for which distinctively Lutheran commitments determine the general shape of the total theological position, in distinction from system-atic theology that merely happens to be done by Lutherans or that gives typically Lutheran answers to certain important questions but is not shaped throughout by distinctively Lutheran commitments? In other words, should there be a "systematically Lutheran" systematic theology? One might waver in response to this question if one views Lutheranism as one way to grasp the gospel, a way organized by certain important, even crucial insights, but also a way with certain blind spots and failings. One would not waver if one viewed Lutheranism as *the* theological perspective uniquely equipped to bring out the evangelical character of the gospel, a character regularly missed by most, perhaps all, other systematic perspectives.

The Joint Declaration calls into question such an unwavering commit-ment to a distinctively Lutheran theology. In the Joint Declaration, Catho-lics and Lutherans agree on "basic truths of the doctrine of justification."

---

1. Geoffrey Wainwright, "Rechtfertigung: lutherisch oder katholisch? Überlegungen eines meth-odistischen Wechselwählers," *Kerygma und Dogma* 45 (1999): 182–206.

Attention has been called to the fact that the Joint Declaration usually says only "basic truths," not "the basic truths." Nevertheless, §5 states that while the agreement "does not cover all that either church teaches about justification," it "does encompass a consensus on basic truths of the doctrine of justification and shows that the remaining differences in its explication are no longer the occasion for doctrinal condemnations." If any remaining differences are not the occasion for doctrinal condemnations, then one can conclude that the remaining differences do not concern matters that could plausibly be called "basic truths." These differences are rather to be understood as "differing explications" (§14) or "differences of language, theological elaboration, and emphasis" (§40). The Joint Declaration should not be taken as saying that Lutherans and Catholics are somehow "really saying the same thing" about justification, simply using different words or conceptualities to elaborate their differing outlooks. Nor is the Joint Declaration asserting that the remaining differences are necessarily complementary. The remaining differences are real and they may represent noncomplementary alternatives, but these differences are encompassed within the larger context of a comprehensive set of agreements and the debate over these remaining differences is the sort of debate that need not divide the church.

The significance of this agreement can be emphasized by juxtaposing two quotations: First, the closing sentence of §15 of the Joint Declaration states, "Together we confess: By grace alone, in faith in Christ's saving work and not because of any merit on our part, we are accepted by God and receive the Holy Spirit, who renews our hearts while equipping and calling us to good works." Place that statement next to this famous quotation from Martin Luther in his Galatians commentary of 1535: "All we aim for is that the glory of God be preserved and that the righteousness of faith remain pure and sound. Once this has been established, namely that God alone justifies us solely by His grace through Christ, we are willing not only to bear the pope aloft on our hands but also to kiss his feet."[2] By Luther's standard, it would appear that the need for a distinct Lutheran movement and a distinct Lutheran systematic theological perspective has disappeared in the wake of the Joint Declaration. Even if one would not draw such a radical conclusion, the Joint Declaration calls for a reappraisal within Lutheran theology.

Lutheran theology has often been what one could call "essentially contrastive." In a sense, contrast is built into any concept. To be one thing in

2. Martin Luther, *Luther's Works*, American ed. (St. Louis: Concordia; Philadelphia: Fortress, 1955), 26:99 [WA 40a:181]).

particular is not to be other things. But we can distinguish this aspect of perhaps all concepts from the specific characteristics of concepts that are essentially bound up with or defined by some contrast. These essentially contrastive concepts are often one side of mutually defining and mutually exclusive polarities. The concept "parent" implies a corresponding concept, "child." Neither the concept "parent" nor the concept "child" makes any sense without its specific contrast with the other. I cannot be both the parent and the child of the same person. Likewise, some things cannot be meaningfully called tall unless some other things are at least relatively short. Nothing can be on my right hand unless there is also a left hand.

Lutheranism, or at least certain significant tendencies within Lutheranism, has almost from its outset been invested in contrastive self-definition. Luther's conclusion, reached no later than 1521, that the pope was the antichrist[3] brought with it a whole way of thinking about the Lutheran movement. The Lutherans were the persecuted remnant of the last days, opposed by the false church of the antichrist, who had set up his throne in the temple of God. The very concept of "persecuted remnant" was embedded in a narrative that contrasted it with the persecuting majority, the false church. Of course, these two groups were mutually exclusive, and ecumenical rapprochement between them unthinkable, for "what agreement does Christ have with Belial?" (2 Cor. 6:15). This apocalyptically colored outlook had a chilling effect on the course of the Reformation. Real rapprochement was incompatible with the contrastive self-identification that went with the apocalyptic narrative accepted by much of sixteenth-century Lutheranism.[4]

This apocalyptic contrastive definition fell away, but it was replaced by others. The debate in Lutheran circles over the Joint Declaration has thrown into relief a form of contrastive self-definition endemic within a prominent strand of contemporary Lutheran theology, typified most clearly by Gerhard Ebeling and Eberhard Jüngel in Europe and Gerhard Forde in the United States, a strand with roots both in the Luther renaissance of the early twentieth century and in dialectical theology, especially its more Bultmannian and Heideggerian side. As David Yeago has noted, true theology is defined for this outlook by a series of analogous dichotomies: law/gospel; letter/spirit; human action/divine action; works/faith. Each dichotomy

3. Scott H. Hendrix, *Luther and the Papacy: Stages in a Reformation Conflict* (Philadelphia: Fortress, 1981), 97–107.
4. See Robin Bruce Barnes, *Prophecy and Gnosis: Apocalypticism in the Wake of the Lutheran Reformation* (Stanford, CA: Stanford University Press, 1988).

represents a mutually exclusive pair: law or gospel, human action or divine action, work or faith.[5]

Decisive for this view is the assertion that these contrasts are definitive of the right understanding of Christian faith. To cite Yeago, these contrasts are taken to be "the prime structuring principle which bounds and orders the conceptual space within which the coherence of Christian belief must be thought out."[6] For this view the mere assertion of these dichotomies is not enough; they must be seen to be determinative of that which is truly Christian. True theology rightly grasps the contrast and allows it to determine all that the theologian says; false theology, usually identified as some gross or subtle form of sub-Christian legalism, fails to grasp the contrast or mistakenly seeks some way to mediate the antitheses.

Contrast is thus built into the formulation of a true theology. True (or Lutheran) theology is defined in an essentially contrastive way. The sort of mediation sought in the Joint Declaration must therefore be anathema. Precisely by challenging the finality of the defining contrasts, such texts challenge something essential. At stake is whether the contrasts by which at least some Lutherans define a true doctrine of justification are final and definitive of a right understanding of Christian faith or can be themselves contextualized and mediated by more comprehensive schemes.

I should stress that while this contrastive self-understanding has been an important strand in Lutheran history, it should not simply be identified with Lutheranism. There have been countertrends, even within the thought of Luther himself. For such a nineteenth-century Lutheran as Nicolai Grundtvig of Denmark, the typical Lutheran dichotomies are themselves to be understood within the larger context of the overarching narrative of creation and redemption.[7] For a twentieth-century theologian of such impeccable Lutheran credentials as Paul Althaus, law and gospel do not form a mutually exclusive pair that structures all Christian discourse, but are to be understood in the context of an ambiguous situation in which the inherently good divine commandment is deformed by human sin and made into an opponent of God's good intention. Law and gospel are mutually

5. David S. Yeago, "Theological Impasse and Ecclesial Future," *Lutheran Forum* 26/4 (November 1992): 36–45.

6. David S. Yeago, "Gnosticism, Antinomianism, and Reformation Theology: Reflections on the Cost of a Construal," *Pro Ecclesia* 2 (1993): 38–39.

7. See Michael Root, "Generous Orthodoxy: Regin Prenter's Appropriation of Grundtvig," in *Grundtvig in International Perspective: Studies in the Creativity of Interaction*, ed. A. M. Allchin, S. A. J. Bradley, N. A. Hjelm, and J. H. Schjørring (Aarhus: Aarhus University Press, 2000), 45–58.

exclusive in one context, but that context is not solely determinative of the entirety of Christian faith and life.[8]

A noncontrastive Lutheran systematic theology would take up the specific insights of the Reformation but would not understand itself as compelled to make them determinative for its general structure or for many of the details of its commitments. It would be open to considering resources from other traditions and limitations within its own tradition. An important but little noted passage in the Joint Declaration comes in §42. The agreement reached, it says, takes nothing away "from the seriousness of the condemnations related to the doctrine of justification. . . . They remain for us 'salutary warnings' to which we must attend in our teaching and practice." Lutherans fully expect that Catholics will hear in Lutheran condemnations a warning of the ways Catholic theology can fall into a sort of works righteousness, despite its best intentions. But are Lutherans ready to hear in the condemnations of Trent a salutary warning about problematic possibilities in our own ways of thinking, especially in those canons of Trent we usually find most problematic, for example, those that condemn any who deny that our good works are not only gifts of grace but also our merits (canon 32, but also 24 and 26)? On the one hand, Lutherans need to make a much better effort to understand what theologians such as Aquinas in fact meant when they spoke of merit.[9] On the other hand, Lutherans need to ask ourselves whether there are aspects of the Christian life we have neglected in our modern rejection of the concept of merit.[10] For Lutheranism, what is "the holiness without which no one will see the Lord" that is mentioned in Hebrews 12:14? Merit may very well be a concept Lutheranism will continue to find at best dangerous and at worst unevangelical, but in the polarized situation of division, have we Lutherans failed to speak of that which merit was used to express, however badly?[11]

The two most impressive examples of Lutheran systematic theology written in the last twenty years—Robert Jenson's (in the United States)[12]

---

8. Paul Althaus, *Gebot und Gesetz: zum Thema "Gesetz und Evangelium"* (Gütersloh: Bertelsmann, 1952); ET, *The Divine Command* (Philadelphia: Fortress Press, 1966).

9. See, e.g., the recent study by Joseph Wawrykow, *God's Grace and Human Action: 'Merit' in the Theology of Thomas Aquinas* (Notre Dame, IN: University of Notre Dame Press, 1995).

10. The concept of merit plays a larger role in the Lutheran confessions than is often noticed. Note Melanchthon's affirmation of merit (though not in relation either to justification or to eternal life) in the octavo edition of the *Apology*, Article 4, in Robert Kolb and Timothy J. Wengert, eds., *The Book of Concord: The Confessions of the Evangelical Lutheran Church* (Minneapolis: Fortress, 2000), 171.

11. I have attempted to deal with merit along these lines in Michael Root, "Aquinas, Merit, and Reformation Theology after the *Joint Declaration on the Doctrine of Justification*," *Modern Theology* 20 (2004): 5–22.

12. Robert W. Jenson, *Systematic Theology* (New York: Oxford University Press, 1997).

and Wolfhart Pannenberg's (in Germany)[13]—fit the model of a Lutheran systematic theology that is noncontrastive. Lutheran insights are taken up, but they are not all-determinative, nor are they treated as beyond question. In the preface to the first volume of his *Systematic Theology* Jenson states:

> To live as the church in the situation of a divided church—if this can happen at all—must at least mean that we confess we live in radical self-contradiction and that by every churchly act we contradict that contradiction. Also theology must make this double contradiction at and by every step of its way. . . . A theologian who described her or his own work as "Lutheran" or "Reformed" or whatever such, and meant by that label to identify the church the work was to serve, would either deny the name of church to all but his or her own allegiance or desecrate the theological enterprise.[14]

If there is to continue to be a distinctly Lutheran systematic theology, it will avoid being sectarian only if it systematically seeks to contradict the contradiction of Christian division.

Justification as Criterion

In relation to the fundamental nature and character of systematic theology, the most prominent issue raised in the debate over the Joint Declaration concerned the role that justification (or the message of justification or the doctrine of justification) should play in systematic theology. Here the abstract question of contrastive or noncontrastive approaches to theology takes on specificity.

In §18 of the Joint Declaration, Catholics and Lutherans together affirm that the doctrine of justification "is more than just one part of Christian doctrine. It stands in an essential relation to all truths of faith, which are to be seen as internally related to each other. It is an indispensable criterion which constantly serves to orient all the teaching and practice of our churches to Christ." The text then goes on to note a Lutheran-Catholic difference: "When Lutherans emphasize the unique significance of this criterion, they do not deny the interrelation and significance of all truths of faith. When Catholics see themselves as bound by several criteria, they do not deny the special function of the message of justification."

13. Wolfhart Pannenberg, *Systematische Theologie* (Göttingen: Vandenhoeck & Ruprecht, 1988); ET, Wolfhart Pannenberg, *Systematic Theology* (Grand Rapids: Eerdmans, 1991).

14. Jenson, *Systematic Theology*, 1:vii.

This paragraph was at the center of the intense debate over the Joint Declaration among German Lutherans. Eberhard Jüngel of Tübingen, one of the sharpest of the critics, led the way with an article in the *Zeitschrift für Theologie und Kirche* titled "Um Gottes willen, Klarheit!" (For God's Sake, Clarity!), although he later came to support the Joint Declaration after the Annex was developed. As will become clear, Jüngel's arguments were rooted in his own distinctive theology, but his arguments were both so widely influential and sufficiently typical that they can serve as the focus for an analysis of the issue.

Despite the title of Jüngel's article, what is most striking about the Lutheran debate over justification as a criterion is its lack of conceptual clarity. This unclarity appears in three separate areas. First, rarely do the authors involved consistently adhere to a specific definition of the content or subject matter of the doctrine of justification. Justification seems to function as an accordion concept, expanding and shrinking as the occasion demands. When called on to defend their statements about the centrality of justification, Lutherans have a tendency initially to take a specific definition of the article and then expand it to include the entirety of soteriology. For example, Jüngel states, "The Easter hymn summarizes it most powerfully and profoundly: If he had not risen, the world would have perished. If you have grasped that, you have grasped the doctrine of justification."[15] In light of this statement, does justification mean anything more specific than "Jesus saves by means of his resurrection"? Jüngel, in another context, states that God's word to Cain that he will place a mark on him so that others will not kill him is "the first word of justification, the first text that deals with the justification of the sinner."[16] Does this indicate that justification can mean even less than "Jesus saves"? Without some clear and plausible account of what is meant by justification (or the message or doctrine of justification), arguments about justification's function in theology are almost certainly pointless.

Second, rarely are distinctions made between a necessary criterion, a sufficient criterion, and a necessary and sufficient criterion. A necessary but not sufficient criterion would be a criterion needed to identify some particular thing, but not perhaps adequate by itself to identify that thing. A sufficient criterion would be sufficient by itself to identify some thing, but may be one of a number of such criteria, no one of which is necessary.

---

15. Eberhard Jüngel, *Justification: The Heart of the Christian Faith: A Theological Study with an Ecumenical Purpose*, trans. Jeffrey F. Cayzer (Edinburgh: T & T Clark, 2001), 13; trans. of Eberhard Jüngel, *Das Evangelium von der Rechtfertigung des Gottlosen als Zentrum des christlichen Glaubens: Eine theologische Studie in ökumenischer Absicht* (Tübingen: Mohr Siebeck, 1998), 11.

16. Jüngel, *Justification*, 11 (*Evangelium der Rechtfertigung*, 9).

A necessary and sufficient criterion would be both. It is simply pointless to debate whether justification is "a" or "the" criterion in theology without any further elaboration of what sort of criterion is meant.

Third, Lutheran advocates of a significant criteriological role for the doctrine of justification often conflate the notions of a criterion, an axiom, and a hermeneutical key. A criterion is simply something used to distinguish some specific thing from other things. A ruler is a criterion of length; it distinguishes that which is a certain length from that which is not. The canon of the Bible distinguishes books that are scriptural from books that are not. To say that the doctrine of justification is a criterion is simply to say that it serves to distinguish one thing from another, usually the gospel from that which is not gospel. A criterion is quite different from an axiom, a statement or principle from which other statements or principles might be derived. Sometimes, even if not often, justification (usually conceptually reshaped to some degree) is said to be an axiom from which all theology derives; Eilert Herms, for example, makes this claim.[17] More often a criterion is confused with a hermeneutical key, that is, some principle or statement that constitutes an interpretive perspective through which some reality is interpreted.

Justification could be a criterion—necessary, sufficient, or both—without being a hermeneutical key. The doctrine of justification would be a necessary criterion if every Christian assertion or practice needed to be tested for consistency with it. Justification could have such a criteriological role, however, without having any particular hermeneutical role. During the debate on the Joint Declaration, the distinction between the possible criteriological and hermeneutical roles of justification was regularly overlooked. The Joint Declaration itself ran criteriological and hermeneutical functions together by stating (§18) that the doctrine of justification is "an indispensable criterion which constantly serves to orient all the teaching and practice of our churches to Christ."

During the debate on the Joint Declaration, extreme claims were made for the doctrine of justification both as criterion and as hermeneutical

---

17. "Es ist darauf zu insistieren, dass alle Einzelsätze der reformatorischen Theologie sich analytisch als Implikate *eines* Grundsatzes müssen verstehen lassen" (Eilert Herms, "Stellungnahme zum dritten Teil des Lima-Dokumentes 'Amt,'" *Kerygma und Dogma* 31 [1985]: 69). In this essay, this one "Grundsatz" seems directly to concern the word-character of revelation more than it does the acceptance of the sinner by the righteous God. On at least one occasion, Dorothea Wendebourg comes close to describing the doctrine of justification as a sort of axiom from which all other teaching must be derived: Dorothea Wendebourg, "'Kirche und Rechtfertigung': Ein Erlebnisbericht zu einem neueren ökumenischen Dokument," *ZTK* 93 (1996): 90.

key. Again, Jüngel is typical. On justification as criterion, he stated, "The doctrine of justification is the one and only criterion for all theological statements."[18] On justification as an interpretive category, he said, "In the justification article all these statements [the contents of the Creed] come to a head. The decision is made here first of all [allererst] as to who this God is, and what it really means to be creatively active."[19] Similarly, in relation to the classical christological affirmations, "It is only when explained by means of that doctrine [of justification] that Christology becomes a materially appropriate [sachgemäß] Christology at all [überhaupt]."[20] Justification plays this decisive hermeneutical role because it makes clear the soteriological, *pro nobis* character of the contents of the Christian message. The doctrine of justification serves "to bring to bear [zur Geltung zu bringen] the (objective) truth of the gospel as the truth which makes the sinner true [die den Sünder wahrmachende Wahrheit]."[21]

Both the hermeneutical and criteriological versions of this claim are deeply implausible. Note that it is not claimed that a Reformation doctrine of justification lays bare permanently important aspects of the faith to which any comprehensive theological scheme must do justice in some way. For such a claim the explicit doctrine of justification is not hermeneutically decisive; what is decisive is some aspect of that to which it refers or some more general rule of theology that it instantiates. This approach can claim some permanent significance for the particular perspective of the Reformation, but still grant that quite different theological perspectives, in which justification plays little explicit role, may adequately represent the essential truth.

Jüngel's claim is more extreme. He seems to be saying that without a hermeneutical use of the doctrine of justification, any Christology is not sachgemäß and thus inadequate at best. He concedes that the doctrine of justification may be at work even when its terminology is missing.[22] Such a concession may make sense in interpreting, say, Luther in the Catechisms,

18. Eberhard Jüngel, "On the Doctrine of Justification," *International Journal of Systematic Theology* 1 (1999): 25–52. On another occasion, however, Jüngel stated, "The cross of Jesus Christ is the ground and measure [Grund und Maß] of the formulation of metaphors which are appropriate to God" (Eberhard Jüngel, *Entsprechungen: Gott—Wahrheit—Mensch; Theologische Erörterungen*, 3rd ed. [Tübingen: Mohr Siebeck, 2002], 151; ET, Eberhard Jüngel, *Theological Essays*, trans. J. B. Webster [Edinburgh: T & T Clark, 1989], 65). Of course, cross and justification are closely related, but neither the realities referred to nor the doctrines that interpret them are simply identical. Again the lack of clarity of the extent of the reference of the terms "justification" or "doctrine of justification" makes argument difficult.

19. Jüngel, *Justification*, 16 (*Evangelium der Rechtfertigung*, 13).

20. Ibid., 29 (24).

21. Eberhard Jüngel, "Um Gottes willen—Klarheit!" *ZTK* 94 (1997): 394–406, at 404.

22. Jüngel, *Justification*, 21 (*Evangelium der Rechtfertigung*, 17).

where justification seems to play a shaping role even when the language of justification is not used, but it is unlikely to be convincing in interpreting John of Damascus, Vladimir Lossky, or John Zizioulas—or it will convince only by expanding justification to mean little more than that all salvation comes from Christ. Are such Christologies to be condemned to the outer darkness as *nicht sachgemäß* simply because the doctrine of justification is neither explicitly nor implicitly determinative within them? At this point, Lutheranism, against the intentions of the Reformers, becomes sectarian.

Jüngel's claim that the doctrine of justification is the one and only criterion of all theological statements is even more implausible. Consider the following statements:

- Marriage is a divinely instituted order of human life to be entered into by a man and a woman, not by two men or two women.
- Baptism carried out without any use of water, but only with the laying on of hands (as has been done in the Kimbanguist church of Central Africa), is not a valid baptism for it does not conform to baptism as divinely instituted.
- In eternal life, we will have no genuinely new experiences, but will receive back the experiences of this life in a new form.
- We cannot confidently assert whether or not Judas Iscariot will be included in God's final redemption (a claim by Karl Barth in vol. 2, part 2, of the *Church Dogmatics*).

These all would seem to be theological statements. Jüngel's criteriological claim seems to imply that if one wishes to determine the truth or "Christianness" of any of these statements, the only question one rightly can ask is how they relate to the doctrine of justification. It would appear that one could not ask: What is the place of sexual differentiation in human life and in what sense can it be said to be divinely willed? What is the right exegesis of passages in the New Testament that speak of Judas? How do we relate baptism with water to "baptism with the Spirit"? How does this life relate to eternal life? One would think that the answers to these questions would be among the criteria that would determine whether the sentences above are theologically acceptable. Following Jüngel, however, it would appear that they could play such a role only if these questions were in fact indirect means of asking about the relation of the above sentences to the doctrine of justification. It is hard to believe that Jüngel intends such an implausible result, but his words seem to dictate such.

When a theologian as brilliant as Jüngel says something so prima facie odd, the question should be asked whether the statements in question mean something other than what they seem to mean. Jüngel's assertions can be read in another light, but a light that still casts into question his more extreme statements.[23] The nature of truth is a subtle and elusive matter philosophically and even more difficult within theology, where truth in relation to God must be considered.[24] When Jüngel speaks of the doctrine of justification as a criterion of truth, he may not mean "truth"or "true" in precisely the same sense as when we say that the statement "Abraham Lincoln was born in Kentucky" is true or that "Karl Rahner was born in South Bend" is false. As noted, Jüngel says that the doctrine of justification concerns "the truth which makes the sinner true." The doctrine of justification perhaps is not a criterion for theological statements considered in every possible way, but a criterion for whether these statements bear a right relation to this truth that makes the sinner true. Understood in this way, Jüngel's exclusive claim for the criteriological role of justification is less baffling, but still not self-evident. On the contrary, does the doctrine of justification uniquely and exhaustively lay bare this saving truth? Might theological traditions that have made little appeal to the concept "justification" (for example, Orthodox theology) have their own ways of expressing this saving truth? Even read in this way, however, Jüngel has argued only for justification as a necessary criterion. This criterion would still need to be supplemented by other criteria. For example, an adequate theological discussion of human sexuality would need at least to be compatible with (and at best itself expressive of) a right understanding of justification as the truth that makes the sinner true. But it would also need to ask, "What is God's creative intention in the differentiation of the sexes?" With sufficient hermeneutical ingenuity, a theologian might be able to expand the doctrine of justification to take in this latter question also, but would such an expansion of justification do justice to the specificity of the question?

Extreme versions of the criteriological and hermeneutical claims for the doctrine of justification also raise questions about the normative role of the Bible in Lutheran systematic theology. If the doctrine of justification becomes the hermeneutical lens through which the Bible is comprehensively

23. The following paragraphs moderate my critique of Jüngel in "Continuing the Conversation: Deeper Agreement on Justification as Criterion and on the Christian as *simul iustus et peccator*," in *The Gospel of Justification in Christ: Where Does the Church Stand Toady?*, ed. Wayne Stumme (Grand Rapids: Eerdmans, 2006), 46–54.

24. On the theological interpretation of "truth," see Bruce D. Marshall, *Trinity and Truth*, Cambridge Studies in Christian Doctrine (Cambridge: Cambridge University Press, 1999).

interpreted and the sole criterion of true theology, is the result a hermeneutical circle of such tightness that the Bible can play no critical role in
relation to this interpretive scheme? Walter Kasper, still at the time Bishop
of Rottenburg-Stuttgart, raised this question to Jüngel. Jüngel responded
that, on the one hand, the Reformation understanding of justification was
itself developed out of a reading of the Bible. On the other hand, Jüngel
continued, "the subject matter [Sache] of Scripture is, according to the
Reformation understanding, identical with the article of justification. Accordingly, the article of justification is the authentic object of theology
('homo reus et perditus et deus iustificans vel salvator' [a quotation from
Luther on the object of theology])—a determination which was made on
the basis of Holy Scripture and which must anew be brought to bear within
Holy Scripture, if necessary against the canon of holy scriptures."[25] The
relation between the interpretive commitments brought to a text and the
linguistic and conceptual material that is present in the text as an artifact
independent of such commitments is, of course, complex. But the enterprise
of interpretation becomes arbitrary when the text can provide no check on
its own interpretation. If a Reformation understanding is identified with
the true Sache of Scripture in so a priori a manner, worries must arise about
the norms and sources that determine the systematic theology that flows
from such an understanding.

Worry expands when one reads Jüngel's dismissal of concerns for attend-
ing to the entire canon. He gives a brief exposition of Paul on justification
along traditional Lutheran lines, rejecting most recent Pauline scholarship
in a page and a half of the preface to the second edition of his recent book
on justification.[26] Jüngel then adds, "If you take this exposition of Paul
seriously, you will not be troubled by the question whether the rest of the
New Testament witness can be reconciled with the Pauline doctrine of
justification. Such a question presupposes a ban on any internal criticism of
biblical material."[27] To insist that theology attend to the range of the canon
is not to place a ban on any internal criticism. It is to say that the biblical
norm under which systematic theology operates obligates the theologian
to take into account the widest possible range of biblical material and that
the capacity to account for a wide range of biblical material on some topic
is to be taken as a virtue (though not the only virtue) in judging different
theological approaches. That Jüngel believes that the systematic rejection

25. Jüngel, "Klarheit," 401.
26. Jüngel, Justification, xxxi–xxxii.
27. Ibid., 20 (Evangelium der Rechtfertigung, 16).

of such an approach is dictated by Lutheran commitments on justification is at least worrisome.

The question of the canon extends beyond detailed matters of how we reconcile this or that outlook. It touches fundamental questions of how we read the Bible as constituting a single whole so that it may be coherently and consistently used as a norm in theology. Charles Wood has analyzed the way theology must engage in a "canonical construal," a decision about how the Bible constitutes a single, usable norm.[28] Is Lutheranism tied to a canonical construal that forces it to ignore much of the complexity of the biblical text? Karl Barth, in his first systematic theology lectures, noted (and criticized) the Lutheran tendency to "view revelation as a cone with a point which consists of a single communication of God to us: Your sins are forgiven you."[29] Luther himself was willing, at least on occasion, to take a rather different view: "The gospel is and should be nothing other than a chronicle, a history, a story of Christ, who he was, what he did, said, and suffered, which one person describes at length, and another briefly, one person in one way and another in another."[30] Perhaps the Christian faith or the revelation of God or the Bible is not like a cone that comes to a point, but rather, as the quotation from Luther suggests, a narrative that has its center in Christ but which stretches from creation through the history of Israel into the church (as the inclusion of Acts in the canon demonstrates) and on to the consummation of all things. This story cannot be read in just any way and still be gospel, but it can be read in a variety of evangelical ways. No one conceptual criterion determines the content and meaning of every aspect of that narrative, even if some (justification, incarnation, Trinity) constitute indispensable criteria for its right comprehension.

The question of how the normative role of Scripture is realized in theology relates directly to the question of the criteriological role of justification. Does justification's criteriological role undercut the normative authority of the canon of Scripture? Lutherans have criticized Catholic understandings of magisterial tradition as the normative interpretation of the Bible on the grounds that they leave insufficient room for Scripture to criticize and potentially correct magisterial tradition. But do Lutherans run the danger of placing an aspect of their own specific tradition, a Reformation understanding of justification, beyond the reach of scriptural

28. Charles M. Wood, *The Formation of Christian Understanding: An Essay in Theological Hermeneutics* (Philadelphia: Westminster, 1981), 99.

29. Karl Barth, *The Göttingen Dogmatics: Instruction in the Christian Tradition*, trans. Geoffrey W. Bromiley (Grand Rapids: Eerdmans, 1990), 171.

30. WA 10a, 9:15–18.

criticism and correction? The debate over justification as a criterion makes one worry.

Two Substantive Matters

The Joint Declaration not only confronts the Lutheran theologians with questions about the nature and method of Lutheran systematic theology; it also highlights certain substantive problems, only two of which can be mentioned—not fully discussed—here.

Most obviously, the Joint Declaration calls for a renewed discussion of the *simul iustus et peccator*, the assertion that the justified person is and remains a sinner in this life.[31] The explicitly Lutheran paragraph on this topic in the Joint Declaration (§28) is the longest and most tortuous in the text. For all the difficulty in drafting this paragraph and in the subsequent debate, the issues here should not be intractable. Lutheran-Catholic differences on this assertion are primarily a function of differing conceptual schemes and differing judgments about what problematic assertions are most to be avoided. Agreement would be aided by a close attention to Luther's detailed discussion of this question in his *Against Latomus* of 1521, where he explicitly developed the *simul* both in the sense of the Christian as totally just and totally sinful and in the sense of the Christian as partially just and partially sinful.[32] Since the Joint Declaration, significant progress has already been made on this topic in a comprehensive study on the *simul iustus et peccator* by the Catholic-Protestant Ökumenischer Arbeitskreis in Germany, the group that carried out the earlier study of doctrinal condemnations that played an important background role for the Joint Declaration. The group achieves a substantive consensus on the issue.[33]

A far more difficult issue raised for Lutheran systematic theology by the Joint Declaration is the role of human action in justification. The difficulties are implicit in §21 of the Joint Declaration. On the one hand, it states that Lutherans "do not deny that believers are fully involved personally in their faith," and they "do not deny that a person can reject the working of grace." On the other hand Lutherans insist that the saved are justified "strictly passively" (Latin *mere passive*) and cannot cooperate in their salvation because "they actively oppose God and his saving actions." But in the

---

31. I discuss the *simul* in "Continuing the Conversation," 54–59.
32. Luther, *Luther's Works*, 32:133–260 [WA 8:43–128].
33. Theodor Schneider and Gunther Wenz, eds., *Gerecht und Sünder zugleich? Ökumenische Klärungen*, Dialog der Kirchen 11 (Freiburg i.B.: Herder, 2001).

justified, this active opposition must be something other than rejection. That we are moved by grace is agreed. But the Lutheran confessions are clear that grace does not move us like a block or stone.[34] What is the nature of our personal engagement in our justification? In traditional terms, what is the role of the will in the reception of grace? There is more diversity in the history of Lutheranism on this question than is often recognized. Various Scandinavian theologians have been more willing than other Lutherans to speak of a role of the will in the reception of justification, as long as it is in no sense understood to be meritorious.[35] In American Lutheranism, the predestination controversy of the late nineteenth century involved similar questions.[36] When Philip Melanchthon suggested that the three causes of conversion were the Holy Spirit, the word of God, and the human will, he may very well have made a fundamental mistake in seeming to put these three on the same causal level, but was he simply wrong in trying to see a role for the human will within justification? Recent popular Lutheran discussions such as that by Gerhard Forde exclude the will so entirely that it is not clear that human reception of the gospel actually plays any significant role in justification.[37] It is precisely here that careful systematic work needs to be done.

⌒⌇⌒

An ecumenism that does not call for change in all our churches is an ecumenism that is not honest. We must not sacrifice unity for truth, but the truth that unity is given us in Christ and that we are called "to maintain the unity of the Spirit in the bond of peace" (Eph. 4:3) must not be sacrificed for the sake of maintaining the comfort of our divisions. The Joint Declaration is a challenge to theology, Lutheran and Catholic, to reconsider its methods and contents in the light of an agreed understanding of our salvation in the righteousness of Christ.

The Scriptures are the touchstone for such an ecumenical reevaluation. Ecumenism will thus always require the careful work of both theologians and biblical scholars. An attempt by Catholics and Lutherans to "reread

---

34. *Formula of Concord*, Solid Declaration, Article 2:59–60 (Kolb and Wengert, *Book of Concord*, 555).

35. See Regin Prenter, "Luthers 'Synergismus'?" in *Theologie und Gottesdienst: Gesammelte Aufsätze* (Aarhus: Forlaget Aros, 1977), 222–46. Prenter cites Ragnar Bring as arguing along the same line.

36. See the selections in Theodore G. Tappert, ed., *Lutheran Confessional Theology in America: 1840–1880*, Library of Protestant Thought (New York: Oxford University Press, 1972), 166–226.

37. Gerhard O. Forde, *Justification by Faith—A Matter of Death and Life* (Philadelphia: Fortress, 1982), 22.

Paul together" will thus need the engagement of both disciplines. The distance between the theological and biblical departments of contemporary seminaries and graduate schools can sometimes appear to be as great as that between the confessions. May the building of both ecclesial and disciplinary bridges continue.

4

Justification by Faith in Pauline Thought

A Catholic View

JOSEPH A. FITZMYER, S.J.

In light of the noteworthy signing of the Joint Declaration on the Doctrine of Justification by Lutherans and Roman Catholics on October 31, 1999, it is fitting to consider once again how our common reading of Pauline letters made that noteworthy event possible. No little part of the basic agreement was the preparatory work of almost thirty-five years of bilateral dialogue, both national and international, as well as the joint publication of the national document, *Justification by Faith* (1985) and of the international document, *Church and Justification* (1994). Both of these texts made clear our common understanding of the important Pauline teaching about justification by grace through faith. That fundamental teaching became the topic of our colloquium at the University of Notre Dame.

I have been asked to set forth a Catholic understanding of that important Pauline doctrine, and my further remarks on this topic will be made under four headings: (1) the Old Testament background of righteousness and justification; (2) the Christ-event and its effects; (3) Pauline justification in Romans and Galatians; and (4) other Pauline texts.

The Old Testament Background

The Pauline notion of justification was built on what the Hebrews of old had taught their people about the righteousness of God and his dealings with a sinful people, and about their righteousness with one another. *Tsedeq* or *tsedaqah* was predicated both of human beings and of God.

Per se, words of this root express a proper relationship between human beings in their interaction with one another, or between human beings and God.[1] This relationship is understood as what is right, fair, equitable, or honest in the interplay of human society: in the family, clan, tribe, or kingdom, whether as kings or commoners, kinsfolk or neighbors. It thus connotes a societal or judicial relationship, sometimes ethical and often forensic (i.e., related to law courts).[2]

Because the ancient Hebrews enjoyed a covenant with God, *tsedeq* expresses at times their responsibility to their transcendent partner in that pact. It also denotes God's expectations for Israel. One has only to read the first chapter of Isaiah, as the prophet quotes God's words to Judah and Jerusalem, to see how this was phrased: "How the faithful city has become a harlot, she that was full of justice! Righteousness [*tsedeq*] used to lodge in her, but now murderers" (Isa. 1:21).

Many Old Testament passages ascribe this quality to God, speaking of the righteous God as *tsaddiq* (Exod. 9:27; Deut. 32:4; Dan. 9:14; Job 34:17). They predicate *tsedaqah* of God, not only in his being, but also in his dealings with humanity (Ps. 36:7; 71:19). Especially in the older writings of the Old Testament, *tsedeq* expresses the quality whereby God, involved in a lawsuit with rebellious Israel, passes judgment on it and thereby upholds

---

1. See further G. Quell and G. Schrenk, "*dikē, dikaios, ktl,*" *TDNT* 2:174–225; J. J. Scullion, "Righteousness (OT)," *ABD* 2:724–36. Cf. J. A. Fitzmyer, "What Do the Scriptures Say about Justice?" in *Jesuit Education 21: Conference Proceedings on the Future of Jesuit Higher Education 25–29 June 1999,* ed. M. R. Tripole (Philadelphia: Saint Joseph's University Press, 2000), 98–112; J. Reumann, *Righteousness in the New Testament: "Justification" in the United States Lutheran–Roman Catholic Dialogue,* with responses by Joseph A. Fitzmyer and Jerome D. Quinn (Philadelphia: Fortress; New York/Ramsey, NJ: Paulist Press, 1982), 12–26, 197–202; D. H. van Daalen, "Paul's Doctrine of Justification and Its Old Testament Roots," *SE* 6 (TU 112, 1973): 556–70; H. Gross, "'Rechtfertigung' nach dem Alten Testament: Bibeltheologische Beobachtungen," *Kontinuität und Einheit: Für Franz Mussner* (Freiburg im B.: Herder, 1981), 17–29; Walter Klaiber, *Gerecht vor Gott: Rechtfertigung in der Bibel und heute,* Biblisch-theologische Schwerpunkte 20 (Göttingen: Vandenhoeck & Ruprecht, 2000); P. Stuhlmacher and D. A. Hagner, *Revisiting Paul's Doctrine of Justification: A Challenge to the New Perspective* (Downers Grove, IL: InterVarsity, 2001); C. H. Talbert, "Paul, Judaism and the Revisionists" *CBQ* 63 (2001): 1–22.

2. See Deut. 25:1 ("If there arises a dispute between human beings and they go to court, and the judges decide between them, acquitting [*wehitsdiqu*] the innocent and condemning the guilty . . ."); cf. Gen. 18:25–26.

his righteousness (Ps. 35:23–24; Jer. 12:1; Hos. 4:1–2). It thus denotes a forensic or judicial attribute of God the Judge, as he "judges the world with righteousness" or rewards Israel for its conduct in the covenantal relationship with him (Ps. 9:9). With alliteration and assonance, Isaiah expresses what God seeks from individual Israelites: "For he looked for what is right [mishpat], and behold bloodshed [mispakh]; for righteousness [tsedaqah], and behold a wailing cry [tse'aqah]" (5:7).

In the postexilic period, however, tsedeq as a quality of God acquired an added nuance, especially in Deutero-Isaiah, as it came to describe God's execution of his role in the covenant, acquitting his rebellious people, manifesting toward them his gracious salvific activity in a just judgment. In the words of Deutero-Isaiah, "I bring near my righteousness; it is not far off; my salvation will not tarry!" (Isa. 46:13). Here tsidqathi (my righteousness) stands in poetic parallelism with teshu'athi (my salvation), revealing the salvific nuance that God's righteous judgment has assumed.[3] Without the parallelism the same notion of God's salvific righteousness is found also in Isaiah 50:8; 53:11; 54:14, 17.

Although Noah is the first human being to be declared "a righteous man, blameless in his generation," because he "walked with God" (Gen. 6:9),[4] the adjective tsaddiq came to denote one who stood acquitted or vindicated before a judge's tribunal (Exod. 23:7; 1 Kings 8:32). It also is used to describe the covenantal status of righteousness achieved in God's sight by the observance of the statutes of the Mosaic law (Ps. 119:1–8, 75, 137–44). The Old Testament often notes, however, how difficult it was to achieve such a status (Job 4:17; 9:2; Ps. 143:2; Ezra 9:15). Yet Josephus could imagine nothing "more righteous" than obeying the statutes of the law (Ag. Ap. 2.41 §293).

Many of the Hebrew nuances of tsedeq, tsedaqah are likewise found in the Septuagint, where these words are regularly rendered by dikaiosynē, the adjective tsaddiq by dikaios, and the cognate verb by dikaioō. In this way all the passages I quoted above are regularly translated. It is important to note, however, how some passages fared as they were rendered into Greek in the

3. The same parallelism is found in Isa. 45:8; 51:5, 6, 8; 56:1; 61:10; 62:1–2; Ps. 40:10–11 (NRSV translates tsidqatheka "your saving help"); 98:2. See further J. J. Scullion, "Sedeq-Sedaqah in Isaiah cc. 40–66 with Special Reference to the Continuity in Meaning between Second and Third Isaiah," Ugarit-Forschungen 3 (1971): 335–48; J. N. Oswalt, "Righteousness in Isaiah: A Study of the Function of Chapters 55–66 in the Present Structure of the Book," in Writing and Reading the Scroll of Isaiah: Studies of an Interpretive Tradition, VTSup 70/1–2, ed. C. C. Broyles and C. A. Evans (Leiden: Brill, 1997), 1:177–91, esp. 179, 186.

4. This is said of Noah in a context that antedated the Mosaic law.

third–second century BCE. Thus Isaiah 56:1b, "For my salvation [*yeshu'athi*] is near and coming, my righteousness [*tsidqathi*] about to be revealed," becomes in Greek: *ēngisen gar to sōtērion mou paraginesthai kai to eleos mou apokalyphthēnai.* Here *tsedaqah* is translated by *eleos* (mercy, compassion), which usually renders Hebrew *khesed* and is a different quality often attributed to God in his deal-ings with human beings. Such a translation reveals, however, the softening nuance detected in the postexilic sense of God's *tsedaqah*, already mentioned. This is not an isolated instance of such translation, for it also occurs in Ezekiel 18:19, 21, where *mishpat utsedaqah* becomes *dikaiosynē kai eleos.*[5]

It is especially this postexilic nuance of God's saving *tsedaqah* that is echoed often in the later Palestinian Jewish writings of the Qumran com-munity in pre-Christian times. In the community rule book, one reads:

> As for me, I belong to wicked humanity, to the assembly of perverse flesh; my iniquities, my transgressions, my sins together with the wickedness of my heart belong to the assembly doomed to worms and walking in darkness. No human being sets his own path or directs his own steps, for to God alone belongs the judgment of him, and from his hand comes perfection of way. . . . And I, if I stagger, God's grace is my salvation forever [*khsdy 'l yshw'thy l'd*]. If I stumble because of a sin of the flesh, my judgment is according to the righteousness of God [*btsdqth 'l mshpty*], which stands forever. . . . In his mercy he has drawn me close [to him], and with his favors will he render judgment of me. In his righteous fidelity he has judged me; in his bounteous goodness he expiates all my iniquities, and in his righteousness he cleanses me of human defilement and of human sinfulness, that I may praise God for his righteousness and the Most High for his majesty. (1QS 11:9–15)[6]

Three things should be noted about this Qumran text. First, how it syn-thesizes in a remarkable way the Old Testament teaching about human sinfulness and God's righteous reaction to such sinfulness. Second, how its insistence on God's predestinating mercy provides an excellent Palestin-ian Jewish background to Pauline teaching about human righteousness and justification by grace, even though it is not entirely identical with the Pauline doctrine, as we shall see. Third, even though the Pauline phrase *dikaiosynē theou* (the righteousness of God) is found verbatim nowhere in the Old Testament, it does turn up here (*btsdqth 'l*, 1QS 11:12).[7] Such, then, is

---

5. One should also recall how often *tsedeq* or *tsedaqah* becomes in the Septuagint *eleēmosynē* (alms), which is a still further and later extension of the word's meaning in such passages as Greek Deut. 6:25; 24:13; Ps. 24:5; 33:5; 35:24; 103:6; Isa. 1:27; 28:17; Dan. 4:24; 9:16.

6. See also 1QH 4:30–38; 7:28–30; 9:32–34; 14:15–16.

7. It also occurs in 1QS 10:25.

the Old Testament and the Palestinian Jewish background of the concept of righteousness and justification as it will be used by Paul.

The Christ-Event and Its Effects

Building on such Old Testament and Palestinian Jewish understandings of righteousness, Paul introduces a new element, a reference to the historical event of the death of Jesus of Nazareth and of faith in him as the risen Lord. For Paul, Jesus Christ, the risen Lord, has become the unique way in which the "righteousness of God" is to be revealed henceforth in the Christian gospel. And so his basic teaching is a christocentric soteriology.

Paul speaks of Jesus as one descended from David (Rom. 1:3) and as *heis anthrōpos* (one man: Rom. 5:14, 17, 19), thus emphasizing what Jesus did as an individual human being in the course of his earthly life on behalf of all humanity.[8] Moreover, for Paul, Jesus is the Messiah born of Israelites: "From them by natural descent comes the Messiah, who is God over all, blest forever! Amen" (Rom. 9:5). Therefore, he acknowledges "Jesus our Lord, who was handed over [to death] for our trespasses and raised for our justification" (Rom. 4:25). He speaks often of Jesus' death (Rom. 5:5, 8, 10; 6:3, 5, 10; 8:34; 14:15), or of the shedding of his blood (Rom. 5:9). "Through his blood God has presented him a means of expiating sin for all who have faith" (Rom. 3:25). Moreover, Paul sees there an intimate connection between Jesus' cross and his resurrection, and this becomes the basis of his proclamation and explanation of Christian faith.[9]

"Christ-event" is a short way of referring to the complex of decisive moments of the earthly and risen life of Jesus Christ. Three moments are of foremost importance for Paul: Jesus' passion, death, and resurrection. But three other moments also have to be included: Jesus' burial, exaltation, and heavenly intercession, for he sees significance in these as well. That is why Paul understands Christian believers as identified with such preeminently salvific moments in his use of verbs compounded with the preposition *syn*, for instance: *sympaschein* (suffer with), *systaurousthai* (be crucified with), *synapothnēskein* (die with), *synthaptesthai* (be buried with), *syndoxasthai* (be

---

8. He is viewing Jesus' existence *kata sarka*, as he says in Rom. 1:3; 9:5.

9. See further H. Weder, *Das Kreuz Jesu bei Paulus*, FRLANT 125 (Göttingen: Vandenhoeck & Ruprecht, 1981); C. B. Cousar, *A Theology of the Cross: The Death of Jesus in the Pauline Letters*, OBT (Minneapolis: Fortress, 1990); D. M. Stanley, *Christ's Resurrection in Pauline Soteriology*, AnBib 13 (Rome: Biblical Institute, 1961).

glorified with).[10] Paul gives no evidence of having known Jesus personally in his earthly ministry,[11] and so he never speaks of the Christian "being born" with Christ or "walking with" Christ. Not having been an eyewitness of that ministry, he emphasizes rather those decisive moments of Jesus' existence, and they make up for him the Christ-event.

When Paul looked back at the Christ-event, he realized what Jesus Christ had accomplished for humanity, Jew and Greek alike. These are the *effects* of the Christ-event, or what later systematic theologians have often called the "objective redemption." Paul sums up those effects under ten different images: justification, salvation, reconciliation, expiation, redemption, freedom, sanctification, transformation, new creation, and glorification. Each of these images expresses a distinctive aspect of christocentric soteriology.

One might query whether there is really any difference among the ten images, and in reality I would have to admit that they are simply different ways of conceiving the basic mystery of Christ and his role. If the Christ-event is conceived of as a decahedron, a ten-sided solid figure, one can understand how Paul, gazing at one panel of it, might use one image to express its effect (e.g., he justified us), whereas he might use another image when gazing at another panel (e.g., he reconciled us). Each of the ten panels would be expressing only one aspect of the whole.

It is also necessary to realize that multiple images have been derived from Paul's Hellenistic and Jewish backgrounds and have been applied by him to the Christ-event and its effects.[12] In studying each of them, one has to consider its origin or background, its meaning for Paul, and the occurrences of it in his writings.

The image most frequently used by Paul to express an effect of the Christ-event is "justification" (*dikaiōsis, dikaioō*).[13] Years ago Albert Schweitzer called Pauline justification "a subsidiary crater, which has formed within the rim of the main crater—the mystical doctrine of redemption through the being-in-Christ" or a teaching that is "incomplete and unfitted to stand alone."[14] In making such a judgment, Schweitzer failed to distinguish ad-

---

10. From the deutero-Paulines one may add *synegeiresthai* (be raised with).

11. Not even 2 Cor. 5:16 need imply that he did.

12. See further J. A. Fitzmyer, *Paul and His Theology: A Brief Sketch*, 2nd ed. (Englewood Cliffs, NJ: Prentice Hall, 1989) 59–71 (§§67–90).

13. T. Söding, ed., *Worum geht es in der Rechtfertigungslehre? Das biblische Fundament der "Gemeinsamen Erklärung" von Katholischer Kirche und Lutherischem Weltbund*, QD 180 (Freiburg im B.: Herder, 1999); T. Schneider and G. Wenz, eds., *Gerecht und Sünder? Ökumenische Klärungen* (Freiburg im B.: Herder; Göttingen: Vandenhoeck & Ruprecht, 2001).

14. Albert Schweitzer, *The Mysticism of Paul the Apostle*, 2nd ed. (London: Black; New York: Macmillan, 1953; repr., New York: Seabury, 1968), 225–26.

equately the different Pauline images and subsumed justification under "redemption" or "being-in-Christ," as if they did not bear their individual or specific nuances. In contrast, Ernst Käsemann maintained that "justification is the heart of the Christian message."[15] That is obviously going too far; Käsemann unduly reduced the other effects of the Christ-event almost to irrelevance.[16] In order to appreciate the multifaceted soteriology in Pauline thought, one has to reckon with all these images and with their specific differences, for they are all expressions of the gospel.

Romans and Galatians

For anyone who reads Paul's letters to the Galatians and Romans, justification is clearly the effect of the Christ-event that claims pride of place. This image is drawn from Paul's Old Testament and Jewish backgrounds, as I have indicated above. It is necessary to stress this because the verb *dikaioō* in the Greek world otherwise meant "to make or set right" or "to deem right." When used with a personal direct object, it meant to "do someone justice," usually in the case of someone who has been unfair, violent, or wrong; hence it normally denoted "to pass sentence against, condemn, punish."[17] This negative sense prevailed in classical Greek, and only rarely did one find the positive sense, "to set right an injustice suffered."[18]

When *dikaioō* was used in the Septuagint to translate Hebrew *hitsdiq*, which always meant to "acquit, vindicate, declare innocent, justify,"[19] the Greek verb *dikaioō* took on a nuance that it did not normally have in extrabiblical Greek that is not dependent on the Greek Old Testament or New Testament.[20] The closest example in extrabiblical Greek to the Pauline usage is found in the (second- or third-century CE) *Corpus Hermeticum* (ed. W. Scott) 13.9: "For aside from judgment see how she has driven out

15. Ernst Käsemann, "Some Thoughts on the Theme 'The Doctrine of Reconciliation in the New Testament,'" in *The Future of Our Religious Past: Essays in Honour of Rudolf Bultmann*, ed. J. M. Robinson (New York: Harper & Row, 1971), 49–64, esp. 63.

16. See further J. A. Fitzmyer, "Reconciliation in Pauline Theology," in *To Advance the Gospel: New Testament Studies*, 2nd ed. (Grand Rapids: Eerdmans; Livonia, MI: Dove, 1998), 162–85, esp. 170–75.

17. So in Herodotus, *History* 1.100; 3.29; Aeschylus, *Agamemnon* 393; Plato, *Laws* 11.934b; Thucydides, *Peloponnesian Wars* 3.40.4; Aristotle, *Nicomachean Ethics* 5.9.2 §1136a.

18. Pindar, *Fragment* 169.3, quoted in Plato, *Gorgias* 484b; Polybius, 3.31.9.

19. E.g., Exod. 23:7; Deut. 25:1; Ps. 82:3; Isa. 5:23; 43:26.

20. The negative sense is not found in the Septuagint in any writings that depend on Hebrew usage, except perhaps in deuterocanonical Sir. 42:2, where *dikaiōsai ton asebē* renders Hebrew *lhtsdyq rsh'*, probably meaning "to pass sentence against the impious."

iniquity . . . we have been made righteous [*edikaiōthēmen*], my child, now that iniquity is absent." Here the verb connotes some kind of ethical change.[21] This means, therefore, that when Paul employs the verb *dikaioō* it generally has the Septuagintal judicial connotation, which is derived from the Hebrew hiphil *hitsdiq*, and that clearly reveals the Old Testament background of his image of justification. It is also colored by the Palestinian Jewish usage that I have already noted in the Qumran writings.[22]

When Paul speaks of Christ Jesus justifying the sinner, he means that because of the Christ-event the sinner stands before God's tribunal and hears a verdict of "not guilty." The process of justification thus starts in God, who is "righteous" and who "justifies" the godless sinner as a result of what Christ Jesus has done for humanity. Thus Paul is using *dikaiosynē theou* in the postexilic salvific sense of God's *tsedaqah* and is echoing the "righteousness of God" (*tsdqth 'l*) of the Qumran writings.[23]

The sinner is pronounced *dikaios* (Rom. 5:7) and stands before God's tribunal as "righteous, acquitted." For this reason Paul speaks of Christ as "our righteousness" (1 Cor. 1:30), since he is the "one man" through whose obedience "the many will be made righteous" (*dia tēs hypakoēs tou henos dikaioi katastathēsontai hoi polloi*, Rom. 5:19).[24]

The action whereby God "justifies" the sinner has been the subject of no little debate. Does the Pauline verb *dikaioō* mean "to declare righteous" or "to make righteous"? One might expect that *dikaioō*, being a verb belonging to the *-oō* class of contract verbs, would have the causative or factitive meaning typical of such verbs: *dēloō* (make clear), *douloō* (enslave), *nekroō* (mortify). Thus it would mean "to make righteous." Normally in the Septuagint, however, *dikaioō* has a declarative, forensic meaning: "declare righteous."[25] At times, the declarative sense seems to be, indeed, the meaning in Paul's letters (Rom. 2:13; 3:4, 20; 8:33). Some of these cases are quotations of or allusions to the Greek Old Testament, but others are simply ambiguous.

---

21. See further D. Hill, *Greek Words and Hebrew Meanings: Studies in the Semantics of Soteriological Terms*, SNTSMS 5 (Cambridge: Cambridge University Press, 1967), 101–2.

22. See further M. A. Seifrid, *Justification by Faith: The Origin and Development of a Central Pauline Theme*, NovTSup 68 (Leiden: Brill, 1992).

23. See further J. A. Fitzmyer, "Alonso Schökel and *Dikaiosynē Theou*," *EstBíb* 56 (1998): 107–9.

24. Compare 1 Cor. 6:11; Rom. 5:18.

25. So Schrenk, *TDNT* 2:212–14. Cf. D. R. Hillers, "Delocutive Verbs in Biblical Hebrew," *JBL* 86 (1967): 320–24; N. M. Watson, "Some Observations on the Use of *dikaioō* in the Septuagint," *JBL* 79 (1960): 255–66. Watson observes, "the LXX translators intended *dikaioō* to carry substantially the same range of meanings as that carried by *hitsdiq*, and that, when they used the Greek verb, they did have the picture of a judge as clearly in their minds as did the authors of the Hebrew Bible when they used the Hebrew equivalent" (266).

The effective sense of the verb seems to be supported by Romans 5:19 just quoted: *dia tēs hypakoēs tou henos dikaioi katastathēsontai hoi polloi*, "through the obedience of one [man] the many will be made [or constituted] righteous."[26] Those who so argue often quote the Old Testament idea of God's effective or performative word in Isaiah 55:10–11. Moreover, if Käsemann's idea about *dikaiosynē theou* connoting God's "power" is correct, it might be invoked to support this effective sense of justification.[27]

From patristic times on, the effective sense of *dikaioō* (make righteous) has been used. John Chrysostom explained it as *dikaion poiēsai* (to make [someone] righteous).[28] Similarly Augustine employed *iusti facti* or *iusti efficimur*.[29] Because of such statements, A. E. McGrath concluded that "righteousness, effected in justification, is regarded by Augustine as *inherent* rather than *imputed*, to use the vocabulary of the sixteenth century."[30] The debate became acute in the Reformation period, but even then no less a person than Philip Melanchthon said, "Because of Christ by faith itself we are truly accounted righteous or acceptable before God. And 'to be justified' means to make unrighteous men righteous or to regenerate them, as well as to be pronounced or accounted righteous. For Scripture speaks both ways. Therefore we want to show first that faith alone makes a righteous man out of an unrighteous one, that is, that it receives the forgiveness of sins."[31]

In any case, no matter how one resolves the issue of the sense of the verb, the important idea for Paul is that sinners are justified by God's grace through faith.[32] His main assertion about this conviction is found in Romans 3:21–26:

26. BDAG (492) defines *kathistēmi* here as "cause someone to experience someth., make, cause," with a possibly legal nuance. See also F. W. Danker, "Under Contract: A Form-Critical Study of Linguistic Adaptation in Romans," in *Festschrift to Honor F. Wilbur Gingrich, Lexicographer, Scholar, Teacher, and Committed Christian Layman*, ed. E. H. Barth and R. E. Cocroft (Leiden: Brill, 1972), 91–114, esp. 105–7. Cf. B. J. Korošak, "'Costituti peccatori' (Rom 5,19)," *Euntes Docete* 40 (1987): 157–66.

27. See E. Käsemann, "The 'Righteousness of God' in Paul," in *New Testament Questions of Today* (Philadelphia: Fortress, 1969), 168–82. Cf. M. L. Soards, "Käsemann's 'Righteousness' Re-examined," *CBQ* 49 (1987): 264–67.

28. *In ep. ad Romanos* 8.2 (PG 60.456); *In ep. II ad Corinthios* 11.3 (PG 61.478).

29. *De Spiritu et littera* 26.45; 32.56 (CSEL 60.199, 215). Cf. *Sermo* 131 19 (PL 38.733).

30. A. E. McGrath, *Iustitia Dei: A History of the Christian Doctrine of Justification*, 2 vols. (Cambridge: Cambridge University Press, 1986), 1:31 (his italics). He also maintained that this sense persisted throughout the early and late medieval period (184).

31. *Apology* 4.72; Theodore G. Tappert, ed. and trans., *The Book of Concord: The Confessions of the Lutheran Church* (Philadelphia: Fortress, 1959), 117. Compare also the modern debate about its meaning between Presbyterian B. M. Metzger (review of E. J. Goodspeed, *Problems of New Testament Translation, Theology Today* 2 [1945–46]: 561–63) and Baptist E. J. Goodspeed ("Some Greek Notes," *JBL* 73 [1954]: 84–92, esp. 86–91).

32. See further K. Kertelge, *"Rechtfertigung" bei Paulus: Studien zur Struktur und zum Bedeutungsgehalt des paulinischen Rechtfertigungsbegriffs*, NTAbh ns 3 (Münster: Aschendorff, 1967).

But now, independently of the law, the righteousness of God has been dis-
closed, even though the law and the prophets bear witness to it, the righteousness of God that comes through faith in Jesus Christ toward all who
believe, toward all, without distinction. For all alike have sinned and fall
short of the glory of God; yet all are justified freely by his grace through the
redemption that comes in Christ Jesus. Through his blood God has presented
him as a means of expiating sin for all who have faith. This was to be a
manifestation of God's righteousness for the pardon of past sins committed
in the time of his forbearance, a manifestation of his righteousness also at
the present time to show that he is upright and justifies the one who puts
faith in Jesus.

In this passage far more problems call for comment than I can possibly
handle here; I will limit my comments to the following six points.

First, Paul's emphasis falls on justification as an effect of the Christ-event,
even though two other effects are also mentioned: "redemption" (*apolytrōsis*,
3:24) and "means of expiating sin" (*hilastērion*, 3:25).

Second, *dikaiosynē theou* (the righteousness of God) is mentioned twice
in this passage, echoing the thematic proposition of Romans 1:16–17: "Now
I am not ashamed of the gospel. It is God's power [unleashed] for the salvation of everyone who believes, for the Jew first, but also for the Greek.
For in it is revealed the righteousness of God through faith and for faith."
There I understand the phrase to have a subjective genitive and to denote
an attribute of God, which is the beginning of the process of justification.[33]
Although some commentators have preferred to follow Luther in understanding *theou* to be a genitive of origin and to mean "the righteousness that
comes from God,"[34] I insist on the attribute-meaning in all places where
the phrase occurs in the Epistle to the Romans.[35]

I also admit that righteousness as a gift given to human beings is found
in Pauline theology, viz., in 2 Corinthians 5:21: "that we might become
through him the righteousness of God" (*hina hēmeis genōmetha dikaiosynē*

33. In this I am following A. Schlatter, *Romans: The Righteousness of God* (Peabody, MA: Hendrickson, 1995), along with Käsemann "The 'Righteousness of God' in Paul," as well as S. Lyonnet, "De
'iustitia Dei' in epistola ad Romanos 3,25–26," *VDom* 25 (1947): 129–44, 193–203, 257–63; Kertelge,
"*Rechtfertigung*" *bei Paulus*, 1–14; and P. Stuhlmacher, *Gerechtigkeit Gottes bei Paulus*, FRLANT 87
(Göttingen: Vandenhoeck & Ruprecht, 1965), 175.

34. See Martin Luther, *Preface to Latin Writings* (1545), WA 54.185–86. Luther was following
Augustine, *De Trinitate* 14.12.15 (CCSL 50A.443); *De Spiritu et littera* 1.9.15; 1.11.18 (CSEL 60.167,
171). Cf. R. Bultmann, "*Dikaiosynē Theou*," *JBL* 83 (1964): 12–16; G. Klein, "Righteousness in the
NT," *IDBSup*, 750–52; C. E. B. Cranfield, *The Epistle to the Romans*, 2 vols., ICC (Edinburgh: T & T
Clark, 1975, 1979), 1:98–99.

35. See further J. A. Fitzmyer, *Romans*, AB 33 (New York: Doubleday, 1993), 257–63.

theou en autō). Here an abstraction is used for a concrete expression: that we might become righteous through him as God's gift. Some interpreters have also related Philippians 3:9 to this idea, but that text reads, "not having any righteousness of my own based on the law, but that which comes through faith in Christ, the righteousness from God, depending on faith" (*tēn ek theou dikaiosynēn epi tē pistei*). Even though it may express the same idea of righteousness as a God-given gift, it uses the preposition *ek* and does not have a simple genitive. So it says little about the meaning of *dikaiosynē theou*.

Third, Paul emphasizes the sins of which all human beings are guilty (*pantes gar hēmarton*), an idea that he will repeat in Romans 5:12. In this regard, Paul is echoing a Jewish conviction mentioned in the Essene text quoted above.

Fourth, the gratuity of justification is twice affirmed: by *dōrean* (freely) and by *tē autou chariti* (by his grace). Thus Paul stresses the merciful benevolence of God the Father, who has initiated this process of justification. Such a dependence on grace likewise echoes an Essene conviction mentioned above, even though Paul's view lacks the nuance of predestinating mercy that was present there.

Fifth, the sinner is said to appropriate the effect of justification "through faith" (*dia tēs pisteōs*, 3:25; *dia pisteōs Iēsou Christou*, 3:22). In the latter instance I understand *Iēsou Christou* to be an objective genitive (faith in Jesus Christ), as also in Philippians 3:9. Even though Paul does not explain what he means by "faith" in this passage, it has to be understood as the response to the gospel or the preached word, as he describes it in Romans 10:8–10: "the word of faith that we preach: if you profess with your lips that 'Jesus is Lord,' and believe in your heart that God raised him from the dead, you will be saved. Such faith of the heart leads to righteousness; such profession of the lips to salvation." In introducing this important element of faith in Christ, Paul is distancing himself clearly from the Essene teaching on justification. For "Christ" and "faith in him" were scarcely part of that teaching. In other words, the sinner who is justified in God's sight acquires that status only through faith in the Son of God.

Sixth, that Pauline idea of faith is not complete as it appears in Romans; one has also to relate to it what Paul says in Galatians 5:6 about a faith that "works itself out through love" (*pistis di' agapēs energoumenē*).

These are the main aspects that emerge from this important passage in Romans.[36] Another Pauline passage, however, must also be cited to cor-

36. For a consideration of the implications of this Pauline teaching, one can consult J. Lambrecht and R. W. Thompson, *Justification by Faith: The Implications of Romans 3:27–31*, Zacchaeus Studies, NT (Wilmington, DE: Glazier, 1989).

roborate what is asserted in Romans and bring out other aspects of the Apostle's teaching on justification, viz., Galatians 2:15–16:

> We [Peter and Paul], who are Jews by birth and not sinners from among the Gentiles, know that no human being is justified by deeds of the law but through faith in Jesus Christ, even we have believed in Christ Jesus in order that we may be justified by faith in Christ, and not by deeds of the law, because by deeds of the law no human being will be justified [*ex ergōn nomou ou dikaiōthēsetai pasa sarx*].

This is echoed in Romans 3:28:

> For we maintain that a human being is justified by faith apart from deeds of the law.

Once again the relation of justification to faith in Christ Jesus is asserted— three times, in fact. Noteworthy, however, is the relation asserted here of justification by faith to *erga nomou* (deeds of the law), that is, concrete human acts demanded by the (Mosaic) law.[37] The phrase also occurs in Romans 3:20, 28; 9:32 (in some manuscripts); Galatians 3:2, 5, 10; and in abbreviated form in Romans 3:27; 4:2, 6; 9:32; and possibly 9:11. The meaning of the phrase emerges from Paul's use of it in Romans 3:20, where he has just concluded his *testimonia*, the catena of ten verses drawn from "the oracles of God" (Rom. 3:2) that have been entrusted to Israel. Ten verses from the Old Testament have been strung together by him to declare the utter sinfulness of all human beings. As he ends this indictment of humanity, Paul paraphrases Psalm 143 to declare, "No human being will be justified before him through deeds of the law; for through the law comes the real knowledge of sin" (Rom. 3:20). Using words of Psalm 143:2, Paul writes, *ou dikaiōthēsetai pasa sarx enōpion autou*,[38] but he boldly prefixes to them *ex ergōn nomou*. He thus accommodates the psalmist's cry of unworthiness to his own idea of justification and to a specific problem not envisaged by the psalmist. Because Paul has just quoted ten verses from the Old Testament (from Psalms, Proverbs, Isaiah, and Ecclesiastes), he is clearly thinking of prescriptions found in such writings and sums them up as "the law" (3:19). Hence he uses *nomos* in the broad sense of the whole Old Testament, as he does again in 3:31.

---

37. See E. Käsemann, *Commentary on Romans* (Grand Rapids: Eerdmans, 1980), 64.

38. The Septuagint reads rather *ou dikaiōthēsetai enōpion sou pas zōn*, which reflects more accurately the MT, *lo' yitsdaq lephaneka kol khay*, with which 11QPs[a] 25:8 also agrees. Cf. 4QPs[p] 1–2:1.

This understanding of "deeds of the law" means that I would not agree with J. D. G. Dunn, who maintains that the phrase functions as "boundary markers" that divide Jews from Gentiles and that refer to such things as "circumcision and food laws" that set those "within the law . . . apart as people of the law."[39] Besides the use of the phrase in Romans 3:20 just explained, which gives a function to "deeds of the law" different from Dunn's interpretation, the Hebrew equivalent of *erga nomou* has turned up in a significant way in the Dead Sea Scrolls.

Toward the end of the Halakhic Letter (4QMMT) occurs the phrase *mqtst m'sy htwrh* (C 27), which the editors translated, "some of the precepts of the Torah."[40] More literally it would be "some deeds of the law," that is, prescriptions of the Mosaic law.

The Pauline phrase has always sounded like a well-known Jewish slogan, but it has never been found in the Old Testament or in later rabbinic literature. Now that the Hebrew form occurs in a Palestinian Jewish text, 4QMMT, it shows that Paul knew whereof he was speaking.[41] In the Halakhic Letter, a leader of the Qumran community, possibly the Teacher of Righteousness, addresses leaders of Jews who were outsiders and who disagreed with teachings of the community. The letter formulates over twenty different *halakhôt* derived from the Torah that are examples of "deeds" prescribed by the law. In the letter's epilogue, the writer concludes, "We have written to you [about] some of the deeds of the law [*mqtst m'sy htwrh*], which we consider for your welfare and that of your people, because w[e recognize that] you have prudence and knowledge of the law." Then he adds the sage remark, "It will be reckoned to you as righteousness, as you do what is upright and good before him for your welfare and [that] of Israel" (C 31–32).[42] Thus one

39. *Romans 1–8* (WBC 38A; Dallas: Word Books, 1988), 154; see also his articles, "Works of the Law and the Curse of the Law (Gal 3. 10–14)," *NTS* 31 (1985): 523–42; "Yet Once More—'The Works of the Law: A Response,'" *JSNT* 46 (1992): 99–117 (Dunn replies to the criticism of C. E. B. Cranfield, "'The Works of the Law' in the Epistle to the Romans," *JSNT* 43 [1991]: 89–101).

40. See E. Qimron and J. Strugnell, *Qumran Cave 4. V: Miqsat Ma'aśe ha-Torah*, DJD 10 (Oxford: Clarendon, 1994), 62–63.

41. Before 4QMMT was made known in a preliminary report by E. Qimron and J. Strugnell ("An Unpublished Halakhic Letter from Qumran," in *Biblical Archaeology Today: Proceedings of the International Congress on Biblical Archaeology, Jerusalem, April 1984* [Jerusalem: Israel Exploration Society, 1985], 400–407), another text from Qumran Cave 4 was often cited as having the Hebrew equivalent: 4QFlorilegium 1:7 (*m'sy twrh*). However, some interpreters have contested the reading there and claimed that the second word is actually *twdh* (thanksgiving), but that reading of the word is far from certain, and 4QMMT supports the original reading of J. M. Allegro, "Further Messianic References in Qumran Literature," *JBL* 75 (1956): 174–87, esp. 182–86.

42. The Hebrew text runs: *wnkhshbh lk ltsdqh b'[swthk] hyshr whtwb [lpnw] ltwb lk wly[sr'l]*. See Qimron and Strugnell, *Qumran Cave 4*, 62.

finds here not only the Hebrew equivalent of Paul's phrase, but also its use in a context of acquiring the status of *tsedaqah* or righteousness in the sight of God by doing "deeds of the law." Observance of precepts prescribed by the Mosaic law was indeed a mode of acquiring the status of righteousness in God's sight in at least one form of pre-Christian Palestinian Judaism.[43]

The trouble with Paul's use of *erga nomou* is that he does not always use the full phrase. Sometimes he abbreviates and speaks only of *erga*, as in Romans 3:27; 4:2, 6; 9:12, 32. For instance, Paul says, "If Abraham was justified by deeds, he has reason to boast" (Rom. 4:2); or again, "David uttered a beatitude over the human being to whom God credits righteousness apart from deeds" (Rom. 4:6). In both these instances, Paul is thinking of "deeds of the law," but his tendency to abbreviate and generalize the expression is precisely what gave rise eventually to the antinomian caricature of Pauline teaching that is refuted in the Epistle of James: "You see that a human being is justified by deeds, and not by faith alone" (*ouk ek pisteōs monon*, James 2:24), which sounds like a contradiction of Galatians 2:16.

Two other passages in Romans have to be considered. The first treats of Abraham's righteousness in 4:1–8, which reads:

> What, then, shall we say that Abraham, our forefather according to the flesh, found? If Abraham was justified by deeds, he has reason to boast, but not before God. For what does Scripture say? *Abraham put his faith in God, and it was credited to him as righteousness.* Now when a person labors, wages are not credited to him as a favor, but as what is due. But when one does not labor, yet puts faith in him who justifies the godless, his faith is credited as righteousness. So too David utters a beatitude over the human being to whom God credits righteousness apart from deeds: *Blessed are those whose iniquities have been forgiven, whose sins have been covered up; blessed is the man whose sin the Lord does not credit.*

In Romans 3:21, Paul maintained that his thesis about justification had already been announced by "the law and the prophets." Now he shows that his thesis is exemplified in the story of Abraham, the forefather of Israel. In discussing Abraham, Paul emphasizes the role of faith and grace, reiterating what he had enunciated in 3:24–25. His example exploits Genesis 15:6, as it is rendered in the Septuagint (with the passive verb and with the prepositional phrase *eis dikaiosynēn*). Because Abraham was able to take God at his word and "never wavered in disbelief about God's promise" (Rom.

---

43. See also J. A. Fitzmyer, *According to Paul: Studies in the Theology of the Apostle* (New York: Paulist Press, 1993), 21–23.

4:20), his "faith was credited to him as righteousness," and so he became the father of all "who walk in his footsteps along the path of faith."[44] Paul ends his discussion of Abraham by reminding the predominantly Gentile Christians of Rome, to whom he was writing, that "those words 'it was credited to him' were written not only for Abraham's sake, but for ours too" (4:23–24), many centuries later. Thus he has actualized the meaning of Genesis 15:6.

Second, I note that *dikaiosynē theou* occurs twice in Romans 10:3, where Paul comments on his former coreligionists, the Jewish people, and their reaction to the Christian gospel: "Being unaware of God's righteousness and seeking to set up their own righteousness, they have not submitted to the righteousness of God." My translation of this verse differs from that in the RSV, NRSV, NIV, and NAB, where the identical phrase *theou dikaiosynē*[45] is rendered differently: "For, being ignorant of the righteousness that comes from God and seeking to establish their own, they did not submit/have not submitted to God's righteousness." Shades of the Augustinian translation of *dikaiosynē theou*!

Other Pauline Texts

Paul's main formulation of his teaching on justification is found in the letters to the Galatians and Romans, but a few passages in other letters in the Pauline corpus have to be mentioned to complete the picture. I shall now comment briefly on Philippians 2:12–13; Ephesians 2:8–10; and Acts 13:38–39, the only place where Luke mentions this Pauline doctrine.

Immediately after the famous hymn to Christ as the exalted *Kyrios* in Philippians 2, Paul exhorts his beloved Christians of Philippi: "As you have always obeyed, [do] so now, not only as in my presence, but much more in my absence; work out your own salvation with fear and trembling, for God is at work in you, both to will and to work for his good pleasure" (2:12–13).

Paul speaks here not about justification, but about another effect of the Christ-event, "salvation" (*tēn heautōn sōtērian katergazesthe*), and employs a compound verb of the root *erg-* (work, deed). Verse 12 might sound like an exhortation to works-righteousness with its mention of obedience, fear, and trembling—if it is read out of context. When it is taken with verse 13, however, it is clear that the human will and effort needed for salvation

44. See also M. Cranford, "Abraham in Romans 4: The Father of All Who Believe," *NTS* 41 (1995): 71–88.

45. Save that the first is anarthrous and the second is not.

result only from God's gracious help. When the verses are so read, they reformulate Paul's teaching about justification by grace and speak rather of salvation with God's assistance.

These verses also remind us that even in Romans, where the central teaching on justification, set forth in 3:21–26, echoes the epistolary thesis or proposition in 1:16–17, that thesis has been formulated not in terms of justification but of salvation: *dynamis gar theou . . . eis sōtērian panti tō pisteuonti* (God's power [unleashed] for the salvation of everyone who believes).

Moreover, even before that proposition is positively developed in Romans 3, Paul mentions in 2:5–6 the revelation of "God's just judgment" on the day of wrath (*en hēmera orgēs kai apokalypseōs dikaiokrisias tou theou*),[46] when "he will repay everyone according to his deeds" (*kata ta erga autou*, quoting Prov. 24:12 or Ps. 62:13). Thus Paul confirms the validity of Old Testament teaching about God's eschatological retribution. Similarly, in Romans 14:10–12: "We shall all have to appear before God's tribunal, for it stands written, 'As I live, says the Lord, to me every knee shall bend, and every tongue shall give praise to God.' Every one of us, then, will give an account of himself before God." However, what Paul teaches in Romans 3:21–26, about justification by grace through faith, and in Philippians 2:12–13, about salvation with God's assistance, puts the stern reminder of Romans 2:5–6 and 14:10–12 in its proper perspective.[47] Christians do not work out their salvation alone, apart from God's saving grace, even if one day they will have to answer for their deeds.

Even though the Epistle to the Ephesians may be deutero-Pauline, 2:8–10 reformulates the prime teaching of justification in a way that undoubtedly reflects the understanding of it at a period when the Judaizing problem, which initially gave rise to the teaching, was already a matter of the past. The three verses in Ephesians are important as a brief summary of Paul's teaching, even if it is no longer formulated as "justification," but rather as "salvation": "For by grace you have been saved through faith, and this is not your own doing; it is the gift of God, not the result of deeds, so that no one might boast. For we are his handiwork, created in Christ Jesus for good deeds, which God has prepared in advance that we might live by them." These verses stress in their own way the relation of good deeds,

---

46. Significantly, in this context Paul writes not *dikaiosynē theou*, but *dikaiokrisia tou theou*.

47. See also 1 Cor. 3:13–17; 2 Cor. 5:10. Cf. K. P. Donfried, "Justification and Last Judgment in Paul," *Interpretation* 30 (1976): 140–52; K. L. Yinger, *Paul, Judaism, and Judgment according to Deeds*, SNTSMS 105 (Cambridge: Cambridge University Press, 1999), 143–270; T. Schreiner, "Did Paul Believe in Justification by Works? Another Look at Romans 2," *BBR* 3 (1993): 131–55.

wrought with what later theologians would call God's prevenient grace, to the goal of Christian life, viz., salvation. Along with Philippians 2:12–13, these verses emphasize that Christians are to cooperate with God's grace in working out their salvation. All boasting and works-righteousness are excluded from this view of human destiny.

Finally, Acts reveals how another New Testament writer has echoed Pauline teaching on justification, but reformulated it in terms of his own view of the Christ-event. In the second half of Acts, Luke portrays Paul on his various missionary journeys; in chapter 13 he narrates Paul's evangelization of Pisidian Antioch. When Paul and his companions visit the synagogue in that town, they are asked to address a word of exhortation to the assembled people, and Paul rises to do so. In the course of his address, he says, "So let it be known to you, brothers, that through him [i.e., David's descendant, "whom God has raised up" and who "has not seen decay"] forgiveness of sins is being proclaimed to you, and through him everyone who believes is justified from everything from which you could not be justified by the law of Moses" (13:38–39). With these words, the Lucan Paul proclaims justification by faith apart from deeds of the law, just as Paul did in his letters to the Romans and Galatians. Important too is the admission that justification does not come from "the law of Moses," but rather from David's descendant, the risen Christ.

However, Luke has made this primary Pauline teaching subservient to his own teaching about "the forgiveness of sins" (*aphesis hamartiōn*). That effect of the Christ-event is never found in the undisputed Pauline letters. Along with "salvation," "peace," and "[eternal] life," it is one of the four effects of the Christ-event in Luke-Acts. In other words, Luke has shown that he was aware of Paul's teaching of justification, but he preferred to subsume it under one of his own christological tenets. He simplifies the judicial image of justification and colors it with his own financial image of the remission of debts. So the Lucan Paul mentions "forgiveness of sins" first, and "justification" only as an afterthought. This Lucan effect of the Christ-event also turns up in Colossians 1:14 (*tēn aphesin tōn hamartiōn*) and Ephesians 1:7 (*tēn aphesin tōn paraptōmatōn*) and is usually cited as one of the reasons for regarding these writings as deutero-Pauline.[48]

༄

48. In Rom. 3:25 Paul speaks of *tēn paresin tōn progegonotōn hamartēmatōn*, which I have translated elsewhere "the pardon of past sins," a phrase of highly debated meaning, which does not concern us now. See Fitzmyer, *Romans*, 351–52.

Joseph A. Fitzmyer, S.J.

This sums up the way that I, as a Catholic, read Paul's letters and understand justification by grace through faith in his theology. I consider it a very important Pauline tenet, even though I recognize that there are other ways in which the apostle has described the effects of the Christ-event. The Christian gospel makes all these effects known to human beings, and so that gospel cannot be limited or restricted to justification by faith. Paul's gospel presents a vision of God whose righteousness and fidelity to his promises require of his sin-prone human creatures an acknowledgment in faith of his justifying power and grace made available through his Son, Jesus Christ, in the work of his Holy Spirit.[49]

49. See further B. Byrne, "How Can We Interpret Romans Theologically Today?" ABR 47 (1999): 29–42.

5

Can We Reread Paul Together Any Longer?

Joseph A. Fitzmyer's View of Pauline Justification in Context

RICHARD E. DeMARIS

From the middle of the 19th century to the middle of the 20th century, the phrase "Roman Catholic biblical scholarship" would have been regarded by many as oxymoronic: it may have been Roman Catholic, but was it really scholarship? At the end of the 20th and the beginning of the 21st century, however, the phrase is equally oxymoronic: no one doubts the quality of the scholarship, but in what sense is it any longer "Catholic"?

Certainly, Catholics would now contribute more positively toward ecumenism, not only because they could work with Protestant scholars using the same methods, but above all because the retrieval of the literal sense, stripped of the accretions of dogmatic and polemical interpretations, would help overcome historic antipathies.

Luke Timothy Johnson, *The Future of Catholic Biblical Scholarship*[1]

However much one may differ with the way Luke Johnson characterizes Catholic biblical scholarship since Pius XII's encyclical *Divino Afflante Spiritu* (1943), his comments give voice to a perception that

---

1. Luke Timothy Johnson and William S. Kurz, *The Future of Catholic Biblical Scholarship: A Constructive Conversation* (Grand Rapids: Eerdmans, 2002), 4, 9.

some have of biblical studies today, and not just in Catholic circles. There is apprehension that for all the benefits the historical-critical method or scientific exegesis has brought, they have come at a price. Among other things, biblical scholarship has become increasingly detached from its intellectual and institutional moorings, from theology and from the church and church-related academic institutions. Accordingly, Johnson wonders whether there is anything distinctively Catholic about the biblical scholarship coming from contemporary Catholic exegetes.

One could dismiss Johnson if it were not for other voices singing the same tune. The more critical among them express alarm and point out the deep flaws in the historical-critical method. One such critic, Cardinal Ratzinger, asserts that biblical studies is in crisis because biblical scholars have failed adequately to critique and correct the historical-critical method. As a result, they have not recognized the method's limitations or the implications of its theoretical presuppositions.[2] While Ratzinger does not advocate abandoning the historical-critical method, he sees nothing redeeming in forms of it that dissect or atomize the biblical text; he finds the method as a whole in need of thorough rethinking. To put the critique more bluntly—in this case by Protestant biblical scholar Paul S. Minear—a method focused on history alone is not adequate for grasping the full significance of the Bible, which is, finally, a deeply theological book that makes profound theological claims.[3]

More constructive voices, while not unaware of the limits of critical biblical studies, stress the useful insights that the historical-critical method has produced and fit it (and them) into a larger program of biblical interpretation. Thus, Peter S. Williamson acknowledges the historical-critical method as an indispensable part of how Roman Catholics interpret Scripture, which he lays out in a detailed, systematic fashion.[4] Likewise, though much more briefly, Douglas E. Oakman draws extensively from critical biblical scholarship as he begins his exploration of Christian symbols and contemporary Lutheran hermeneutics.[5]

2. Joseph Cardinal Ratzinger, "Biblical Interpretation in Crisis: On the Question of the Foundations and Approaches of Exegesis Today," in *Biblical Interpretation in Crisis: The Ratzinger Conference on Bible and Church*, ed. R. J. Neuhaus, Encounter Series 9 (Grand Rapids: Eerdmans, 1989), 1–23.

3. Paul S. Minear, *The Bible and the Historian: Breaking the Silence about God in Biblical Studies* (Nashville: Abingdon, 2002), 37–57.

4. Peter S. Williamson, *Catholic Principles for Interpreting Scripture: A Study of the Pontifical Biblical Commission's "The Interpretation of the Bible in the Church,"* SubBib 22 (Rome: Pontifical Biblical Institute, 2001). Williamson summarizes the study in "Catholic Principles for Interpreting Scripture," CBQ 65 (2003): 327–49.

5. Douglas E. Oakman, "The Promise of Lutheran Biblical Studies," *CurTM* 31/1 (February 2004): 40–52.

Apart from fundamentalists, no one wants to ban critical biblical studies. Nevertheless, the historical-critical approach does not enjoy the wide and ready acceptance it once did. In this new atmosphere it is worth considering whether the benefits that the approach brought about will continue. A key benefit Johnson notes, namely, promoting ecumenism and overcoming historic antipathies, is underscored by one of the greatest proponents and practitioners of the historical-critical method in the twentieth century. Raymond E. Brown affirms, "I believe historical biblical criticism has made important contributions to ecumenical church discussions and can continue to do so."[6] He continues:

> The use of biblical criticism enabled Lutheran–Roman Catholic dialogues in which I participated to recognize that, since both Lutheran and Tridentine theologians of the sixteenth century were too absolute in assuming what the Bible clearly taught, without being unfaithful to either there can be a nuanced affirmation that did not occur to our ancestors.[7]

Will the ecumenical enterprise fostered by the common embrace of historical criticism thrive in the new climate just described? It seems unlikely. No matter how important articulating a distinctive Catholic or Protestant approach to the Bible might be, the pursuit of distinctiveness opens the door to the "provincialization" of biblical studies, which is potentially antagonistic to building bridges between Christian traditions.

It does not necessarily follow that the decentering of the historical-critical method will endanger ecumenical undertakings. Yet defining a distinctive kind of biblical studies or interpretive approach downplays what it has in common with other approaches, which in turn erodes common ground. Worse, differentiating one approach from another may set up oppositions, which is precisely what happens when Johnson attempts to plot the future of Catholic biblical scholarship. Johnson is troubled by what he calls the "either/or" mentality that drives critical biblical studies to distinguish early traditions from late, authentic parable from allegorical overlay, and historical fact from theological embellishment. Such sorting out is not purely an Enlightenment-inspired program in historical analysis. Rather, Johnson sees a Protestant perspective at work because of the values attached to the findings: the early, authentic, and historical reflect the beginnings of the

---

6. Raymond E. Brown, "The Contribution of Historical Biblical Criticism to Ecumenical Church Discussion," in *Biblical Interpretation in Crisis: The Ratzinger Conference on Bible and Church*, ed. R. J. Neuhaus, Encounter Series 9 (Grand Rapids: Eerdmans, 1989), 31.

7. Ibid., 33–34.

church; the late, the developed, and the embellished represent a departure from the original.[8]

Some of what Johnson claims about the pedigree of the historical-critical method is correct. In offering this analysis as prelude to a Catholic program of "both/and" biblical studies, however, he has effectively reintroduced historic antipathies between Catholicism and Protestantism. After all, stigmatizing a Protestant orientation as "either/or" may simply be a repackaging—intended or not—of an old charge, that Protestantism is sectarian and dualistic. In any case, stressing the Protestant heritage of the historical-critical method and then using it as a foil for defining Catholic biblical studies does nothing to promote an ecumenical spirit. On the contrary, it sparks suspicion and discourages collaboration.

Convergence in the Face of Divergence

What these opening paragraphs have described is the growing debate, fostered by critics in and outside the guild of biblical scholars, over how (and where and by whom) biblical scholarship should be done. Against this backdrop, where consensus is unraveling and divergence expanding, the Joint Declaration on the Doctrine of Justification and the fruitful dialogue between Protestant and Catholic biblical scholars that led to it stand out in vivid relief. For in the face of all the charges about what historical criticism cannot do or has failed to do, the Joint Declaration and the biblical scholarship behind it demonstrate what it has done, namely, foster common purpose and facilitate the convergence of two traditions.

Is this claiming too much for the historical-critical method? My experience as a doctoral student in New Testament suggests not. As I look back some twenty-five years, what comes to mind is not a specific incident or occasion at Union Theological Seminary but the general atmosphere and orientation of the New Testament program there. There we were, both Protestant and Roman Catholic students, studying with Protestant Lou Martyn and Catholic Ray Brown, whom we saw working in harmony and with common purpose. We saw no conflict in how they approached a biblical text. When they disagreed about an interpretation, a Protestant-versus-Catholic viewpoint did not appear to be the cause. In fact, it would never have dawned on us to frame their disagreements in such terms.

8. Johnson and Kurz, *Future of Catholic Biblical Scholarship*, 15–27.

Is there a connection between the spirit of cooperation that typified the biblical studies enterprise at Union (and elsewhere, I presume) and that characterizes the Joint Declaration and the biblical spadework behind it? That is difficult for me to say, because at Union that cooperation was simply a given; it is what I found there and no one felt the need to account for it. But I think it fair to say that the Joint Declaration is in some way the natural, though certainly not inevitable, outcome of a joint enterprise operating in the New Testament guild for as long as I have known it. Protestant and Catholic scholars have shared the historical-critical approach to the Bible for decades, so despite the differences between Protestant and Catholic hermeneutics, a common method has provided a lingua franca for conversation and collaboration between them.

Conversation can produce discord as easily as concord, of course, but in this case consensus about method enabled scholars socialized in very different theological worlds to approach key biblical passages on common ground, a first and necessary step toward reaching agreement about their interpretation. Consequently, I am convinced that Vatican II's embrace of ecumenism[9] would not have led to the ecumenical breakthrough that the Joint Declaration represents without Rome's acceptance of that method, which was well under way by the middle of the twentieth century.[10] The Joint Declaration may not have been inevitable, but from my perspective as a New Testament scholar and ecumenist, it was not a surprise but a hoped for, perhaps even expected, outcome, the culmination of a decades-long dialogue.

Joseph A. Fitzmyer's treatment of justification by faith in Pauline thought reflects this dialogue and thus provides an excellent example of how critical biblical scholarship serves as a basis for the convergence of Roman Catholic and Protestant thought. It is best appreciated from that vantage point. The treatment begins like a typical historical-critical study of Pauline righteousness or justification—the Greek *dikaiosynē* lies behind both English terms—with a diachronic philological analysis that sets the stage for establishing precisely what Paul meant by the term. Fitzmyer thinks that an ancient Israelite and Palestinian Jewish understanding of righteousness, particularly as that notion develops in the postexilic period, provides the most illuminating background to Paul's thought. Accordingly, his philological presentation focuses on the Hebrew terms *tsadiq*

---

9. As expressed in the Decree on Ecumenism (*Unitatis Redintegratio*) in *The Documents of Vatican II*, ed. W. M. Abbott (New York: America Press, 1966), 341–66.

10. On this last point, see Raymond E. Brown and Thomas Aquinas Collins, "Church Pronouncements," *NJBC*, 1166–74.

(righteous) and *tsedaqah* (righteousness) in the Hebrew Bible and Qumran literature. The Christ-event takes Paul's thinking about righteousness in a new direction, of course, yet for Fitzmyer the frame of reference remains decidedly Jewish.

When Fitzmyer turns to Paul, the scholarly analysis continues, yet with a Catholic shading. While he agrees that justification is central to Paul's letters to the Galatians and Romans, he is quick to note that justification is only one effect of the Christ-event in Paul's thinking. Paul's understanding of salvation comes to expression in other ways, too, which explains why some of his letters articulate what Christ accomplishes for humankind and the cosmos in different terms: reconciliation, expiation, transformation, and so forth. So while justification is central in Paul's thinking, it is but one aspect or expression of a very rich christocentric soteriology.

From the perspective of ecumenical dialogue, Fitzmyer's study of justification represents what Raymond Brown called "nuanced affirmation" at its best. Throughout the study, a historical-critical orientation stimulates Fitzmyer to put Pauline justification in broad perspective. The result is a fine diachronic analysis that highlights how justification (*tsedaqah/dikaiosynē*) runs like a red thread through the biblical tradition. From one viewpoint, the study amounts to an implicit endorsement of the Protestant emphasis on righteousness. At the same time, Fitzmyer's scholarly attentiveness to a broad perspective provides the basis for giving this counsel to his Protestant interlocutor: "If you emphasize justification too much, you risk diminishing the Christ-event and distorting Paul." Fitzmyer conducts a remarkable balancing act, whereby critical biblical study and a Catholic sensibility combine to promote ecumenical convergence.

If Critical Biblical Scholarship Gave, Can It also Take Away?

Fitzmyer's presentation of justification in Paul needs to be set in a second context, namely, that of late-twentieth- and early-twenty-first-century Pauline scholarship. Fitzmyer kept such contextualizing to a minimum, for his contribution was not meant to be a report about the state of Pauline studies. Nevertheless, the Joint Declaration makes claims about Paul's thinking and writing, and it is the product of vigorous intellectual dialogue among biblical scholars and theologians. While the Declaration is first and foremost a document of the church, many of those who contributed to its making belong to the professoriate, so placing it against the background of contemporary Pauline scholarship is appropriate.

Fitzmyer notes that preparatory work for the Declaration included some thirty-five years of bilateral dialogue. From this perspective, the time that elapsed from the conclusion of talks about righteousness in the New Testament (*"Righteousness" in the New Testament: "Justification" in the United States Lutheran–Roman Catholic Dialogue* appeared in 1982) and about justification by faith (*Justification by Faith*, Lutherans and Catholics in Dialogue 7, appeared in 1985) to the signing of the Joint Declaration in 1999 is not great.[11] Yet from the standpoint of New Testament studies, an aeon has passed, for the last twenty years have brought dramatic change to the field. The study of Paul and of the New Testament generally is in the midst of a major transition that began in the late 1970s and early 1980s.[12] Fitzmyer and other biblical scholars who were party to the dialogues that led to the Joint Declaration witnessed the beginning of this paradigm shift, and they engaged it.[13] Still, they were concluding their work as Pauline studies began a major change in course. The question such a change prompts is this: if a common understanding of Paul was foundational to the bridge building between Protestants and Catholics, what happens to the bridge if the scholarly consensus about Paul shifts, or worse, crumbles altogether?

The question is not hypothetical. One can detect steady erosion in the longstanding scholarly consensus about the centrality of justification merely by looking chronologically at chapter and section headings of review literature on Pauline scholarship from the last two decades. "Justification by Faith" is the fourth chapter of Joseph Plevnik's six-chapter look at Pauline scholarship in 1986, *What Are They Saying about Paul?*[14] A year later H. Hübner's review of postwar scholarship on Paul appeared in *Aufstieg und Niedergang der römischen Welt*. There treatment of Pauline justification appears in a section titled "Rechtfertigung als Mitte paulinischer Theologie?" ("Justification at the Heart of Paul's Theology?"), and what follows is a lengthy presentation of alternative centers.[15] More recently, in Veronica

11. John Reumann, *"Righteousness" in the New Testament: "Justification" in the United States Lutheran–Roman Catholic Dialogue*, with responses by Joseph A. Fitzmyer and Jerome D. Quinn (Philadelphia: Fortress/New York: Paulist Press, 1982); H. George Anderson, T. Austin Murphy, and Joseph A. Burgess, eds., *Justification by Faith*, Lutherans and Catholics in Dialogue 7 (Minneapolis: Augsburg, 1985).

12. Richard A. Horsley, "Innovation in Search of Reorientation: New Testament Studies Rediscovering Its Subject Matter," *JAAR* 62 (1994): 1127–66; Elisabeth Schüssler Fiorenza, *In Memory of Her: A Feminist Theological Reconstruction of Christian Origins* (New York: Crossroad, 1983), 68–95, esp. 70–71.

13. Both Fitzmyer and John Reumann took issue with E. P. Sanders's *Paul and Palestinian Judaism: A Comparison of Patterns of Religion* (Philadelphia: Fortress, 1977). See Reumann, *"Righteousness" in the New Testament*, 120–23, 217–18.

14. Joseph Plevnik, *What Are They Saying about Paul?* (New York: Paulist Press, 1986), 55–76.

15. "Paulusforschung seit 1945: Ein kritischer Literaturbericht," *ANRW* 2.25.4:2649–2840.

Koperski's *What Are They Saying about Paul and the Law?* we find a chapter titled "The New Center?" It opens with these words: "There is emerging an increasing consensus that justification by faith alone can no longer be considered the center of Paul's theology."[16] The trend is obvious, and if Koperski's assessment of it is accurate, it would appear that Protestants and Catholics have reached agreement about a matter of secondary importance to Paul. Is the Joint Declaration thereby diminished in significance? Or worse, does the dissolution of scholarly consensus about the centrality of justification in Paul's thought undo the Joint Declaration and move the ecumenical enterprise back to square one?

The question can be restated in light of the positive contribution critical biblical scholarship has made to ecumenical dialogue up to this point. One could legitimately and poignantly ask, "If biblical scholarship gave, can it also take away?"

Challenges to the centrality of justification in Paul have arisen from many quarters, but perhaps the most serious comes from the so-called New Perspective on Paul, a label that sprang from a 1983 essay of the same name by James D. G. Dunn.[17] Taking a seminal essay by Krister Stendahl about the perils of reading Paul through Luther and E. P. Sanders's groundbreaking reexamination of Judaism at the time of Paul as points of departure,[18] Dunn has reexamined justification, particularly in Romans and Galatians, and has written extensively about it.[19] Fitzmyer took issue with Dunn in his study, when he objected to Dunn's understanding of Paul's phrase "deeds of the law" (*erga nomou*) as a reference primarily to particular observances of the law like circumcision and the food laws, which Dunn sees functioning as identity and group boundary markers for Judaism. But this is only one aspect of what constitutes a sweeping reinterpretation of Paul. Along with a restricted understanding of the law goes a decentering of justification by faith. The latter, Dunn holds, emerged as a corollary to Paul's mission to

16. Veronica Koperski, *What Are They Saying about Paul and the Law?* (New York: Paulist Press, 2001), 93.

17. James D. G. Dunn, "The New Perspective on Paul," *BJRL* 65 (1983): 95–122; repr. with an additional note in *Jesus, Paul, and the Law: Studies in Mark and Galatians* (Louisville: Westminster John Knox, 1990).

18. Krister Stendahl, "The Apostle Paul and the Introspective Conscience of the West," *HTR* 56 (1963): 199–215; repr. in *The Writings of St. Paul: Annotated Text and Criticism*, ed. W. A. Meeks, Norton Critical Editions in the History of Ideas (New York: W. W. Norton, 1972). Sanders, *Paul and Palestinian Judaism*.

19. E.g., James D. G. Dunn, *The Theology of Paul the Apostle* (Grand Rapids: Eerdmans, 1998); idem, *The Epistle to the Galatians* (Peabody, MA: Hendrickson, 1993); idem, *Romans 1–8*, WBC 38A (Waco: Word Books, 1988); idem, *Romans 9–16*, WBC 38B (Waco: Word Books, 1988).

the Gentiles, as a way of defending their inclusion in the household of God against Jewish objections. Understood in this way, justification by faith loses its primacy and universality in Pauline thought.

Dunn and other proponents of the New Perspective have drawn heavy scholarly fire. One can cite several titles intended primarily to dispute Dunn and his allies, and others will undoubtedly appear.[20] A determined rebuttal of Dunn, however, does not mean the field's rejection of the New Perspective. On the contrary, the frequency of such rejoinders, especially from conservative biblical scholars, points to how widely accepted and prominent the New Perspective has become in the field. It is so well established that some scholars now take it as a point of departure for their work.[21] Consequently, we need to take seriously a development in mainstream Pauline scholarship that threatens to shake the biblical basis of the Joint Declaration, or at the very least diminish its significance.

If we conclude that a decentering of justification poses a threat to the Joint Declaration, we can take some consolation in knowing that a resource for counteracting the threat may already be at hand in the Roman Catholic understanding of justification. In contrast to the longstanding German Protestant placement of justification at the center of Paul, indeed, at the heart of the Christian message, Fitzmyer argues that justification is one of several ways Paul and other early Christians talked about the effects of the Christ-event. Nestling justification in a bulwark of interrelated aspects—Fitzmyer asks us to picture a decahedron—instead of insisting that it stand alone, is a wiser strategy against the onslaught of the New Perspective. Yet this very understanding was the basis for the common reading of Paul that lies behind the Joint Declaration.

Still, however one deals with the New Perspective, there are clouds on the horizon. There is enough ferment in Pauline scholarship at the moment to prompt the question whether we can reread Paul together and expect anything like the consensus that was foundational for the Joint Declaration. Besides the position taken by Heikki Räisänen and others that the many contingencies Paul had to address led to incoherence in his thought, there has emerged uncertainty across the field about finding a theological

20. Recent examples include Peter Stuhlmacher, *Revisiting Paul's Doctrine of Justification: A Challenge to the New Perspective*, with an essay by Donald A. Hagner (Downers Grove, IL: InterVarsity, 2001); Seyoon Kim, *Paul and the New Perspective: Second Thoughts on the Origin of Paul's Gospel* (Grand Rapids: Eerdmans, 2002); A. Andrew Das, *Paul, the Law, and the Covenant* (Peabody, MA: Hendrickson, 2001).

21. E.g., Brendan Byrne, "Interpreting Romans Theologically in a Post–'New Perspective' Perspective," *HTR* 94 (2001): 227–41; Simon Gathercole, "After the New Perspective: Works, Justification and Boasting in Early Judaism and Romans 1–5," *TynBul* 52 (2001): 303–6.

center or centers in Paul.[22] Between 1991 and 1997 there appeared four volumes of papers previously presented and discussed in the Pauline Theology
Consultation, a group formed under the auspices of the Society of Biblical
Literature in 1985. Its task was to reassess the way Pauline theology should
be conceived. The preface to the first volume describes the undertaking
as a response both to the collapse of traditional models for understanding
Paul and to the claim that Paul's theology lacks coherence.[23]

What has resulted from this consultation, undertaken by a distinguished
panel of Pauline scholars? In volume 2 Jouette Bassler notes:

> If Paul was not a *systematic* theologian, there seems nevertheless to be a pat-
> tern, a center, a commitment, a conviction, a vision, an underlying structure, a
> core communication, a set of beliefs, a narrative, a coherence—something—in
> Paul's thoughts or behind them that dispels any abiding sense of mere opportun-
> ism or intellectual chaos on the part of the apostle. Yet nowhere, it seems, does
> this core, center, vision, etc. come to expression in a noncontingent way.[24]

In the fourth volume, as he summarizes over a decade of work by the consultation, Paul W. Meyer admits that, despite careful and intensive study, "the
task of understanding the apostle's theology remains unfinished," and that
"there is no consensus at the end of this stage of the inquiry."[25] Accordingly,
his contribution to the final volume bears the title "Pauline Theology: A
Proposal for a Pause in Its Pursuit."

Such inconclusiveness undercuts consensus building, and it has opened
the door to a host of fundamental reappraisals. A case in point is John
Ashton's recent book on the religion of Paul, in which he rejects "concep-
tualist" interpretations of Paul altogether, turning instead to Paul's religious
experience—which Ashton sees as matching a shamanic career—as the
best way to get to the heart or center of Paul. Here we see a scholar casting
about for something more basic and determinative in Paul than theological
or doctrinal formulation.[26]

22. Heikki Räisänen, *Paul and the Law* (Philadelphia: Fortress, 1986).

23. Jouette M. Bassler, ed., *Pauline Theology*, vol. I, *Thessalonians, Philippians, Galatians, Philemon*
(Minneapolis: Fortress, 1991), ix.

24. Jouette M. Bassler, "Paul's Theology: Whence and Whither?" in *Pauline Theology*, vol. 2, *1 and
2 Corinthians*, ed. D. M. Hay (Minneapolis: Fortress, 1993), 6.

25. Paul W. Meyer, "Pauline Theology: A Proposal for a Pause in Its Pursuit," in *Pauline Theology*,
vol. 4, *Looking Back, Pressing On*, ed. E. E. Johnson and D. M. Hay, SBLSymS 4 (Atlanta: Scholars
Press, 1997), 140.

26. John Ashton, *The Religion of Paul the Apostle* (New Haven: Yale University Press, 2000).

The second divergence—the unraveling of the scholarly consensus about what is central to Paul—poses a second and more serious threat to the type of ecumenically minded scholarship one finds in Fitzmyer and other chapters in this volume.

A Charter for What Lies Ahead

The balkanization of biblical studies and the centrifugal inclination of contemporary Pauline studies may hinder or prevent future cooperation between Protestant and Catholic biblical scholars and theologians. If the two divergences I have described can be successfully addressed, however, it is worth considering how the Joint Declaration and the biblical scholarship on justification can serve as the basis of continuing ecumenical dialogue. In other words, how does the Joint Declaration serve not as a conclusion or endpoint to a significant ecumenical undertaking but as a point of departure for future undertakings?

Another way of approaching Fitzmyer's view of Pauline justification is to assess its place in the continuing convergence of the Catholic and Protestant traditions, the third and last context this chapter will consider. I take seriously the language in the closing paragraph of the Response of the Catholic Church to the Joint Declaration, where it calls for renewed effort on the part of Lutherans and Catholics to "find a language that can make the doctrine of justification more intelligible . . . for men and women of our day."[27] As we reread Paul together, I propose one way of reading him that will make the Joint Declaration a charter for future ecumenical cooperation in the world today.

My proposal would require Fitzmyer to push treatment of justification (*dikaiosynē*) beyond the bounds of Jewish thought. He notes that *dikaioō*, the verb related to *dikaiosynē*, had a mostly negative sense in Greek literature—to correct wrong, to punish, and so forth—and that the Septuagint provides the likeliest background for the positive sense it has in Paul. Yet the noun *dikaiosynē* had a very positive sense in the Greek and Roman world, which Frederick Danker has explored exhaustively in the epigraphical and literary record of the ancient Mediterranean.[28] He finds the term

27. Response of the Catholic Church to the Joint Declaration of the Catholic Church and the Lutheran World Federation on the Doctrine of Justification, Clarification no. 8, titled, "Prospects for Future Work."

28. Frederick W. Danker, *Benefactor: Epigraphic Study of a Graeco-Roman and New Testament Semantic Field* (St. Louis: Clayton Publishing House, 1982), 343–48; idem, "*dikaiosynē*," BDAG, 247–49.

typically connected with the exercise of executive privilege in conferring a benefit, whether it is God or the gods benefiting human beings or a human patron bestowing gifts on clients. Justice or righteousness was, in other words, a cardinal virtue of the benefactor, divine or human, and Paul could well have had this context (along with other contexts) in mind as he characterized God in Romans. Certainly the Roman recipients of his letter would have located *dikaiosynē* in the world of benefaction. If so, we have a basis in Romans itself for exploring the relationship between justification and social relationships, which the Joint Declaration enjoins us to do (§43): "There are still questions of varying importance which need further clarification. These include . . . the relation between justification and social ethics."

How can Romans be a resource for ecumenical initiatives in the arena of social justice? Let us consider Paul's language of justification in the letter in the context of other justification talk of the time. For instance, as Augustus's summary of his public activities, the *Res Gestae*, comes to a close, it tells of the recognition he received for bringing peace and order to the world. The senate and people of Rome gave him many awards to acknowledge his courage, clemency, justice (*dikaiosynē, iustitia*), and piety (34.2).[29] This is the language of imperial propaganda and it resonated throughout the empire. In my study of the archaeological record of Corinth, for example, I have come across several inscriptions to the deified Augustus. One of these honors Augustus for his justice.[30]

Paul's claims about divine *dikaiosynē* must be set alongside the public discourse about imperial *dikaiosynē* of his day. When Paul wrote about the righteousness of God in his letter to the Romans, he may well have been setting it up in opposition to the "divine" righteousness of the Roman world, that is, the widely acknowledged justice that the deified emperor had established. N. T. Wright makes this very point in comments about Romans in an essay on empire and gospel:

> So, without losing any of its deep-rooted Jewish meanings of the covenant faithfulness of the creator God, with all that this means for God's dealing with sin and justification of those who believe, Paul's declaration that the

---

See also Bruce J. Malina and Jerome H. Neyrey, *Portraits of Paul: An Archaeology of Ancient Personality* (Louisville: Westminster John Knox, 1996), 44–45, 96, 209.

29. P. A. Brunt and J. M. Moore, eds., *Res Gestae Divi Augusti: The Achievements of the Divine Augustus* (London: Oxford University Press, 1967), 34.

30. John Harvey Kent, *Corinth*, vol. 8, part 3, *The Inscriptions, 1926–1950* (Princeton, NJ: American School of Classical Studies at Athens, 1966), 32, no. 52.

gospel of King Jesus reveals God's *dikaiosynē* must also be read as a deliberate laying down of a challenge to imperial pretension.[31]

Following this lead, one can imagine contemporary situations in which an appeal to God's justice might be a fitting retort to nationalistic claims of "justice for all."

A broadened understanding of *dikaiosynē* may, at least, save Paul's justification language from being read narrowly, as it often is in America's religious culture, as though it were meaningful only in the arena of religion and bore solely on the individual and her or his being made right with God. If the Joint Declaration is to have real significance for contemporary human societies, justification/righteousness language must become a resource for addressing issues of right and just relationships between peoples and nations. The Declaration can be such a resource, if we read Paul's justification language broadly, not just in a Jewish context but with the larger Roman world in mind.

31. N. T. Wright, "Paul's Gospel and Caesar's Empire," in *Paul and Politics: Ekklesia, Israel, Imperium, Interpretation: Essays in Honor of Krister Stendahl*, ed. Richard A. Horsley (Harrisburg, PA: Trinity Press International, 2000), 171–72. See also Dieter Georgi, "God Turned Upside Down," in *Paul and Empire: Religion and Power in Roman Imperial Society*, ed. Richard A. Horsley (Harrisburg, PA: Trinity Press International, 1997), 148–57; Neil Elliott, *Liberating Paul: The Justice of God and the Politics of the Apostle*, The Bible and Liberation Series (Maryknoll, NY: Orbis, 1994), 190–92.

6

Justification by Faith in Pauline Thought

A Lutheran View

JOHN REUMANN

For much of the last century the Bible has been an ecumenical meeting ground,[1] even at points where it had once been a battleground. Such is the case with the doctrine and experience of justification by faith. Scripture study, like ecumenism, involves both individual efforts and team projects. Behind the Lutheran–Roman Catholic Joint Declaration on Justification by Faith (1999), with which other churches may now identify, there existed, on the one hand, pioneering studies such as those by Hans Küng,[2] Karl Kertelge,[3] Rudolf Bultmann,[4] and Ernst Käsemann and his pu-

1. I explored this area, noting how inclusive-language debates cut across confessional lines in "The Bible: Ecumenical Meeting Ground or Inclusive Language Battle Ground?" in *The Papin Gedenkschrift: Dimensions in The Human Quest: Essays in Memory of Joseph Papin*, vol. 2, *Scriptural Dimensions*, ed. J. Armenti (Ann Arbor, MI: University Microfilms International, 1986), 519–52.

2. Hans Küng, *Justification: The Doctrine of Karl Barth and a Catholic Reflection* (German 1957; New York: Thomas Nelson, 1964; 2nd ed., Philadelphia: Westminster, 1981). Küng was not much cited in the dialogue because Lutherans regarded his theology as Calvinist and Küng's later image in Rome scarcely made even his earlier work helpful. In *Justification by Faith*, ed. H. G. Anderson, T. A. Murphy, and J. A. Burgess, Lutherans and Catholics in Dialogue 7 (Minneapolis: Augsburg, 1985), cf. Common Statement §72 and notes 127 and 131.

3. Karl Kertelge, *"Rechtfertigung" bei Paulus: Studien zur Struktur und zum Bedeutungsgehalt des paulinischen Rechtfertigungsbegriffs*, NTAbh. N. F. 3 (Münster: Aschendorff, 1967; 2nd ed., 1971); Kertelge, *"dikaiosynē," "dikaioō," "dikaiōma,"* EDNT 1 (1990): 325–35 (German: EWNT Lieferung 7/8, 1979).

4. Rudolf Bultmann, *"dikaiosynē theou,"* JBL 83 (1964): 12–16.

pils.[5] On the other hand, there were bilateral statements by Lutherans and Catholics internationally, in Europe, and the United States.[6] The volume titled *"Righteousness" in the New Testament: "Justification" in the United States Lutheran–Roman Catholic Dialogue* was the work of three individuals, but it was discussed by the full dialogue team during a two-year period.[7] Such efforts were harvested in the Joint Declaration.

In academia, we benefit from the contributions of individual scholars and at times from corporate efforts like the Society of Biblical Literature Pauline Theology Group or a Society for New Testament Studies seminar.[8]

Such a synergy is reflected in this colloquium volume by attention to an official document of the churches, the Joint Declaration, and presentations of individual scholars, in this case, "Justification by Faith in Pauline Thought: A Lutheran View." For something more official—*the* Lutheran view—one

5. Ernst Käsemann, "The Righteousness of God in Paul," in Käsemann, *New Testament Questions of Today* (German 1961; Philadelphia: Fortress, 1969), 168–82. C. Müller, *Gottesgerechtigkeit und Gottes Volk*, FRLANT 86 (Göttingen: Vandenhoeck & Ruprecht, 1964). P. Stuhlmacher, *Gerechtigkeit Gottes bei Paulus*, FRLANT 87 (Göttingen: Vandenhoeck & Ruprecht, 1965).

6. "Report of the Joint Lutheran–Roman Catholic Study Commission on 'The Gospel and the Church,' 1972 ('Malta Report')," *LW* 19 (1972): 259–73; *Worship* 46 (1972): 326–51; repr. without footnotes in *Growth in Agreement: Reports and Agreed Statements of Ecumenical Conversations on a World Level*, ed. H. Meyer and L. Vischer, Faith and Order Paper No. 108 (Geneva: World Council of Churches; New York: Paulist Press, 1984) 168–89, esp. §§26–30. Lutheran–Roman Catholic Joint Commission, *Church and Justification: Understanding the Church in the Light of the Doctrine of Justification* (Geneva: Lutheran World Federation, 1994), esp. §§1–9; repr. in *Deepening Communion: International Ecumenical Documents with Roman Catholic Participation*, ed. W. G. Rusch and J. Gros (Washington, DC: U.S. Catholic Conference, 1998), 73–176, and in *Growth in Agreement II: Reports and Agreed Statements of Ecumenical Conversations on a World Level 1982–1998*, ed. J. Gros, H. Meyer, and W. G. Rusch, Faith and Order Paper No. 187 (Geneva: WCC; Grand Rapids: Eerdmans, 2000), 485–565. K. Lehmann and W. Pannenberg, eds., *The Condemnations of the Reformation Era: Do They Still Divide?* (German 1988; Minneapolis: Fortress, 1990). See also Anderson et al., eds., *Justification by Faith.*

7. John Reumann, *"Righteousness" in the New Testament: "Justification" in the United States Lutheran–Roman Catholic Dialogue*, with responses by Joseph A. Fitzmyer and Jerome D. Quinn (Philadelphia: Fortress; New York: Paulist Press, 1982) xiii, xvi; Anderson et al., eds., *Justification by Faith* 11–12, summary by J. Fitzmyer, 77–81.

8. J. M. Bassler, ed., *Pauline Theology*, vol. 1, *Thessalonians, Philippians, Galatians, Philemon* (Minneapolis: Fortress, 1991); D. M. Hay, ed., *Pauline Theology*, vol. 2, *1 and 2 Corinthians* (Minneapolis: Fortress, 1993); D. M. Hay and E. E. Johnson, eds., *Pauline Theology*, vol. 3, *Romans* (Minneapolis: Fortress, 1995); E. E. Johnson and D. M. Hay, eds., *Pauline Theology*, vol. 4, *Looking Back, Pressing On*, SBLSymS 4 (Atlanta: Scholars Press, 1997). From a Studiorum Novi Testamenti Societas seminar, note K. P. Donfried and J. Beutler, eds., *The Thessalonians Debate: Methodological Discord or Methodological Synthesis* (Grand Rapids: Eerdmans, 2000), with which compare the earlier collection of essays, some from SNTS and SBL seminars, K. P. Donfried, ed., *The Romans Debate* (Minneapolis: Augsburg, 1977), rev. and expanded ed. (Peabody, MA: Hendrickson, 1991), esp. 299–345 on theology. Cooperative efforts involving Scripture and Systematic Theology scholars on justification are rarer, but cf. J. Reumann and W. Lazareth, *Righteousness in Society: Ecumenical Dialog in a Revolutionary Age* (Philadelphia: Fortress, 1967).

must turn to the sixteenth-century confessions, subsequent church statements, and bilateral findings, in a hierarchy of authorities.

A (and the) Lutheran View

Any Lutheran view on our topic should be consonant with sound scriptural interpretation, in light of critical studies over the long haul and today of *dikaiosynē* and related concepts, with confessional positions articulated with regard to *iustitia/Rechtfertigung*, in the *Augsburg Confession*, *Apology*, *Smalcald Articles*, and the *Formula of Concord*, and should be aware of past and current critical analyses of these documents.[9]

In my work, "'Justification by Grace through Faith' as an Expression of the Gospel: The Biblical Witness to the Reformation Emphasis," I was well aware of serving two masters: academic biblical scholarship and confessional commitment—or four or more masters, if you wish, should we add broader Lutheran, Protestant, and Catholic scriptural studies and dogma.[10]

One should not assume that these areas were as fixed in the 1970s when we worked on the topic as might be supposed, for the Roman Catholic world was still in the heady days following the Second Vatican Council. Yet many other currents were swirling as well. This was, for example, a period when justice was more prominent than justification, especially in Liberation Theology.

Lutheranism was by no means as centered on a clear understanding of *die Rechtfertigungslehre* as one might think today. The influence was considerable from Krister Stendahl's oft-reprinted article, "Paul and the Introspective Conscience of the West," which seemed to downgrade justification and find fault with Luther and Augustine,[11] and from E. P. Sanders's *Paul*

9. *Die Bekenntnisschriften der evangelisch-lutherischen Kirche* (Göttingen: Vandenhoeck & Ruprecht, 1930; 2nd ed. 1952; 11th ed. 1992), T. G. Tappert et al., eds. and trans., *The Book of Concord: The Confessions of the Evangelical Lutheran Church* (Philadelphia: Muhlenberg Press, 1959), with which the translation edited by R. Kolb and T. J. Wengert (*The Book of Concord: The Confessions of the Evangelical Lutheran Church* [Minneapolis: Fortress, 2000]) should now be compared.

10. Reumann, *"Righteousness" in the New Testament*, 1–192. Cf. my paper to the Lutheran Professors and Graduate Students breakfast at the 1997 SBL/AAR meeting in San Francisco (November 25), published in shortened form as "Serving Two Masters: Teaching and Writing between Academy and Church," in *Intersections* (Columbus, OH: ELCA Division for Higher Education & Schools) 9 (2000) [unpaged, final article].

11. *HTR* 56 (1963): 199–215; repr. in K. Stendahl, *Paul among Jews and Gentiles* (Philadelphia: Fortress, 1976), 78–96. Cf. my comment in Reumann, *"Righteousness" in the New Testament*, 119 n. 128: "Note . . . in that volume 'Justification Rather than Forgiveness,' pp. 23–40, and pp. 129–32 where Stendahl denies that he meant Paul's doctrine of justification was primarily polemical and regrets

and Palestinian Judaism,[12] with its assault on what to this day is sometimes dismissed as "the Lutheran Paul" and the replacement of justification with what Sanders called "eschatological participation." This was a period when the Lutheran World Federation had experienced what was widely regarded as a fiasco in trying at its 1963 Assembly in Helsinki to restate for the present day "the doctrine on which the church stands or falls."[13] It was a time when "reconciliation" was far more popular as a Pauline theme, witness the *Presbyterian Confession of 1967*.[14] A colleague and I used to ask ourselves at times if we were the only American Lutherans in biblical studies who still believed justification had something of its traditional significance in Paul.[15] Defense by American Lutherans of "the Lutheran Paul" has not been extensive.

For such reasons, in beginning presentations to the American dialogue in 1980, I prefaced a paper with a section, "The Reformation Claim Reviewed."[16] While often enriched by what Luther or Melanchthon said in sermons or wrote in *Loci*, Lutheran commitment is fundamentally to pertinent sections in the *Book of Concord*, in light of "a history of development, debate, and openness on certain matters" since 1580.[17] One can debate whether justification is "the one central theme and doctrine in light of which all else is to be understood" or is "part of a constellation of articles and doctrines, such as [*Augsburg Confession* articles] 3 and 4 (Christology

being forced to choose, as a Lutheran theologian, between justification and salvation history, his real interest for Rom 9–11 and for Christian-Jewish relations." In *Final Account: Paul's Letter to the Romans* (Minneapolis: Fortress, 1995), Stendahl wrote, after pondering the epistle over forty years for "the commentary of my dreams" that he was never able to write, "In Romans the principle of justification by faith is a principle of mission—of understanding how it is possible to become part of God's scheme, and plan, and people" (14).

12. Subtitled *A Comparison of Patterns of Religion* (Philadelphia: Fortress, 1977), on which see Reumann, *"Righteousness" in the New Testament*, 120–23, and (J. Fitzmyer) 217–18.

13. Cf. Reumann, *Justification by Faith*, Common Statement §§82–85; I am more positive about what was accomplished at Helsinki regarding justification than many were.

14. Text in *The Book of Confessions* (Philadelphia: General Assembly of the United Presbyterian Church in the United States of America, 1967), and in E. A. Dowey Jr., *A Commentary on the Confession of 1967 and an Introduction to "The Book of Confessions"* (Philadelphia: Westminster, 1968), 13–25. On "reconciliation" and the confusion that often results from the German "Versöhnung" (expiation-atonement; reconciliation), see Reumann, *"Righteousness" in the New Testament*, §§201–2 (and J. Fitzmyer's comment in §407).

15. Reflecting the situation in Roman Catholic critical biblical studies in this period, cf. R. Brown, ed., *The Jerome Biblical Commentary* (Englewood Cliffs, NJ: Prentice Hall, 1968) §79:94–97, where "justification" is listed as the last of four effects of the salvation event; contrast *NJBC* §82:68–70.

16. Reumann, *"Righteousness" in the New Testament*, §§5–23.

17. Ibid., §18. The ancient ecumenical creeds do not mention righteousness/justification, but there is considerable material on it in patristic and medieval theology.

and justification) or 3–4–5 (the Holy Spirit), or 4–5–6 (faith), among other possibilities."[18]

I preferred a broader view of justification, as in the *Augsburg Confession*, where *regeneratio* (rebirth) and *vivificatio* (making alive) are said to "mean the same thing" as justification, not the more limited sense in the *Formula of Concord*. There justification becomes a step between "(1) repentance, contrition, or conversion," and "(3) regeneration, vivification, or sanctification, and the good works that follow," above all, love, in an *ordo salutis*.[19] As to *sola fide*, "faith *alone* is involved," "not to the exclusion of word or sacraments but solely to exclude any claim of merit on our part."[20]

Lutherans expect justification to be "forensic," a pronouncement or declaration, reflecting a judgment or law court setting, as at God's final assize. That means also an understanding of ourselves as sinners before God, prior to and even after God's declaration (*simul iustus et peccator*), till the transformation at the last day. This involves what New Testament studies sometimes call Paul's "eschatological reservation."[21] But believers are not only "pronounced or regarded as righteous"; " 'to be justified' means that out of unrighteous people righteous people are made or regenerated. . . . Scripture speaks both ways."[22]

To such things the Lutheran view is confessionally committed, but with considerable openness in the interplay between the perennial task of scriptural study and ongoing analysis of the Confessions.

These colloquium essays provide the opportunity for individuals to read and teach about Paul together, while exploring the assertion in Joint Declara-

18. Reumann, *"Righteousness" in the New Testament*, §22, with reference in n. 12 to debate over the hermeneutical center of the Augsburg Confession.

19. Ibid., §15 and n. 8, citing *Apology*, Article 4:72, 75, 78, 97, 117, 196, 250, and 7:31; *Formula of Concord*, Solid Declaration 3:24; Epitome 3:5, 8. To say, with the *Formula of Concord*, that "justification," though an important step, is but one step of many on the way to salvation, is a view frequently heard with regard to Paul (long ago and typically in A. M. Hunter), once steps in an "order of salvation" are distinguished. Cf. K. P. Donfried, "Justification and Last Judgment in Paul," *ZNW* 67 (1976): 90–110 (cf. "Justification and Last Judgment in Paul," *Int* 30 [1976]: 140–52), separating justification (as past), sanctification (present), and salvation (future) as a "Pauline pattern"; Reumann, *"Righteousness" in the New Testament*, §398.

20. Reumann, *"Righteousness" in the New Testament*, §12. Cf. K. Kertelge, "Paulus zur Rechtfertigung allein aus Glauben," in T. Söding, ed., *Worum geht es in der Rechtfertigungslehre? Das biblische Fundament der "Gemeinsamen Erklärung" von katholischer Kirche und Lutherischem Weltbund*, QD 180 (Freiburg: Herder, 1999), 64–75, where, for the "Sola-fide-Prinzip," the work of O. Kuss in *Der Römerbrief I* (Regensburg: Pustet, 1957), 177 (cf. *LTK*² 9 [1963], 860–61 [K. Haendler]), is lifted up (Rom. 3:28 calls for "allein durch den Glauben"), in the face of the criticisms of the Joint Declaration draft in 1998 by some 160 German Protestant theologians, including E. Jüngel, "Um Gottes willen—Klarheit!" *ZTK* 94 (1997): 394–406. *Sola fide* stands with *solus Christus*.

21. See below, p. 127 n. 73.

22. *Apology* 4:72 (ed. Kolb and Wengert, 132); Reumann, *"Righteousness" in the New Testament*, §18.

tion §13 that dialogue together "has led to a notable convergence concerning justification, with the result that this *Joint Declaration* is able to formulate a consensus on basic truths concerning the doctrine of justification." We note first the considerable biblical work in and behind the Joint Declaration and then explore the experience of justification by faith in Paul from the angle, not of Galatians or Romans, but Philippians—in a Lutheran view and beyond, toward the future.

Biblical Data in the Joint Declaration

There has been discussion and criticism on the use of the Bible in Joint Declaration §§8–12, "The Biblical Message of Justification," earlier in reviews of *"Righteousness" in the New Testament* in 1982,[23] reactions to the American dialogue volume *Justification by Faith* (1985), and debate among individuals, groups, and churches, especially in Germany, on the Joint Declaration itself.[24] Some critiques are scholarly, reasoned, theological; others, popular, even vociferous. Among those to be noted are *Worum geht es in der Rechtsfertigungslehre?* (1999); *Gerecht vor Gott* (2000) by Ernst Käsemann's pupil, now a Methodist bishop, Walter Klaiber; and ecumenical and conservative evangelical treatments.[25]

23. G. Sloyan, *JES* 20 (1983): 670; D. J. Harrington, *CBQ* 46 (1984): 361–62; C. Graesser, *CurTM* 11 (1984): 190.

24. I have taken into consideration responses available to the dialogue and the U.S. Lutheran–Roman Catholic Coordinating Committee, from within the Lutheran World Federation and member churches and the Congregation for the Doctrine of the Faith and Pontifical Council for Promoting Christian Unity, and responses from churches in Germany, often unpublished, although there were sometimes news releases concerning them. Professor Fitzmyer and I responded, separately, to criticisms from the Tübingen faculty in 1998 to the Joint Declaration draft, in light of a negative statement about the document signed by 160 "Lutheran" (often other Protestant) theologians in Germany. For the Lutheran Church–Missouri Synod, see, in addition to official and seminary faculty statements, R. Preus, *Justification and Rome* (St. Louis: Concordia Academic Press, 1997), on the 1995 draft of the Joint Declaration.

25. Söding, *Worum geht es in der Rechtsfertigungslehre?* includes U. Wilckens, "Die 'Gemeinsame Erklärung zur Rechtfertigungslehre' (GE) und ihre biblische Grundlage," 27–63; Kertelge, "Paulus zur Rechtfertigung allein aus Glauben," 64–75; H. Hübner, "Die paulinische Rechtfertigungslehre als ökumenisch-hermeneutisches Problem," 76–105; K.-W. Niebuhr, "Die paulinischen Rechtfertigungslehre in der gegenwärtigen exegetischen Diskussion," 106–30; M. Theobald, "Der Kanon von der Rechtfertigung (Gal 2,16; Röm 3,28)—Eigentum des Paulus oder Gemeingut der Kirche?" 131–92; T. Söding, "Kriterium der Wahrheit? Zum theologischen Stellenwert der paulinischen Rechtfertigungslehre," 193–246. W. Klaiber, *Gerecht vor Gott: Rechtfertigung in der Bibel und heute* (Göttingen: Vandenhoeck & Ruprecht, 2000). T. Schneider and G. Wenz, eds., *Gerecht und Sünder zugleich? Ökumenische Klärungen*, Dialog der Kirchen 11 (Göttingen: Vandenhoeck & Ruprecht; Freiburg: Herder, 2001). Bilaterale Arbeitsgruppe der Deutschen Bischofskonferenz und der Kirchenleitung der VELKD, *Communio Sanctorum: Die Kirche als Gemeinschaft der Heiligen* (Paderborn/Frankfurt, 2000), 53–63, on

One complaint is that the Joint Declaration contains too little Scripture (4 paragraphs out of 44), that the American dialogue volume in 1985 was deficient here (27 paragraphs out of 165, on "The Biblical Data" as part of "Perspectives for Reconstruction," thought perhaps the chief means for such joint reconstruction). Klaiber suggested that "the results of exegetical labor were little asked about . . . in the vigorous debate over the Joint Declaration."[26] Such criticisms fail to follow the footnotes back to the 1982 volume, where every New Testament passage using *dikaio-* terms was discussed against the Old Testament background of over five hundred instances of *sdq* words in Hebrew. A Joint Declaration footnote mentioned the Reumann-Fitzmyer-Quinn volume, with the misleading statement, "At the request of the U.S. dialogue on justification, the non-Pauline NT texts were addressed in *"Righteousness" in the New Testament* . . ."[27]; the Pauline texts were treated too. Under "Sources" for the Joint Declaration, the biblical treatment by the American dialogue is not listed. In *Justification by Faith*, the "Background Paper" by Father Fitzmyer summarizes *"Righteousness" in the New Testament* in five pages; there were also papers in round 7 on merits and rewards according to Scripture by J. D. Quinn and J. Burgess.[28] But the dialogue and Joint Declaration did not make clear

justification; ET version, *Communio Sanctorum: The Church as the Communion of Saints,* trans. Mark Jeske et al., Unitas Books (Collegeville, MN: Liturgical Press, 2004). Papers on the Joint Declaration in *JES* 38 (2001): 1–108, from the 2001 Annual Conference of the North American Academy of Ecumenists, seldom stress Scripture. But cf. G. Wainwright, "Scope from a Methodist Point of View," 21–32 (a Methodist "swing-voter," now with Lutherans, now with Catholics, for "the compatibility of Methodist doctrine with the Joint Declaration); L. Turcescu, "An Orthodox Perspective," 64–72, esp. 64–66, 69–70 ("deification"; contrast G. Vandervelde, "Justification and Deification—Problematic Synthesis: A Response to Lucian Turceseu," 73–78, esp. 73–74, 78); and J. J. Ripley, "Covenantal Concepts of Justice and Righteousness, and Catholic-Protestant Reconciliation: Theological Implications and Explorations," 95–108 (which covenant is unclear; OT *mishpat* and *tsedaqah* are emphasized, against later distortions). A. N. Lane, *Justification by Faith in Catholic-Protestant Dialogue: An Evangelical Assessment* (Edinburgh: T & T Clark, 2002).

26. Klaiber, *Gerecht vor Gott,* 5. The "Response of the Catholic Church" (Congregation for the Doctrine of the Faith and the Pontifical Council for Promoting Christian Unity, printed, among other places, in KNA Dokumentation Nr. 5, 30.6.1998, pp. 1–4): "Particularly desirable would be a deeper reflection on the biblical foundation that is the common basis of the doctrine of justification by faith both for Catholics and for Lutherans. This reflection should be extended to the New Testament as a whole and not only to the Pauline writings" (§7, repr. in F. Reckinger and L. Scheffczyk, *Teilkonsens mit vielen Fragenzeichen: Zur Gemeinsamen Erklärung über die Rechtfertigungslehre und ihrem Nachtrag* [St. Ottilien: EOS-Verlag, 1999], 71).

27. Joint Declaration, §9, n. 10; cf. the comment of the "Response of the Catholic Church" cited in the previous note.

28. J. D. Quinn, "The Scriptures on Merit," 82–93; J. A. Burgess, "Rewards, but in a Very Different Sense," 94–110. These papers in Anderson, Murphy, and Burgess, *Justification by Faith,* were resources for Joint Declaration §4.7, "The Good Works of the Justified," though what the Joint Declaration cites

how much time and energy in the American dialogue and how many pages (295) of publication were devoted to Scripture and to Paul. Such biblical work done in an ecumenical context is often overlooked by the academy; *"Righteousness" in the New Testament* is not always cited in treatments of *dikaiosynē*.[29] A further problem is that dogmaticians often regard biblical scholars as "mere philologists," not pertinent to "theology"; biblical and later theologies do not meet.

A second criticism calls Joint Declaration §§8–12, "The Biblical Message of Justification," confusing in structure, incomplete, and unsatisfactory, a "potpourri" of biblical texts. It is difficult to sum up briefly the rich scriptural data, making connections with the many interrelated topics in the Old and New Testaments, with an eye to centuries of later interpretation and dispute. The Joint Declaration includes seven areas where a common understanding has emerged, in each instance with Catholic and Lutheran nuances. Items like law and gospel, sin, and assurance of salvation could not be covered in the "Biblical Message" section. Paragraphs 8–12 in the Joint Declaration had a complicated drafting history.[30] The initial version (1994) sought comprehensiveness yet a certain freshness. "Too long," said the drafting committee; it was cut sharply. As the draft document was circulated, a number of churches and groups called for "more Bible." In 1996 Professor Fitzmyer and I put together the present form. Editing in Rome and Geneva sometimes resulted in infelicities.

The five paragraphs aim to show that "listening together" to the word of God in Scripture has led to new insights about the good news, summed up in the "little gospel" of John 3:16, in light of an Old Testament background "about human sinfulness" and "God's 'righteousness' . . . and judgment." Old Testament references were meant to be representative (§8).

Paragraph 9 indicates how Matthew, John, Hebrews, and James provide differing treatments on "'righteousness' and 'justification.'" Even in Paul

---

under "Sources" for 4.7 (38–39) are from Lehmann-Pannenberg, *Condemnations*, 66ff., and the "Position Paper" of the United Evangelical Lutheran Church in Germany (VELKD) 90ff.

29. *EDNT* 1:330 added it in its bibliography of the German *EWNT*, written prior to 1982. In *ABD* (1992) 5:736–73, "Righteousness, Early Judaism; Greco-Roman World; New Testament"; *HBD* (1996): 558–59 ("justification") and 935–36 ("righteousness"); and *Eerdmans Dictionary of the Bible* (Grand Rapids: Eerdmans, 2000), 757–58 and 1129–30, I was able to build on and expand the 1982 treatment for the dialogue in an academic context, and in a biblical theology context in D. E. Gowan, ed., *Westminster Theological Wordbook of the Bible* (Louisville: Westminster John Knox, 2003), "Just, etc.," 262–71. Cf. now Hans Hübner and Bruce D. Marshall, "Justification," in *The Encyclopedia of Christianity* (Grand Rapids: Eerdmans; Leiden: Brill), 3:90–100.

30. Unpublished papers for the U.S. Lutheran–Roman Catholic Coordinating Committee in 1994 (October 24–26) and 1995 (March 24–26) trace this history. The coordinating committee dealt with the reception process in the United States for what became the Joint Declaration.

there is diversity, where "the 'justification' of sinful human beings by God's grace through faith" is, however, called "chief" among the Apostle's ways of describing "the gift of salvation." Five other Pauline ways are freedom, reconciliation, new creation, life in Christ, and sanctification.

Paragraphs 10–12 deal with Paul in detail, especially §10, which is based chiefly on Romans.[31] From Romans 1:16–17 on, *dikaiosynē* references are treated, with cross-references to other Pauline epistles, including Ephesians 2:8–9. Paragraph 11 presents what justification means in Paul and Luke, including forgiveness of sins; liberation from sin, death, and law; communion with God; union with Christ; reception of the Spirit in baptism; and incorporation into the body of Christ.

The final paragraph (§12) speaks of living by faith, faith that comes from the word of God and is active in love. Assaults on the justified from within and without and falling into sin are noted, so that God's promises must be heard anew; salvation is worked out as God works in believers. The good news as God's act in Christ, as righteousness leading to justification and life for all, is reiterated. Such is the biblical summary on which the common understanding in the Joint Declaration builds.

A third criticism is that the Joint Declaration fails to reflect the latest "state of the art" methods and positions of end-of-the-century New Testament studies. It must be realized that the Joint Declaration is a harvest of earlier statements, not a *Forschungsbericht* or the creation of individual scholars in the 1990s. The *Malta Report* was completed in 1971, the American biblical volume in 1980–1981. The drafting process had no warrant to bring in newer subdisciplines in literary, rhetorical, or social-world criticism, though there was awareness, for example, of rhetorical analysis for Galatians by H. D. Betz, who was in turn indebted to Luther and Melanchthon.[32] Crafting the Joint Declaration did not call for analyzing all the proposals of the last two decades of the twentieth century, quite apart from whether the so-called new methods would be helpful for the theological solution of sixteenth-century differences, for it is unclear whether the "assured results" in biblical scholarship 2000 CE will have any payoff ecumenically or will simply reflect the subjectivity of each reader's response.[33]

31. Fitzmyer's commentary, *Romans*, AB 33 (New York: Doubleday), had appeared in 1993. I completed in 1997 a brief treatment for the *Eerdmans Commentary on the Bible* (Grand Rapids: Eerdmans, 2003), 1277–1313.

32. Reumann, *"Righteousness" in the New Testament*, 53 n. 68. In Betz, *Galatians*, Hermeneia (Philadelphia: Fortress, 1979), cf. 14–25 n. 97, and the Luther quotation on page v.

33. Cf. J. Reumann, "After Historical Criticism, What? Trends in Biblical Interpretation and Ecumenical, Interfaith Dialogues," *JES* 29 (1992): 55–86; rhetorical and social-world approaches seem to

Trends in scholarship may be illustrated here by debate over the genitive in the *pistis Christou* statements by Paul. Traditionally *Christou* has been taken as an objective genitive, "faith in Christ." Periodically *Christou* has been taken as a subjective genitive, "Christ's faith," the way Jesus believed or trusted. In the 1982 American volume neither Professor Fitzmyer nor I inclined to the subjective genitive.[34] The Joint Declaration offers no occasion to take the matter up, though nowadays some think the subjective sense is so firmly established as to exclude any other option. Often it is connected with quests for the historical Jesus, stressing how Jesus trusted God;[35] for Paul, it would mean Jesus Christ's own faith, not the faith of the justified in Christ. But "the faith of Christ" is so variously interpreted that it threatens to become a cypher veiling a number of positions.

I once asked two Lutheran systematicians what difference adopting a subjective genitive interpretation would make. They replied that it would make none at all for their work. It would simply make salvation even more objective; Jesus does it all, even believing for us. But for the Joint Declaration a subjective genitive, consistently applied, would make "faith" a work of Christ for us, almost *ex opere operato*, not response to "the saving action of God in Christ," on the part of sinners, whereby they place "trust in God's gracious promise," a faith on their part then "active in love" (Joint Declaration §25). Joint Declaration §4.3, "Justification by Faith and through Grace," could scarcely have been written about human response if only

offer promise, but results differ as much or more among themselves than much-maligned "historical" criticism ever did. Further, J. Reumann, "Biblical Studies at the Threshold of the Third Millennium," in *At the Threshold of the Third Millennium*, ed. F. A. Eigo (Villanova, PA: Villanova University Press, 1998), 31–71.

34. Reumann, *"Righteousness" in the New Testament*, 53 n. 68; §99 (Gal. 2:16); 75 n. 80 (Rom. 3:25); cf. §§52, 100, 105. Fitzmyer, *Romans*, 345–46, cites much of the extensive secondary literature, which includes, for the subjective genitive, J. Haussleiter, *Der Glaube Jesu Christi und der Christliche Glaube* (Erlangen: Deichert, 1891); P. Valloton, *Le Christ et la foi* (Geneva: Labor et Fides, 1960); R. B. Hays, *The Faith of Jesus Christ: An Investigation of the Narrative Substructure of Galatians 3:1–4:11*, SBLDS 56 (Chico, CA: Scholars Press, 1983; 2nd ed., Grand Rapids: Eerdmans; Dearborn, MI: Dove, 2002); idem, *"Pistis* and Pauline Christology: What Is at Stake?" in Johnson and Hay, *Pauline Theology* 4:35–60; for the objective genitive, J. D. G. Dunn, "Once More, *Pistis Christou*," in Johnson and Hay, *Pauline Theology* 4:61–81, and his *Theology of Paul the Apostle* (Grand Rapids: Eerdmans, 1998), §14.8, 379–85. P. O'Callaghan, *Fides Christi: The Justification Debate* (Dublin/Portland, OR: Four Courts Press, 1997), does not touch on this issue.

35. E.g., E. Fuchs, *Studies in the Historical Jesus*, SBT 42 (London: SCM, 1964), 11–31, 48–64, 167–90; L. E. Keck, *A Future for the Historical Jesus* (Nashville: Abingdon, 1971; repr. Philadelphia: Fortress, 1981). This background for emphasis on a "Jesus story" has not always been acknowledged in discussions.

Jesus' faith, or even just God's faithfulness, are involved.[36] See below on the crux passage Philippians 3:9.

There are, of course, insights since 1980 or so that one wishes could have been included in the Joint Declaration. German Evangelical and Catholic New Testament scholars have in the last fifteen years come to see Galatians 2:16 as a doctrinal statement, a principle, or basic proposition, "A person is justified not by works of the law but through faith in Jesus Christ" (NRSV). This is not a theological statement Paul has created, but the communal property (*Gemeingut*) of the church. Similarly with Romans 3:28, "A person is justified by faith apart from works prescribed by the law."[37] Jürgen Becker can be credited with working out the case that others have endorsed and expanded:[38] "Galatians 2:16 includes as unquestioned church knowledge the assertion that a person is not justified by works of the law but only through faith in Jesus Christ, a consensus statement of Antiochene theology that also appears in Romans 3:28." Linguistic and other clues are noted[39] that identify here a *Lehrsatz* (doctrinal statement) in the oral tradition, like Galatians 3:28 (on baptism) and Galatians 6:15 ("Neither circumcision

36. Klaiber, *Gerecht vor Gott*, 123 n. 147: "Trotz immer wieder neuer Versuche den Gen. *pistis I sou Christou* als 'Glaube' oder 'Treue Jesu Christi' zu interpretieren, ist an der Übersetzung 'Glaube an Jesus Christus' festzuhalten."

37. Cf. C. Burchard, "Nicht aus Werken des Gesetzes gerecht, sondern aus Glauben an Jesus Christus—seit wann?" in *Geschichte—Tradition—Reflexion*, FS M. Hengel, ed. H. Lichtenberger (Tübingen: Mohr Siebeck, 1996), 3:405–15: in Gal. 2:16, "we" = Peter, Paul, and other Jewish Christians in Antioch; this *Grund-Satz* or *Fundament* could go back, respectively, to Peter's Easter-vision "call" at 1 Cor. 15:5 and Paul's "Damascus Road" experience, Gal. 1:15–16; the prior history may have also involved the Hellenist circle around Stephen in Jerusalem; the verse is as much a building stone in early Christianity as 1 Cor. 11:23–25 and 15:3–5; M. Theobald, "Der Kanon von der Rechtfertigung (Gal 2,26; Röm 3,28)—Eigentum des Paulus oder Gemeingut der Kirche?" in Söding, ed., *Worum*, 131–92; in the same volume, Kertelge, "Paulus zur Rechtfertigung allein aus Glauben," 69–72; Söding, "Kriterium der Wahrheit?" 213. On the prior and later history, cf. P. Stuhlmacher, *Biblische Theologie des Neuen Testaments*, vol. 1 (Göttingen: Vandenhoeck & Ruprecht, 1992), 234–52.

38. *Paul Apostle to the Gentiles*, trans. O. C. Dean Jr. (German 1989; Louisville: Westminster John Knox, 1993), 96, cf. 283 on Rom. 3:28.

39. Note the introduction: "we know" (Gal. 2:16, *eidotes hoti*), "we hold" (Rom. 3:28, *logizometha hoti*); the absence of the definite article (*anthrōpos* in both examples = *tis* [anyone], a statement in "the timeless present," characteristic of rules); the opposition of the phrases "works of the law" (cf. *ioudaïzein*, Gal. 2:14, i.e., practice circumcision and observe food laws) and "faith in Christ"; the verb *dikaiousthai* in the passive, *passivum divinum* or *theologicum*, an "eschatological passive" (M. Reiser, *Die Gerichtspredigt Jesu*, NTAbh 23 [Münster: Aschendorff, 1990], 255–61); the way 16a–b, "Yet we know that a person is justified not by the works of the law but through faith in Jesus Christ," is parenthetical or an insertion between 2:15 and 16c, "We ourselves are Jews by birth and not Gentile sinners . . . we too [*kai hēmeis*] have come to believe in Christ Jesus [chiasm with "Jesus Christ" in 16b], so that we might be justified by faith in Christ, and not by doing the works of the law." Then follows in 2:16 a final clause, from Ps. 143:2, as scriptural support (Rom. 3:29–30 brings in the Shema of Deut. 6:4, *heis theos*, for the One God of Jews and Gentiles).

nor uncircumcision is anything, but a new creation is everything"). Such statements are what can be called a "rule" (Greek *kanōn*, Gal. 6:16) for Jewish as well as Gentile Christians. The matrix was the mission theology of the church at Antioch.[40]

In *Righteousness in the New Testament*, I proposed some half dozen early, pre- and non-Pauline formulations on righteousness/justification that present the meaning of Christ's cross and resurrection for us (§§59–76). These were called "part of the common apostolic faith, in Jewish and more particularly Jewish-Hellenistic communities," not "the original work of some one theologian like Paul" (§76, pp. 39–40). To these one can now add Galatians 2:16 (Rom. 3:28) as a basic doctrinal assertion going back to the church of Peter and Paul in Antioch, a piece of apostolic church teaching, not simply a Pauline peculiarity or *proprium*.[41]

Michael Theobald notes that this church teaching on justification was only partly received in subsequent centuries. It is not, for instance, found in the classic creeds. But the doctrine "makes history" when a Luther or Karl Barth takes it up. Whenever *solus Christus* is threatened with being overshadowed by ecclesiology or in some other way, Paul steps up.[42]

Righteousness/Justification in Philippians

Romans and Galatians are usually the starting points for treating justification by faith in Pauline thought.[43] They contain sixty-three and thirteen examples of *dikaio-* terms, respectively, compared with seven in 2 Corinthians and six in Philippians.[44] But Philippians contains as many instances of *dikaiosynē* as does Galatians (four each). Romans and Galatians focus

40. This fundamental proposition (*Grundsatz*) can be traced further in its usage by Paul in his doctrine of justification. Its transformations appear in Acts (13:38–39; 15:10–11; cf. 3:12, 16), Ephesians (2:5, 8–9), and the Pastoral Epistles (2 Tim. 1:8–9; Titus 3:4–7); protest against it surfaces in James 2:14–26.

41. None of these German discussions mention, let alone endorse, *pistis Christou* as "the faith of Jesus"; Christ is instead the object of faith, as Gal. 2:16 makes clear in the statement directly after the *kanōn*, "we too believed in [*episteusamen eis*] Jesus Christ."

42. So Theobald, "Kanon von der Rechtfertigung," 192.

43. So, e.g., Mark Seifrid, *Justification by Faith: The Origin and Development of a Central Pauline Theme*, NovTSup 68 (Leiden: Brill, 1992); idem, *Christ Our Righteousness: Paul's Theology of Justification*, New Studies in Biblical Theology 9 (Downers Grove, IL: InterVarsity, 2000); Kertelge, "Paulus zur Rechtfertigung allein aus Glauben," 64.

44. Statistics, among other places, in Reumann, *"Righteousness" in the New Testament* §78; those in *ABD* 5:747 include *adikia* terms also, raising the totals respectively for the four letters to seventy-two (Romans), fourteen, eleven, and six (Philippians).

on righteousness over a number of chapters; in Philippians, references are concentrated in 3:6–9, in a contrast between Torah-righteousness and faith-righteousness. Philippians reflects a number of purposes, perhaps because the canonical document is a composite, made up from three letters.[45]

New themes burst upon the readers in 3:2, after Paul had moved toward an epistolary conclusion. Verse 2 erupts with the warning, "Beware the dogs! Beware the evil workers! Beware 'the incision' [*katatomē*]" or "those who mutilate the flesh" (NRSV). Then in 3:3 follows a threefold claim with which ecclesiology finds it difficult to reckon: "We—Paul and the Philippian Christians—are the circumcision [*peritomē*], we serve by the Spirit of God, we make our boast in Christ Jesus and do not put our confidence in the flesh."

This abrupt new letter body reflects conflict, as do the treatments of righteousness/justification in Galatians and, more calmly, in Romans. But we need not suppose Paul took up "the righteousness of God" and "how sinners are rightwised" only at the prodding of opponents (contra Albert Schweitzer). For earlier (often Jewish-Christian) formulas about the death of Jesus justifying sinners appear throughout New Testament letters in a variety of settings (1 Cor. 6:11; 2 Cor. 5:21; Rom. 3:24–26a; 4:25; cf. 1 Peter 3:18; 1 Tim. 3:16).[46] In his churches the Apostle likely taught the effects of the death and resurrection of Jesus as including righteousness/justification for believers. In doing so he certainly used his Bible, what we call the Old Testament, in its Greek form, texts like Habakkuk 2:4 and Genesis 15:6, plus cultic ideas like the *hilastērion* (Rom. 3:25, from Exod. 25:17–22; 31:7; 35:12; 37:7–9) and the sin offering of Isaiah 53:10, cf. Leviticus 6:25 (in 2 Cor. 5:21), and the Servant figure of Isaiah

45. Details appear in standard commentaries and my Anchor Bible commentary on Philippians (forthcoming), more briefly in "The Theologies of 1 Thessalonians and Philippians: Contents, Comparison, and Composite," in *SBL 1987 Seminar Papers*, ed. K. H. Richards, SBLSP 26 (Atlanta: Scholars Press, 1987), 521–36, 528 (§3.4). For issues that will be reflected in the commentary, see my "Contributions of the Philippian Community to Paul and to Earliest Christianity," *NTS* 39 (1993): 438–57; "Philippians, Especially Chapter 4, as a 'Letter of Friendship': Observations on a Checkered History of Scholarship," in *Friendship, Flattery, and Frankness of Speech: Studies on Friendship in the New Testament World*, ed. J. T. Fitzgerald, NovTSup 82 (Leiden: Brill, 1996), 83–106; "Justification and the *Imitatio* Motif in Philippians," in *Promoting Unity: Themes in Lutheran-Catholic Dialogue*, Festschrift for Johannes Cardinal Willebrands, ed. H. G. Anderson and J. R. Crumley Jr. (Minneapolis: Augsburg, 1989), 17–28; and "Christology in Philippians, Especially Chapter 3," in *Anfänge der Christologie: Festschrift für Ferdinand Hahn zum 65. Geburtstag*, ed. C. Breytenbach and H. Paulsen (Göttingen: Vandenhoeck & Ruprecht, 1991), 131–40.

46. Reumann, *"Righteousness" in the New Testament* §§59–76; *ABD* 5:752–54, drawing on Kertelge, S. K. Williams, and others; against A. Schweitzer, *The Mysticism of Paul the Apostle* (London: A. & C. Black; New York: Henry Holt, 1931; repr. New York: Seabury, 1968). Add now Gal. 2:16 as a *Basissatz*.

53 (esp. vv. 5, 6, 11, 12). Such imagery would not be strange to a Jewish Christian audience. How Gentile Christians responded we may be able to see in Philippians.

The identity of Paul's opponents in Philippians 3, described there as "enemies of the cross of Christ" (3:18), has long been debated.[47] I would distinguish them from the preachers mentioned in 1:14–18, Christians in the city of Paul's imprisonment (Ephesus, in my opinion), who act out of rivalry and envy toward Paul, yet who proclaim a gospel quite acceptable to Paul. I would also distinguish them from the intimidating opponents in 1:28, who are Roman, civic officials in Philippi. The menacing figures in chapter 3 seem more like those Paul faced in Galatia than those with whom he disputed in 2 Corinthians. They loom on the horizon but are not yet in Philippi. Paul writes to firm up his beloved Philippians against such people lest they be taken in, if and when these enemies of the cross invade his favorite congregation.

One must finally note, by way of introduction to this passage, that Paul writes and speaks here in the first person, as elsewhere in Philippians. That is not a matter of egotism, as Robert Fortna once charged,[48] but reflects situation and genre. In 1:12–26 Paul must speak in the first person when telling of his situation (jailed, threatened with death). In 4:10–20 he must write about himself with regard to gifts and friendship from the Philippians, and his own self-sufficiency in the face of possible patron-client reciprocity. Here in chapter 3 he turns to his autobiography, not Scripture as in Galatians and Romans, to assert his identity in Christ as one with "the righteousness that comes from God based on faith."

In the rhetorical comparison or *synkrisis*[49] of verses 4–11, Jewish credentials, sevenfold, are presented for Saul of Tarsus. They are listed in a remarkably positive way: (1) "circumcised on the eighth day" and so a proper Jew from birth, a member of the Mosaic covenant community; from

47. The literature and hypotheses are extensive. For what follows, see *SBL 1987 Seminar Papers*, ed. K. H. Richards, SBLSP 26 (Atlanta: Scholars Press, 1987), 527–28 (§3.1–3), with P. Perkins, among others.

48. Robert Fortna, "Philippians: Paul's Most Egocentric Letter," in *The Conversation Continues: Studies in Paul and John in Honor of J. Louis Martyn*, ed. R. T. Fortna and B. Roberts Gaventa (Nashville: Abingdon, 1990), 220–34. Compare B. Dodd, *Paul's Paradigmatic "I": Personal Example as Literary Strategy*, JSNTSup 177 (Sheffield: Sheffield Academic Press, 1999).

49. S. K. Stowers, "Friends and Enemies in the Politics of Heaven," in *Pauline Theology I*, 115–17; B. Dodd, *Paul's Paradigmatic "I,"* 181 n. 39; W. Harnisch, "Die paulinische Selbstempfehlung als Plädoyer für den Gekreuzigten: Rhetorisch-hermeneutische Erwägungen zu Phil 3," in *Das Urchristentum in seiner literarischen Geschichte*, Jürgen Becker, ed. U. Mell and U. B. Müller, BZNW 100 (Berlin: de Gruyter, 1999), 135–36; on the device earlier in Philippians, see S. Vollenweider, "Die Waagschalen von Leben und Tod: Zum antiken Hintergrund von Phil 1,21–26," *ZNW* 85 (1994): 93–115.

(2) the race of Israel, (3) the tribe of Benjamin; and (4) a Hebrew born of Hebrews. These items were the inheritance of a true Jewish male. Then the "encomiastic comparison"[50] goes on with three accomplishments that marked the particular manner of life Saul forged for himself: (5) as to the law—a Pharisee. His standard was Torah, "in, with, and under" which the Pharisee lives.[51] This places him within "covenantal nomism," though how much Saul's emphasis was on *nomos* and how much on (Mosaic) "covenant" is impossible to tell. (6) "As to zeal, a man persecuting the church." His zeal for the law led to an onslaught against the community of Jesus' followers. (7) "As to righteousness," the final, climactic term, "the righteousness called for in the law, blameless" in conduct. Like the rich young ruler of Mark 10:20 and parallels, Saul and other good Jews believed one could keep all the commandments of God, from *alef* to *tav*. But many an expositor has regarded such a claim as outrageous, "human striving to make oneself righteous before God."[52] Sanders uses such responses by Protestants (and Catholics) to claim that Judaism has often been caricatured by Christians, for such conduct has to do with "staying in" the covenant, not "getting in" the covenant relationship with God.[53] For Greek hearers the term *dikaiosynē* here might suggest a classic virtue; being "blameless" was no impossibility among Greeks.[54]

In this self-description, Saul of Tarsus does not blacken his past or depreciate his time in Judaism. Torah is given high place (*nomos* twice in v. 6, flanking "zeal"). Saul could "walk the walk" that God willed for the people of the covenant. The verse puts a question mark over the notion that Israel was, in its own opinion, "in exile" and under the curse of Deuteronomy 27:26 because Israel (as N. T. Wright holds)[55] or at least Saul had not kept Torah. But it does suggest a separation "*of* Judaism *from the other nations*"

50. B. J. Malina and J. H. Neyrey, *Portraits of Paul: An Archaeology of Ancient Personality* (Louisville: Westminster John Knox, 1996), 52–55.

51. O. Betz, "Paulus als Pharisäer nach dem Gesetz: Phil 3,5–6 als Beitrag zur Frage des frühen Pharisäismus," in *Treue zur Tora: Beiträge zur Mitte des christlich-jüdischen Gesprächs*, FS G. Harder, ed. P. von der Osten-Sacken, Institut Kirche und Judentum bei der Kirchlichen Hochschule Berlin 3 (Berlin: Institut Kirche und Judentum, 1977), 57.

52. J. Gnilka, *Die Philipperbrief*, 3rd ed., HTKNT 10/3 (Freiburg: Herder, 1980), 190–91.

53. Sanders, *Paul and Palestinian Judaism*, 33–59.

54. On Greco-Roman understandings, cf. J. Reumann, *ABD* 5:742–45, and "Justification and Justice in the New Testament," *HBT* 21 (1999): 26–45. The adjective *amemptos* occurs in Greek inscriptions, including civic decrees of honor; cf. J. H. Moulton and G. Milligan, *The Vocabulary of the Greek New Testament Illustrated from the Papyri and Other Non-Literary Sources* (London: Hodder and Stoughton, 1930), 26; F. W. Danker, *Benefactor* (St. Louis: Clayton Publishing House, 1982), 354.

55. N. T. Wright, *The Climax of the Covenant: Christ and the Law in Pauline Theology* (Minneapolis: Fortress, 1992), 137–56.

and a separation of some "*within* Judaism *from other Jews*" (J. D. G. Dunn).[56] Not "all Israel" but "I, Saul" is the subject.

Yet along with this high estimate of his life as involving the best of Judaism, Paul has also struck an ominous note with regard to the very badge of identity for a Jewish man, the mark of the Mosaic covenant, by his polemic in verse 2 against circumcision as *katatomē* ("mutilation," in Greek eyes) and the counterclaim, "We"—the church he once persecuted—"are the *peritomē*." This is an audacious assertion for communal identity "in Christ." Paul Minear recognized it as "a clear-cut ecclesiological designation,"[57] though few have developed this "Israel term," and some see it as a claim by opponents taken over by Paul and set in antithesis with "the essential mark of Christian existence,"[58] the Spirit and possessing righteousness from God.

Paul's own judgment, now "in Christ," about what he once regarded as "gains" or pluses on the balance sheet, is swiftly and devastatingly given in verses 7–8: "These things I have come to consider loss because of Christ." They are "crap" (8), to use an expression that includes the possible meanings of both "garbage" and "excrement." The "great reversal" in Saul's thought and life came *propter Christum* (7, Vulgate). The name "Christ" occurs four times in the next five verses, plus six pronoun forms referring to Paul's new Lord. Veronica Koperski regards 3:7–11 as "one of the strongest christological statements in Christian Scripture," as strong as or stronger than 2:6–11.[59] Nonetheless J. C. Beker has called *dikaiosynē* "[t]he key term in Philippians 3:4–11."[60] We must not lose the thread of our argument on justification amid the many themes in the passage: Pauline autobiography, the kerygma or Christ-story, and influences from opponents in chapter 3, to say nothing of the term *gnōsis* ("knowing Christ," vv. 8, 10) and eschatology.

56. Dunn, *Theology of Paul the Apostle*, 349–50.

57. Paul Minear, *Images of the Church in the New Testament* (Philadelphia: Westminster, 1960), 76.

58. W. Klaiber, *Rechtfertigung und Gemeinde: Eine Untersuchung zum paulinischen Kirchenverständnis*, FRLANT 127 (Göttingen: Vandenhoeck & Ruprecht, 1982), 28–29, with J. Jervell and others.

59. Veronica Koperski, *The Knowledge of Christ Jesus My Lord: The High Christology of Philippians 3:7–11*, CBET 16 (Kampen: Pharos, 1996). The Christology here is, however, more about Christ's "work" than "person," and really about believers knowing and gaining Christ. Cf. Melanchthon's *Christum cognoscere, beneficia eius cognoscere* (*Loci Communes* 1521, ed. H. Engelland, 2:7, "to know Christ is to know his benefits."

60. J. C. Beker, "Paul the Theologian," *Int* 43 (1989): 361. This is to deny that the *dikaiosynē* references in 3:9 are a secondary intrusion in the argument; the reference to *dikaiosynē* in v. 6 speaks against that. Righteousness/justification should not be made to oppose the christological emphasis in the passage, for Paul's doctrine of justification is his "functional Christology" (Reumann, *"Righteousness" in the New Testament*, §216).

In verse 9, Paul's contrasting term to the Torah-righteousness that characterized his days in Judaism is introduced. It is "the righteousness of God" (*tēn ek theou dikaiosynēn*), a possibly technical term[61] that is not found in Galatians. At Philippians 3:9 the phrase is surrounded by two references to faith (*pistis*). The initial one describes this righteousness as *tēn dia pisteōs Christou*, traditionally rendered the God-kind of righteousness[62] "that comes through faith in Christ" (objective genitive, *Christou*). The alternative, subjective genitive has now made it into the NRSV margin, "through the faith of Christ."[63] The phrase here obviously stands in contrasting parallel with "a righteousness of my own that comes from the Torah." Is the implication from "my own" (*emēn* in Greek) that the righteousness by faith is through "my own faith"? Or shall we stress not "of my own" but rather "the faith of Christ"? The subjective genitive would offer an odd contrast with regard to a Jew like Jesus of Nazareth, namely believing or trusting but not with regard to covenant or Torah. It is weakened by the fact that the Gospels never use "Jesus" as the subject of the verb *pisteuein*. If one tries to make it "faithfulness" on Jesus' part, his obedience "unto death" (Phil. 2:8), Paul has a different word (at 2:8 *hypēkoos*; elsewhere *hypakoē*) for the obedience that comes from faith. The real interest of some who champion the subjective genitive is to weave Jesus' own faith or faithfulness into a "story of Jesus," as a model for Paul and us in Philippians, involving above all 2:6–11 as "story."[64] This section of chapter 3 could be taken as part of a story about Jesus who was circumcised, obeyed the law, lived within the Mosaic covenantal relationship, and so on. But such analogies would be contrary to the points Paul wants to make against the enemies threatening the church in Philippi. For these and other reasons, amply argued elsewhere, notably by J. D. G. Dunn, it seems best to accept the objective genitive here.

But the matter is complicated by the other phrase about faith just after the reference to "the righteousness of God," at the end of verse 9, namely *epi tē pistei*. The NRSV takes it as "the righteousness from God based on

61. Cf. P. Stuhlmacher, *Paul's Letter to the Romans: A Commentary* (Louisville: Westminster John Knox, 1994), 29–32, reflecting his *Gerechtigkeit Gottes bei Paulus* (above, n. 5).

62. The phrase is A. T. Robertson's, *Paul's Joy in Christ: Studies in Philippians* (New York: Fleming H. Revell, 1917), 192. Cf. Rom. 1:17 (note: *ek theou . . . dia pisteōs Christou*).

63. See n. 34 above for the literature.

64. Among other treatments, cf. R. B. Hays, *The Faith of Jesus Christ: An Investigation of the Narrative Substructure of Galatians 3:1–4:11*, SBLDS 56 (Chico, CA: Scholars Press, 1983; 2nd ed., Grand Rapids: Eerdmans; Dearborn, MI: Dove, 2002); idem, "*Pistis* and Pauline Christology" (with only passing reference to Philippians); and S. E. Fowl, *The Story of Christ in the Ethics of Paul: An Analysis of the Function of Hymnic Material in the Pauline Corpus*, JSNTSup 36 (Sheffield: JSOT Press, 1990), 49–102 (without reference to Hays).

faith" (with no marginal alternative adopting the subjective genitive), then punctuates with a period. This means that in verse 10 the words "I want" must be added before "to know Christ." Those who support a subjective genitive five words back find that interpretation more difficult at the end of verse 9, especially when a period follows (as in NRSV), because "Christ" is not mentioned. But the article in Greek before *pistei* can signal "*the* well-known faith" just mentioned. But that can cut two ways, for others regard *epi tē pistei* at the end of the verse as repeating the sense of the objective genitive interpretation, "faith in Christ," to reinforce the point. Some commentators try to have it both ways, first "through the faithfulness of Christ" but secondly that "which is based on the responding faithfulness of the believer."[65] Gordon Fee retorts, "One wonders how the Philippians could possibly have caught on to such a radical shift of subject and object" here.[66] There remains a possible interpretation that goes back to the Greek fathers:[67] to connect "on the basis of faith" at the end of verse 9 with what follows in verse 10, "on the basis of faith to know Christ and the power of his resurrection." This is to be preferred, as in the NAB Revised New Testament, "depending on faith to know him."

Thus far we have translated *dikaiosynē* in verses 6 and 9 as "righteousness," a rendering that fits well for the *dikaiosynē* that is in the law and for the phrase "righteousness of God." But in both Hebrew and Greek one root serves for what we in English term either "righteousness" (from the Anglo-Saxon) or "justification" (from Latin). Occasionally commentators remark that "righteousness through faith" here means "justification" (Vulgate, *iustitia in fide*), and even see in verse 9 an "unambiguous instance . . . of a justification 'pronounced' on the basis of the believer's faith."[68] But again, readers in Philippi could have heard, in light of the Roman imperial cult, the notion of an upright world order under Caesar and God's beneficent righteousness and justice[69]—until they grasped that such notions about

65. M. Bockmuehl, *The Epistle to the Philippians*, BNTC (London: A. & C. Black; Peabody, MA: Hendrickson, 1998), 211, among others.

66. Gordon Fee, *Paul's Letter to the Philippians*, NICNT (Grand Rapids: Eerdmans, 1995), 325 n. 45.

67. John Chrysostom, *Hom. Phil.* 11 (PG 62: 265.57–266; *NPNF*[1] 13:235–36); so also Erasmus, Ewald, and, among others, J.-F. Collange, *The Epistle of Paul to the Philippians* (French CNTXa, 1973; London: Epworth, 1979), 130–31, who notes that Paul gives a definition: "Faith is . . . a form of knowledge," resting "upon a tradition or 'catechism'" that concerns the righteousness of God.

68. C. H. Cosgrove, "Justification in Paul: A Linguistic and Theological Reflection," *JBL* 106 (1987): 667 n. 34.

69. U. Luck, "Die Bekehrung des Paulus und das Paulinische Evangelium: Zur Frage der Evidenz in Botschaft und Theologie des Apostels," *ZNW* 76 (1985): 187–205. While conflict with the Roman

Caesar were shattered in Paul's letter by the references to Christ and to *nomos* as Torah and to circumcision. However we translate it, Paul is setting forth faith-righteousness, from God, attained by believing, obedient trust in Christ.

A striking feature of 3:10 is the appearance of resurrection language in the hendiadys "the power of [Christ's] resurrection [*anastasis*] and participation in his sufferings" and, in verse 11, Paul's hope "to attain to the resurrection [*exanastasis*] of the dead." As part of the future eschatology of chapter 3 (cf. 3:20–21, about the transformation that will occur only when Christ the Savior comes at the parousia), Paul mentions the resurrection for the first time in Philippians.

This is one of several places where Paul is supplementing, if not correcting,[70] the "hymn" (better, "encomium") in 2:6–11.[71] That passage I take as a composition by the Philippians, to set forth the gospel they received from Paul, employing their own terms for evangelization in a Hellenistic, Roman world.[72] Their composition does not mention the resurrection but speaks rather of exaltation or apotheosis for Jesus (2:9–11), just as it may not have mentioned the cross till Paul added it at the end of verse 8 (*thanatou de staurou*: the death of the unnamed figure in vv. 6–8 was on a cross). How natural for Greek converts addressing a Greek world to speak of God exalting Jesus as Lord—likely as a counterclaim to Caesar exalted as *dominus*! Paul corrects their depiction with the biblical idea of resurrection, indeed bodily resurrection (Phil. 3:21), which he also associates with righteousness/justification elsewhere (Rom. 4:25).

One more point from verses 12–16 is pertinent to Paul's experience of righteousness/justification, a factor in the ethical paraenesis that begins at verse 16 and for which Paul serves as illustration. The pronoun "I" is expanded in the process from the Apostle's autobiographical *egō* to a sense that applies to all who are justified and found "in Christ": in verse 15, "let *us*

state is sometimes overstated for Philippians, there is considerable evidence to see the rival lordships of Caesar and Christ (2:11) as a factor in the situation.

70. "Resurrection in Philippi and Paul's Letter(s) to the Philippians," in *Resurrection in the New Testament*, Festschrift for Jan Lambrecht, ed. R. Bieringer, V. Koperski, and B. Lataire, BETL 165 (Leuven: Peeters, Leuven University Press, 2002), 407–22.

71. The trend since I examined criteria for hymns in "Philippians 3.20–21—a Hymnic Fragment?" *NTS* 30 (1984): 593–609, has shifted away from the form-critical category of "hymn," even for 2:6–11; e.g., G. Kennel, *Frühchristliche Hymnen? Gattungskritische Studien zur Frage nach den Liedern der frühen Christenheit*, WMANT 71 (Neukirchen: Neukirchener Verlag, 1995); R. Brucker, *"Christenhymnen" oder "epideiktische Passagen"?* FRLANT 176 (Göttingen: Vandenhoeck & Ruprecht, 1997).

72. J. Reumann, "Contributions," *NTS* 39 (1993): 442–46, with W. Schenk, *Die Philipperbriefe des Paulus: Kommentar* (Stuttgart: Kohlhammer, 1984), 173–75, 192–93, 195, 202, 209, 336; idem, "Der Philipperbrief in der neueren Forschung (1945–1985)," *ANRW* 2.25.4:3299–3308, and others.

then think in this way." The verses speak against Christians who claim to be "already perfected" (12; *teleioi*, 15) by the power of the resurrection, though likely without suffering; against those who think they have already attained (12); perhaps even claiming to be "already transformed," something against which 3:21 speaks, for the transformation occurs only in the future.

Paul speaks repeatedly here, paradigmatically, of how he has not yet attained the goal (12), has not "made it my own" (13)—the goal, the finish. And if not Paul, who then has attained? The admonition is to "press on" (12), to stretch forward to what lies ahead (13), to run in pursuit of the goal (14), to continue on the same course that has been begun (16).

These emphases have sometimes been called Paul's "eschatological" or "future reservation," his reservations about Christians here and now obtaining all that God has promised.[73] He knows it's not all here as yet, during earthly life. The situation is sometimes summed up in the words, "no longer-not yet." Paul is "no longer" what he was (as Saul), but "not yet" what he will be (when he will be "with Christ"). Meanwhile, he is "justified," "in Christ," and *in via*, always "on the way." A classical Reformation way of expressing this liminal state is the *simul* formula: simultaneously *iustus* yet *peccator*; threatened by shame, "earthly things," wrong gods, and destruction (3:19). In the language of 3:12, he is "successfully taken hold of by Christ" but not yet having made salvation his own. Hence the famous admonition of 2:12–13, "With fear and trembling, continue working out what your salvation means, for the one at work in and among you [plural] is God."

While more could be said about righteousness/justification in Philippians 3, several points stand out. First, the Apostle is describing his own experience in coming to know (and be "in") Christ as his personal Lord, in terms of the new life in Christ. He expects such an experience to fit his hearers, even if their background does not begin in Judaism but with counterparts in their Greco-Roman world.[74] Second, he does so above all in terms of two kinds of righteousness, formerly that of law (Torah, though the Roman world knew well the place of *lex*) and now by faith in Christ. Third, it is justification *propter Christum*, particularly stressing, within the "Jesus story," the cross (2:8; 3:18) and resurrection (3:10–11). Fourth, faith is emphatically stressed on our reading of *pistis* as the way believers respond to the Christ-event and the gospel. If *pistis Christou* ever has a subjective

73. Käsemann, among others, emphasized that Paul had reservations about how completely the fulness of life with God in the new age is already being fulfilled in this life and the present age; cf. Dunn, *Theology of Paul the Apostle*, 479–80.

74. P. Pilhofer, *Philippi*, vol. 1, *Die erste christliche Gemeinde Europas*, WUNT 87 (Tübingen: Mohr Siebeck, 1995), 126–27.

genitive sense, it is likely Christ's faithfulness in the working of justification. Fifth, the *simul* is suggested in 3:12–16. Sixth, some object that *sola gratia* is strikingly absent, but "grace" is not at issue. Never in Philippians is *charis* a major theme. God's favor can be assumed, however, in the covenantal relationship Saul knew as well as in the gains Paul finds in Christ. Seventh, Paul presents his gospel gained in Christ without disparaging the Mosaic law: the contrast is not between what is "bad" and what is "good," but between "good" and "better."[75] Eighth, Scripture—anything from the Septuagint or Hebrew Bible—is missing from the argument addressed to this Greco-Roman audience in Philippi. Ninth, the final judgment, regularly a part of forensic justification, runs through the passage and all of Philippians; it becomes explicit as a climax to the chapter in 3:20–21. Tenth, ethical aspects begin to appear in 3:16 and, by implication, in Paul's modeling what it means to be right with God. Eleventh, Paul goes into righteousness/justification because he fears the Philippian church community might be vulnerable to opponents if its own message is lacking in references to cross, resurrection, justification/righteousness as a result of the Christ-event, and future expectation of the end-time coming of the transforming Lord.

To begin study of justification in Pauline theology with some or all of these pointers would provide no mean basis for approaching the often more complicated treatments in Galatians and Romans.

There is a final, disputed area in Pauline studies on which Philippians 3 sheds light. Traditionally the reversal of values in 3:7–11[76] has been termed a result of Paul's conversion in Luke's triple account of the "Damascus road" event. Krister Stendahl, among others, has argued against the term "conversion," preferring to speak of Paul's "call," his assignment to a new task; this would avoid any notion of a "change of 'religion.'"[77] The desire is partly to preserve continuity with Israel, partly to avoid anti-Semitism in Christian origins.

A new possibility has been injected into the "conversion-call" debate by application of Victor Turner's concept of "liminality," from anthropology

---

75. Cf. John 1:17, "The law indeed was given through Moses; grace and truth came through Jesus Christ" (NRSV), where there is neither a *de* (but) nor a *kai* (and) between the clauses. This is a case of "step parallelism." Its effect is to contrast the origins of "law" on the one hand and "grace and truth" on the other. R. Bultmann says that "grace" here is "Pauline" (*The Gospel of John* [Philadelphia: Westminster, 1971], 40–41).

76. Harnisch, "Die paulinische Selbstempfehlung als Plädoyer für den Gekreuzigten," 137, regards v. 7 as the *propositio* after the *narratio* in 4b-6, with 8–14 as *argumentatio*. Others see vv. 9–11 as *propositio*.

77. Krister Stendahl, "Call Rather Than Conversion," in idem, *Paul Among Jews and Gentiles* (Philadelphia: Fortress, 1976), 7–23. Cf. also B. Roberts Gaventa, *From Darkness to Light: Aspects of Conversion in the New Testament*, OBT 20 (Philadelphia: Fortress, 1986), 17–51, esp. 29–33.

and the study of rituals and symbols in society.[78] Application to Philippians 3 has been made especially by Christian Strecker, in *Die liminale Theologie des Paulus*, approaching Pauline theology from a cultural-anthropological perspective.[79] The concept comes from Arnold van Gennep; others prior to Strecker had applied "liminality" to Paul.[80] The case is developed by Strecker with regard to 3:2–21, not just 3:2–11 as in Beverly Gaventa's treatment of "conversion."[81]

Instead of "conversion" or "calling," one should speak of an "initiation process" involving transformation.[82] The process occurs in three stages: "separation" out of one group, "aggregation" into a new, transformed structure, with the middle phase of "liminality" the most important one. Liminality is the "betwixt and between," the "threshold period" (Latin *limen*, *liminis*), the door or dwelling through which one passes. Strecker applies the concept to, among other things, the phrase *en Christō*, with the sense of *Christus communitas*, the community into which one enters by faith and baptism, on the way from Judaism or some other community.[83] The ultimate, final aggregation is what Philippians 3:21 calls the *politeuma* in the heavens, where Christ is Lord and Savior.

To apply this initiation-scenario to the narrative in Philippians 3, Paul's preliminal phase or past status, from which he separates, is indicated in verses 4b–6. The liminal phase is presented in verses 7–16, with typical initiation themes, namely *gnōsis*, death, suffering, and resurrection (cf. Rom. 6:3–11 on baptism). The postliminal aggregation is glimpsed in the *politeuma* of 3:20–21.

78. Victor Turner, *The Ritual Process: Structure and Anti-Structure* (Chicago: Aldine, 1969); *Drama, Fields, and Metaphors: Symbolic Action in Human Society* (Ithaca, NY: Cornell University Press, 1974); summary in *ER* 12:382–86, including Turner's definitions of terms.

79. Christian Strecker, *Die liminale Theologie des Paulus: Zugänge zur paulinischen Theologie aus kulturanthropologischer Perspektive*, FRLANT 185 (Göttingen: Vandenhoeck & Ruprecht, 1999).

80. A. van Gennep, *The Rites of Passage*, trans. M. B. Vizedom and G. L. Caffee (French 1909; Chicago: University of Chicago Press, 1960); cf. *ER* 12:382 (separation, transition, incorporation). S. C. Barton remarks on Paul's "liminal lifestyle" in *Dictionary of Paul and His Letters* (Downers Grove, IL: InterVarsity, 1993), 898–99; N. R. Peterson, *Rediscovering Paul: Philemon and the Sociology of Paul's Narrative World* (Philadelphia: Fortress, 1985), 151–70, is "convinced that if Turner had not created the concepts of structure and anti-structure, we would have to invent them . . . to account for what we see in Paul's letters" (197 n. 165). By "structure" is meant "the system of hierarchically and segmentarily differentiated roles that can be played by a society's members" in its system of social relationships, and their inversion in a non- or antihierarchical *communitas* (152).

81. Gaventa, *From Darkness to Light*.

82. Strecker, *Die liminale Theologie des Paulus*, 83–157. Chapter 6 deals with Paul's transformation (Gal. 1:11–17; Phil. 3:2–21 [pp. 112–37]; 2 Cor. 4:6–12; 1 Cor. 9:1; 15:8–10).

83. This interpretation of *en Christō* combines features of E. P. Sanders's "participatory" model, the ecclesiological model (Bultmann), and the "heilsgeschichtlich-historisierende" model of Neugebauer. It is anchored in the rite of baptism and provides the liminal phase for all believers.

Much can be said about what Strecker has done with this pattern, and some criticisms can be made.[84] But the model does justice to both "conversion" and "calling" aspects. It fits this passage, with its move from covenantal nomism and Paul's considerable status therein to an inversion of that value-system, a new status, world, and being "in Christ." That there is controversy over initiation rites and group identity is signaled at the outset by the references to circumcision in 3:2–3; then to the new status by Spirit (3), justification, and being found "in Christ," with its vertical, horizontal, ecclesial, and social implications. The break with Saul's past is complete. One cannot, even for a moment, think of the Philippians accepting circumcision in the flesh. They have an identity through the gift of the Spirit and justification. Yet "we"—the Philippians and Paul—have not yet attained all that is promised. There is the call upward (14), for the present, in their liminal existence, to think and walk accordingly. Christian existence till the parousia is, to use phrase other than *simul*, their "permanent liminality"[85]—till the glorious transformation of the body comes.

⌒⌣⌒

The phrase "the 'Lutheran' Paul" has been bandied about in the last two and a half decades, in many ways an inexact term for what some New Testament scholars think Luther thought about Paul (chiefly from his Galatians commentary). It also fits positions of Augustine, Calvin, and others, embracing Reformed, Catholic, and other theologies. Its many aspects include justification and faith, but also sin, anthropology, the relation of Paul's gospel to the several covenants in Israel's history, and *Heilsgeschichte* (now seen under terms like "story" or "narrative"). The considerable literature, in treatments in Europe and by North American Evangelicals, con and pro, is summed up in a number of places. Stephen Westerholm, in treating the debates, has made a respectable case for a "Lutheran" Paul who is by no means all wrong exegetically; "Lutherans" (the term includes many in Protestantism and Catholicism) have "rightly captured Paul's rationale and basic point" with regard to justification by faith.[86]

84. Cf. J. Karrer, *TLZ* 126 (2001): 172–75; R. DeMaris, *BTB* 31 (2001): 79; J. Schröter, *RBL* 10/8/2001, available online at http://www.bookreviews.org. Schröter is critical of Strecker's application to Christ's "transformation" in 2:6–11 but holds that on Paul's "apostolic self-understanding" the approach contributes to "the 'new perspective' on Paul."

85. Strecker, *Die liminale Theologie des Paulus*, 113: "die andauernde Liminalität" is in 3:2–21 more emphasized and theologically based for all Christian believers than in Gal. 1:11–17.

86. Stephen Westerholm, *Perspectives Old and New on Paul: The "Lutheran" Paul and His Critics* (Grand Rapids: Eerdmans, 2004), 445, with varying views summarized and criticized, but little analysis of ecumenical work like the Joint Declaration.

7

A Conversation among Friends

A Roman Catholic Response to John Reumann

MARGARET M. MITCHELL

Professor Jack Reumann's chapter brings to us the plentiful results (and some insider secrets) from the intensive ecumenical dialogue between Lutheran and Catholic New Testament scholars and theologians since Vatican II that has sought to chart a new way forward into Christian cooperation, a way that leaves behind the tactics of condemnation, repudiation, and polemical caricature that ensure that the "other side" is presented in the most adverse light possible, and moves instead toward articulating and celebrating "common ground," both doctrinal and experiential. I must begin by expressing profound gratitude, admiration, and respect for Prof. Reumann's scholarship and its intentional and honest positioning so as to be accountable and serviceable to both church and academy. His career and the history of this cooperative Joint Declaration are a testimony to many things: uncountable hours of painstaking exegetical labors over the texts of the New Testament and Hebrew Bible, endless committee and consultation meetings (which must make any scholar yearn for the solitude of a private study and silent lexicon study partners!), and likely even more ceaseless rounds of interpretive and mediatorial work behind and in front of the scenes as the agreement took shape and garnered support, and then, naturally, also elicited informal and formal dissent. The chapter to which I am giving this written response represents the fruits of all three types of endeavors.

In addition, Prof. Reumann's work, and this informative chapter in particular, also demonstrates, especially in the footnotes, one more essential ingredient in the path forward in ecumenical cooperation—friendship—which I think deserves to be held up for admiration and emulation in this context. I myself suspect that diplomatic advances—whether of the geo-political or ecclesial variety—are forged as much by personal friendships across boundaries of entrenched alienation as by any other factor. Hence friendship is not only a result of such work, but is perhaps also its precondition. This coheres as well with the ancient concepts of friendship (which Prof. Reumann, rightly in my opinion, sees as operative in Paul's Letter to the Philippians), in which, as the commonplace has it, *panta koina tois philois* (all things are in common among friends). Once scholars and church leaders take this as their mantra (one found close at hand in that biblical text, which urges fully four times: "that you might think the same thing, having the same love, with a common soul, thinking with one mind" [Phil. 2:2]), then scholarship and church teaching can, and must, look different. Those who seek to yield fruits from the labors of these pioneers must find ways to "water" the seeds of friendship so well planted by Profs. Reumann, Fitzmyer, and others, to issue forth in the "increase" of scholarly advance and ecclesial mutual enrichment.

Conversation Partners

Out of this cluster of considerations comes the choice for the title of my essay—*enteuxis philōn*—a Greek phrase that means "an act of reading among friends," or equally, "a conversation among friends," for the Greek word *enteuxis* quite aptly and suggestively can mean both "conversation" and "reading or study."[1] The phrase therefore nicely captures the ciccadian rhythm of a scholarly life rotating between private study (reading) and public presentation (conversation); it also suggests that when we "read" Paul we engage in "conversation" with a lively, provocative person and thinker.[2] Yet conversational harmony, like church unity, does not mean

1. LSJ, 576.
2. I have explored the dynamics of Paul as coming to life in the reading of his letters in my book, *The Heavenly Trumpet: John Chrysostom and the Art of Pauline Interpretation*, Hermeneutische Untersuchungen zur Theologie 40 (Tübingen: Mohr Siebeck, 2000; Louisville: Westminster John Knox, 2002).

unanimity; thus, in my response I shall debate Prof. Reumann, in what I hope is a *philikōs* manner, on some exegetical and hermeneutical points about our mutual friend, Paul.

But first I should introduce myself as a friend joining the conversation in reading. I have been invited to write this chapter, "A Roman Catholic Response," in reply to Prof. Reumann's chapter. What does this mean? I am a Roman Catholic laywoman (my parents, rest their souls, would want me to say "*Irish* Catholic"), a scholar of the New Testament and early Christian literature who received doctoral training at the University of Chicago (founded as a Baptist institution of higher education), where my major intellectual influences were a German Reformed Pauline scholar (Hans Dieter Betz) and an Orthodox Jewish scholar of Hebrew Bible and rabbinics (Jon Levenson). From that cauldron of ecumenical seasoning I went to teach at McCormick Theological Seminary (a seminary of the Presbyterian Church [U. S. A.]) for twelve years, before returning to the faculty at the University of Chicago six years ago, where I teach graduate and undergraduate students from a wide range of religious commitments, noncommitments, enthusiasms, and aversions. I hold appointments both in the Divinity School and in the Division of the Humanities, and I teach courses and students from both in the same room. Is this the right *cursus honorum* to qualify as a "Catholic" voice in a conversation? I do not know. Yet I was born and will be buried as a Catholic and would be foolhardy to claim that my professorial and confessional selves are completely hermetically sealed from each other, although I regard myself neither as teaching "the Catholic take on Paul" (or on the New Testament, or on patristics) nor, I should add, as propounding simply the "new common understanding of Paul" that the Joint Declaration represents. My job, as I see it, entails introducing my students to complex and ambiguous texts and to the long history of conflicted interpretation of them, so that they can take their place as readers who are informed by the past, yet also free to move the conversation on these texts, which are of perennial importance, forward in new ways.

Consequently, I do not want to claim that I am somehow a "typical Catholic voice," even as I am not sure who would qualify to be such. Therefore, on the basis of biography, like Prof. Reumann, I would want to insist on the indefinite article in the title, "A Roman Catholic Response." And I would like to stress this caution, not just as a protective personal caveat to my own remarks, but as an illustration of the sociological, ecclesiological, and pedagogical facts in which we are now enmeshed with one another, which are markedly different from the state of affairs just decades ago. My confessionally mixed background and foreground are not unusual for the current scene, but are becoming more and more the norm. The scholars who are now taking up the task of Pauline interpretation have been conspicuously formed already in an ecumenically sensitive way. The current conversational context, in sum, becomes muddier and muddier if what we seek, from ourselves and from others, are pure pedigrees of confessional and pedagogical adherence, with predictable results. I take this as a sign of remarkable progress and tremendous opportunity (the sheer demographics of our pedagogical situations are moving ecumenism forward "on the ground"), even as it admittedly provides much impetus for identity crises and conversational confusion.

My Roman Catholic "perspective" is furthermore complicated by my scholarly research interests, because I have for more than a decade been immersed in the Pauline interpretation of John Chrysostom, who was claimed by both Roman Catholics and Protestants in the Reformation (despite the fact that Luther called him "nur ein Weffscher" [only a gossip!] in the *Tischreden*)[3] but is most thoroughly identified with Greek Orthodoxy. That perspective at the very least reminds us that all of Christianity is not encompassed in the Protestant-Catholic divide, let alone the Lutheran-Catholic divide, though the present conversations do not include any Greek Orthodox, non-Chalcedonian, or other Christian readers of Paul outside of the usual Western map of post-Reformation denominationalism. Chrysostom speaks directly to Reumann's chapter and to the present situation, for his fate in modern Pauline scholarship in the West has (at least until recently) been seriously hampered by the fact that the famous Antiochene preacher has been deemed deficient precisely in his lack of understanding or appreciation of the Pauline doctrine of justification by faith.[4] Some scholars, such as Ernst Benz, have characterized the East-West divide as a split between "Pauls": the West, following Augustine and then Luther, views him through Galatians and Romans, while the East turns to the Corinthian correspondence, interested more in mysticism and practical ethics than in forensic soteriology.[5] Later in this chapter I shall introduce into this conversation with one John (Reumann) my fourth-century friend John (Chrysostom) to further our conversation on a shorter letter, Philippians, which stands outside this traditional configuration of the *Hauptbriefe*[6] and its legacy for Pauline theology, East and West.

3. *Tischreden* no. 252; text: *Luther's Works*, ed. Weimar, trans. T.G. Tappert (Philadelphia: Fortress, 1967), 54.34.
    4. Discussion in Mitchell, *Heavenly Trumpet*, 8–18.
    5. Ernst Benz, "Das Paulus-Verständnis in der morgenländischen und abendländischen Kirche," ZRGG 3 (1951): 289–309.
    6. This German term refers to what are traditionally considered the four "main letters" of Paul: Romans, 1 and 2 Corinthians, and Galatians.

Methodological Considerations

John Reumann's chapter has three parts: (1) a methodological and historical preamble ("A [and the] Lutheran View"); (2) an exploration and
defense of some critiques of the role of biblical data in the Joint Declaration;
and (3) righteousness/justification in Philippians. The three sections show
a consistency of perspective and form a unified presentation of our topic
of justification by faith in Paul. I would like to focus my response initially
on four methodological issues raised by what Reumann has articulated and
has modeled in this chapter. Then I would like to join him, and my fourth-
century guest interpreter, in rereading Philippians 3:2–16.

First, Reumann identifies his methodological principle at the outset:
"Any Lutheran view on our topic should be consonant with sound scriptural interpretation, in light of critical studies . . . of *dikaiosynē* and related
concepts, [and] with confessional positions articulated with regard to *iusti-
tia/Rechtfertigung*." This principle of double consonance, if I may call it that,
is later enacted, Reumann says, in "considerable openness in the interplay
between the perennial task of scriptural study and ongoing analysis of the
Confessions." While he bemoans the alienation that still exists between
biblical scholars and systematic theologians, on the one hand, and between
academic biblical scholarship and that carried out in ecumenical contexts
on the other, he also celebrates the "new insights about the good news"
that have come from "'listening together' to the word of God in Scripture."
I would like to probe further here, and ask whether it is possible to locate
these new insights more specifically in relation to the dual threads of this
enterprise: the exegetical and the confessional.

Is a fresh "common reading" of Paul indeed the basis for the new theo-
logical-confessional unity celebrated in the Joint Declaration? One reason
I find this rather a frightening prospect is that, if true (and I am not sure
it is), it might establish an unwise and unwieldy precedent for ecumenical
advance: the precondition of consensus among New Testament scholars![7]
But in addition to the strategic role and limitations of biblical scholarship
in ecumenical work, there are considerable intellectual issues here that re-

---

7. After the SBL Pauline Theology group sessions in the 1990s, we can hardly be optimistic about
such a prospect. This group published four volumes as a record of their discussions and debates (often of
highest value when genuine disagreements were named and explored): Jouette M. Bassler, ed., *Pauline
Theology*, vol. 1, *Thessalonians, Philippians, Galatians, Philemon* (Minneapolis: Fortress, 1991); David
M. Hay, ed., *Pauline Theology*, vol. 2, *1 and 2 Corinthians* (Minneapolis: Fortress, 1993); David M. Hay
and E. E. Johnson, eds., *Pauline Theology*, vol. 3, *Romans* (Minneapolis: Fortress, 1995); E. E. Johnson,
ed., *Pauline Theology*, vol. 4, *Looking Back, Pressing On* (Atlanta: Scholars Press, 1997).

quire more careful consideration: issues of hermeneutics (where is meaning located: in text, author, reader, communities, etc.?), of epistemology (how do we know what we know, and if we gain new insights, does that mean the old were wrong, and if so, what was the source of the error?), and of tradition (what is the relationship between words of the past and realities of the present, both in terms of the writings of Paul and of the anathemas pronounced in the sixteenth century?). These questions have a special pertinence, I think, in Reumann's way of addressing the critique that the Joint Declaration did not make use of "'state of the art' methods and positions of end-of-the-century New Testament studies." Reumann rightly replies that the goal of the Joint Declaration was not a *Forschungsbericht* (report on research), but he also appears diffidently cautious about "whether the so-called new methods would relate helpfully to the theological solution of sixteenth-century differences." But if the problem here is anachronism or at least historical distance, as this sentence implies, then we must ask why *any* post-Enlightenment methods, including the historical-critical methodologies most employed here, could with any confidence be expected to do so. Further, I am unsure why his wariness about the possible ecumenical pay-off of the results of biblical scholarship of this sort is associated with concerns about "the subjectivity of each reader's response" when that criterion does not appear to be employed to critique historical, philological, or other methods applied in the construction of the Joint Declaration, or of this chapter.

For example, how can an exegesis of Philippians 3:2–11 that has as its guiding star "not los[ing] the thread of our argument on justification" not be in some sense subjective in its chosen focus and concentration (after all, who is the "our" of the quotation?), even if the author has named some of the other—perhaps equally important—elements in the passage, such as the term *gnōsis* (knowledge), which will stand outside his investigation due to time limitations? The way one chooses to spend the finite time one has is always a subjective choice to some degree, based on selected criteria that come from somewhere—in this case, strongly reinforced from the confessional side. So the methodological question remains: from which side of the dual enterprise does the agenda arise, and does that matter for the enterprise?

Second, what is the relationship between the "doctrine" and the "experience" of justification by faith for Reumann, or for Paul? Reumann has noted the degree to which this polemically generated passage, at the very least in Philippians 3:5–6, has an encomiastic structure marked by *synkrisis* (rhetorical comparison), with which I agree, in that it lists what the rhetoricians would call *ta kephalaia* (rhetorical headings) in the category of *ta exōthen*[8] (the external circumstances of a person's life: family, homeland, education), alongside the major topoi of *psychē* (soul) and *sōma* (body; interesting in a context where "having confidence in the flesh" is the central topic).[9] We could say much more on this, but it seems crucial to ask whether and how we can get at Paul's experience of justification from a passage with such complex literary purposes and rhetorical subtleties (much more is going on here than is indicated in Reumann's remark that "the Apostle is *describing his own experience*"). And what is the weight of that experience even if recoverable? To formulate my question in general terms, what is the relationship between Paul's experience, Paul's rhetoric, and the Pauline thought of Reumann's title? And how does that triad function in the tasks of contemporary systematic and constructive theology?

This leads me to a third consideration: the force of the word "Pauline" before "thought" in this study. One of the points of Prof. Reumann's essay strikes me as curious on two fronts. It has to do with his interpretation of what is surely the crux of any argument on justification by faith in Paul's letters—Galatians 2:16—which he refers to with the appositional trinity "a doctrinal statement, a principle, or basic proposition." Reumann argues, with Jürgen Becker and a few others, that Paul has not created this theological statement; rather, it is the communal property (*Gemeingut*) of the church, a consensus statement of Antiochene theology. The force of this argument is that the teaching on justification by faith is not, strictly speaking, "Pauline," but Antiochene.

The exegetical arguments in support of this hypothesis seem unconvincing. For one thing, the participial phrase *eidotes hoti* (knowing that) is thought to be like Romans 3:28, which Reumann cites as *logizometha hoti* (we reckon that), claiming that this is one of several such statements in Paul's letters that are quotations of traditions going back to the Antiochene

---

8. For full discussion of these terms and their place in ancient rhetorical theory, see Mitchell, *Heavenly Trumpet*, 200–206, and passim.

9. Confirming this reading, John Chrysostom, the rhetorically trained Antiochene exegete and preacher, recognizes this scheme. First, he acknowledges its encomiastic nature when he defends Paul for composing an encomium to himself. The language John uses is a topos: Paul "says great things about himself" because of "necessity," to avoid "offense"; on which see Margaret M. Mitchell, "A Patristic Perspective on Pauline *periautologia*," *NTS* 47 (2001): 354–71. Second, John divides Paul's encomium into two parts: *ta aproaireta* (things that are not a matter of choice), which he identifies with the traditional topic of *eugeneia* (noble birth), and *ta tēs proaireseōs* (things that one has chosen) (*Hom. Phil.* 10.2 [PG 62.258]); on this language, and its place in ancient encomia, see Mitchell, *Heavenly Trumpet*, 249–50.

church. But the Romans passage does not read *hoti* (that), but instead has an indirect discourse with infinitival construction; hence the grammatical parallelism named is not actually there. Moreover, the hanging participle *eidotes* in Galatians 2:16 can hardly bear all the weight placed on it by Becker and Reumann to infer that what follows asserts "as unquestioned church knowledge . . . that a person is not justified by works of the law but only through faith in Jesus Christ, a consensus statement of Antiochene theology that also appears in Romans 3:28."

The lack of definite article on *anthrōpos* (human being) in both Galatians 2:16 and Romans 3:28 is taken as characteristically apodictic; perhaps so, but that is irrelevant to the authorship of the sentence, for Paul is capable of issuing statements of "holy law," as Ernst Käsemann long ago demonstrated,[10] and can formulate general statements with anarthrous *anthrōpos* all on his own, such as 1 Corinthians 11:28. Moreover, the verbal parallels that do exist between Romans 3:28 and Galatians 2:16 do not tell us anything about pre-Pauline authorship, but instead point to common locutions in the same author when talking about the same topic—just what we would expect, unless there are serious reasons for doubting that this author could have written these two, quite similar, statements. Finally, even if Reumann and Becker are right that 2:16 reflects some pre-Pauline Antiochene agreement, that does not explain what any of the parties meant by the enigmatic *ean mē* ("but" or "except" or "unless").

So I am not convinced by the evidence offered that some type of formal church consensus statements underlie these two Pauline sentences. Furthermore, the argument falters on contextual exegetical grounds, which Reumann has not addressed here. Of the triad of designations he gives the verse (doctrinal statement, principle, or basic proposition), the last is the one that is historically and rhetorically most accurate: Galatians 2:16 is the proposition (*hypothesis*) to the argument[11] that extends from 2:16 through at least 5:12, if not 6:17. Famously this proposition "bleeds over" from the direct discourse to Cephas that begins in 2:14, without a clear demarcation (before 3:1) to show when Paul actually stops reciting what he had said on that past occasion and shifts to the Galatian addresses directly. Consequently, the argument proceeds seamlessly from the historical exemplum. In addition to effecting a remarkably

10. Ernst Käsemann, "Sentences of Holy Law in the New Testament," in idem, *New Testament Questions of Today* (New Testament Library; Philadelphia: Fortress, 1969), 66–81.

11. Cf. Hans Dieter Betz, *Galatians* (Hermeneia; Philadelphia: Fortress, 1979), 113–27, who regards 2:15–21 entire as the *propositio*. I regard 2:16 as the proposition, with 2:17–21 being the explication and opening argument in its favor. The end result of the two positions is not very different.

smooth *transitio*, Paul's rhetoric here allows him to avoid the expectation that, in true narrative fashion, he would recount Cephas's response to his statements. Presumably Paul takes this tack because there was nothing in Cephas's response that was useful for Paul's case. If 2:16 did represent "a consensus statement of Antiochene theology,"[12] surely Cephas/Peter would have had to acknowledge it as such—especially on the home turf of Antioch—and Paul would have quoted him to that effect as he appears to do earlier in 2:7–10, by reference both to confirming words and actions (the handshake). But Paul did not do so in 2:15–16, apparently because he did not win the fight described in 2:11–14 and consequently he does not have Cephas on record as agreeing with the proposition formulated here. Rather than being a pre-Pauline statement of Antiochene church theology, the more logical and historically plausible solution, to my mind, is that Paul himself is responsible for 2:16, and the issue of justification is *his* way of characterizing what is at stake in the "false gospel's" compulsion of Gentile converts to become circumcized. It is Paul who introduced the dichotomy, in line with his consistent mode of antithetical argumentation in Galatians.[13] Surely his opponents in Galatia would never have agreed to such a dichotomy, for they did not see some measure of Torah observance as conflicting with faith in Jesus Christ.[14] But neither, apparently, did Cephas, at least on occasion. One must reckon with the fact that if all the Antiochenes stood with Paul on this, undoubtedly he would have said so (with much more vehemence than the hanging participle *eidotes*).[15] Other Christians may have used justification language as one of a series of terms for the effects of the death and resurrection of Christ (1 Cor. 6:11 may point to this), but I think it is quite clearly Paul who accents it, and surely Paul who considers it to be actuated *only* by *pistis Iēsou Christou*, "faith in Jesus Christ."

12. Jürgen Becker, *Paul: Apostle to the Gentiles*, trans. O. C. Dean Jr. (Louisville: Westminster John Knox, 1993), 96, cited by Reumann, *"Righteousness" in the New Testament: Justification in the United States Lutheran–Roman Catholic Dialogue* (Philadelphia: Fortress; New York: Paulist Press, 1982), 17.

13. The argument is structured on pairs of binary opposites that Paul sets up, stacks up, and uses to render self-evident his antithetical logic, which disallows any coalescence or compromise: works of law/faith in Jesus Christ; destroy/build up; dying/living; flesh/spirit; blessing/curse; slavery/freedom.

14. I am substantially in agreement with Profs. Reumann and Fitzmyer on the objective genitive, by the way, so we shall not have to debate that thorny issue here. For a defense of the "faith[fulness] of Jesus" position, and entrée into the considerable literature, see Richard B. Hays, *The Faith of Jesus Christ: the Narrative Substructure of Gal 3:1–4:11* (Chico, CA: Scholars Press, 1983; 2nd ed., Grand Rapids: Eerdmans; Dearborn, MI: Dove, 2002).

15. One might add to this argument the striking fact that later Antiochene tradition speaks loudly against any such coherent Antiochene view on *dikaiosynē*. In addition to the radically different view of the Gospel according to Matthew (e.g., 5:20; 6:1, 33; 12:37), often thought to be Antiochene in origin, even more tellingly, Ignatius of Antioch, perhaps the most thoroughly Pauline thinker and writer in the earliest church, never mentions justification by faith, indeed directly coalescing faith with other things through which one may be justified (Ign. *Phld.* 8.2).

Nevertheless, I am raising this issue not simply for the exegetical discussion—though I'd enjoy engaging that further—but rather to bring forward what to me is a puzzlement in Reumann's mode of intersecting historical data and theological merit. If the criterion for biblical theology is the presence of a doctrine or teaching in the biblical text, especially in view of the Lutheran criterion of *sola scriptura*, why is it deemed necessary to bolster the testimony of any single statement in the text by a reconstructed, underlying plural authorship (and therefore collegial authority) other than Paul himself? It seems to me that that is just the force of the argument Reumann has presented when he finds here "a basic doctrinal assertion going back to the church of Peter and Paul in Antioch, a piece of apostolic church teaching, not simply a Pauline peculiarity or proprium." What hermeneutical assumptions underlie this claim to apparently "higher octane" authority for 2:16 on the basis of the conclusion that it is not just Paul's private or idiosyncratic position? Is this an argument by appeal to historical priority, and therefore greater claim to the truth than later "accretions"?[16] If so, it is a classic Reformation argument, to be sure, but also it contains an irony: it involves an end run around *sola scriptura* to conciliarism as the basis for authority. Hence my question: does the authority of scriptural truth in this instance rely on prescriptural consensus?

Fourth, how much does Reumann's method and exegesis rely on Luke and the Lukan portrait of Paul? Certainly the reconstruction of Antiochene Christianity (à la Becker and as appropriated here) depends very heavily on Acts for the depiction of the Hellenists, for the Pauline itinerary, and for connecting Paul (and Barnabas) with Antioch prior to the "Jerusalem Council" in the first place.[17] If we had only Galatians—and here I stand with my Chicago predecessor John Knox in insisting that we first deal with the evidence of the letters on their own terms[18]—we would not assume that Paul was, as Becker has him, twelve years in Antioch, the leading Christian thinker there. A curiosity of Becker's reconstruction is that pre-Pauline winds up being just "early Pauline," as he himself states, though without perhaps sufficient appreciation of the irony.[19] It is difficult to claim Paul the Antiochene innovator and the Antiochene loyalist in the same breath!

16. The theological question, rooted in the dynamic I articulated above on the meanings of "tradition," is this: must theological truth always entail a return to an ideal past, or can it be an advance over or beyond the past?

17. See Becker, *Paul*, 83–124.

18. John Knox, *Chapters in a Life of Paul*, rev. ed. (Macon, GA: Mercer, 1987).

19. See Becker, *Paul*, 104.

Reumann's strong reliance on Acts,[20] therefore, extends both to the particulars of historical reconstruction (with Becker), and the church conciliar model that governs his assessment of the power of these theological statements. The important questions remain: what is "Pauline" about "Pauline thought" on justification, and what is due to "Paul's experience," and what to his Antiochene traditioning? I think there is some tension among the various claims of Reumann's chapter in these respects.

The issue of Acts also becomes acute in Reumann's exegesis of Philippians 3, in which we hear him repeatedly enshrining the Lukan name change Saul/Paul, though the author of Philippians offers no Jewish name for himself,[21] no onomastic overturnings. Yet Reumann uses the Acts name shift to typologize the experience he thinks Paul is describing in Philippians 3, as though the Saul/Paul divide took place at the moment of his "conversion" or "call."[22] But even in Acts no name shift takes place in Acts 9, in the moment or aftermath of the "Damascus road incident," but only later, in 13:9, is it told to the reader as an aside: *Saulos de, ho kai Paulos* (Saul, aka Paul). And it is mentioned in a rather unlikely place: in the middle of the curse against Bar-Jesus. The Victor Turner liminality model Reumann incorporates into his analysis (with Christian Strecker) appears to be more pressed into the service of Acts 9 (also 22 and 26) than of Philippians 3:2–21, as can be seen at the very least from the fact that the three-stage process is mapped only to 3:4–6, 7–16, and 20–21.

Rereading Philippians 3 among Friends

Turning from explicitly methodological concerns to the exegesis of Philippians 3, I would like to say first that I am in agreement with many, perhaps most, of Reumann's eleven exegetical observations about righteousness/justification in Philippians 3, which do not in large measure stand outside scholarly consensus on the letter.[23] But I would like to note

20. This merging of Paul and Luke is found as well in the Joint Declaration, §11, as also quoted in Reumann's chapter, which harmonizes the concepts of justification and forgiveness of sins.

21. Paul does say he is of the "tribe of Benjamin" (3:5), whose famous ancestor was King Saul, but does not thereby claim a personal name for himself.

22. I am referring to the famous essay of Krister Stendahl, "Paul among Jews and Gentiles," part 2, "Call Rather than Conversion," in idem, *Paul Among Jews and Gentiles* (Philadelphia: Fortress, 1976), 7–22.

23. The major exception to this is Reumann's consensus-defying claim (with reference to Reumann's earlier article on this topic, and the work of W. Schenk) that the "hymn" in Phil. 2:5–11 was composed by the Philippians, who sent it to Paul, who then edited it into conformity with his theology

for further discussion an odd unevenness in the application of the methodological principle of double consonance between Scripture and the Lutheran
Confessions. Whereas Reumann translates what he understands as Paul's
eschatological reserve in 3:12–16 into the Reformation language of *simul
iustus et peccator*, he does not do so in the case of the law in 3:6–7 (i.e., by
bringing in Luther's stark and stinging law/gospel dichotomy).[24] On the
contrary, Reumann confidently states (his point 7) that "Paul presents his
gospel gained in Christ [orally he added here: "in contrast to Galatians and
Romans"] *without disparaging the Mosaic law*: the contrast is not between
what is 'bad' and what is 'good,' but between 'good' and 'better'" (italics
added). This is a move perhaps surprising on the Lutheran level, where one
might expect the stance of the *Confessions* and other documents to insist
on a stronger contrast between law and gospel, but not so on another level
of ecumenical engagement—that with Jews and Judaism—which one can
only deem laudable here, even though it does illustrate how difficult it is
(for all of us) to be multiply ecumenical at the same time.

However, the exegetical basis for Reumann's quick assertion that Paul does
not in fact disparage the law in Philippians 3 has not been sufficiently offered
here. In grappling with this question I would like to consult my promised
exegetical friend, John Chrysostom (347–407 CE), presbyter at Antioch
and later bishop of Constantinople, who says he understands Paul so well
because he loves him so much,[25] and bring him into this conversation about
and with Paul. Chrysostom, though hardly worried about offending Jews
(he was the author of the notoriously bitter invectives *Adversus Judaeos*),[26]
nonetheless displays considerable angst about Paul's words concerning the
law in Philippians 3, because it might appear that the Apostle is terming it
skybala ("crap," as Reumann aptly translates the term), among *ta panta* (all
things, 3:8–9). Chrysostom's anxiety is not merely hypothetical, but designed
to address a real-life usage of this passage among some fourth-century Christian interpreters, probably Marcionites, whom John terms *hoi hairetikoi* (the
heretics), who say, "look, the law is a loss; look, it is called 'crap'! How then
do you say it is God's law?"[27] John's interpretive method is the one we should

and included it in his letter of reply. I do not find this suggestion very plausible, either on exegetical
or historical grounds, but cannot take up that argument here.

24. See the chapter by Randall Zachman in this volume.

25. See Mitchell, *Heavenly Trumpet*, 1, 38–40, 429, with references and hermeneutical discussion
of the concept of "love hermeneutics."

26. On which see Robert L. Wilken, *John Chrysostom and the Jews: Rhetoric and Reality in the Late 4th
Century*, Transformation of the Classical Heritage 4 (Berkeley: University of California Press, 1983).

27. *Hom. Phil.* 11.1 (PG 62.263–64) (my translation, as throughout this chapter).

adopt: "Let's attend with precision to what is being said."[28] When he does, his solution is—remarkably—precisely that offered by our contemporary John in his contribution to this book:

> It is not a loss, but is [merely] considered a loss now, since grace is so much better. Just as one who is poor, living in famine, when he has silver, escapes from starvation, but when he finds gold, and he is not able to hold onto both and considers holding onto silver a matter of loss, he lets it go and takes the gold. He lets it go, not because the silver is a loss—because it isn't—but because it is not possible to hold onto the two [i.e., grace and law] at once, but it is necessary to leave the one behind.[29]

However, despite this precise correlation between our two readers named John, it would be premature to baptize Chrysostom a Lutheran just yet. For he also finds a way in this passage to explicate what he understands to be Paul's ethical requirements for *dikaiosynē* (justification), not just in the "eschatological reserve" of 3:12–16, where Reumann sees ethical aspects in the passage, but earlier, in 3:10–11, because John understands the attaining of the resurrection of the dead to be conditional upon[30] having *koinōnia tōn pathēmatōn autou* (participation in [Christ's] sufferings) and becoming *symmorphizesthai tōi thanatōi autou* (coformed to his death). For John, one does this by dying to sin and enduring persecution and sufferings,[31] "making up what is lacking in the sufferings of Christ" (he twice quotes Col. 1:24 to make the point).[32] Hence John can go on to say, in most un-Lutheran terms,[33] "You see that it

28. The concept of exegetical *akribeia* (precision, accuracy) is very important in early Christian biblical hermeneutics, and can profitably be appreciated and modeled by modern interpreters; see the valuable study of Robert C. Hill, "Akribeia: A Principle of Chrysostom's Exegesis," *Colloquium* 14 (1981): 32–36.

29. *Hom. Phil.* 11.1 (PG 62.264).

30. See the clear expression of the condition, and its logic: "For if you have not died, you have not risen again" (*Hom. Phil.* 11.3 [PG 62.267]).

31. See *Hom. Phil.* 11.2 (PG 62.266): "For just as Christ suffered from people, so also I . . . 'I make up what is lacking in the afflictions of Christ in my flesh' (Col. 1:24). That is: the persecutions and these sufferings create that image of [his] death. For he was not seeking his own advantage, but that of the many. Therefore, both the persecutions and the afflictions and the oppressions not only should not upset us, but they should cheer us, because through these we are being co-formed to Christ's death."

32. The key exegetical variance here is that Chrysostom emphatically does not regard "the power of his resurrection and the participation in his sufferings" as a hendiadys, as Reumann does. Rather, he thinks that it is faith in the power of the resurrection that generates the latter: "For from faith comes the participation in his sufferings. How? For if we did not believe [*pisteuein*], we would not suffer. If we did not believe [*pisteuein*] that by enduring we shall co-reign, we would not undergo the sufferings" (*Hom. Phil.* 11.2 [PG 62.266]).

33. This despite the fact that just earlier in the same homily Chrysostom accented the free gift of God in terms any Lutheran would applaud: "This justification [*dikaiosynē*] is of God. This is completely

is not necessary for there to be simply faith, but [it must be] through works [*Horas hoti ouch haplōs dei tēn pistin einai, alla di' ergōn*]. For this is the person who most believes [*malista pisteuei*] that Christ rose—the one who perilously gives him/herself over to dangers, the one who is a partner with Christ in his sufferings."[34]

I offer Chrysostom's exegesis here both for its substance, and to illustrate—once again—the multivalence of these texts, the interpretation of which is always influenced by a whole host of factors in the text, the reader, the audience, the moment, the genre, and the purpose of the interpretive endeavor. I am not championing an endlessly relativistic hermeneutic; I do not believe the text can imitate Paul in being "all things to all people" (1 Cor. 9:22). But the long history of varied and rich interpretation of Pauline texts should make us appropriately cautious about proclaiming new hegemonious readings that will "settle" old debates, for those other readings, once possible, will always be possible. This is what it means to have a tradition of interpretation: the conscious preservation of alternative points of view in the reading of the texts, passed on to each new generation. For me this is one of the strongest arguments for the centrality of justification by faith as an important vantage point from which to read Paul. While exegetically I am not convinced that Paul isolates justification by faith in his letters to the degree Luther does, or that he sets it in some hierarchical position over his other soteriological terms (salvation, sanctification, reconciliation, redemption), I nonetheless cannot read Paul's letters as though Luther had not read them. My own view is that the ten terms Joseph Fitzmyer identifies as different aspects of the Christian gospel do not in fact signify different effects of the Christ-event but rather are different metaphorical means, deliberately taken from a variety of cultural loci (military, cultic, diplomatic, economic), for expressing the same, single salvific reality that Paul understands Christ's death and resurrection to have made possible for humanity. Hence I would propose that instead of a decahedron of salvific effects, we think of these as different templates or transparencies that can be overlaid in viewing what is for Paul the singly central Christ-event.[35]

---

a gift. The gifts of God to such a great degree surpass the paltriness of the good deeds which come about by our zeal" (*Hom. Phil.* 11.2 [PG 62.265]).

34. *Hom. Phil.* 11.2 (PG 62.266).

35. In this view I am influenced by Fitzmyer's classic statement: "[Paul] spoke of the effects of [Christ's] accomplishment under ten different images. . . . For each of these images expresses a distinctive aspect of the mystery of Christ and his work. If the Christ-event is conceived of as a decahedron, a ten-sided solid figure, one can understand how Paul, gazing at one panel of it, would use one image to express an effect of it, whereas he would use another image when gazing at another panel. Each one expresses an aspect of the whole" (*Paul and His Theology: A Brief Sketch*, 2nd ed. [Englewood Cliffs,

Paul chose which metaphorical complex to use, as a type of brilliantly effective rhetorical shorthand,[36] depending on the contingent situation he faced. Hence, for instance, at one point in the conflicted situation with the Corinthians, Paul emphasized reconciliation terminology (2 Cor. 5:18–20), but even there it sits comfortably alongside the language of justification (from the forensic realm). It is true that in the preserved letters Paul drew more often and with more concentrated argumentative attention on the justification metaphor than any other (in Galatians, Romans, and Philippians), due to the conflicts he faced in defending his mission to the Gentiles. But it is not clear to me that the historical Paul set justification into competition with his other linguistic fields denoting salvation, redemption, sanctification, and so on, for the latter terms are used even in arguments in which justification plays a large role. Yet the Lutheran argument that justification is the article "by which the church stands or falls" presses this question and therefore must be taken as an important respect in which the later history of interpretation of these texts—for all readers—has indelibly and unforgettably marked them for later generations of readers. And this is especially the case when we read among friends.

NJ: Prentice Hall, 1989], 59). Yet I do not think these are separate "effects" so much as distinct ways of articulating one unified result of the Christ-event; hence I shift the image from ten panels to ten transparencies over a single entity. And I emphasize that the generative moment of these images is not only Paul's contemplative gaze but, crucially, his dialogical and persuasive interaction with diverse audiences in specific situations.

36. For a more detailed investigation of the dynamics of Paul's use of theological shorthand to incorporate the gospel into his arguments, see my article, "Rhetorical Shorthand in Pauline Argumentation: The Functions of 'The Gospel' in the Corinthian Correspondence," in *Gospel in Paul: Studies on Corinthians, Galatians and Romans for Richard N. Longenecker*, ed. L. Ann Jervis and Peter Richardson, JSNTSup 108 (Sheffield: Sheffield Academic Press, 1994), 63–88. Of course, "justification by faith" is itself an elliptical shorthand of a shorthand.

8

Interpretations of Paul in the Early Church

David M. Rylaarsdam

The interpretations of Paul in the early church constitute a daunting topic. Its magnitude is made manageable only by drawing on superb studies from the last few decades that have significantly advanced our understanding of patristic interpretations of Paul. These studies indicate that three general theories about early Pauline reception are very questionable. First, the notion of a smooth, linear reception of Paul into the theology of the early church seems untenable.[1] Rival interpretations of Paul were likely commonplace from the first century onward. Various Jewish and Gentile Christian groups, as well as Marcion, Christian Gnostics, Manicheans, Neoplatonists, Arians, and all those who reacted in various ways to such interpreters, together created, in the words of Karlfried Froehlich, "a constant back and forth of assertions and reactions, endorsements and rejections, in short, a much more colorful palette of normative images of Paul" than has been recognized. He continues:

1. See references in Karlfried Froehlich, "Which Paul? Observations on the Image of the Apostle in the History of Biblical Exegesis," in *New Perspectives on Historical Theology: Essays in Memory of John Meyendorff*, ed. Bradley Nassif (Grand Rapids: Eerdmans, 1996), 287–90.

Which Paul influenced the beginnings of Christian theology? Which Pauline "school" upheld the true Paul against distortions? To which church was which Pauline theology adapted? There are no easy answers to these bewildering questions.[2]

There is not a single Pauline tradition. Instead, we see the Apostle accomplishing posthumously through the diverse reception of his epistles what he deeply desired during his lifetime, namely, to be "all things to all people" (1 Cor. 9:22).[3]

If the theory of a smooth, linear reception of Paul into the theology of the early church is unlikely, so too is a second theory, that Paul was merely a marginal figure. Several scholars have convincingly argued that there is no solid basis for the idea that Paul was unimportant, forgotten, suppressed, or even rejected by the mainstream church until at least the mid-second century, when Marcion forced the issue of Pauline interpretation.[4] From the first century onward, Paul seems to be a constituent element of developing ecclesiastical tradition.[5] Although the Apostolic Fathers, for example, do

2. Ibid., 288. Cf. François Bovon, "Paul comme document et Paul comme monument," who describes the second century as "le temps de la réception polychrome des épîtres pauliniennes" (in *Chrétiens en conflit: l'épître de Paul aux Galates, Dossier pour l'animation biblique*, ed. J. Allaz et al. [Paris: Labor et Fides, 1987], 54). See also Walter Bauer, who comments on the "elasticity" of Paul's views: "In the long run, almost any gentile Christian could attach himself to the Apostle to the Gentiles so as to receive legitimation from him" (*Orthodoxy and Heresy in Earliest Christianity*, trans. Robert A. Kraft and Gerhard Krodel [Philadelphia: Fortress, 1971], 233–34). It should be no surprise that Paul's letters were interpreted in a variety of ways. The "particularity" of his letters means "that reading them is analogous to listening to only one side of a telephone conversation" (Martinus de Boer, "Comment: Which Paul?" in *Paul and the Legacies of Paul*, ed. William S. Babcock [Dallas: Southern Methodist University Press, 1990], 54).

3. Froehlich, "Which Paul?" 290.

4. Maurice Wiles, *The Divine Apostle: The Interpretation of St Paul's Epistles in the Early Church* (Cambridge: Cambridge University Press, 1967), 139; Froehlich, "Which Paul?" 287; Andreas Lindemann, "Paul in the Writings of the Apostolic Fathers," in Babcock, ed., *Paul and the Legacies of Paul*, 44–45; de Boer, "Comment: Which Paul?" 45–47. See also Ernst Dassmann, *Der Stachel im Fleisch: Paulus in der frühchristlichen Literatur bis Irenaeus* (Münster: Aschendorff, 1979); Karl Hermann Schelkle, *Paulus, Lehrer der Väter: Die altkirchliche Auslegung von Römer 1–11*, 2nd ed. (Düsseldorf: Patmos-Verlag, 1958); Andreas Lindemann, *Paulus im ältesten Christentum: Das Bild des Apostels und die Rezeption der paulinischen Theologie in der frühchristlichen Literatur bis Marcion*, Beiträge zur historischen Theologie 58 (Tübingen: Mohr Siebeck, 1979); and David Rensberger, "As the Apostle Teaches: The Development of the Use of Paul's Letters in Second-Century Christianity" (Ph.D. diss., Yale University, 1981).

5. Also, Paul was not the sole authority for Gnostic forms of Christianity: see de Boer, "Comment: Which Paul?" 45–46; and Lindemann, *Paulus im ältesten Christentum*, 1–6. Cf. Martinus de Boer, "Images of Paul in the Post-Apostolic Period," *CBQ* 42 (1980): 359–80; and Hans von Campenhausen, *The Formation of the Christian Bible*, trans. J. A. Baker (Philadelphia: Fortress, 1972), who claims that Paul was known simply and approvingly as "the apostle" and that his letters played a unique and positive role in the development of ecclesiastical tradition. For recent theories on the origin and transmission of the Pauline corpus, see David Trobisch, *Die Entstehung der Paulusbriefsammlung: Studien zu den Anfängen*

not make extended use of Paul or write commentaries or draw systematic conclusions from his thought, they do tend to name Paul more often than any other person and use his letters more often than any other texts or traditions from the beginnings of Christianity.[6]

A third theory, often held in conjunction with the second, is that the Greek Christian tradition's understanding of Pauline soteriology was fundamentally deficient, that the true thought of Paul was eclipsed until Augustine began to expel the darkness of the Greek East's Pelagian world. Whether Paul was rightly construed by his diverse interpreters within the church prior to Augustine depends, of course, both on one's judgment of the central theme(s) of Paul's theology and on one's judgment of the patristic interpreters' understanding and application of Paul's thought within their particular historical contexts. The former debated issue, regarding the right understanding of Paul's central theme(s), can be left to the judgment of biblical scholars. Some light can be shed on the latter issue—the patristic interpretation of Paul—by summarizing the ways in which he is represented by Origen, Chrysostom, and Augustine. These three influential interpreters have left substantial commentary on Paul, making conclusions about their understanding of the Apostle's versatile theology more reliable than is possible with interpreters before the third century. Moreover, these particular interpreters offer very distinct colors on the patristic palette of images of Paul, colors created by a variety of factors, including each interpreter's personal experience, historical context, and selection of key Pauline texts in shaping a broad theological vision. In order to limit the scope of this study, only some of the Pauline soteriological themes pertinent to the Joint Declaration on the Doctrine of Justification[7] will be highlighted in the context of each interpreter's broader thought.

Origen

Origen constructed his understanding of Paul in response to philosophical determinism, particularly to gnostic appropriation of the Apostle that emphasized that human beings are, by election, classed into three groups

---

christlicher Publizistik (Freiburg/Schweiz: Universitätsverlag; Göttingen: Vandenhoeck & Ruprecht, 1989); and E. H. Lovering, "The Collection, Redaction, and Early Circulation of the Corpus Paulinum" (Ph.D. diss., Southern Methodist University, 1988).

6. Lindemann, "Paul in the Writings of the Apostolic Fathers," 27–28, 44–45.

7. Joint Declaration on the Doctrine of Justification: The Lutheran World Federation and the Roman Catholic Church (Grand Rapids: Eerdmans, 2000).

and those who will be saved are saved by grace alone.[8] Origen was convinced that the gnostic idea of fixed natures not only posed a moral problem by contradicting the biblical teaching of human responsibility and free will but also, and more important, determinism threatened the justice and goodness of God.[9] Rejection of free choice raised a host of pressing questions about an electing God. Is an electing God good and just? What is his relation to evil? Does God govern the universe purposefully and for beneficent ends? What is the manner and meaning of salvation? Such questions, Origen believed, were also central concerns of Paul in the Epistle to the Romans. As Peter Gorday convincingly argues, "Origen saw Paul as a theologian of *election*," as a theologian who sought, in terms of the salvation-history of Judaism and Gentile Christianity, to understand and defend a God who elects his people to salvation.[10] Origen repeatedly wrestles with Romans 9–11, because these chapters seemed to support deterministic gnostic thinking.[11] He does not avoid the electing God presented by Paul, but he does not interpret election, as Augustine will later, in terms of God's inscrutable choice of some people to salvation without providing equal opportunity to all. Instead, Origen spreads election out within the entire divine *oikonomia*, that is, the entire

8. Elaine Pagels, "The Valentinian Claim to Esoteric Exegesis of Romans as a Basis for Anthropological Theory," *Vigiliae Christianae* 26 (1972): 242–43.; H. Jonas, *The Gnostic Religion* (Boston: Beacon Press, 1963), 46–47, 270–77; von Campenhausen, *The Formation of the Christian Bible*, 144–46; Marguerite Harl, "Les 'mythes' Valentiniens de la création et de l'eschatologie dans le langage d'Origène: Le mot *hypothesis*," in *The Rediscovery of Gnosticism*, ed. Bentley Layton, Studies in the History of Religions 41 (Leiden: E. J. Brill, 1980), 1:417–25; Kurt Rudolph, *Gnosis: The Nature and History of Gnosticism*, trans. Robert M. Wilson (San Francisco: Harper & Row, 1983), 194–95. By the time of Origen, philosophical determinism had a long tradition; see Martha Nussbaum, *The Fragility of Goodness: Luck and Ethics in Greek Tragedy and Philosophy* (Cambridge: Cambridge University Press, 1986); David Amand, *Fatalisme et liberté dans l'antiquité grecque* (Louvain: Bibliothèque de l'Université, 1945); Max Pohlenz, *Die Stoa: Geschichte einer geistigen Bewegung*, 2 vols. (Göttingen: Vandenhoeck & Ruprecht, 1948–1949), 1:111–57; Franz Cumont, *Astrology and Religion among the Greeks and Romans*, trans. J. B. Baker (New York: Dover, 1960).

9. Origen makes this connection at the beginning of his discussion of free choice in *De Principiis*. It is urgent to discuss free choice, he says, because it is tied with the church's teaching of God's righteous judgment (3.1.1; see also 1.pref.5 and 3.1.2). See Robert L. Wilken, "Justification by Works: Fate and the Gospel in the Roman Empire," *Concordia Theological Monthly* 40 (1969): 385.

10. Peter Gorday, *"Paulus Origenianus:* The Economic Interpretation of Paul in Origen and Gregory of Nyssa," in Babcock, ed., *Paul and the Legacies of Paul*, 161–62; also, Gorday, *Principles of Patristic Exegesis: Romans 9–11 in Origen, John Chrysostom, and Augustine*, Studies in the Bible and Early Christianity 4 (New York: Edwin Mellen, 1983), 51–52.

11. The importance of the issues raised in these chapters is stated up front in Origen's commentary; see *Comm. Rom.* praef. (unless otherwise noted, all references to Origen's *Comm. Rom.* are from the translation of Rufinus found in PG 14). Texts such as Rom. 9 "disturb ordinary people with the thought that a human person is not a free agent (*autexousion*), but that it is God who saves and destroys whom he will" (*Princ.* 3.1.7 [SC 268.42]; G. W. Butterworth, trans., *Origen: On First Principles* [New York: Harper & Row, 1966], 168).

drama of a good and purposeful God's activity in relation to the cosmos. In contrast to the gnostic hypothesis of a foolish and immoral God and of a deterministic redemption, Origen strives to develop a coherent scenario of the divine *oikonomia* in which the one, loving God deliberately plans to use the corporeal order as the arena in which the process of the restoration of the cosmos is graciously worked out.[12]

Since Origen's thought is more foreign to us than that of Chrysostom or Augustine, we will review it in three stages, working our way from his broadest theological framework, the divine economy, to his primary soteriological metaphor, divinization, and finally to the specific soteriological themes of grace, faith, and works. According to Origen's scenario of the divine economy, God creates all souls from the same lump and with the possibility that free will may lead them astray. When a premundane fall occurs, each soul is enfleshed according to the degree of its sin. In the penal and therapeutic state of corporeality, enfleshed souls freely struggle with good and evil in order to be morally purified for a return to the spiritual world. In his providential care for the spiritual progress of his creatures, God is like a doctor who administers the process of healing or like a pedagogue who administers instruction and discipline. For Origen, Romans 9–11 illustrates this benign providence in the process of redemption both on a cosmic and on an individual level. According to the salvation history presented in Romans 9–11, God, by his gracious governance, includes the Gentiles within his people because of Jewish hardness. Despite the Jews' rejection of the gospel, God continues to work on their behalf and will ultimately include unbelieving Israel within his providential mercy as he did the Gentiles. According to Origen, God's providential goodness uses human freedom, including the misuse of that freedom, to move the cosmos forward to the restoration of all things, when "God will be all in all" (1 Cor. 15:28). As Romans 11:32 sums up salvation history, God has included all within sin in order that all may be subject to redemption. For Origen, chapters 9–11 are the climax of Paul's argument in Romans, a logical and necessary conclusion to his description of salvation history.[13]

12. Gorday, "*Paulus Origenianus*," 162–63; William S. Babcock, "Introduction," in idem, ed., *Paul and the Legacies of Paul*, xxi. On *oikonomia*, see George L. Prestige, *God in Patristic Thought*, 2nd ed. (London: SPCK, 1964), 57–67; Gorday, *Principles of Patristic Exegesis*, 34–39; John Reumann, "*Oikonomia* as 'Ethical Accommodation' in the Fathers, and Its Pagan Backgrounds," in *Texte und Untersuchungen* 78 (*Studia Patristica* 3), ed. F. L. Cross (Berlin: Akademie-Verlag, 1961), 370–79; and John Reumann, "The Use of *oikonomia* and Related Terms in Greek Sources to about A.D. 100, as a Background for Patristic Applications" (Ph.D. diss., University of Pennsylvania, 1957).

13. Gorday, *Principles of Patristic Exegesis*, 87–94.

These chapters are crucial for Origen's understanding not only of salvation history but also of the spiritual progress of individual human beings. The dying and rising of Israel in Romans 9–11 is analogous to the redemptive process experienced by individuals. Take Pharaoh, for example. Concerning the hardening of hearts referred to in Romans 9:14 and following,[14] Origen maintains human freedom by claiming that God's selection of who will be hardened is based on and justified by his foreknowledge of how he will be received by different souls. Origen also emphasizes the goodness of the sovereign God, for he contends that the divine hardening of Pharaoh was for Pharaoh's ultimate benefit. Such hardening is the providential, pedagogical process by which hearts are purified through punishment and suffering. Hardening, not a rapid and superficial relief, enables people to know their own sin and God's righteousness. It is both penal and medicinal. Although God is not the author of Pharaoh's specific evil acts, he is an accomplice in evil, the hardener of Pharaoh's heart. According to God's purposeful design of creation, human beings will spiritually progress through various instruments, including evil.[15]

Within Origen's vision of the divine economy, the primary image of salvation is divinization or deification (*theopoiēsis/theopoieō*), not justification (*dikaiosynē/dikaioō*).[16] Although the notion has Platonic roots, divinization in Origen and in other patristic authors is not the accomplishment of the philosophical soul but the work of God's grace. Moreover, the idea is tied up with biblical texts such as John 10:34 and 2 Peter 1:4, as well as several biblical themes, including persons being created in God's image, believers being adopted children of God, exhortations to imitate God, and the

14. Origen interprets this passage as the words of a person debating Paul, thereby relieving Paul of the more extreme statements (*Comm. Rom.* 7.16). In his commentary on Romans, Origen was the first to suggest this interpretation. For Origen's interpretation of Pharaoh's hardening, see W. J. P. Boyd, "Origen on Pharaoh's Hardened Heart: A Study of Justification and Election in St. Paul and Origen," *Studia Patristica* 7 (*Texte und Untersuchungen* 92) (1966): 434–42; and Marguerite Harl, "La mort salutaire du Pharaon selon Origène," in *Studi in onore di Alberto Pincherle*, 2 vols. (Rome: Ateneo, 1967), 1:260–68.

15. *Princ.* 3.1.7–22 and *Comm. Rom.* 7.16. Gorday, "*Paulus Origenianus*," 146–47. Similarly, when he comments on Rom. 9:9–13, Origen argues that God's choice of Isaac and of Jacob instead of their brothers was based on his foreknowledge of their merit. Moreover, Ishmael and Esau were not selected because they needed to be purged of sins from a prior state of existence (*Comm. Rom.* 7.15).

16. Although Origen does speak of justification as well as a variety of other soteriological images (such as healing, forgiveness, and purification), divinization receives the primary emphasis. Cf. Einar Molland, *The Conception of the Gospel in Alexandrian Theology* (Oslo: Jacob Dybward, 1938), 170–72. Panagiotis N. Trembelas's material on justification as a concept in the Greek Fathers is misleading because it implies a systematic presentation of the idea by patristic authors (*Dogmatique de l'Église Orthodoxe Catholique*, trans. P. Dumont [Chevetogne: Desclée de Brouwer, 1967], 2:288–377).

glorification of human nature.[17] According to Origen's understanding of divinization within the divine *oikonomia*, humans are created after the Image of God, the Logos. The Logos is the only perfect Image (Col. 1); human beings are "after the Image." Being "after the Image" is a gift of God and is participation in God. Because of the fall, the Logos, in the *kenōsis* of the incarnation (Phil. 2), descends through the ontological distance between God and human beings.[18] As part of its redemptive work, the Word forms itself in the believer, first purifying the soul by restoring the image of God in it (Rom. 8:29) and then, with the believer, cultivating a life of virtue. Divinization, it seems, is both a gift and a process. The purified soul, using its free will, struggles to live the Christian life, to choose the way of the spirit and not the flesh. As progress is made in virtue, the soul increasingly resembles the divine, and faith becomes knowledge. The Word, through its self-disclosures in Scripture and in the cosmos, progressively guides the soul through the stages of knowledge, moving from knowledge of earthly to heavenly things, and from knowledge of the humanity of Christ to knowledge of the divinity. The Logos is the perfect image through which the soul contemplates God and ultimately progresses to face-to-face knowledge of God. In this final beatitude of knowledge or union or love, a person made "after the image" of God attains the likeness of God, the gift of divinity.[19]

Origen's concern, in his antignostic polemic, to understand God's cosmic, providential activity, including the divinization of human beings, should be seen as the context within which Origen interprets the Pauline themes of grace, faith, and works.[20] Grace, for Origen, is the pedal point of the entire divine *oikonomia*, from our creation as rational creatures to the final restoration.[21] As for the relationship between grace and human faith,

17. William G. Rusch, "How the Eastern Fathers Understood What the Western Church Meant by Justification," in *Justification by Faith*, Lutherans and Catholics in Dialogue 7 (Minneapolis: Augsburg, 1985), 133–35. Cf. G. Bardy, "Divinisation, II and III," *Dictionnaire de spiritualité, ascétique et mystique* 3 (1957), 1375–98; P. B. T. Bilaniuk, "The Mystery of *Theosis* or Divinization," *Orientalia Christiana Analecta* 195 (1973): 337–59.

18. Karen Jo Torjesen, *Hermeneutical Procedure and Theological Method in Origen's Exegesis* (New York: Walter de Gruyter, 1986), 115–16 on *Hom. Num.* 27.3.

19. Henri Crouzel, *Origen*, trans. A. S. Worrall (San Francisco: Harper & Row, 1989), 88–99, 113–17; Karen Jo Torjesen, "Pedagogical Soteriology from Clement to Origen," *Origeniana Quarta* 4 (1987): 370–78, esp. 375–77.

20. For Origen's interpretation of these concepts in his Romans commentary, I am largely indebted to Wiles's reliable analysis (*Divine Apostle*, esp. 103–6, 114–17).

21. *Comm. Rom.* on Rom. 4:1–8 (*Le Commentaire d'Origène sur Rom. III.5-V.7 d' après les extraits du papyrus No 88748 du Musée du Caire et les fragments de la Philocalie et du Vaticanus Gr. 762* [Greek text], ed. Jean Schérer [Cairo: Institut Français d'Archéologie Orientale, 1957], 184; see also the Greek fragments on Rom. 4:1–8 in "The Commentary of Origen on the Epistle to the Romans," ed. A. Ramsbotham, *Journal of Theological Studies* 13 [1912]: 357; also *Comm. Rom.* 4.1 [PG 14.963–64]);

both are necessary for salvation, but grace is more essential. Comparing the phrase "justified by his blood" in Romans 5:9 with "justified by faith" in 5:1, Origen writes: "Neither our faith without the blood of Christ, nor the blood of Christ without our faith justifies us; we are justified by both but much more by the blood of Christ than by our faith."[22] Moreover, Origen asserts that divine grace as manifested in Christ's incarnation and death is logically prior to faith even though human faith is logically prior to God's foreknowledge.[23]

Faith itself is both a gift of God and a work of human beings, although Origen is not consistent or at least is imprecise about the way in which both parties are involved. Sometimes he sees faith as first and foremost the gift of God.[24] At other times, Origen seems to distinguish between two types of faith, an initial germ of faith, which lies within a person's own power, and a complete faith, which is necessary for justification and is possible only through God's grace. Complete faith is a gift of God, given according to the proportion of a person's faith. It seems that a person's initial element of faith is rewarded and reinforced by God's grace. Being graciously reinforced, the beginnings of faith lead through hope to love, thereby culminating in a completion of faith.[25]

Works, for Origen, play a significant role in salvation. In fact, true faith can never be without works. That the two are inseparable is evident from Origen's understanding of the believer's union with Christ. Since Christ does not merely possess but *is* his attributes, according to Origen, a person united to Christ in faith does not need to supplement his faith with works. Faith automatically includes the adoption of Christ's virtues.[26] Perfection is not immediate, however. Being "in Christ" in his death and resurrection is both a once-for-all past event and a continual process of daily renewal and growth in virtue. Union with Christ must be progressively realized. Although the conversion of a person's will may be immediate, consistently good actions are developed only gradually.[27] In this pilgrimage of growth,

---

on Rom. 4:16–17 (Schérer, *Commentaire*, 204; *Comm. Rom.* 4.5 [PG 14.974]). Cf. Gorday, "*Paulus Origenianus*," 354 n. 21.

22. *Comm. Rom.* 4.11 (PG 14.1001).

23. Ibid.

24. *Comm. Rom.* on Rom. 4:16 (Schérer, *Commentaire*, 204–6; Ramsbotham, "Romans," 359–60; *Comm. Rom.* 4.5 [PG 14.974–75]); *Jo.* 20.32.

25. *Comm. Rom.* on Rom. 4:1–9 (Schérer, *Commentaire*, 182–88; Ramsbotham, "Romans," 357; *Comm. Rom.* 4.1 [PG 14.963]); on Rom. 4:18–22 (Schérer, *Commentaire*, 212–14); *Comm. Rom.* 9.3 (PG 14.1212–13).

26. *Jo.* 1.22; 1.34; 6.6; 32.127; *Comm. Rom.* 3.7; 8.2; *Cels.* 5.39.

27. *Comm. Rom.* 6.9; 6.11; *Princ.* 3.1.17; 4.4.2.

believers are guided by moral precepts such as those given by Paul. These moral rules are God's gift and are adapted to people at the different stages of their advancement along the road to perfection.[28] As people make progress in virtue they merit or deserve further grace from God or, as Origen sometimes puts it, people receive greater gifts because they are more fit for them, they have reached a capacity sufficient to receive them.[29]

Origen's understanding of merit is not clear. Although Origen occasionally speaks of merit as human achievement that is apparently distinct from the grace of the Holy Spirit, at least three factors contradict or undermine the potential force of such statements. First, his most striking examples of merit language exist only in Latin translation; it has been argued that the Latin terms used (from *mereo*) may carry a stronger implication of "merit" than the original Greek words did.[30] Second, Origen clearly speaks of good works that people do as the fruits of the justification that God gives:

> This faith when justified, like a root taking in the rain, goes down into the soil of the soul, so that when cultivated by the law of God, there will rise up out of it shoots which will bear the fruits of works. Therefore, the root of justice is not from the works but the fruit of the works grows from the root of justice, that root of justice, indeed, by which God brings justice without works.[31]

Third, when Origen comments on Paul's distinction in Romans 4:4 between that which is received by gift and that which God renders as due, Origen states:

> No one . . . is so capable of doing what is right that the reward given by God to those who do rightly is not by grace but by due [*opheilēma*]. For I would even say that nothing of what God gives to the created nature does he give as being due; rather, he bestows all things as grace; and all who are shown

28. *Fr. 1 Cor.* on 1 Cor. 6:12 and 7:25.
29. *Fr. Eph.* on Eph. 4:7.
30. E.g., *Comm. Rom.* 6.12 (PG 14.1096). As Wiles points out, Greek terms that Origen uses (*axios* and *kataxiōmai*) are also found in the New Testament (Rev. 3:4; Luke 20:35; 2 Thess. 1:5) in relation to one's worthiness for heaven (*Divine Apostle*, 118–19). Cf. Benjamin Drewery, *Origen and the Doctrine of Grace* (London: Epworth Press, 1960), 193–206; and Alister McGrath, *Iustitia Dei: A History of the Christian Doctrine of Justification*, 2nd ed. (Cambridge: Cambridge University Press, 1998), 14–15.
31. *Non ergo ex operibus radix iustitiae, sed ex radice iustitiae fructus operum crescit, illa scilicet radice iustitiae, qua Deus accepto fert iustitiam sine operibus* (*Comm. Rom.* 4.1 [PG 14.965]), trans. Robert B. Eno, "Some Patristic Views on the Relationship of Faith and Works in Justification," *Recherches augustiniennes* 19 (1984): 6.

kindness receive kindness not from a kindness owed them, but rather God wills by his own grace to show kindness on whomever he shows kindness.[32]

Note that Origen's language here echoes the words of Romans 9. He seems to be reading Romans 4, in part, through the lens of Romans 9, a text that reminds us of Origen's fundamental concern to understand the electing God.

In sum, gnostic interpretation of Paul likely pushed Origen to realize that it was not simply the current of philosophical determinism in third-century culture that posed a threat to human freedom and therefore God's goodness, but also the freely willing God described by Paul in Romans 9. Given Origen's gnostic context, it should perhaps not be surprising that his articulation of the divine and human roles in faith and works is no more precise than the Apostle's. For Origen, the problem posed by Paul's letters was not justification by grace through faith, but the goodness of a God who could freely select Jacob and Esau before either had been born.[33] Using Paul, especially Romans 9–11 but also 1 Corinthians 15, Colossians 1, and Philippians 2,[34] Origen sought to offer a coherent scenario of the electing God's providential goodness in the cosmic drama of redemption.

Chrysostom

During the century and a half that separates Origen and Chrysostom, a number of writers were influenced by Origen's interpretation of Paul, but since only fragments of commentaries on Paul's epistles survive from this period, the degree of direct influence is unknown. Continuities between Origen and Chrysostom are evident, including an emphasis on the soteriological significance of the incarnation, the freedom of human beings, and the importance of moral development.

The most distinctive characteristic of Chrysostom's Pauline exegesis is his concern for the person of Paul. In her superb work on Chrysostom, Margaret Mitchell analyzes how Chrysostom's exegesis of Paul is exegesis of both the person and thought of the author. His interpretation of the

32. *Comm. Rom.* 6.1 (Schérer, *Commentaire*, 184), trans. Robert L. Wilken, "Free Choice and the Divine Will in Greek Christian Commentaries on Paul," in Babcock, ed., *Paul and the Legacies of Paul*, 132. Cf. Gorday, "*Paulus Origenianus*," 354 n. 21.

33. See Wilken, "Free Choice and the Divine Will," 127–29, 132–33, 139, who demonstrates that Greek commentators on Paul freely adopted Paul's description of a freely willing God even though it weakened their defense of human freedom.

34. Gorday, "*Paulus Origenianus*," 145–52.

Apostle's words is inherently interwoven with his perception of Paul's character and biography.[35] Chrysostom has a strong claim to being Paul's most ardent admirer in the patristic era.[36] His obsession with the person of the Apostle[37] is due in part to his understanding of Paul as a premier model for imitation.[38] Paul, in Chrysostom's estimation, is more virtuous and has reached a higher degree of sanctity than any other human.[39] In fact, Paul is more imitable than Christ; whereas Christ's humanity is predominated by his divinity, Paul is human exactly as we are.[40] As Mitchell demonstrates, Chrysostom believes that all people can imitate or portray (*mimeomai*) Paul by contemplating his epistles, for the Apostle paints self-portraits in his letters. Referring to 2 Corinthians, Chrysostom comments, "Writing in the form of a letter, Paul was compelled there to compose for us a portrait of his good deeds, one by one."[41] The epistles, Chrysostom declares confidently, provide the reader with an opportunity to "gaze into Paul's soul, just as into

35. Margaret M. Mitchell *The Heavenly Trumpet: John Chrysostom and the Art of Pauline Interpretation* (Tübingen: Mohr Siebeck, 2000).

36. Margaret M. Mitchell, "The Archetypal Image: John Chrysostom's Portraits of Paul," *Journal of Religion* 75 (1995): 15; Wiles, *Divine Apostle*, 21–22.

37. See, e.g., *Hom. Isa.* 45:7; *Hom. Gen.* 11.17; Chrysostomus Baur, *John Chrysostom and His Time*, trans. M. Gonzaga, 2 vols. (Westminster, MD: Newman Press, 1959), 1:291–93.

38. "I have an intense regard for this man," Chrysostom blurts out in his homilies on Genesis. "I do not cease bringing him constantly to mind, fixing my eyes on his soul as though on some exemplary model" (*Hom. Gen.* 11.13 [PG 53.95]).

39. In the early church, unqualified claims regarding Paul's moral perfection reach their greatest frequency and intensity in Chrysostom's homilies. Paul possessed all angelic virtues (*Laud. Paul.* 1.1; 1.13–14), he lived on earth as though he were in heaven (*Hom. Gen.* 34; *Laud. Paul.* 2.8; *Hom. Gen.* 4.5), "Paul was a heaven" (*Hom. Act.* 55 [PG 60.383]), he was higher than any heavens above the heavens and went up to God himself (*Hom. Heb.* 16.8), and "Paul's heart was Christ's heart, and a tablet of the Holy Spirit, and a book of grace" (*Hom. Rom.* 32 [PG 60.679–80]). Such assertions are found throughout Chrysostom's homilies, but especially in *De laudibus sancti Pauli apostoli*. For further references, see Mitchell, *The Heavenly Trumpet*; David M. Rylaarsdam, "The Adaptability of Divine Pedagogy: *Sunkatabasis* in the Theology and Rhetoric of John Chrysostom" (Ph.D. diss., University of Notre Dame, 1999), 239–53, 266–78. On Chrysostom's many different strategies for preserving Paul's virtuous character against charges of inconsistency, see Mitchell, "'A Variable and Many-sorted Man': John Chrysostom's Treatment of Pauline Inconsistency," *Journal of Early Christian Studies* 6.1 (1998): 93–111.

40. Rylaarsdam, "Adaptability of Divine Pedagogy," 260–61. On the "unequal union of [Christ's divine and human] natures" (*Quatr. Laz.* [PG 50.642–43]), see Melvin Lawrenz, "The Christology of John Chrysostom" (Ph.D. diss., Marquette University, 1987), 92–108; and C. Hay, "St. John Chrysostom and the Integrity of the Human Nature of Christ," *Franciscan Studies* 19 (1959): 298–317.

41. *Hom. Rom.* 4 (PG 60.163), trans. Mitchell, "Archetypal Image," 27 n. 54. Actually, Paul's self-portrait was made possible by Christ's grace: "This tablet [of Paul's soul] was not long ago lying covered with soot, full of cobwebs. (For nothing is worse than blasphemy.) But when the one who refashions everything came, and saw that it was not through carelessness and laziness that Paul was drawn this way, but through inexperience, and his not having the bright colors of piety (for he had zeal, but the colors were not there, because he did not have 'the zeal according to knowledge'), he gives him the

a certain archetypal image."[42] When a person imitates Paul, one is imitating Christ, as Paul exhorts in 1 Corinthians 4:16 and 11:1: "Be imitators of me as I am of Christ." Through Paul a person is able to imitate Christ indirectly but exactly, for Paul is the perfect copy of Christ.[43] Chrysostom assumes that one of his tasks as a preacher is to hold up this model of virtue before the eyes of his listeners. Employing his considerable rhetorical skills, Chrysostom sketches a gallery of portraits of Paul[44] in order to make the dead saint a virtually living, moving presence, a vivid image that people can see and imitate.[45]

Another reason for Chrysostom's preoccupation with the person of Paul is his sense of the pastoral and theological challenges that he shares with the Apostle:[46] he reads his own experiences into and from Paul's epistles. He sees Paul as a zealous teacher who, amid the many difficulties of public ministry, pursues and advocates the monastic ideal, relentlessly seeking to bring his charges to greater faith and virtue. More precisely, Paul as a teacher is the consummate guide of souls. Chrysostom incessantly traces Paul's psychagogy, his leading of souls to salvation, particularly his weaving of harsh and gentle rhetoric as he coaxes his listeners forward down the path of ever greater maturity: "Paul varied his discourse according to the need of his learners, at one time cutting and cauterizing, at another applying a gentle medicine."[47] Chrysostom sees this mixed method of exhortation everywhere; his common refrain is: "because Paul had attacked them sharply, he refreshes them again."[48] The Apostle is pictured as virtually omniscient.[49] Perfectly anticipating with each word or turn of phrase the overstrained or

---

bright color of the truth, that is, grace. And all at once he exhibited the imperial portrait" (*Hom. 1 Cor.* 13.3 [PG 61.110], trans. Mitchell, "Archetypal Image," 27).

42. *Hom. Gen.* 11.4 (PG 53.95), trans. Mitchell, "Archetypal Image," 22.

43. *Hom. 1 Cor.* 13.5; cf. *Laud. Paul.* 2.10 (SC 300.158) regarding Paul as an "archetype of virtue."

44. "Here we are painting royal portraits . . . by means of the colors of virtue. . . . The pencil moreover is the tongue, and the Artist the Holy Spirit" (*Hom. Act.* 30 [PG 60.227–28]). Cf. *Hom. 1 Cor.* 13.3.

45. For a catalog of Chrysostom's Pauline portraits—miniatures, somatic, psychic, and biographical—see chapters 3–6 of Mitchell, *The Heavenly Trumpet.*

46. Their lives share challenges such as conflict within the church, Judaizing Christians, the relationship between Christians and culture, and physical and emotional sufferings, especially during Chrysostom's exile (Mitchell, "Archetypal Image," 42 n. 159).

47. *Comm. Gal.* 1.1 (PG 61.612).

48. For references, see Rylaarsdam, "Adaptability of Divine Pedagogy," 277–85. On the Greco-Roman practice of psychagogy, see Clarence Glad, *Paul and Philodemus: Adaptability in Epicurean and Early Christian Psychagogy* (New York: E. J. Brill, 1995); and Pierre Hadot, *Philosophy as a Way of Life: Spiritual Exercises from Socrates to Foucault* (New York: Blackwell, 1995).

49. For examples of this apparent omniscience, see Rylaarsdam, "Adaptability of Divine Pedagogy," 246–48.

sluggish spiritual state of his listeners, Paul oscillates between severity and tenderness.[50] Such rhetorical variation is one way in which he becomes all things to all people. A key text in Chrysostom's interpretation of Paul is 1 Corinthians 9:19–23.[51]

As Chrysostom traces the ebb and flow of Paul's benevolent harshness, he provides the Apostle's soteriological reasons for this method, interpreting Paul's understanding of repentance, grace, the process of becoming holy, the work of the Holy Spirit, and so on. The most prominent image of Chrysostom's soteriology is union with God, a union made possible in the incarnation. The soteriological efficacy of the incarnation, for Chrysostom, is centered less in Christ's obedience or our imitation of Christ than in the union of divinity and flesh in Christ that makes our renewed association with God possible. The birth of Christ contains "the sum of the whole *oiko-nomia*"; it is the foundation of salvation because it joins "God's nature with humanity's, the things that are his with ours."[52] The Word "became the Son of Man, though he was the true Son of God, in order that he might make children of men children of God."[53] Although such language sounds similar to Origen's notion of salvation as divinization, Chrysostom understands human union with God in moral terms rather than metaphysical:[54] virtue

50. The following excerpts from a few Migne columns of Chrysostom's second homily on the exordium of the Corinthian correspondence are typical: "[1:6] . . . Through praises and thanksgiving, he attacks them sharply. . . . These are the words of one both reproving and simultaneously winning them over. . . . Although the praises are not very close to the truth, they are inserted as a precaution, preparing the way for his discourse. For whoever says unpleasant things at the outset ruins his chances of being heard by the weaker: those hearers who are equal to him in status will be angry and those who are inferior will be annoyed. To avoid this, he begins with what seem to be praises. . . . He dwells on the lovingkindness of God so that he may more fully purge them of their malady. . . . [1:7] . . . Consider Paul's wisdom, how withdrawing them from consideration of human things, he terrifies them by mentioning the fearful judgment seat. . . . [1:8] . . . Here he seems to court them, but the saying is free from all flattery, for he knows also how to attack them. Moreover, he is covertly accusing them. . . . [1:9] . . . Paul, by a kind of divine art, inserts these things early, so that after the fury of the rebukes they will not fall into despair" (*Hom. 1 Cor.* 2.3–8 [PG 61.17–19]).

51. See Rylaarsdam, "Adaptability of Divine Pedagogy," 254–60, 266–78.

52. *Hom. Matt.* 2.3 (PG 57.27). The core truth of the gospel, says Chrysostom in the preceding homily, is "God on earth, man in heaven, and all become mingled together . . . and reconciliation is made between God and our nature" (*Hom. Matt.* 1.2 [PG 57.15]). The union of human and divine is assured when the flesh is glorified in Christ's ascension: see *Hom. Jo.* 11.2 and *Hom. Heb.* 5.1. In the Eucharist, as in the incarnation, our human nature is mingled with Christ; see *Hom. Jo.* 46.1–2 and *Hom. Matt.* 82.5.

53. *Hom. Jo.* 11.1 (PG 59.79).

54. Rowan Greer, *The Captain of Our Salvation: A Study in the Patristic Exegesis of Hebrews* (Tübingen: Mohr Siebeck, 1973), 274–76.

makes human beings like God so that they begin to dwell as if in heaven even while on earth.[55]

God's grace has made union with him possible: "what the Only-begotten was by nature, this too human beings became by grace."[56] For Chrysostom, as for Origen, grace plays a larger role than human effort in the process of salvation. "The gifts of God's grace," says Chrysostom on Romans 5, "are many and various; our part—also essential but much smaller—is faith alone."[57] The unequal contribution of the divine and human in Chrysostom's soteriology coincides both with the "unequal union of the natures" in his Christology[58] and with the divine predominance in the authorship of Scripture.[59] Although Chrysostom admits that even human free choice is assisted by God's grace, he is concerned to demonstrate that Paul's conception of grace does not eliminate the individual's responsibility to respond to God's call. Paul is not a precise theologian, Chrysostom reminds his listeners, but a pastor whose occasional, apparent overemphasis on God's grace is intended to teach proper humility before God. Paul's goal when he speaks about election is that his readers will think more of their dependence on God's grace than their own achievements.[60] Election is based on God's foreknowledge, argues Chrysostom; it cannot be arbitrary and irrational or determined by a person's created nature.[61]

55. Unlike Origen, Chrysostom does not envision a long process of moral purification "as the endless and enormous ages slip by" (*Princ.* 3.6.6), but instead emphasizes an imminent final judgment and retribution; see Brian E. Daley, *The Hope of the Early Church: A Handbook of Patristic Eschatology* (Cambridge: Cambridge University Press, 1991), 47–64 and 105–9. For a much more complete discussion of Chrysostom's soteriology and its relationship to his Christology, see Rylaarsdam, "Adaptability of Divine Pedagogy," 177–90 and 223–36.

56. *Hom. Rom.* 15 (PG 60.541), trans. adapted from Panayiotis E. Papageorgiou, "A Theological Analysis of Selected Themes in the Homilies of St. John Chrysostom on the Epistle of St. Paul to the Romans" (Ph.D. diss., Catholic University of America, 1995), 77.

57. *Hom. Rom.* 9.2 (PG 60.468). Similarly, on Rom. 1:17, "it is not your own righteousness, but that of God. . . . For you do not achieve it by toilings and labor, but you can receive it as a gift from above, contributing one thing only, namely 'believing'" (*Hom. Rom.* 2 [PG 60.409], trans. Frances M. Young, *From Nicaea to Chalcedon: A Guide to the Literature and Its Background* [Philadelphia: Fortress, 1983], 150). Based on his study of Chrysostom's homilies on Hebrews, Greer concludes that Chrysostom's homiletical emphasis seems to be on free will, but "there is no doubt that grace is the prior concept for Chrysostom and that his theological emphasis is upon this aspect of the matter" (*Captain of Our Salvation*, 272). Papageorgiou's detailed study of Chrysostom's homilies on Romans also draws the conclusion that the divine and human contribution toward redemption are not of equal measure ("Theological Analysis," 87–91).

58. *Quatr. Laz.* (PG 50.642–43).

59. See Rylaarsdam, "Adaptability of Divine Pedagogy," 126–39, 170.

60. Preaching on Eph. 1:4–5, Chrysostom argues that if God's love were the only cause of salvation, then everyone would automatically be saved (*Hom. Eph.* 1.2).

61. Wiles, *Divine Apostle*, 94–96. See *Hom. Rom.* 15.1 and 16.5–6.

Although grace, for Chrysostom, is the dominant theme in the process of redemption, he is not precise about the way in which the divine and human contribute to faith. He simply insists that both grace and a free human response are necessary. Whereas it is an act of God alone that liberates us from the devil, Christ's persuasion of captives to take advantage of the freedom that he has made available is not his work alone. Faith is a joint work that is actually the more wonderful part of Christ's work, because it is easier to accomplish an act that lies in one's own power than an act that requires the free cooperation of others.[62]

Good works are the fruit of faith.[63] Paul bases his moral exhortations on what God has done, says Chrysostom, because a person's faith in the fact and extent of salvation is the root of humility, which is a root of virtuous living.[64] Unlike Origen, Chrysostom does not present faith as automatically entailing the adoption of Christ's virtues. Instead, faith brings a change of inclination or ruling purpose (*proairesis*).[65] Christ and his Spirit transform a believer as if from a leper to a handsome youth[66] so that now, Chrysostom exclaims, "it is even possible for one who has a mortal body not to sin. Do you see how abundant is the grace of Christ?"[67] By cooperating with God in cultivating a life of virtue, a believer becomes like God, fulfilling God's creational intent. From the beginning, God created humans for lives of virtue.[68] Created "in God's image," which includes the attributes of reason and freedom,[69] humans are expected to become perfect "according to God's likeness." Virtues, especially love, make believers like God.[70]

To recapitulate: Chrysostom reads Paul as a mirror and model of his own ministry. Paul is relentlessly seeking to persuade his listeners to take advantage of the freedom that Christ has made available by grace. He seeks to inculcate a robust virtue-producing faith in his listeners through two prominent means: by rhetorically becoming all things to the varying

---

62. Putting it anachronistically, cooperative grace, Chrysostom implies, is a greater grace than operative grace.

63. Papageorgiou, "Theological Analysis," 99, 203; Louis Meyer, *Saint Jean Chrysostome: Maitre de perfection chrétienne* (Paris: G. Beauchesne et ses fils, 1933), 44.

64. Wiles, *Divine Apostle*, 131. See *Hom. Eph.* 9.2 and 10.1.

65. Wiles, *Divine Apostle*, 125. See *Hom. Eph.* 13.2; *Hom. Col.* 8.1.

66. *Hom. Eph.* 1.3.

67. *Hom. Rom.* 11 (PG 60.486), trans. Papageorgiou, "Theological Analysis," 75.

68. *Hom. Gen.* 23.5.

69. *Dianoia* and *proairesis/exousia/autexousion*. See Papageorgiou, "Theological Analysis," 80–87, for many references.

70. E.g., *Hom. Rom.* 9 (PG 60.474). Regarding the perfection of the likeness of God in humans according to Chrysostom, see Meyer, *Saint Jean Chrysostome*.

needs of all people (1 Cor. 9:19–23) and by providing himself as a model for imitation (1 Cor. 11:1). Paul seeks to persuade his listeners that, through God's dominant grace and their own grace-assisted zeal, they can become more and more like God.

Augustine

Augustine's interpretation of Paul evolved over the course of his life. Before his conversion, Augustine was a Manichee who saw Paul as an inconsistent thinker. As a newly baptized convert, Augustine read Paul as a Neoplatonist, envisioning the spiritual life as an ascent to perfection.[71] Human beings are free: they sin voluntarily and they can take the initiative in an ascent to God. In the early 390s, Augustine's philosophizing exegesis of Scripture was challenged by the Manichees. Their biblically based arguments rejecting the attribution of moral responsibility to human free will pushed Augustine to nuance his understanding of the will. Adam had completely free will but, Augustine now asserted, ever since the fall the efficacy of the human will was adversely affected. Sin is freely willed, but it is habit-forming.[72] Against the Manichean critique of the Old Testament, Augustine also developed his understanding of salvation history and the four stages of humans: before the law, under the law, under grace, and at peace.[73] Although individuals cannot move from law to grace on their own, their faith does empower them to call on Christ for assistance.[74] Augustine's concern for freedom of the will and God's fairness also shaped his understanding of election. God hated Esau and hardened Pharaoh because he foreknew that they would not have had faith. Election is God's reward for the merit of freely willed faith.[75]

By 397, less than two years after making this interpretation of Romans 9, Augustine had changed his mind. He now argued that election is not based on faith, as if it were a reward for merit. In the words of Romans 9:16, "It does not depend on human desire or effort, but on God's mercy." Based on his judgment made before time, God graciously and mysteriously elects some sinners from humanity, which is a damned mass (*massa peccati*) as a result

71. Peter Brown, *Augustine of Hippo: A Biography* (Berkely: University of California Press, 1967), 151.

72. *Fort.* 22.

73. *Exp. prop. Rom.* 13–18.

74. Ibid., 44.

75. Ibid., 55, 62.

of Adam's sin.[76] God's justice in choosing some and not others is hidden.[77] Augustine's remarkable shift in thought seems to have been brought about, at least in part, by Paul's biography. The ruthless persecutor did not call on Christ; God inscrutably called him.[78]

Not until many years later, when Augustine struggled with the Pelagians, did he fully discern the new view of God's relation to humanity that he had gained through Paul by 397. The difference between his views of 397 and those held against the Pelagians was one of degree and not of kind. What is Augustine's more developed understanding of human freedom, grace, faith, and justification? Fallen humans are responsible agents, Augustine asserts, because they enjoy the power of free choice, *liberum arbitrium*. However, they do not possess authentic freedom (*libertas*), the ability to use the power of choice properly.[79] Since the power of free choice has been captivated (*liberum arbitrium captivatum*), humans are saddled with "a cruel necessity of sinning."[80] Authentic freedom (*libertas* or *vera libertas*) can be restored only by divine grace.[81]

From the fallen mass of humanity God chooses some for salvation.[82] By divine mercy alone God's call evokes and secures a voluntary response of faith. Against the Pelagians, Augustine insists that faith is a divine gift even while defending its voluntary character. He does so by distinguishing between the will and its exercise.[83] The beginning of faith at the point of conversion (*initium fidei*), Augustine insists, is a divine gift alone.[84] Grace is necessary for any good willing. The good will by which a person begins

76. In his interpretation of Paul's clay metaphor in Rom. 9:21, Augustine used *massa* as a synonym for *conspersio* (lump).

77. *Simpl.* 1.2.8–17.

78. Ibid., 1.2.22. For Augustine, Christ's compelling Paul was a model for Catholic use of state force against the Donatists. J. Patout Burns argues that the conflict with the Donatists also provided conditions within which election was quickly accepted in North Africa. Augustine's doctrine was questioned or rejected in Europe, where there was not conflict over the sacraments and therefore not uncertainty about the economy of salvation. See "The Atmosphere of Election: Augustinianism as Common Sense," *Journal of Early Christian Studies* 2.3 (1994): 325–39.

79. *Spir. et litt.* 5.7 (CSEL 60.159) and 33.58 (CSEL 60.216); *Nat. grat.* 64.77 (CSEL 60.291). See J. Ball, "Libre arbitre et liberté dans saint Augustin," *L'année théologique* 6 (1945): 368–82; and E. Gilson, *The Christian Philosophy of Saint Augustine*, trans. L. E. M. Lynch (New York: Random House, 1983), 185–216.

80. *Perf.* 9 (CSEL 42.8). Cf. *Nat. grat.* 55.65 (CSEL 60.282); 66.79 (CSEL 60.293).

81. *Nat. grat.* 3.3 (CSEL 60.235); *Spir. et litt.* 30.52 (CSEL 60.208–9).

82. *Enchir.* 100.

83. For Augustine's understanding of the will, I am largely indebted to Marianne Djuth's excellent entries on "*initium fidei*," "liberty," and "will" in *Augustine through the Ages: An Encyclopedia*, ed. Allan Fitzgerald (Grand Rapids: Eerdmans, 1999), 447–51, 495–98, and 881–85, respectively.

84. *Praed.* 4.8; *Enarrat. Ps.* 35.1; 70.2.

to will to believe comes from outside the will; it is a divine gift that acts on the will, converting the will's unrighteous exercise. The act that results from the reception of this gift is freely chosen, but it is a good act because the divine gift provides the will with the freedom or strength to act well.[85] In other words, 1 Corinthians 4:7 ("what do you have that you have not received?") pertains to faith also, "not because it is not in the choice of the human will to believe or not to believe, but because in the elect the will is prepared by the Lord."[86]

Faith in God, for Augustine, is personal adherence to God or movement toward God through good use of the will.[87] Through faith sins are forgiven.[88] Although Augustine sometimes says that faith itself is a kind of righteousness,[89] he typically emphasizes that the only faith that justifies is the faith that is "active through love" (Gal. 5:6). The faith of demons knows Christ, but lacks *caritas*. Demons do not believe so that they may be united to Christ but in order to avoid him.[90] Only *caritas* can unite us with God, and this love is from God himself, his supreme gift, his Spirit.[91] As Romans 5:5, Augustine's most cited Pauline text, states, "Love for God has been poured into our hearts through the Holy Spirit that has been given to us."[92] By dwelling in us, God moves us to love him; he loves himself through us.[93] As a gift of God, love endows the human will with liberty, with a new desire to do good out of love for God, with a striving for good deeds of love such as righteousness, justice, and peace.[94]

Although the indwelling of the Spirit makes the will capable of loving God and the good for their own sake, liberation from self-love and concupiscence is not complete. The believer is divided in spirit between self-love and the love for God, as described by Paul in Romans 7:14–25. The most remarkable shift in Augustine's reading of Paul after 397 is his reinterpretation of this passage.[95] He decides that Paul is not picturing a

85. *Persev.* 13.33; *Praed.* 2.4; 8.15.

86. *Praed.* 5.10 (PL 44.968).

87. *C. ep. Pel.* 1.3.

88. *C. du. ep. Pelag.* 3.5; *Serm.* 143.2.

89. See A. C. De Veer, "Rom. 14,23b dans l'oeuvre de saint Augustin (*Omne quod non est ex fide, peccatum est*)," *Recherches Augustiniennes* 8 (1972): 145–85; Christine Mohrmann, "Credere in Deum," in *Mélanges Joseph de Ghellinck, S.J.*, 2 vols. (Gembloux: J. Duculot, 1951), 1:277–85.

90. *Ep.* 194.11 (CSEL 57.185).

91. *Spir. et litt.* 17.29 (CSEL 60.183); *Trin.* 15.18 (CCL 50A.507–08).

92. On Rom. 5:5, see A. M. La Bonnardière, "Le Verset paulinien Rom. V, 5 dans l'oeuvre de S. Augustin," in *Augustinus Magister* (Paris: Études augustiniennes, 1954), 2:657–65.

93. *Serm.* 128.2.

94. *Spir. et litt.* 8.13; 30.52; *Enchir.* 31.117; *Praed.* 3.7.

95. *Nat. grat.* 57.67.

person under the law but a believer under grace. The Apostle is not speaking rhetorically, but autobiographically. Paul is the believer who still suffers because of the concupiscence of the flesh. Since the Pelagians misread the person of Paul in Romans 7, they misread Paul's entire text.[96] Augustine related his rereading of Paul to the story of his own experience at the hands of God's grace.[97]

So great is the inner struggle pictured in Romans 7, according to Augustine, that a person will choose and accomplish the good only through great effort. This cooperation of a believer with God's grace acquires merit. But merit is itself a gift. As Augustine's famous dictim puts it, "When God crowns our merits, he crowns nothing but his own gifts."[98] In fact, a person can continue in good willing and working until the end of life only through the gift of perseverance. This operation of the Spirit, according to Augustine, is a gift given only to the elect, not every believer.[99]

Against the Pelagians, Augustine develops a history of redemptive grace, a process of justification, that stretches from the beginning of a faith that is active through love to glorification, the reaching of final perfection in the eschatological city.[100] This history of a person under grace seems equivalent to Augustine's notion of justification, the gracious process by which God restores human beings to justice, that is, to giving to God and neighbor the love that is their due (Matt. 22:40), to loving God and neighbor for the sake of God.[101] Augustine understands *iustificare* to mean "to make just or righteous."[102] A person is made just by the justice given by God in Christ and by faith in Christ, both of which are gifts of God. But through faith, a person also participates in the healing process by which they become just, for faith in Christ's saving work exercises the human soul so that it is drawn toward the proper love of God and neighbor, thereby making gradual progress

96. C. du. ep. Pelag. 1.8; see Paula Fredriksen, "Augustine's Early Interpretation of Paul" (Ph.D. diss., Princeton University, 1979), 278–80.

97. Persev. 20.53.

98. Ep. 194.5 (CSEL 57.190). Cf. J. N. Bakhuizen van den Brink, "Mereo(r) and Meritum in Some Latin Fathers," in Studia Patristica 3 (Berlin: Akademie-Verlag, 1961), 333–40; and John Burnaby, Amor Dei: A Study of the Religion of St. Augustine (London: Hodder & Stoughton, 1938), 219–52.

99. Corrept. 8.18.

100. Ibid., 7.13.

101. For this idea of justice, see, for example, Trin. 8.9; 9.9; Civ.11.17.

102. McGrath points out that this interpretation is quite distinct from the Hebrew concept underlying dikaioun, namely, "to consider as righteous, to acquit" (Iustitia Dei, 4–16, 29–31). Similarly, the iustitia Dei, the justice of God, is understood by Augustine to be that justice of God by which he justifies sinners, not that justice by which he himself justly judges human beings (Jo. ev. tr. 26.1; Trin. 14.15; Serm. 169.11; 170.6). See also Basil Studer, "Le Christ, notre justice, selon saint Augustin," Recherches Augustiniennes 15 (1980): 99–143, esp. 116–21.

in holiness.[103] Sometimes Augustine speaks of this process of justification in terms of deification.[104] The later Augustine often uses phrases that sound like those Eastern figures, the Cappadocians.[105]

As we have listened to Augustine's reading of Paul in the middle of the Pelagian controversy, we have heard him stress that redemption depends on God's mercy alone, for there is nothing we have that we have not received. Only through Christ's gift of the Spirit are we able to have a faith that is active through love. But even with this gift believers fight within themselves, struggling to obey the law of love. Texts such as Romans 5:5, 7:14–25; 9:16; 1 Corinthians 4:7; and Galatians 5:6 are often heard explicitly or as overtones in Augustine's articulation of the Apostle's thought.

Comparisons and Conclusions

Origen, Chrysostom, and Augustine offer different interpretations of Paul. Obviously Origen and Chrysostom—and the Greek East more generally—share some tendencies that are not stressed by the late Augustine. Origen and Chrysostom tend to ground their understanding of the economy of salvation in creation, emphasizing the gift of God's image in humanity and the potential for human beings to advance continually in union with God. Through the union of divinity and humanity in the incarnation, the creational intent of growth in participation with God is renewed and brought to fulfillment. For Origen and Chrysostom, as Patout Burns puts it, the process of redemption is more "continuous" and "developmental" than interventionist.[106] By contrast, Augustine tends to emphasize the definitive divine intervention of grace in Christ that liberates the elect from the guilt of Adam's sin and gives the Holy Spirit, whose love enables works of justice. Grace, for Augustine, is centered in the third of four stages in salvation history. Yes, God endowed humanity at creation with his image, but this gift is greatly disrupted by human misuse of it. Although Origen and Chrysostom believe that sin exercises a powerful dominion over fallen creatures, they

103. *Perf. iust.* 8.19; *Spir. et litt.* 9.15.
104. On the theme of divinization in Augustine's soteriology, see Gerald Bonner, "Augustine's Concept of Deification," *Journal of Theological Studies* 37 (1986): 369–86.
105. E.g., *Serm.* 192.1; *Enarrat. Ps.* 49.2; *Trin.* 14.12. See Berthold Altaner, "Augustinus, Gregor von Nazianz und Gregor von Nyssa," *Revue Bénédictine* 61 (1951): 54–62; and Berthold Altaner, "Augustinus und die griechische Patristik: Eine Zusammenfassung und Nachlese zu den quellenkritischen Untersuchungen," *Revue Bénédictine* 62 (1952): 201–15.
106. See J. Patout Burns, "The Economy of Salvation: Two Patristic Traditions," *Theological Studies* 37 (1976): 598–619.

do not see God's creational intentions so easily and decisively undermined by humans. Their conception of human beings as created with God's gift of his image perhaps explains, in part, their lack of precision in defining the role of grace and human freedom in the act of faith, because the response of faith made to God's call is not the response of a person as over against God but the image of God in a person.[107]

Although there are similarities between Origen and Chrysostom, there are also clear differences in their interpretation of Paul. Chrysostom's understanding of the process of redemption is less "interventionist" than Augustine, but it is certainly less "continuous" than Origen. In contrast to Origen's vision of the consummation of the world as occurring gradually until all human souls are saved, Chrysostom repeatedly paints the scene of Christ's final judgment of humans with relish and makes clear his belief in the finality of damnation.[108] Chrysostom also differs from Origen in his lack of speculation on cosmological metaphysics or on the purposes, mechanics, and ultimate intentions of God's will. Although Chrysostom defends human free will and divine sovereignty in the progressive unfolding of salvation history, he does not attempt to elaborate thoughtfully the complexities of the interplay between these two. Instead of the largely theocentric focus of Origen, who sought to understand the activity of the sovereign God in salvation history, Chrysostom's thought is more anthropological, oriented to the issue of how an enfleshed, mortal human being can be united to the divine through a life of obedient faith. Like many of his late fourth-century contemporaries, Chrysostom is interested in the individual Christian's pursuit of spiritual perfection.[109] Chrysostom's anthropological focus is more similar to the later Augustine than to Origen. Against the Pelagians, Augustine is not without concern for the goodness and justice of God, but his focus is on the nature of righteousness within a person, how a person becomes righteous, and the inner struggle of a person under grace.

The early church offers many different interpretations of Paul, not simply an Eastern and Augustinian, not even one interpretation per author in many cases. The reason for such diversity is obvious: countless factors shape exegesis. The life experience of the interpreter is one factor. Chrysostom reads his own experience as a priest into and from Paul's text. Augustine's

---

107. Wiles, *Divine Apostle*, 136, makes this important point.

108. See S. Schiewietz, "Die Eschatologie des hl. Johannes Chrysostomus und ihr Verhältnis zu der origenistischen," *Der Katholik* 4.12 (1913): 445–55; 4.13 (1914): 45–63, 200–216, 271–81, 370–79, 436–48; F. Leduc, "L'Eschatologie, une préoccupation centrale de saint Jean Chrysostome," *Proche-Orient Chrétien* 19 (1969): 109–34.

109. Gorday, *Principles of Patristic Exegesis*, 134–35.

fundamental shift in thinking by 397 and his later rereading of Romans 7 are both influenced, at least in part, by his autobiographical engagement with the person of Paul.[110] As Mitchell points out, both Chrysostom and Augustine identify personally with Paul, but different images of the Apostle result. Whereas for Chrysostom Paul is fighting against all opposition to win the world for the gospel, for Augustine the Apostle is fighting against the lustful forces of his own nature. Paul is not the archetype of virtue for Augustine, but the exemplum of perpetual inner moral struggle.[111]

Textual selection, too, affects the exegesis of Origen, Chrysostom, and Augustine. In each author's interpretation of Paul, a unique set of Pauline texts is emphasized. These texts, along with other biblical texts and philosophical ideas, contribute to the broader theological framework within which Paul is read. Even when two interpreters both see a particular text as key, the placement of the text in relation to others yields different interpretations of Paul. For example, Peter Gorday argues that Augustine uses Romans 9–11 as a locus of predestination, an appendix to or restatement of Romans 1–8, while Origen understands chapters 9–11 as the climax or logical conclusion of the redemptive history of both Jews and Gentiles outlined in Romans 1–11.[112] Sometimes not only particular passages but entire epistles may hold more sway than others. In Chrysostom's exegesis, for example, the Corinthian correspondence is perhaps more central to his understanding of Paul's person, work, and objectives than is Romans.

Another factor that contributes to different interpretations of Paul is historical context, including particulars such as past exegetical or theological controversies, social-political circumstances, and an interpreter's immediate opponents. We have not had opportunity to unfold these influences properly in our limited survey, but writing apologetic works and commentaries in a gnostic context at Alexandria prior to fourth-century theological developments obviously shapes exegesis in a quite different way than spurring on nominal believers through homilies in the context of the imperial state church after receiving rhetorical training in the schools of Antioch.

In short, many factors contribute to the distinct interpretations of Paul provided by Origen, Chrysostom, and Augustine. Putting any ancient interpretation of Paul into its various contexts inhibits facile generalizations about the Greek East or anachronistic theological judgments.[113] Of course, even

110. Mitchell, Heavenly Trumpet, 411–23.

111. Ibid., 418–19.

112. See esp. Gorday, Principles of Patristic Exegesis, 231–35.

113. For examples of such generalizations and theological judgments, see Eva Aleith, Paulus-Verständnis in der alten Kirche (Berlin: A Töpelmann, 1937). Thomas Torrance, The Doctrine of Grace

when a person reads sympathetically an ancient interpretation will exhibit weaknesses when judged by that person's own understanding of Paul's central theme(s). But a contextualized reading will also reveal strengths of ancient interpretations capable of challenging or complementing modern ones. Ecumenical dialogue in the twenty-first century can profit from drawing on the strengths of a very colorful palette of early Pauline interpretations.

---

in the Apostolic Fathers (Edinburgh: Oliver and Boyd, 1948); and McGrath, Iustitia Dei. Aleith has undefended assumptions about what an accurate interpretation of Paul's theology should have been. Torrance does not adequately take historical context (purposes and circumstances of composition, potential opponents, etc.) into account. McGrath agrees with Krister Stendahl's generalization that Paul meant "relatively little for the thinking of the church during the first 350 years of its history" (Stendahl, Paul among Jews and Gentiles [Philadelphia: Fortress, 1983], 83, quoted by McGrath, Iustitia Dei, 19). Cf. Jacques Rivière, The Expansion of Christianity in the First Three Centuries according to the Conclusions of Harnack (London: B. Herder, 1915).

9

Medieval and Reformation Readings of Paul

RANDALL C. ZACHMAN

The reading of Paul in the Middle Ages was decisively shaped by the legacy of Augustine of Hippo, the great father of Latin theology. The central theological issue for Augustine had to do with the correspondence of the order of our love with the order of being and reality. Since God is the being of beings, and the highest good, we should love God for the sake of God alone. Since human beings are created in the image of God, we should love ourselves and other human beings, not for their own sakes, but for the sake of God. All love should be referred to God alone, and the way we love should direct others to love God as well. Hence the central concern dominating the reading of Paul after Augustine was how to love God, others, and ourselves in a rightly ordered, and hence just, way.[1]

The Reformation represents the first major challenge to this Augustinian reading of Paul in the Latin West and reflects the impact of Martin Luther in particular. For Luther, the central theological issue shifted from how we are rightly to love God for the sake of God and ourselves and others for the sake of God, to how we as sinners are to know with certainty that God loves

1. See in particular Anselm of Canterbury, Bernard of Clairvaux, Thomas Aquinas, Bonaventure, and Duns Scotus.

us. Luther's reading of Paul developed in the context of his experience of a terrified conscience. Luther started out under the influence of Augustine's understanding of rightly ordered love but soon became convinced that the terrified conscience could not be consoled by means of our love for God, for our love could never have the power to remove the sense of sin, and hence of the wrath of God, from our conscience. Only God's love for us in Jesus Christ had the power to console the terrified conscience, as that love is revealed to us in the death and resurrection of Christ and proclaimed in the gospel. Luther was opposed by Roman theologians who rightly saw that Luther was departing from the Augustinian reading of Paul, without being able to see the legitimacy of Luther's divergent reading of Paul. These two ways of reading Paul—the Augustinian and the Lutheran—remain with us to this day, and represent the context in which we must all learn to reread Paul together.

The Augustinian and Latin Reading of Paul

The reading of Paul bequeathed to the Latin West by Augustine was framed by the summary of the law given by Jesus in the Synoptic Gospels: we are to love the Lord our God with all our mind, soul, and strength, and love our neighbors as ourselves. Augustine further developed the meaning of this summary of the law by means of an ontology basically derived from the Neoplatonic tradition. In this ontology God is viewed as the highest good, the goodness in which all good beings participate. Human beings are created in the image and likeness of God so that they might participate in God by knowing and loving God with their minds and hearts, and this participation would form their true and eternal happiness. However, because God is the highest good, God cannot be loved so that we might be happy, for this would mean loving God for the sake of ourselves. Rather, God must be loved for the sake of God, and this will make us happy. Moreover, it is not enough to know God as the highest good, as the being in which all beings participate, or as the light in which all rational creatures see light, for such knowledge, far from making us love God, could rather inflate us with pride. Hence even though we cannot love God without knowing God, it is not enough to know God as the highest good unless we also love God for the sake of God. Knowledge is therefore ordered entirely toward love and is fulfilled only when we rightly love the truth that we know.

Within this framework, sin is the perversion of the order of love, in which God is not loved for the sake of God but is loved for the sake of the one claiming to love God. Sin redirects our love from the highest good to a good that is only good by participation in God. Ironically, it is the goodness of all things that makes sin possible, for their goodness can attract our love to them so that we love them for their own sake, and not for the sake of God, in whose goodness all good things participate and exist. Sin can either be directed to ourselves, in which case it expresses itself as self-love (*amor sui*), or it can be directed toward the goodness of creatures outside of us, in which case it expresses itself as concupiscence (*concupiscentia*). However, since only God is able to make human beings happy, our attempt to find happiness by loving ourselves or other creatures will end in failure, leaving us with the sense that we are always seeking something that we are never able to find, leading ultimately to our temporal and eternal death. Hence sin becomes its own punishment, as God hands us over to our desire to seek a happiness apart from God that we can find only in God. In this paradigm, the wrath of God expresses itself in handing us over to the order of love we choose for ourselves, in the knowledge that our misdirected love will never make us happy, but will form its own punishment.[2]

If sin were misdirected love, then grace would be the gift that would rightly order love within us. In particular, grace would bestow upon us the ability to love God for the sake of God, which would free us from loving ourselves and/or others for their own sake. Such love would make it possible for us to render to God what we owe to God as the highest good, and hence would make us just. Since love is rooted primarily in the will, justice would be a rightly ordered will. The gift of love would free the will from consenting to the desire to love itself or other creatures for their own sake instead of God, but it would not free the will from being tempted by these desires. However, such desires would not condemn us if we did not consent to them, but rather resisted them through the divine gift of grace. Because we have the ability to love God by grace, we have reason to hope, but because we are surrounded by the temptation to love ourselves and/or other creatures in place of God, we also have good reason to fear. Hence the way of salvation passes between the Scylla of presumption and the Charybdis of despair.[3]

2. See in particular *The City of God*, translated by R. W. Dyson (Cambridge: Cambridge University Press, 1998), book 14.

3. See in particular *On the Spirit and the Letter*, in *Augustine: Later Writings*, trans. John Burnaby (Philadelphia: Westminster Press, 1980), and *On the Trinity*, translated by John E. Rotelle (Brooklyn, NY: New City Press, 1990), book 4, preface.

Texts Highlighted by the Augustinian and Latin Reading of Paul

The Augustinian reading of Paul that I have traced above had the effect of highlighting certain texts in Paul in light of its narrative of creation, sin, and redemption. These texts were formative both of the medieval reading of Paul and of the Roman reaction to the Reformation reading of Paul. In the following section I would like to highlight those texts and also comment on the variant readings of these texts that developed in the Latin West after Augustine. This will give us a template to use in illuminating the distinctive nature of the Reformation reading of Paul. As we shall see, the reading of Paul is in large part shaped by the larger theological and ontological framework in which such reading takes place.

"Therefore . . . sin came into the world through one man and death through sin, and so death spread to all because all have sinned" (Rom. 5:12). According to the Augustinian reading of Paul, the descent into self-love and concupiscence took place in Adam, in whom all people sinned. All of us manifest the effects of the sin of Adam, and are unable through our own efforts to free ourselves from sin and death. As the Pelagian controversy framed the way Augustine and his successors understood the nature of human sin, the understanding of sin tended to focus on the baptism of infants, which the Pelagians and their opponents both practiced. Infants inherit the sin and death of Adam and are condemned to temporal and eternal death unless the Holy Spirit that is imparted to them in baptism frees them from sin and death. This focus on original sin and baptism will manifest itself in the Council of Trent, which will focus its discussion of infant baptism around the issue of original sin, and its definition of justification around the sacrament of adult baptism.

"Therefore God gave them up in the lusts of their hearts to impurity" (Rom. 1:24). For Augustine and his heirs, the wrath of God manifests itself primarily by handing sinners over to the objects of their desire. Since they in sin choose to love themselves and the world rather than God, God punishes them by allowing them to seek for happiness where it can never be found. Hence the wrath of God is not described by the medieval Latin tradition as an experience of anger and condemnation by God, but rather as a state of being passed over by the mercy of God, so that one is subject to the future one has chosen for oneself.

"So they are without excuse; for although they knew God they did not honor him as God" (Rom. 1:20–21). Since in the Augustinian reading of Paul sin primarily impacts the will, the medieval readers of Paul had little problem acknowledging that Gentile sinners could come to the true knowledge of God by means of their reason and/or the manifestation of God in creation. Augustine would say that the Platonists came to the knowledge of the true God, but this knowledge did not lead them to find their happiness in God, but rather served to make them more proud.[4] The knowledge of God does not of itself have the power to conquer the sin of self-love but can rather serve to increase it. Hence the Latin readers of Paul would highlight Paul's contrast between knowledge and the genuine love of God. "Knowledge puffs up, but love builds up" (1 Cor. 8:1).[5]

"I would not have known what it is to covet if the law had not said, 'You shall not covet'" (Rom. 7:7). Even as the knowledge of God may increase the problem of human pride inherited from Adam, so the law of God actually works to increase the very concupiscence it forbids. According to Augustine, the law is unable to give us what it commands of us, and this serves only to increase the sin and death we have brought upon ourselves. Apart from the Spirit, which gives the love that the law commands, the law can only reveal our sin, especially our concupiscence: "for the letter kills, but the Spirit gives life" (2 Cor. 3:6). This function of the law, so crucial to Augustine's argument against the Pelagians, tends to disappear among the medieval readers of Paul, perhaps due to the focus on the removal of original sin in infant baptism. If all Christians are baptized as infants and receive the Holy Spirit at that time, there seems to be no need to discuss the way the written code of the law kills by increasing the very sin it prohibits. The difference between the letter and the Spirit comes instead to describe the difference between the old covenant with Israel and the new covenant in Christ, as one sees in scholastic theologians such as Thomas.

"For the law of the Spirit of life in Christ Jesus has set you free from the law of sin and of death" (Rom. 8:2). Since neither the knowledge of God, nor the written code of the law, can free us from the pride and concupiscence that lead us to death, only the grace of God can free us from sin, through the Spirit that is given to us through Christ Jesus. In the Augustinian reading of Paul, the focus is not so much on what Christ himself does on our behalf to free us from sin but rather the way Christ brings the Spirit, which alone gives us the ability to fulfill the law of love. "For God has done what the law, weakened by the flesh, could not do: by sending his own Son in the likeness of sinful flesh, and to deal with sin, he condemned sin in the flesh, so that the just requirement of the law might be fulfilled in us, who walk

---

4. See in particular *Confessions*, translated by John K. Ryan (New York: Image, 1960), book 7.

5. This distinction is fundamental to Anselm's theological method. See *Cur deus homo* 2.1 for his assumption regarding the knowledge of God in fallen reason.

not according to the flesh but according to the Spirit" (Rom. 8:3). The *telos* of the saving work of Christ is attained only when the Spirit gives us the ability to will and do what the law requires, so that we might fulfill the law and thereby be made righteous. "For just as by the one man's disobedience the many were made sinners, so by one man's obedience the many will be made righteous" (Rom. 5:19). By meriting the gift of the Spirit for us by his death, Christ makes it possible for sinners to be made righteous by turning their wills from the love of creatures to the love of God for the sake of God alone.

"God's love [or "love for God"] has been poured into our hearts through the Holy Spirit that has been given to us" (Rom. 5:5). According to the Augustinian reading of Paul, the primary meaning of the grace of God is the love for God that the Holy Spirit pours or infuses into our hearts, which gives us the ability to do what the law requires of us. Without this freely given love, neither the knowledge of God nor the law of God can free us from sin, but with this free gift we can fulfill the law of love and therefore be made righteous. "Love does no wrong to a neighbor; therefore, love is the fulfilling of the law" (Rom. 13:10). Since Christ alone gives the Spirit, faith must seek this gift from Christ. However, since the gift of love alone frees us from sin and makes us righteous, faith without love profits us nothing. "And if I have prophetic powers, and understand all mysteries and all knowledge, and if I have all faith, so as to remove mountains, but do not have love, I am nothing" (1 Cor. 13:2). Such love frees us from the dominion of pride and concupiscence that led to our death. However, the temptation to sin remains in those who have been given love for God by the Holy Spirit, leading to a state of war in their souls that will not cease until they die.[6]

"For I delight in the law of God in my inmost self, but I see in my members another law at war with the law of my mind, making me captive to the law of sin that dwells in my members" (Rom. 7:22–23). Once we have been given the ability to love God for the sake of God, we become conscious of all the desires that war against this love, threatening to take us captive yet again. We cannot free ourselves from the law of sin in our members in this life, but if we struggle against the sin in our members by the love given us by the Holy Spirit, we will not be condemned. "So then, I of myself serve the law of God with my mind, but with my flesh I serve the law of sin. There is therefore now no condemnation for those who are in Christ Jesus" (Rom. 7:25–8:1). Augustine succeeded in convincing readers of Paul after him that

---

6. See especially *Confessions*, book 10.

the state described in Romans 7 applied to those who had been freed from the dominion of sin by the Holy Spirit, but he did not resolve the question of whether such desires remaining in the saints were really and truly sinful. On the one hand, Augustine claimed that such desires do not condemn us if we, by the Spirit, do not consent to them, however tempted we might be by them, following the injunction of Paul: "Live by the Spirit, I say, and do not gratify the desires of the flesh" (Gal. 5:16). If we withhold our consent, such desires will have no dominion within us. "Therefore, do not let sin exercise dominion in your mortal bodies, to make you obey their passions" (Rom. 6:12). On the other hand, Augustine could insist that such desires, even when we do not consent to them, really are sin, and really need to be confessed to God. Such desires will not condemn if we confess them before God, for such confession keeps us humble, and humility is essentially related to love. The refusal to confess such desires as sin would reveal the sin of pride, which would be the violation of love.[7]

There were at least two factors that led the medieval readers of Paul to deny that such desires of the flesh are really sin. First, there was the gloss of Jerome that was incorporated into the *Glossa Ordinaria* of the twelfth century, which says that the sin remaining in our flesh is not really sin, but is rather the occasion of sin, that will truly become sin only if we consent to it. The authority of this gloss is revealed in the way the fathers at Trent insist that the church has never understood such desires to be sin even though Paul calls the concupiscence in the baptized "sin." Here we can see how the voice of Jerome completely eclipsed Augustine in the reading of Romans 7. Second, there was the rise of private confession in Europe, brought to the continent by the Celtic missionary monks of the seventh century. Confession was to be for sins that arose from the consent of the will, not for those sinful desires to which we had not consented. Hence Augustine's insistence that we need to confess the desires of the flesh in order not to be condemned by them was eclipsed by the pastoral practice of confessing only those sins that arose from an intention of the will that directly contradicted love for God. However, for both Augustine and the later medieval readers of Paul, the presence of such desires in those who had been given the gift of love for God meant that the whole of life is a battle in which we can never think we are safe.

"Work out your own salvation with fear and trembling; for it is God who is at work in you, enabling you both to will and to work for his good pleasure" (Phil. 2:12–13). If the grace of God means the gift of love poured into our

7. See in particular Augustine's *Homilies on First John*, in *Augustine: Later Writings*.

hearts by the Holy Spirit, then the work of salvation must be entirely due to the work of God within us, both to will and to work the love that is the fulfilling of the law. However, since we have been given the ability to fulfill the law of God by grace, the work of salvation must also be entirely due to what we do by that grace, though with fear and trembling, as we are aware of the weakness that remains even in those given the gift of love for God. Because we know the power of God's grace and mercy, we have good reason to hope; yet because we also know our own weakness, and the difficulty of discerning our true motivations, we also have good reason to fear. As Paul reminded the Corinthians, "So if you think you are standing, watch out that you do not fall" (1 Cor. 10:12). The Augustinian reading of Paul describes the faithful as always living in the field of tension created by fear and hope, given the twin dangers of pride and concupiscence. The godly are to hope in the mercy of God, but they can never be certain that they are the beloved children of God. "I do not even judge myself. I am not aware of anything against myself, but I am not thereby acquitted" (1 Cor. 4:3–4). We are to hope in the grace and mercy of God, but without presumption, and we are to fear on the basis of our own weakness, but without despair.

"If you sow to your own flesh, you will reap corruption from the flesh; but if you sow to the Spirit, you will reap eternal life from the Spirit" (Gal. 6:8). Following Augustine, the Latin reading of Paul highlighted the theme of sowing and reaping, along with the theme of running to obtain the prize. The grace of God sets the believer on the path of salvation, but it is up to the believer to strive to sow according to the Spirit, so as to reap eternal life from the Spirit. Eternal life is thus entirely the work of the Spirit within us, and the work of the person sowing to the Spirit.[8] Moreover, it is always possible to sow more to the Spirit in order to reap more from the Spirit unto eternal life. "The point is this: the one who sows sparingly will also reap sparingly, and the one who sows bountifully will also reap bountifully" (2 Cor. 9:6). According to this reading, Paul himself gave up marital relations for the sake of the Lord, though he never condemned marriage; those who do not marry do better because they sow even more to the Spirit. "So then, he who marries his fiancée does well; and he who refrains from marriage will do better" (1 Cor. 7:38).

The Latin tradition combined the theme of sowing and reaping with the theme of running and competing to obtain a crown. Just as athletes disci-

---

8. See *Grace and Free Will*, trans. Robert P. Russell (Washington, DC: Catholic University of America Press, 1968). This is especially clear in the beginning article of the second part of the *Summa Theologiae* of Thomas Aquinas.

pline themselves in order to compete more effectively, Paul exhorts all the saints to subdue their flesh so that they might obtain the crown of eternal life. "Do you not know that in a race all the runners compete, but only one receives the prize? Run in such a way that you may win it. Athletes exercise self-control in all things; they do it to receive a perishable wreath, but we an imperishable one" (1 Cor. 9:24–25). Those who, like Paul, run the race and subdue their flesh with self-control can hope like him to receive the crown of eternal life. "I have finished the race, I have kept the faith. From now on there is reserved for me the crown of righteousness, which the Lord, the righteous judge, will give me on that day, and not only to me but also to all who have longed for his appearing" (2 Tim. 4:7–8). However, the hope that we will reap what we sow unto eternal life, and will win the crown of eternal life in the race we are running, must always be tempered by the awareness that all this is due to the grace of God within us, and not due to our own power and ability, lest we once again become proud.

"What do you have that you did not receive? If you received it, why do you boast as if it were not a gift?" (1 Cor. 4:7). The Augustinian reading of Paul was ever attentive to the threat of human pride, even in the one who had been given the ability to love God and thereby begin to fulfill the law of love. We must always acknowledge that the only reason we are crowned at the end of the race is that the grace of God has been at work in us, both to will and to work to God's good pleasure. Hence when God gives the crown of eternal life to those who have run the race set before them, God is really crowning God's own gift within them. Once again we are placed in the field of tension created by the need to strive, on the one hand, and the danger of boasting, on the other. The grace of God is effective within us so that we can sow in the hope of reaping eternal life; yet we must never boast, lest we fall back into the pride that leads to eternal death. "For by grace you have been saved through faith; and this is not your own doing; it is the gift of God—not the result of works, so that no one may boast. For we are what he has made us, created in Christ Jesus for good works, which God prepared beforehand to be our way of life" (Eph. 2:8–10).

"He chose us in Christ before the foundation of the world to be holy and blameless before him" (Eph. 1:4). In order to avoid all boasting, and yet to find a solid basis of hope, we must acknowledge that all striving for eternal life by the grace at work within us is ultimately due to the eternal election of God. What distinguishes us is not due to our own ability, but is rather due to the predestination of God, which chooses some in mercy as vessels of glory, and passes over others in justice as vessels of wrath (Rom. 9:22–23). Our salvation is thus ultimately due to the free grace and mercy of God, and not to our own efforts. "For he says to Moses, 'I will have mercy on whom I have mercy, and I will have compassion on whom I have compassion.' So it depends not on human will or exertion, but on God who shows mercy" (Rom. 9:15–16). However, even here we must avoid the danger of pride, by falling into the presumption that we know we are elected. We must rather acknowledge that election itself is a mystery that transcends all our ability to understand it, to keep us humble, even as it is the only source of our hope for salvation and eternal life. "O the depth of the riches and wisdom and knowledge of God! How unsearchable are his judgments and how inscrutable his ways! 'For who has known the mind of the Lord? Or who has been his counselor?' 'Or who has given a gift to him, to receive a gift in return?'" (Rom. 11:33–35).[9]

We must, of course, acknowledge that the medieval reading of Paul was not entirely uniform, especially in its reading of the relationship between human striving and the work of God within us. Due to the influence of another gloss on Paul first found in the *Glossa Ordinaria*, the idea arose that God does not deny grace to those who do what is within them. Once this gloss arose, every subsequent reader of Paul would have to address this issue, even if he later came to insist that "doing what is within oneself" is based entirely on the grace of God already at work in the person, as in the later theology of Thomas. The interpretation of Paul was further complicated by the rise in interest in the relationship between nature and grace. As Scotus reasoned, if the grace of God does not destroy but rather perfects nature, then love for God for the sake of God must correspond to the essential human nature of every human being, no matter how hardened a sinner he or she appears to be. If this were true, then the reason of every human being must command him or her to love God for the sake of God, for otherwise they would not be guilty of failing to love God. Finally, if reason commands us to love God for the sake of God, then it must be possible for the will to obey this command of love, even in the state of sin, or else the command would be absurd, by commanding what cannot be done. "When Gentiles who have not the law do by nature what the law requires, they are a law to themselves, even though they do not have the law" (Rom. 2:14). Those who obey this command to love, elicited in their will by the command of reason, will not be denied grace, and those who do what is within them by the grace of God at work within them will not be denied the reward of eternal life.[10]

9. See in particular *The Predestination of the Saints*, in *Four Anti-Pelagian Writings*, trans. John A. Mourant and William J. Colligne (Washington, DC: Catholic University of America Press, 1992).

10. See *Duns Scotus on the Will and Morality*, trans. Alan B. Wolter (Washington, DC: Catholic University of America Press, 1998).

"For he will repay according to each one's deeds: to those who by patiently doing good seek for glory and honor and immortality, he will give eternal life; while for those who are self-seeking and who obey not the truth but wickedness, there will be wrath and fury." (Rom. 2:6–8). This emphasis on the greater role of human striving was nonetheless tempered by the claim that none of our striving profits unto eternal life without the grace of God within us, and by the insistence that our eternal salvation is due entirely to the mercy of God, either in terms of the election and acceptance of the saints, as in Scotus, or in the gratuitousness of the covenant made with humanity, as in Biel.

The Lutheran and Evangelical Reading of Paul

Even though it is true, as we shall see, that the reading of Paul that gave greater stress to human striving formed the proximate context for the Evangelical reading of Paul in the sixteenth century, it must nonetheless be said that the Evangelical reading of Paul represents a sharp break with the Augustinian reading of Paul as a whole, even that reading that stresses the grace and mercy of God over and above any and all human striving. For reasons that ultimately elude historical investigation, the Augustinian reading of Paul failed to meet the spiritual needs of many readers of Paul, beginning with but not limited to Martin Luther.[11] For these readers it was no longer sufficient to understand the grace of God as the love for God that is poured into our hearts by the Holy Spirit that is given to us. These readers turned their attention from the grace of God at work *within* the faithful, to the grace of God that is manifested in what God has done *for* us in Jesus Christ, especially in his death and resurrection. As Melanchthon and Luther both said in 1521, the term *gratia* should be understood as the love that God has for us, in distinction to the gift of God that is at work within us.[12]

Whereas the Evangelical reading of Paul includes many more voices than that of Luther, it is nonetheless true that his experience and teaching provided the catalyst for these other voices to emerge.[13] Luther's reading

11. Such readers would include Philip Melanchthon, Martin Bucer, Ulrich Zwingli, Oecolampadius, Heinrich Bullinger, John Calvin, and Thomas Cranmer, to name but the most prominent.

12. Philip Melanchthon, *Loci Communes* (1521), in *Melanchthon and Bucer*, ed. Wilhelm Pauck (Philadelphia: Westminster, 1969); Martin Luther, *Against Latomus* (1521), LW 32.

13. Ulrich Zwingli and Menno Simons, among others, credit Luther's boldness at the Leipzig Debate of 1519 and in *The Babylonian Captivity* of 1520 with giving them the courage to break with Rome. Melanchthon, Bucer, Bullinger, Calvin, and Cranmer all credit Luther with bringing them to the Evangelical position.

of Paul derived from his experience of sin and confession in particular, and centered on the status of concupiscence in the baptized. Luther initially accepted the Augustinian and Latin reading of Paul, according to which sin is removed by the gift of love infused into the hearts of the faithful. Luther also accepted the teaching of the medieval church on penance, according to which all sins that afflict the conscience should be confessed to one's confessor. However, as Luther dutifully tried to remove the sense of sin from his conscience in this way, he found that the sense of sin only increased, to the point that his conscience was terrified by the wrath of God that is threatened against all the ungodly. "For the wrath of God is revealed from heaven against all ungodliness and wickedness of those who by their wickedness suppress the truth" (Rom. 1:18). The experience of the terrified conscience led Luther away from the Augustinian sense of wrath, in which a sinner is handed over to their disordered love, toward an understanding of wrath as the active will of God to punish and condemn sinners, as one begins to see in the theology of Tauler and *The German Theology*. His task then became how to understand the grace of God in relation to the sense of sin and wrath in his conscience.[14]

His first conclusion on the basis of his experience of the terrified conscience was to resolve decisively the ambiguity surrounding the desires of the flesh in the Augustinian reading of Paul. Luther concluded that the concupiscence left in the faithful is still sin, even if they do not consent to it, and as such it deserves to be punished under the wrath of God. He thus rejected the gloss of Jerome, that such concupiscence is not sin, but is rather the tinder (*fomes*) of sin. Over against this interpretation, Luther intensified the sinfulness of concupiscence even beyond the position of Augustine, insisting that concupiscence is mortal sin, even when we resist it and do not consent to it. Far from removing the sense of sin, the infusion of love for God reveals for the first time how sinful concupiscence really is. The infusion of grace is therefore experienced as the diffusion of sin and wrath on the believer. One may out of love for God willingly consign oneself to hell as a sinner under wrath, as Luther claimed between 1515 and 1519, but the infusion of love does not have the ability to remove the sense of sin and wrath from the conscience.[15]

The decisive breakthrough to a new paradigm for the reading of Paul came in the years between 1519 and 1520, and had to do with the distinc-

14. See in particular Martin Becht, *Martin Luther: His Road to Reformation, 1483–1521*, trans. James L. Schaaf (Minneapolis: Fortress, 1981).

15. Luther states this position with particular boldness in his *Lectures on Romans* of 1515–1516, LW 25.

tion Luther drew between Moses and the law, and Christ and the gospel. Through his reading of Paul in light of his terrified conscience, Luther concluded that it was not the infusion of grace that revealed sin, but rather the law of God. Indeed, the law is limited to this power to reveal sin, and to terrify the conscience with the awareness of sin and wrath. This is done so that we might despair entirely of all that we might do to save ourselves from wrath and attain eternal life, including what we might do by the gift of God at work within us. We must turn instead to Jesus Christ, and to the gospel that offers Christ and his work to us. When we do, we will discover that Christ frees us from sin by bearing our sins in his body and by putting them to death on the cross in order to give us righteousness and eternal life in their place. The gospel proclaims that our sin is forgiven not by the gift of God within us, but by the cross of Christ, and eternal life is freely given to us not on the basis of our striving by the grace of God within us but by the resurrection of Christ. The shift from the grace of God as the work of God within us by the Holy Spirit to the grace of God as the work of God for us in Jesus Christ created a new narrative for the reading of Paul, one that both highlighted texts neglected by the Augustinian reading and neglected texts highlighted by the Augustinian narrative. We will now turn to the texts highlighted by the Evangelical reading of Paul in order to see how this new reading replaced the Augustinian reading of Paul, at least for Luther and his followers, while acknowledging that the Augustinian reading lived on in Luther's Roman opponents.

Texts Highlighted by the Lutheran and Evangelical Reading of Paul

"For 'no human being will be justified in his sight' by deeds prescribed by the law, for through the law comes the knowledge of sin" (Rom. 3:20). According to Luther and the new Evangelical reading of Paul, the attempt to remove the sense of sin and wrath in the conscience by doing works of the law, even under the influence of the grace of God within us, is doomed to failure because the law has the power only to reveal sin and can never remove sin. God gave the law precisely to reveal sin, and thereby humble the pride of those who think that they can free themselves from sin by their own works. "Yet, if it had not been for the law, I would not have known sin" (Rom. 7:7). If the law reveals sin, then it also reveals the wrath of God against sin. "For the law brings wrath, but where there is no law, neither is there violation" (Rom. 4:15). Luther and his followers understood such wrath as being actively cursed by God, and not simply as being handed over to the consequences of the sinful desires of our hearts. "For all who rely on the works of the law are under a curse; for it is written, 'Cursed is everyone who does not observe and obey all the things written in the book of the law'" (Gal. 3:10). The revelation of sin by the law is thus the revelation of the wrath and curse of God that sentences sinners to death. "The sting of death is sin, and the power of sin is the law" (1 Cor. 15:56). The revelation of sin, death, and wrath by the law is not an end in itself, however, but is intended by God to drive us outside ourselves to seek God's mercy and love in Jesus Christ.

"For God has done what the law, weakened by the flesh, could not do; by sending his own Son in the likeness of sinful flesh, and to deal with sin, he condemned sin in the flesh" (Rom. 8:3). Once the law has fulfilled its function of revealing sin, Luther and his followers direct our attention to those passages in Paul that speak of the sending of the Son to take the burden of sin upon himself. The law makes this burden intolerable in the conscience; only Christ has the power to remove this burden from the conscience. Christ does this by transferring our sin to his own flesh in order to free us from it. "For our sake he made him to be sin who knew no sin, so that in him we might become the righteousness of God" (2 Cor. 5:21). By taking our sin upon himself Christ also takes upon himself the curse of God lying upon our sin. "Christ redeemed us from the curse of the law by becoming a curse for us—for it is written, 'Cursed is everyone who hangs on a tree'" (Gal. 3:13). By taking on our sin and curse Christ frees us once and for all from the condemnation of the law, making it possible for condemned sinners to become children of God. "But when the time had fully come, God sent forth his Son, born of woman, born under the law, in order to redeem those who were under the law, so that we might receive adoption as children" (Gal. 4:4).[16]

In exchange for our sin and death Christ freely gives us his own righteousness and life. "Therefore just as one man's trespass led to condemnation for all, so one man's act of righteousness leads to justification and life for all" (Rom. 5:18). Luther and his followers decisively depart from the entire Augustinian tradition of reading Paul by highlighting those passages in which eternal life is a free gift of God in Christ Jesus, thereby attempting to eliminate entirely any idea that we might merit eternal life by our life of faith and love. "For the wages of sin is death, but the free gift of God is eternal life in Christ Jesus our Lord" (Rom. 6:23). Our sin was put to death in the death of Christ, and righteousness and life were restored to us in his resurrection, for according to Paul, Christ "was handed over to death for

---

16. See in particular Luther's *Lectures on Galatians* (1535), LW 26, especially chapters 3 and 4.

our trespasses and raised for our justification" (Rom. 4:25). The forgiveness of sin and the inheritance of eternal life both have their source in the free and undeserved love of God for sinners, revealed in the death of Christ.

"But God proves his love for us in that while we still were sinners Christ died for us" (Rom. 5:8). The Evangelical reading of Paul presupposes the experience of the terrified conscience on the part of the reader.[17] In this experience, the key question is not, "How can I be given the ability to love God and thereby fulfill the law of God?" Rather, the central question is, "How can I, a sinner deserving of wrath, know that God loves me?" The pledge of God's love for sinners is found only in the sending of the Son to die for us. "If God is for us, who is against us? He who did not withhold his own Son, but gave him up for all of us, will he not with him also give us everything else?" (Rom. 8:31–32). Faith has as its object this love of God for us, for me, in the death of the Son. "The life I now live in the flesh I live by faith in the Son of God, who loved me and gave himself for me" (Gal. 2:20). Since this love has overcome all that separates us from God—sin, death, and the curse and wrath of God—the faithful are confident that nothing in God or all creation can separate them from this love. "For I am convinced that neither death, nor life, nor angels, nor rulers, nor things present, nor things to come, nor powers, nor height, nor depth, nor anything else in all creation, will be able to separate us from the love of God in Christ Jesus our Lord" (Rom. 8:38–39). The gift of the Holy Spirit, which was central to the Augustinian definition of grace, is no longer understood to give us the ability to love God, but is rather understood as sealing the love of God for us in Christ Jesus on our minds and hearts. This is why hope does not disappoint us: "God's love [for us] has been poured into our hearts through the Holy Spirit which has been given to us" (Rom. 5:5). The field of tension created by hope and fear in the Augustinian reading of Paul is replaced by a bold confidence in the love of God for us in the Evangelical reading of Paul, one that will strike the Roman opponents of the Evangelicals as proud presumption.

"Therefore, since we are justified by faith, we have peace with God through our Lord Jesus Christ" (Rom. 5:1). Only faith in Christ is able to bring peace to the terrified conscience, which becomes the central experiential verification of the right reading of Paul for Luther and his supporters. Such peace arises from the confidence that we have in Jesus Christ, who gives us access to the grace and favor of God toward us. "Through [Christ]

17. This is clearly stated in the *Augsburg Confession*, in *The Book of Concord*, ed. Robert Kolb and Timothy Wengert (Minneapolis: Fortress, 2000). See also Calvin, *Institutes*, 3.xii–xiii.

we have obtained access to this grace in which we stand, and we boast in our hope of sharing the glory of God" (Rom. 5:2). Faith is therefore understood to be a godly confidence and boldness in approaching God, for in Christ Jesus "we have access to God in boldness and confidence through faith in him" (Eph. 3:12). Such boldness is especially evident in the prayer of the faithful, inspired by the gift and testimony of the Holy Spirit within them. "When we cry, 'Abba! Father!' it is that very Spirit bearing witness with our spirit that we are children of God" (Rom. 8:15–16). In contrast to the Augustinian claim that no one can be certain they are a child of God, Luther and the Evangelicals insist that the faithful must know with certainty that they are children of God whom God loves in Christ Jesus, and must boldly and confidently approach God in that faith and certainty. The life of the faithful is acceptable to God only if it is lived out of this bold confidence in the love and mercy of God for us in Christ Jesus. Hence faith, and not love, becomes the central orientation of the lives of the godly.

"For whatever does not proceed from faith is sin" (Rom. 14:23). If both righteousness and eternal life are the free gift of God bestowed upon us in the death and resurrection of Christ, then no form of life can be thought to merit these blessings from God, even if such merit is understood as God crowning God's gifts within us. In the Augustinian reading of Paul, those who sowed more to the Spirit than to the flesh—such as monks, who vowed poverty, chastity, and obedience—could expect to reap more unto eternal life. In the Evangelical reading of Paul, the very thought that the way we live merits any reward from God is a violation of faith, and is therefore sin.[18] This is not to say that the faithful will not live lives of love. The faithful will seek to love others the way God has loved them in Christ. As Christ has borne the burden of our sin, death, and curse, the faithful will seek to do all they can to alleviate the temporal burdens under which their neighbors labor, following the injunction of Paul: "Bear one another's burdens, and in this way you will fulfill the law of Christ" (Gal. 6:2). However, the faithful will not think that this love will win for them a crown of righteousness at the end of their race, for that would be to sin against faith. "For in Christ Jesus neither circumcision nor uncircumcision counts for anything; the only thing that counts is faith working through love" (Gal. 5:6). Rather than fleeing the world of marriage and family to escape to the monastery or a life of celibacy—which the Augustinian model would see as sowing even more to the Spirit in order to reap more unto eternal life—the faithful in

18. See in particular *The Judgment of Martin Luther on Monastic Vows* (1521), LW 44.

the Evangelical reading of Paul will remain in the world, in order to bear the burdens of those around them.[19]

"Let each of you lead the life that the Lord has assigned, to which God called you. This is my rule in all the churches" (1 Cor. 7:17). Whereas the Augustinian focus on love for God emphasized forms of life that were thought to increase love and devotion to God, such as celibacy, the Evangelical emphasis on faith working through love emphasized the relationships of mutual subjection found in the household codes in Ephesians and Colossians.[20] The Evangelicals used Paul to argue against what they saw as self-chosen vocations, such as monasticism, in order to direct our attention to the stations of life to which they claimed God truly calls us. All these vocations can be understood under the rubric of the mutual subjection to which Paul calls us. "Be subject to one another out of reverence for Christ" (Eph. 5:21). The life of faith is to be lived in the various callings of mutual subjection, such as wives and husbands, children and parents, servants and masters, and subjects and rulers. "Let every person be subject to the governing authorities; for there is no authority except from God, and those authorities that exist have been instituted by God" (Rom. 13:1). Not even the calling to serve the church frees one from the mutual subjection of wives and husbands, children and parents, for Paul directs us to "appoint elders in every town as I directed you: someone who is blameless, married only once, whose children are believers, not accused of debauchery and not rebellious" (Titus 1:5–6). The Augustinian reading of Paul looks to those places in which Paul enjoined even greater devotion to the Lord than was possible in marriage and family. "The unmarried man is anxious about the affairs of the Lord, how to please the Lord; but the married man is anxious about the affairs of the world, how to please his wife, and his interest is divided" (1 Cor. 7:32–34). The Evangelical reading of Paul highlights those passages in which Paul assumes all the faithful are already located in webs of relationships involving rulers, parents, spouses, and children. "Let each of you remain in the condition in which he was called" (1 Cor. 7:20). In this reading, the exaltation of celibacy and poverty over marriage and family was yet another sign that the Roman Church had replaced the gospel preached by Paul with the delusions of Satan.

"But even if we or an angel from heaven should proclaim to you a gospel contrary to what we proclaimed to you, let that one be accursed" (Gal. 1:8).

---

19. See especially *The Freedom of the Christian* (1520), LW 31.

20. It is significant that the end of Luther's *Small Catechism* contains a collection of these scriptural references to offices and stations of life. See *The Book of Concord*.

Luther and his followers became convinced that the church of Rome was in fact guilty of preaching a gospel contrary to the one preached by Paul. They thought that the teaching that the gift of the Holy Spirit gave us the ability to fulfill the law of love replaced Paul's teaching of justification by faith with justification by works, which Paul explicitly condemned. "For we hold that a person is justified by faith apart from works prescribed by the law" (Rom. 3:28). They thought that the exaltation of lives of celibacy, poverty, and fasting above the lives of ordinary families and citizens was in fact due to the emergence of the doctrine of demons prophesied by Paul. "Now the Spirit expressly says that in later times some will renounce the faith by paying attention to deceitful spirits and teachings of demons, through the hypocrisy of liars whose consciences are seared wit a hot iron. They forbid marriage and demand abstinence from foods, which God created to be received with thanksgiving by those who believe and know the truth" (1 Tim. 4:1–3). They saw in the mortifications of the flesh in the Roman Church the appearance of sanctity and wisdom of which Paul warned the Colossians: "All these regulations refer to things that perish with use; they are simply human commands and teachings" (Col. 2:22). The source of these teachings was seen to be "the lawless one" whom Paul had prophesied would take his seat in the temple of God. "He opposes and exalts himself above every so-called god or object of worship, so that he takes his seat in the temple of God, declaring himself to be God" (2 Thess. 2:4).

On the other hand, those Roman theologians who defended the Augustinian reading of Paul saw in the Evangelicals a departure from received teaching, again vigorously condemned by Paul.[21] "If any one proclaims to you a gospel contrary to what you received, let that one be accursed" (Gal. 1:9). They rightly detected that the Evangelicals were replacing the Augustinian narrative that had framed the interpretation of Paul for over a thousand years with a new narrative that first emerged from Luther's experience of a terrified conscience. They thought that the Evangelical emphasis on a bold confidence in the mercy of God led to the very pride and presumption against which Augustine had guarded so carefully, summarized in Paul's admonition to "work out your own salvation with fear and trembling" (Phil. 2:12). They thought that the elevation of faith over love constituted a rejection of the more excellent way of love enjoined by Paul himself in 1 Corinthians 13. They thought that the rejection of celibacy,

21. See in particular Johann Eck, *Enchiridion of Common-Places* (1525), trans. Ford Lewis Battles (Grand Rapids: Calvin Theological Seminary, 1978), as well as the *Pontifical Confutation* of the Augsburg Confession (1530), in *The Augsburg Confession: A Collection of Sources with an Historical Introduction*, trans. Johann Reu (Chicago: Wartburg, 1930).

poverty, and other mortifications of the flesh by the Evangelicals led to a betrayal of the life of the Spirit in favor of the flesh, which could lead only to death. "To set the mind on the flesh is death, but to set the mind on the Spirit is life and peace" (Rom. 8:6). They agreed that God sent the Son in the likeness of sinful flesh and for sin to condemn sin in the flesh, but they accused the Evangelicals of forgetting the purpose of this event according to Paul: "that the just requirement of the law might be fulfilled in us, who walk not according to the flesh but according to the Spirit" (Rom. 8:4). Over against the Evangelical claim that Paul made eternal life a free gift in Christ and not a reward for our striving in the Spirit, they set the personal example of Paul himself. "Do you not know that in a race the runners all compete, but only one receives the prize? Run in such a way that you may win it. Athletes exercise self-control in all things; they do it to receive a perishable wreath, but we an imperishable one. So I do not run aimlessly, nor do I box as though beating the air; but I punish my body and enslave it, so that after proclaiming to others I myself should not be disqualified" (1 Cor. 9:24–27). Rejecting the Evangelical reading of Paul that located the inheritance of eternal life in the bestowal of Christ's righteousness and life on us, they reminded the Evangelicals that Paul himself had taught that "all of us must appear before the judgment seat of Christ, so that each may receive recompense for what has been done in the body, whether good or evil" (2 Cor. 5:10). The Evangelicals may delude their followers into thinking that their faith in the mercy of God alone will save them, apart from their works, but Paul taught that God's righteous judgment "will render to every man according to his works" (Rom. 2:6).

For the past four hundred and eighty-two years, these two ways of reading Paul have striven mightily with each other but have basically played to a draw. Neither reading can eliminate and discredit the other, because they both find ample confirmation in the writings of Paul and in the experience of the godly in their respective communities. The hope now is that we can listen more openly to the ways we read the same Paul differently, so that we might come to see the weaknesses in our own readings and the strengths in divergent readings. In this way we might be led from our divergent readings of Paul to the one about whom Paul wrote and so discover our true unity there. "So let no one boast about human leaders. For all things are yours, whether Paul or Apollos or Cephas or the world or life or death or the present or the future—all belong to you, and you belong to Christ, and Christ belongs to God" (1 Cor. 3:21–23).

10

Recent Readings of Paul Relating to Justification by Faith

DAVID E. AUNE

A first reading is something special, like first love. I wish I could come on Saint Paul now by accident and read him for the first time.

Graham Greene, *Monsignor Quixote*

During the course of the twentieth century, New Testament scholars produced a mountain of monographs, articles, and reviews dealing with virtually every aspect of the study of Paul and his letters. In the context of the ongoing debate between Protestants and Catholics on the doctrine of justification, the purpose of this article is not to review the major issues in the study of Paul during the last century, certainly an impossible task. Rather, I intend to survey some, but by no means all, of the more important contributions to the recent study of Paul that have implications for understanding his teaching on justification.

There is one important feature of this review article that is *not* based on any trend in the recent history of Pauline research: the author rejects the assumption that "legalism" (or any of its sanitized synonyms, such as "nomism")[1] should be regarded negatively as it typically has been in much

---

1. Richard N. Longenecker made a careful distinction between legalism and nomism in *Paul: Apostle of Liberty* (New York: Harper & Row, 1964), 78–79. The common element in both terms is

of Protestant New Testament scholarship.[2] By "legalism" I simply mean the religious obligation to obey the laws of God in order to win or maintain divine approbation. Whether the term "legalism" is applied to Judaism ancient or modern or to forms of Christianity ancient or modern, from the standpoint of the history of religions, it is simply one among many ways of conceptualizing the formal relations thought to exist between human beings and the divine.

Few citizens harbor negative attitudes toward the constitutional law governing the nations within which they live. The halakah of the Mishnah, however, is nothing more nor less than a comprehensive system of law formulated by jurists over two centuries and intended to serve as the constitution of the Jewish people. The casuistic formulation of the Mishnah (i.e., using specific cases as the basis for developing general legal principles) is an appropriate form for codifying law in rabbinic jurisprudence.[3] Philip Alexander observes:

> All seem tacitly to regard it as axiomatic that a religion of works-righteousness is inferior to a religion of grace. Weber has accused Judaism of legalistic works-righteousness. They set out to defend it against this charge, but nowhere do any of them radically question the premise that there is something wrong with a religion of works-righteousness.[4]

Many years earlier, George Foote Moore made an analogous observation:

> The prejudice of many writers on Judaism against the very idea of good works and their reward, and of merit acquired with God through them, is a Protestant inheritance from Luther's controversy with Catholic doctrine, and further back from Paul's contention that there is no salvation in Judaism, for "by the

---

"the control of life in conformity to a rule or standard," which is his definition of "nomism." A secondary meaning is "a formal arrangement of the external aspects of life in order to gain righteousness and/or to appear righteous," which is how he defines "legalism." The problem with this distinction is that Longenecker implicitly regards "legalism" as pejorative (he later refers to it as an "egocentric piety," 82), while "nomism" is a neutral or even a positive notion, and he regards it as characteristic of pre-70 CE Pharisaism (84). Ernst Käsemann used the phrase "Jewish nomism" as a negative reality against which Paul fought; see "Justification and Salvation History," in Käsemann, *Perspectives on Paul* (Philadelphia: Fortress, 1971), 72.

2. Simon Gathercole calls attention to the problems involved in an indiscriminate use of the term "legalism" in *Where Is Boasting? Early Jewish Soteriology and Paul's Response in Romans 1–5* (Grand Rapids: Eerdmans, 2002), 29–33.

3. Philip S. Alexander, "Torah and Salvation in Tannaitic Literature," in *Justification and Variegated Nomism*, vol. 1, *The Complexities of Second Temple Judaism*, ed. D. A. Carson, Peter T. O'Brien, and Mark A. Seifrid (Tübingen: Mohr Siebeck; Grand Rapids: Baker Academic, 2001), 261–301, esp. 279–83.

4. Alexander, "Torah and Salvation," 272.

works of the law shall no flesh be justified in his sight." Paul's assertion is the corollary of his first proposition, that the one universal and indispensable condition of salvation is faith in the Lord Jesus Christ.[5]

Historical criticism, the basic method of New Testament scholarship, is inimical to the valorization of one religious system over another when fortified by the presuppositions of cultural relativism. From the perspective of this form of historical criticism, for example, Luther's understanding of Christian soteriology is neither superior nor inferior to that of Trent—it is just *different*.[6]

At the beginning of the twentieth century the agenda for most of the major issues in Pauline studies had been determined largely by the trends of scholarship in the late nineteenth century. The major issues in Pauline study then were primarily historical, though each issue had clear theological implications. There were six important historical questions,[7] all of which have important implications for understanding Pauline thought:

1. What was Paul's relation to Jesus, that is, is Jesus or Paul the real founder of Christianity?
2. How did Paul fit within what is known of first-century Judaism?
3. What was Paul's relationship to Hellenistic culture, particularly Hellenistic religions?
4. What was the nature and meaning of Paul's "conversion"?
5. What can be known about Paul's early ministry and his place in the early church, particularly the Christian communities in Jerusalem and Antioch?
6. Which of Paul's letters are authentic and which are not?

5. G. F. Moore, *Judaism in the First Centuries of the Christian Era: The Age of the Tannaim*, 3 vols. (Cambridge, MA: Harvard University Press, 1927–1930), 2:93–94.

6. As part of a critique of the New Perspective, Donald Hagner declares: "In its best theology, Judaism *is* a religion of grace. Often, however, its gracious foundations are tacitly assumed and often the law takes a place of overwhelming priority. It is not surprising if a religion whose heart lies in praxis rather than theory (theology), a religion dominated by nomism, where the covenant is more presupposed than articulated, inadvertently produces followers who fall into a legalistic mode of existence." This is what Hagner further characterizes as "a natural human tendency toward legalism." See Donald A. Hagner, "Paul and Judaism: Testing the New Perspective," in *Revisiting Paul's Doctrine of Justification: A Challenge to the New Perspective*, ed. Peter Stuhlmacher (Downers Grove, IL: InterVarsity, 2001), 75–105, esp. 87–88. This is clearly a theological rather than a historical assessment in view of the valorization of grace over legalism. Similarly, Thomas R. Schreiner observes, "If some Jews had fallen into legalism in Paul's day, such an error must be ascribed not to the Old Testament itself but to a misunderstanding of the Old Testament" (*Paul, Apostle of God's Glory in Christ* [Downers Grove, IL: InterVarsity; Leicester: Apollos, 2001], 118). Pushing the view of Hagner even further is Bruce Chilton, who maintains that "Legalism is a travesty of Jewish religion" (*The Targum of Isaiah* [Edinburgh: T & T Clark, 1999], xxvii).

7. Victor Paul Furnish, "Putting Paul in His Place," *JBL* 113 (1994): 8.

The specifically theological questions that were topical during the early part of the twentieth century include the following:

1. To what extent was Paul influenced by eschatology or apocalyptic?
2. What constitutes the center of Pauline thought?
3. What is Paul's view of the law?

This last issue, in part because of close connection with Paul's teaching on justification by faith, has been the subject of intense debate since the last quarter of the twentieth century.

The Hellenistic Paul or the Jewish Paul?

During the course of the last century it became increasing clear that the stark alternative posed between Paul the Diaspora or Hellenistic Jew and Paul the Palestinian or Rabbinic Jew led only to an impasse, with impassioned representatives of each position arguing themselves to a standstill on the question. A breakthrough became possible only when it was recognized that Palestinian Judaism was more influenced by Hellenism, to one extent or another, than previously thought,[8] making it clear that the sharp religious and cultural dichotomy between Diaspora or Hellenistic Judaism and Palestinian Judaism, a model dominating scholarly discussion through the 1960s, was an ideal construction.[9]

For many Jewish and some Christian scholars, who have tended to compare Paul with fourth-century Rabbinic Judaism, Paul's critique of the Torah is unintelligible.[10] Some Jewish scholars have therefore proposed that Paul's misunderstanding of the role of the Torah in Judaism was due to his origins as a Hellenistic Diaspora Jew or to the influence of apocalypticism.[11] As

8. The classic work on this subject is by Martin Hengel, *Judaism and Hellenism: Studies in Their Encounter in Palestine during the Early Hellenistic Period*, 2 vols. (Philadelphia: Fortress, 1974); idem, *Jews, Greeks, and Barbarians: Aspects of the Hellenization of Judaism in the Pre-Christian Period* (Philadelphia: Fortress, 1980); idem, *The "Hellenization" of Judaea in the First Century after Christ* (London: SCM, 1990).

9. It is not my intention to deny the utility of the concepts of "Hellenistic Judaism" and "Palestinian Judaism," but simply to argue that these should not be regarded as hermetically sealed from each other.

10. Claude G. Montefiore, "Rabbinic Judaism and the Epistles of St. Paul," *JQR* 13 (1900–1901): 161–217, at 167; Moore, *Judaism*, 3:151; H. J. Schoeps, *Paul: The Theology of the Apostle in the Light of Jewish Religious History*, trans. Harold Knight (Philadelphia: Westminster, 1961), 193–200, 213–18.

11. Joseph Klausner, *From Jesus to Paul* (London: Allen & Unwin, 1942), 450–66; Schoeps, *Paul*, 260–61; Claude G. Montefiore, *Judaism and St. Paul: Two Essays* (London: Max Goschen, 1914), 92–95.

we shall see, one of the achievements of the New Perspective on Paul is its insistence that descriptions of Judaism be based on Jewish texts and not dominated by what Paul has to say about Judaism.

Toward the end of the nineteenth century, early Judaism was widely denigrated among Protestant scholars as a decadent, legalistic, and external religion, antithetical to the enlightened teachings of Jesus and Paul (despite the fact that both were Jews rooted in forms of Judaism), that is, the antithesis of Christianity. The ideological basis for this view was in part provided earlier in the nineteenth century by F. C. Baur, who labeled Judaism a particularistic and legalistic religion and simply a preliminary stage on the road to the development of the universalistic features of Christianity. The scholar who has the dubious honor of providing an influential caricature of Judaism as the antithesis of Christianity was Ferdinand Wilhelm Weber (1836–1879).[12] Using popular negative stereotypes of Judaism as a template for a selective examination of rabbinic literature, Weber produced a unified synthesis of basic Jewish theology that would influence biblical interpretation for generations. Some of the more prominent scholars dependent on Weber's caricature included Emil Schürer, Wilhelm Bousset, Henry St. John Thackeray, and R. H. Charles, to name just a few. Weber's caricature of Judaism was castigated for its inaccuracies and exaggerations, first by Reform Jewish scholar Claude G. Montefiore (1858–1938),[13] and twenty years later by the liberal Christian (Presbyterian) scholar of Judaism, George Foote Moore (1851–1931).[14] Moore himself had erred by arguing for the existence of a relatively unified "normative" Judaism (i.e., Mishnaic Judaism), denigrating the Jewish apocalypses as "extraneous books" contributing nothing to a knowledge of ancient Jewish beliefs.[15] Earlier in the century Montefiore had actually referred to Judaism in the plural when he observed that "several Judaisms, all more or less fluid and growing, existed in the first century."[16] Wilhelm Bousset, dependent on Weber, nevertheless

---

12. Ferdinand W. Weber's first edition of one of his two infamous presentations of Judaism appeared the year following his death: "System der altsynagogalen palästinischen Theologie: Aus Targum, Midrasch und Talmud," ed. by Franz Delitzsch and Georg Schnedermann (Leipzig: Dörffling & Franke, 1880). The second edition of this work, reedited by Delitzsch and Schnedermann, was retitled Jüdische Theologie auf Grund des Talmud und verwandter Schriften, gemeinfasslich dargestellt, 2. verbesserte Auflage (Leipzig: Dörffling & Franke, 1897). A second posthumously published work of Weber, Die Lehren des Talmud, quellenmässig, systematisch und gemeinverständlich dargestellt (Leipzig: Dörffling & Franke, 1886), was also edited by Delitzsch and Schnedermann.

13. Montefiore, "Rabbinic Judaism and the Epistles of Paul," 161–217.

14. George Foote Moore, "Christian Writers on Judaism," HTR 14 (1921): 197–254.

15. Moore, Judaism, 1:126–27.

16. Montefiore, Judaism and St. Paul, 5.

insisted that Jewish apocalypses were a vitally important source for under-standing first-century Judaism and relied on them to the exclusion of the later Tannaitic literature.[17]

During the late nineteenth century and much of the twentieth, schol-ars (largely Protestant) who insisted that Paul must be understood in the context of the Judaism of his day often assumed either that the teachings of Paul stood in contrast to the teachings of Judaism, or they played an enlightened Diaspora Judaism off against Palestinian Judaism, arguing that only the former was the appropriate context for understanding Pauline thought. Though William Wrede was part of the German history-of-religions school (centered at the University of Göttingen), he nevertheless insisted that Paul's thought was incomprehensible unless understood in the context of "late Jewish theology."[18] For Wrede, despite the fact that Paul was born in Tarsus, he was insulated from Hellenism within the local Jew-ish community, and as a disciple of Rabbi Gamaliel, "his culture was the culture of the rabbis."[19] Wrede, rather than contrasting the thought of Paul with that of the rabbis, regarded his Jewish cultural context in a positive light, as would Albert Schweitzer and W. D. Davies in their influential discussions of Pauline thought. More recently, some have recognized the problematic character of an either/or approach to interpreting Paul against a Hellenistic or a Jewish background, and have sought to transcend these antithetical alternatives.[20]

During the first quarter of the twentieth century members of the German history-of-religions school were the strongest advocates of a Hellenistic Paul.[21] The important scholars in this group included Wilhelm Bousset, Albert Eichhorn, Hermann Gunkel, Wilhelm Heitmüller, Rudolf Otto, Alfred Rahlfs, Ernst Troeltsch, Johannes Weiss, and William Wrede. Ru-dolf Bultmann, influenced by this school in his formative years, argued that Hellenistic Christianity constituted the decisive influence on Paul's

17. Wilhelm Bousset, *Die Religion des Judentums im hellenistischen Zeitalter*, ed. H. Gressmann, 3rd ed. (Tübingen: Mohr Siebeck, 1926). Without exception, the Jewish apocalypses were preserved by Christians rather than Jews, one indication of the general Jewish rejection of apocalypticism after the end of the second century CE.

18. William Wrede, *Über Aufgabe und Methode der sogennanten Neutestamentlichen Theologie* (Göt-tingen: Vandenhoeck and Ruprecht, 1897), 76–77; idem, *Paulus*, 2nd ed. (Tübingen: Mohr Siebeck, 1907), 5–7.

19. Wrede, *Paulus*, 7.

20. A clear example of this trend is Troels Engberg-Pederson, ed., *Paul Beyond the Judaism/Hellenism Divide* (Louisville: Westminster John Knox, 2001).

21. Gerd Lüdemann and Martin Schröder, *Die Religionsgeschichtliche Schule in Göttingen: Eine Do-kumentation* (Göttingen: Vandenhoeck & Ruprecht, 1987).

thought.[22] Richard Reitzenstein, a classical philologist who focused his later interest in Gnosticism, argued that Pauline "mysticism" (more recently characterized by the less burdened term "participationism" by E. P. Sanders)[23] was indebted to Hellenistic mysticism, and that the Pauline conceptions of the Lord's Supper and of dying and rising with Christ in baptism had antecedents in the Hellenistic mystery religions.[24] These views were widely influential in subsequent Pauline scholarship. Hans Windisch (1881–1935) considered it indisputable that Pauline religion was a type of mystery religion.[25] Similarly, Kirsopp Lake argued that Christianity became "sacramental" (i.e., a mystery religion) when it moved out of Judaism into a Hellenistic environment, so that baptism for Paul was understood as a "mystery" or "sacrament" that works *ex opere operato*.[26]

A conservative response was inevitable, but this was based not on a positive evaluation of the early Judaism of which Paul was part, but on the positive influence of the Septuagint. Several scholars argued that Pauline theology was entirely explicable under the influence of the Septuagint, and that the hypothesis of any pagan Hellenistic influence on Paul was both unnecessary and inappropriate.[27] While H. A. A. Kennedy and Adolf Deissmann argued that Paul's theology was primarily indebted to the Septuagint,[28] Arthur Darby Nock maintained more broadly that all significant features of Hellenistic Christianity can be traced back to Judaism, making the hypothetical influence of the mystery religions

22. Rudolf Bultmann, *Theology of the New Testament*, trans. Kendrick Grobel, 2 vols. (New York: Scribner, 1951–1955), 1:63. For a similar earlier discussion, see Wilhelm Heitmüller, *Taufe und Abendmahl bei Paulus: Darstellung und religionsgeschichtliche Beleuchtung* (Göttingen: Vandenhoeck & Ruprecht, 1903).

23. E. P. Sanders, *Paul and Palestinian Judaism: A Comparison of Patterns of Religion* (Philadelphia: Fortress, 1977), 440.

24. Richard Reitzenstein, *Die hellenistischen Mysterienreligionen nach ihren Grundgedanken und Wirkungen* (Leipzig: B. G. Teubner, 1927), 417–25 (his entire chapter on Paul [333–93] is still worth reading); ET, *Hellenistic Mystery-Religions: Their Basic Ideas and Significance*, trans. John E. Steely (Pittsburgh: Pickwick Press, 1978), 533–43 (the chapter on Paul occupies pp. 426–500).

25. Hans Windisch, *Paulus und das Judentum* (Stuttgart: Kohlhammer, 1935), 38.

26. Kirsopp Lake, *The Earlier Epistles of Paul: Their Motive and Origin* (London: Rivingtons, 1911), 385.

27. Jonathan Z. Smith, *Drudgery Divine: On the Comparison of Early Christianities and the Religions of Late Antiquity* (Chicago: University of Chicago Press, 1990), 62–84. This approach is alive and well, as exemplified in Larry W. Hurtado, *Lord Jesus Christ: Devotion to Jesus in Earliest Christianity* (Grand Rapids: Eerdmans, 2003), 79–153, where he focuses on the theme of the worship of Jesus in early Pauline Christianity. Hurtado not only refuses to countenance any Hellenistic influence on Paul (e.g., 103, 124), but also implicitly rejects the category of Hellenistic Judaism.

28. H. A. A. Kennedy, *St. Paul and the Mystery-Religions* (London and New York: Hodder & Stoughton, 1913); Adolf Deissmann, *Paul: A Study in Social and Religious History* (German 1912; 2nd [German] ed., revised and enlarged, 1927; New York: Harper & Row, 1957), 99–105.

unnecessary.[29] More recently, Günter Wagner and A. J. M. Wedderburn have produced detailed refutations of the history-of-religions proposal that the Pauline doctrine of baptism was influenced by the mystery religions.[30] In current scholarship, the history-of-religions model of the "dying and rising gods" of the mystery religions, thought so influential on Paul's view of Christian baptism, is widely thought to be "a product of modern imagination," based on an *interpretatio Christiana*.[31]

Since the middle of the twentieth century, and chastised by the horrors of the Holocaust, Protestant New Testament scholars began to understand Paul's Judaism in a more positive light. While relatively positive evaluations of Judaism occasionally surfaced early in the twentieth century, for example in the work of William Wrede and Albert Schweitzer, they were exceptions to the rule. In 1948 W. D. Davies published *Paul and Rabbinic Judaism: Some Rabbinic Elements in Pauline Theology*.[32] This was a revised version of a dissertation supervised by C. H. Dodd and David Daube at Cambridge University. This book, with its positive assessment of the Judaism of Paul, influenced a generation of Pauline scholars and signaled a renewed effort to read Paul and indeed the rest of the New Testament in the context of Judaism. This program was encouraged by the discovery and gradual publication of the Dead Sea Scrolls, which provided a treasure trove of Jewish texts originating in the first century BCE through the first century CE. A negative view of Judaism persisted among many New Testament scholars, however, until E. P. Sanders published *Paul and Palestinian Judaism* in 1977, which in its turn became a major influence on the next generation of scholars. Picking up on the earlier objections of such scholars of Judaism as Claude Montefiore and George Foote Moore, Sanders leveled a devastating critique of the negative attitudes toward Judaism that had persisted in the academy. The last quarter of the twentieth century saw a flood of publications on Paul, most of them abandoning the older

29. A. D. Nock, *Early Gentile Christianity and Its Hellenistic Background* (New York: Harper & Row, 1964). This book contains three essays: two originally appeared in 1928 ("Early Gentile Christianity and Its Hellenistic Background" and "A Note on the Resurrection"), while the third was originally published in 1952 ("Hellenistic Mysteries and Christian Sacraments").

30. G. Wagner, *Die religionsgeschichtliche Problem von Römer 6, 1–11* (Zürich: Zwingli, 1962); translated as *Pauline Baptism and the Pagan Mysteries: The Problem of the Pauline Doctrine of Baptism in Romans VI. 1–11 in Light of Its Religion-Historical "Parallels"* (London: Oliver & Boyd, 1967); A. J. M. Wedderburn, *Baptism and Resurrection: Studies in Pauline Theology against Its Graeco-Roman Background*, WUNT 2.44 (Tübingen: Mohr Siebeck, 1987).

31. Smith, *Drudgery Divine*, 100–101, quoting K. Prümm, "Mystery," in *Sacramentum Verbi: An Encyclopedia of Biblical Theology*, ed. J. B. Bauer, 3 vols. (New York: Herder & Herder, 1970), 2:606.

32. W. D. Davies, *Paul and Rabbinic Judaism: Some Rabbinic Elements in Pauline Theology* (London: SPCK, 1948); a revised edition was published by the same press in 1955.

stereotype of Judaism. The so-called Third Quest of the Historical Jesus made its appearance during the same period; it, too, is characterized by taking the Judaism of Jesus positively and seriously.[33]

Paul's Damascus Experience and Justification by Faith

Throughout the twentieth century Paul's Damascus experience continued to play a central role in shaping the character of his theology in the view of many scholars.[34] Coherent narratives of Paul's Damascus experience are found in three parallel, stylized accounts in Acts, though naturally their historicity has been questioned (9:1–19; 22:4–16; 26:9–19). More important than these secondary sources are Paul's own fragmentary apparent allusions to his Damascus experience, of which the more significant and most widely accepted are Galatians 1:11–17; 1 Corinthians 9:1, 15:1–9; and Philippians 3:5–14. In addition, there are a number of other fragmentary references that a minority of scholars have argued are autobiographical reflections of Paul's Damascus experience (Rom. 10:3–4; 1 Cor. 9:16–17; 2 Cor. 3:4–4:6; 12:1–9), together with a few pertinent secondary references in the later pseudo-Pauline letters (Col. 1:25–27; Eph. 3:1–13).

First, it is important to summarize the major views regarding Paul's Damascus experience, understood either as a "conversion" or a "prophetic call." Then we will turn to a discussion of the extent to which Paul's mission and gospel can be traced back to his Damascus Road vision. The minimalist position, that Paul understood his Damascus experience as a commission to evangelize the Gentiles, is widely accepted. This view is often amplified by suggesting that Paul recognized the messianic status of the crucified Jesus (the christological significance of Paul's conversion) and/or that salvation was available through Christ rather than through the law (the soteriological significance of Paul's Damascus experience), that the law is no longer a valid means to salvation (based primarily on Phil. 3:5–14), often understood to imply that justification is through faith in Christ rather than by the works of the law. Finally, several scholars have gone to the extreme of attributing most, if not all, of Paul's theological insights and program to his conversion experience.

33. Ben Witherington III, *The Jesus Quest: The Third Search for the Jew of Nazareth*, 2nd ed. (Downers Grove, IL: InterVarsity, 1997).

34. Peter Stuhlmacher, *Versöhnung, Gesetz und Gerechtigkeit: Aufsätze zur biblischen Theologie* (Göttingen: Vandenhoeck & Ruprecht, 1981), 172–73.

Conversion or Calling?

While it is certain that Paul's Damascus Road vision produced a great change in his life, during the last forty years there has been a debate about whether this change should be understood as a "conversion," a "calling," or something else. Earlier psychological studies of conversion (such as the 1902 study of William James) maintained that preconversion feelings of self-doubt, unworthiness, sin, and guilt could be overcome by the psychological crisis of conversion.[35] This accords with the traditional Lutheran conception of Paul's conversion, reflected in this description, formulated early in the twentieth century by Johannes Weiss:

> Moreover, the decisive vision itself can only be understood as the final outcome of an inner crisis; it is an explosion, the result of a mighty influence which had left its impression on his troubled heart, the proof of a struggle which had previously been waged within his soul.[36]

Against this view, Krister Stendahl argued that Paul did not experience a conversion followed by a call to apostleship, but rather a prophetic call to work among the Gentiles.[37] The term "conversion" is inappropriate, since no change in religions was involved. Judaism and Christianity were not distinguished as separate religions until late in the first century CE at the earliest.[38] Moreover, Paul regarded himself throughout his life as a Jew, much as Martin Luther continued to regard himself as a Catholic. Karl Olav Sandnes agrees with Stendahl in arguing that the Pauline "conversion" texts are modeled on the literary convention of the prophetic call,[39] a view shared by Thomas Tobin and J. D. G. Dunn, among others.[40] While many, like Jerome Murphy-O'Connor, John Gager, and Mark Seifrid, maintain

35. William James, *Varieties of Religious Experience* (New York: Longmans, Green, 1902).

36. Johannes Weiss, *Earliest Christianity: A History of Period A.D. 30–150*, trans. F. C. Grant, 2 vols. (New York: Harper & Row, 1959), 2:190.

37. Krister Stendahl, "Paul among Jews and Gentiles," in *Paul among Jews and Gentiles* (Philadelphia: Fortress Press, 1976), 7–23; idem, "Paul and the Introspective Conscience of the West," in *Paul among Jews and Gentiles*, 84–85.

38. Daniel Boyarin, *Dying for God: Martyrdom and the Making of Judaism and Christianity* (Stanford, CA: Stanford University Press, 1999); idem, *Borderlines: The Partition of Judaeo-Christianity* (Philadelphia: University of Pennsylvania Press, 2004).

39. Karl Olav Sandnes, *Paul—One of the Prophets? A Contribution to the Apostle's Self-Understanding*, WUNT 2nd series 43 (Tübingen: Mohr Siebeck, 1991), 48–73.

40. Thomas H. Tobin, S.J., *The Spirituality of Paul*, MBS 12 (Wilmington, DE: Michael Glazier, 1987), 43–59; J. D. G. Dunn, "The Theology of Galatians," in *Pauline Theology*, vol. 1, *Thessalonians, Philippians, Galatians, Philemon*, ed. Jouette M. Bassler (Minneapolis: Fortress, 1991), 145; idem, *Jesus, Paul, and the Law: Studies in Mark and Galatians* (Louisville: Westminster John Knox, 1990), 89–107.

that "conversion" is a perfectly accurate description of what happened to Paul,[41] others like Helmut Koester, following Stendahl, argue that the term "conversion" can obscure Paul's own understanding of his vision, which he construed as a call rather than a conversion.[42] Alan Segal, on the other hand, essentially combines both perspectives when he observes that "Paul's experience can be described as a conversion, though he himself used the vocabulary of transformation and prophetic calling to describe it."[43] While Segal recognizes that the psychological term "conversion" is a modern category, after surveying the phenomenon of conversion in the social sciences, he nevertheless argues that it is appropriate.[44] Beverly Gaventa, in her study of conversion in the New Testament, presents a model of three categories of personal change based on social scientific studies: (1) alternation (development from previous behavior), (2) conversion (rejection of past affiliations for a new commitment and identity), and (3) transformation (a cognitive shift reassessing present and past).[45] Focusing on Galatians 1:11–17 and Philippians 3:2–11 (rejecting the possible use of Rom. 7:13–25), Gaventa argues that Paul underwent an abrupt, radical change that she labels a "cognitive shift." She characterizes this change as a transformation, since categorizing it as a "call" is not adequate except insofar as it is a corrective of the category "conversion."[46]

Paul's "Conversion" and His Mission to the Gentiles

The basic inferences of Paul's own autobiographical comments are that he became aware that he was divinely commissioned to proclaim the gospel to the Gentiles (Gal. 1:15–16), and that he had seen the risen Jesus just as had the other apostles (1 Cor. 9:1; 15:8). Paul clearly links his Damascus experience to his mission to proclaim the gospel to the Gentiles in Galatians 1:15–16, a retrospective account written seventeen years after the visionary

41. Jerome Murphy-O'Connor, *Paul: A Critical Life* (Oxford: Oxford University Press, 1996), 71 n. 2; Mark A. Seifrid, *Christ, Our Righteousness: Paul's Theology of Justification* (Downers Grove, IL: InterVarsity; Leicester: Apollos, 2000), 13; John Gager, "Some Notes on Paul's Conversion," *NTS* 27 (1981): 697–704.

42. Helmut Koester, *Introduction to the New Testament*, vol. 2, *History and Literature of Early Christianity* (Berlin and New York: Walter de Gruyter; Philadelphia: Fortress, 1982), 100.

43. Alan F. Segal, *Paul the Convert: The Apostolate and Apostasy of Saul the Pharisee* (New Haven and London: Yale University Press, 1990), 285. Segal is followed by L. J. Lietaert Peerbolte, *Paul the Missionary* (Leuven: Peeters, 2003), 161–62.

44. Segal, *Paul the Convert*, 285–300.

45. Beverly R. Gaventa, *From Darkness to Light: Aspects of Conversion in the New Testament* (Philadelphia: Fortress, 1986), 12.

46. Gaventa, *From Darkness to Light*, 17–46.

experience (allowing ample time for theological reflection on that event): "God, who had set me apart before I was born [alluding to Jeremiah's prophetic call in Jer. 1:5; cf. the similar language of the servant's call in Isa. 49:1, 5–6] and called me through his grace, was pleased to reveal his Son to me, so that I might proclaim him among the Gentiles."[47] Here Paul appears to claim that his experience on the Damascus Road immediately resulted in an awareness of a commission to proclaim the gospel to the Gentiles,[48] and this is indeed how most scholars understand the text.[49] J. D. G. Dunn has frequently discussed the implications of Paul's Damascus Road experience, emphasizing its function as a call to evangelize the Gentiles to the virtual exclusion of its possible christological and soteriological implications.[50] On the other hand, Terence Donaldson has maintained that a radical change in Paul's Christology (e.g., the messianic status of Jesus) and soteriology (e.g., the doctrine of justification by faith) must have preceded his conviction that he was called to the Gentiles.[51] Some, such as Francis Watson, have contended that Paul's initial mission was to the Jews rather than to the Gentiles, and that with the passage of time and the reorientation of the Pauline mission, Paul has read his mission to the Gentiles back into his conversion experience.[52]

Christological Implications: Recognizing Jesus as the Messiah

As mentioned above, one influential view of Paul's Damascus Road experience is that the vision had a christological impact on Paul by revealing

47. In both Jer. 1:5 and Isa. 49:1, 5–6, the call involves a mission to "the nations," i.e., the Gentiles.

48. It is possible to construe the purpose clause, "so that I might proclaim him among the Gentiles," to mean that this implication of his "conversion" became clear to him only later; see Rainer Riesner, *Paul's Early Period: Chronology, Mission Strategy* (Grand Rapids: Eerdmans, 1998), 236.

49. Dunn, *Jesus, Paul, and the Law*, 90–93.

50. J. D. G. Dunn, "Paul's Conversion—A Light to Twentieth Century Disputes," in *Evangelium, Schriftauslegung, Kirche*, ed. Jodstein Ådna, Scott J. Hafemann, and Otfried Hofius (Göttingen: Vandenhoeck & Ruprecht, 1997), 77–93; idem, "'A Light to the Gentiles' or 'The End of the Law'? The Significance of the Damascus Road Christophany for Paul," in *Jesus, Paul, and the Law: Studies in Mark and Galatians* (Louisville: Westminster John Knox, 1990), 89–107 (with an additional note). Seyoon Kim has presented a detailed rebuttal of Dunn's views in *Paul and the New Perspective: Second Thoughts on the Origin of Paul's Gospel* (Grand Rapids: Eerdmans, 2002).

51. Terence L. Donaldson, *Paul and the Gentiles: Remapping the Apostle's Convictional World* (Minneapolis: Fortress, 1997), 250. Donaldson holds that before his Damascus Road experience, Paul attempted to proselytize Gentiles (203–305). Donaldson's proposal is critiqued by Kim, *Paul and the New Perspective*, 35–39.

52. Francis Watson, *Paul, Judaism and the Gentiles: A Sociological Approach*, SNTSMS 56 (Cambridge: Cambridge University Press, 1986), 28–32.

to him that Jesus, whose followers he had been persecuting (1 Cor. 15:9; Gal. 1:13, 23; Phil. 3:6; cf. Acts 8:3; 1 Tim. 1:13), was in fact the Messiah.[53] This is a widely held interpretation and can be exemplified by the words of Arthur Darby Nock:

> Paul's conversion meant for him the recognition that the condemned criminal was in fact the Anointed One of God, living now in the glory of the Spirit world, and that through this Anointed One an imperious call to tell the good tidings had come to him, Paul.[54]

For Jacques Dupont, however, simply recognizing that Jesus was the Messiah is an inadequate basis for understanding Paul's mission to the Gentiles:

> The mission with which Paul knew himself charged for the sake of the Gentiles since the Damascus appearance implied a soteriology wholly suspended on Christ. It could not be adequately explained as arising from belief in the messiahship of Jesus. Its basis could only be located in the faith of the saving, universal and exclusive role of the risen Christ. As Saviour of all men, he must play a benefi-cent role for Gentiles as well as Jews. As a unique Saviour, he takes away all significance from the law as a principle of righteousness and salvation.[55]

Soteriological Implications: Recognizing the Limitations of the Law

Some have argued that Paul's mission to the Gentiles would necessarily entail his reflection on the role of the Torah in such a mission. This, too, is a widely held view, and it is the position maintained by Seyoon Kim:

> But in the Christophany on the road to Damascus Paul received the knowledge of Christ as the end of the law. So he surrendered all his righteousness based on the law to receive God's righteousness which comes from faith in Christ.[56]

Helmut Koester infers that if Paul thought that the time of salvation had begun with the resurrection of Jesus (implied in Paul's vision), and Paul

53. H. G. Wood, "The Conversion of Paul: Its Nature, Antecedents and Consequences," *New Testament Studies* 1 (1954–1955): 276–82; P. H. Menoud, "Revelation and Tradition: The Influence of Paul's Conversion on His Theology," *Interpretation* 7 (1953): 131–41.

54. Arthur Darby Nock, *St. Paul* (New York: Harper & Brothers, 1938), 74.

55. Jacques Dupont, "The Conversion of Paul, and Its Influence on His Understanding of Salva-tion by Faith," in *Apostolic History and the Gospel: Biblical and Historical Essays Presented to F. F. Bruce on His 60th Birthday*, edited by W. Ward Gasque and Ralph P. Martin (Exeter: Paternoster, 1970), 176–94, at 193.

56. Seyoon Kim, *The Origin of Paul's Gospel* (Grand Rapids: Eerdmans, 1981), 4.

himself was called to proclaim the gospel to the Gentiles, then the period of the law had come to an end.[57] However, there is little evidence supporting the existence in the first century CE of the notion that the arrival of the messianic age or the age to come implied the cessation of the Torah,[58] yet some have read Romans 10:4 ("Christ is the end of the law") in support of such a view. Jerome Murphy-O'Connor, a scholar with a very different orientation from that of Kim, combined the christological with the soteriological interpretation by maintaining that Paul's experience revealed to him that Jesus was the Messiah and that Jesus' attitude toward the law must also be correct, that is, the law was *not* the definitive expression of God's will.[59] Some scholars have supposed that pre-Pauline Hellenistic Christians had already rejected the Torah as a means of salvation,[60] and that Paul was persecuting them because they were Jews who had turned their backs on the law (Acts 21:20–21 provides a close analogy).[61]

Another variation on the soteriological approach to Paul's Damascus experience, also widely held, understands justification by faith as the earliest center of Pauline theology rather than as a doctrine developed later in the heat of polemic. Rudolf Bultmann, for example, argued that Paul's conversion involved neither repentance nor an emancipating enlightenment, but rather "obedient submission to the judgment of God, made known in the cross of Christ, upon all human accomplishment and boasting. It is as such that his conversion is reflected in his theology."[62] "Human accomplishment and boasting" is an existential understanding of the widespread notion that Judaism was a legalistic religion of works-righteousness. The theological content of Paul's conversion experience, according to Hans Conzelmann, is Paul's commission to preach the gospel to the Gentiles, as well as "the consequence that the law is finished as a way to salvation" (making the Gentile mission possible).[63]

57. Koester, *History and Literature*, 100. According to W. G. Kümmel, *The Theology of the New Testament according to Its Major Witnesses: Jesus–Paul–John* (Nashville: Abingdon, 1973), 131, Paul was convinced by his vision that "the end-time had broken in through God's action in Christ."

58. W. D. Davies, *Torah in the Messianic Age and/or the Age to Come*, SBLMS 7 (Philadelphia: Society of Biblical Literature, 1952); Peter Schäfer, "Die Torah der messianischen Zeit," ZNW 65 (1974): 27–42.

59. Murphy-O'Connor, *Paul*, 78–79.

60. Bultmann, *Theology of the New Testament*, 1.54, 108; Hans Conzelmann, *An Outline of the Theology of the New Testament*, trans. John Bowden (New York: Harper & Row, 1969), 163–64; Christian Dietzfelbinger, *Die Berufung des Paulus als Ursprung seiner Theologie*, WMANT 58 (Neukirchen-Vluyn: Neukirchener Verlag, 1985), 23, 144.

61. Dupont, "Conversion of Paul," 185.

62. Bultmann, *Theology of the New Testament*, 1:188.

63. Conzelmann, *An Outline of the Theology of the New Testament*, 162–64.

Origin of Paul's Theology?

During the latter part of the nineteenth century, German Protestant scholars like Carl Holsten, followed by H. J. Holtzmann, frequently argued that the fundamentals of Paul's theology arose from his conversion experience,[64] a view more recently revived by Seyoon Kim and Christian Dietzfelbinger.[65] Kim has argued that Paul's Damascus revelation of the exalted Christ as the "image of God" (2 Cor. 4:4) provided the basis for his Adam Christology and his wisdom Christology as well as his transformation soteriology (i.e., the doctrines of justification and reconciliation).[66] For Dietzfelbinger, who knows of Kim's monograph but does not interact with it in any significant way, Jesus had been cursed because of his crucifixion (cf. Deut. 21:23 quoted in Gal. 3:13), motivating Paul the Pharisee not only to object to the proclamation of Jesus as Messiah, but also to persecute followers of Jesus (Gal. 1:13–14; Phil. 3:5).[67] The Damascus event enabled Paul to recognize that Jesus was in fact the Messiah, implying that the Torah that cursed Jesus had itself thereby been rendered null and void.[68] This event was the origin of Paul's theology;[69] the problem of the law dominated his thought from the beginning.[70] Paul's eschatology is based on the conviction that the Torah had come to an end and was no longer valid. A basic criticism by Dunn (that applies to Kim and Dietzfelbinger equally) is that the more significance that is read into the Damascus event (i.e., in terms of a recognition of the end of the law and justification by faith), the less easy it is to understand why the confrontation narrated in Galatians 2 did not take place earlier.[71]

Particularism and Universalism in Pauline Thought

The work of F. C. Baur (1792–1860) exerted enormous influence on nineteenth-century Pauline scholarship, and has continued to influence Pauline studies to this day. Beginning with his conversion, Baur argues, Paul

---

64. Carl Holsten, *Das Evangelium des Paulus*, 2 vols. (Berlin: G. Reimer, 1880–1898); Heinrich Julius Holtzmann, *Lehrbuch der Neutestamentlichen Theologie*, 2 vols. (Freiburg and Leipzig: Mohr Siebeck, 1897), 2:53–65.

65. Kim, *Origin of Paul's Gospel*; Dietzfelbinger, *Berufung des Paulus*.

66. Kim, *Origin of Paul's Gospel*. Dunn has provided a detailed critique of the central thesis of Kim's monograph in *Jesus, Paul, and the Law*, 95–98.

67. Dietzfelbinger, *Berufung des Paulus*, 23.

68. Ibid., 105–6, 118, 125.

69. Ibid., 90, 67–97.

70. Ibid., 115.

71. Dunn, *Jesus, Paul, and the Law*, 98–100.

broke through the barriers of Jewish particularism into the universal idea of Christianity.[72] According to Baur, the important term "righteousness," a conception applicable to both Judaism and Christianity, was for Paul the universal conception of the righteousness of God (*dikaiosynē theou*), which can be realized in two forms: "justification by the works of the law" (*dikaiosynē ex ergōn nomou*), the particularist Jewish form mediated by the law, or "justification by faith" proper (*dikaiosynē ek pisteōs*), a universal notion.[73] Baur thought that the central issue in Pauline theology was Paul's opposition to Jewish exclusivism, in contrast to the traditional Lutheran view, which holds that Paul stood in opposition to Jewish attempts to earn salvation by obeying the law. For many New Testament interpreters in the Reformation tradition (including those influenced by dialectical theology such as Bultmann and Käsemann), Paul was not just attacking Judaism itself, but rather regarded first-century Judaism as a symbol of the universal human error of trying to earn salvation by one's own efforts.

During the last century, a number of scholars (in the spirit of Baur) have understood the contrast in Pauline thought between faith and works and Gentile and Jew as historical symbols for the global issue of cultural particularism versus universalism. One such was W. D. Davies, author of a landmark comparison of the teachings of Paul with those of rabbinic Judaism, significant in part because he was one of the first New Testament scholars to treat Judaism sympathetically rather than as a bête noir. Davies maintained that throughout his life Paul continued to understand himself as a Pharisee, but one who had accepted Jesus as the Messiah.[74] Davies would have agreed with Boyarin's formulation: "Paul lived and died convinced that he was a Jew living out Judaism."[75] For Davies, this entailed the view that Paul thought that he was living in the messianic age preceding the age to come, and shared the rabbinic belief that the Torah would be perfectly observed in the messianic age, and indeed that the Messiah would promulgate a new law that would explain the law of Moses more fully.[76] Paul himself obeyed the law, but he maintained that Gentile followers of Jesus were only obligated to follow the new law of Jesus, not the law of Moses, combining

72. F. C. Baur, *Church History of the First Three Centuries*, 2 vols. (London: Williams and Norgate, 1878–1879), 1.47.

73. F. C. Baur, *Paul the Apostle of Jesus Christ: His Life and Works, His Epistles and Teachings*, 2 vols. (German 1845; London: Williams & Norgate, 1873–1875), 2:134–37.

74. Davies, *Paul and Rabbinic Judaism*, 71.

75. Daniel Boyarin, *A Radical Jew: Paul and the Politics of Identity* (Berkeley: University of California Press, 1994), 2.

76. Davies, *Paul and Rabbinic Judaism*, 72.

the universalist tradition of Judaism with the role of an observant Jew.[77] The religion of the Torah was a nationalistic religion, while Christ was a revelation apart from the law that meant that Gentiles could be followers of Jesus without first becoming Jews.[78] For Paul, accepting the fact that Jesus was the Messiah entailed the universalizing of religion.[79]

Daniel Boyarin, aware of his intellectual kinship with F. C. Baur,[80] emphasizes Paul's universal vision by reading Paul through the hermeneutical key found in Galatians 3:28: "There is no longer Jew or Greek, there is no longer slave or free, there is no longer male and female; for all of you are one in Christ Jesus,"[81] a passage in which Paul signals the abolition of all ethnic, hierarchical, and gender differences. Boyarin argues:

> [Paul] was motivated by a Hellenistic desire for the One, which among other things produced an ideal of universal human essence, beyond difference and hierarchy. This universal humanity, however, was predicated (and still is) on the dualism of flesh and the spirit, such that while the body is particular, marked through practice as Jew or Greek, and through anatomy as male or female, the spirit is universal.[82]

Paul reinterpreted the physical requirements of Torah observance (circumcision, food laws, Sabbath observance) as symbols of universal requirements or possibilities for all humanity, for example, circumcision is a symbol for baptism in the Spirit.[83] This impulse toward universalism informed Paul's allegorical interpretation of the Old Testament. "Works of the law" for Paul primarily involved membership in the historical Israel.[84]

J. D. G. Dunn understands the phrase "covenantal nomism" (coined by E. P. Sanders; see below) as entailing an ethnic identity of the law as coterminous with Israel and served to distinguish Jews (as God's people) from Gentiles.[85] Similarly, the phrase "works of the law" (e.g., Gal. 2:19) refers not to the ethical demands of Torah, but rather to the carrying out of the specific behaviors of the law (e.g., circumcision, food laws, purity laws, Sabbath observance) by members of the covenant community.[86] Paul,

77. Ibid., 73–74.
78. Ibid., 66–67.
79. Ibid., 68.
80. Boyarin, The Radical Jew, 11–12.
81. Ibid., 5–6.
82. Ibid., 7.
83. Ibid., 7.
84. Ibid., 50.
85. Dunn, "Theology of Galatians," 125–46.
86. For critiques of this view, see n. 115 below.

according to Dunn, was concerned about the ways in which covenantal nomism was affecting the Galatians, and he presents three arguments to them: (1) the expression of life within the covenant should be consistent with its beginning (i.e., the original promise given to Abraham was based on faith); (2) "God's promise always had the Gentiles in view from the beginning";[87]and (3) the Galatians misunderstand the purpose of the law. Paul objects to the Jewish understanding of covenantal nomism, because it restricted the covenant to those within the boundaries marked by the law: Jews and proselytes. For Paul the positive function of the law was that it directed Israel until the promise could be fulfilled in Christ. For Judaism, "within the law" = "within the covenant"; for Paul, "within Christ" = "within the covenant" (and thus, "within the law" = "outside the covenant").

The New Perspective on Paul

J. D. G. Dunn coined the phrase "New Perspective on Paul" to describe the interpretation of early Judaism and Paul proposed in the enormously important book by E. P. Sanders, *Paul and Palestinian Judaism: A Comparison of Patterns of Religion* (1977).[88] Sanders, Dunn, and N. T. Wright constitute the triumvirate chiefly responsible for formulating and marketing the New Perspective beginning with the late 1970s, though of course each has his distinctive approach to the issues. However, mention must be made of Krister Stendahl, who has been widely regarded as an important predecessor of the New Perspective.[89] Stendahl argued that it was deceptive to read Paul in the light of Luther's agonized search for relief from a troubled conscience.[90] The Pauline writings themselves, he maintained, reflect a Paul equipped with a rather robust consciousness, since in passages like Philippians 3:6, where Paul speaks of his previous life as a Pharisee, he states, "As to righteousness under the law, [I was] blameless." Here and elsewhere, Stendahl maintains, there is no indication whatsoever that Paul had any difficulty in fulfilling the law or that he had feelings of guilt because of his inability to

87. Dunn, "Theology of Galatians," 132.

88. J. D. G. Dunn, "The New Perspective on Paul," *BJRL* 65 (1983): 95–122, reprinted with an additional eight-page note in Dunn, *Jesus, Paul, and the Law*, 183–214 (further references are to this edition).

89. Several of Stendahl's influential articles have been collectively published with the title *Paul among Jews and Gentiles*.

90. Stendahl, "The Apostle Paul and the Introspective Conscience of the West," *HTR* 56 (1963): 199–215; repr. in idem, *Paul among Jews and Gentiles*, 78–98.

do so.[91] The impossibility of keeping the whole law, in fact, is Paul's decisive argument for a salvation open to both Jews and Gentiles (Rom. 2:17–3:20; Gal. 3:10–12).[92] Bultmann, for whom the Pauline doctrine of justification occupies a central role, is in complete agreement, observing that this view is also foreign to Judaism: "And concerning the issue of being inwardly weighed down through the law, it is quite clear that Paul never speaks of it. In its Lutheran form, this problem is completely foreign to Judaism."[93]

With the appearance of Sanders's *Paul and Palestinian Judaism*, which focused more on Judaism than on Paul,[94] followed by a second work, *Paul, the Law, and the Jewish People* (1983),[95] the theologically laden issues of Paul and Judaism, Paul and the law, and the Pauline doctrine of justification by faith quickly moved to the center of a vigorous debate that has continued unabated to the present.

Sanders attacked the persistent view among Protestants that early Judaism was characterized by a legalistic works-righteousness, the view that salvation is never assured but is attainable only if the final balance of good deeds outweighs the bad.[96] This view of Judaism, argues Sanders, was largely the malevolent invention of nineteenth-century Protestant scholarly imagination, but it achieved almost canonical status through the influential work of such scholars as Emil Schürer, Wilhelm Bousset, Paul Billerbeck, and Rudolf Bultmann. Sanders's rejection of the notion of Jewish legalism was argued earlier by the liberal Protestant scholar George Foote Moore:

91. Stendahl, "The Apostle Paul and the Introspective Conscience of the West," 80; the same position is maintained by Kümmel, *Theology of the New Testament*, 150; Dupont, "Conversion of Paul," 183.

92. Stendahl, "The Apostle Paul and the Introspective Conscience of the West," 80–81.

93. Rudolf Bultmann, "Christus des Gesetzes Ende," in *Glauben und Verstehen: Gesammelte Aufsätze*, 4 vols. (Tübingen: Mohr Siebeck, 1961), 2:34.

94. E. P. Sanders later published a book devoted exclusively to Judaism: *Judaism: Practice and Belief (63 BCE to 66 CE)* (Philadelphia: Trinity Press International, 1992).

95. E. P. Sanders, *Paul, the Law, and the Jewish People* (Minneapolis: Fortress, 1983). A more popular synthesis of Sanders's views on Paul is available in *Paul*, Past Masters (Oxford: Oxford University Press, 1991).

96. If it is appropriate to speak of soteriology at all in ancient Judaism, it was certainly something very different from soteriology in Paul (see Stephen Westerholm, *Perspectives Old and New in Paul: The "Lutheran" Paul and His Critics* [Grand Rapids: Eerdmans, 2004], 295). Judaism had no concept of original sin from which to be saved (Sanders, *Paul and Palestinian Judaism*, 114, 397). Soteriology is what Sanders regards as a convenient category for the essence of Jewish religion or what makes Jewish religion "work" (*Paul and Palestinian Judaism*, 98). In rabbinic literature the final receiving of eternal life is not necessarily called salvation; Moore regards the phrase "a lot in the World to Come" as the closest equivalent to the Christian concept of salvation (*Judaism* 2.94–95). Avemarie prefers the simple term "life" (Friedrich Avemarie, *Tora und Leben: Untersuchungen zur Heilsbedeutung der Tora in der frühen rabbinischen Literatur* [Tübingen: Mohr Siebeck, 1996], 2), while Gathercole uses the term "salvation" in a Jewish context for "the topic of final vindication in the *eschaton*" (*Where Is Boasting?*, 22).

It should be remarked, further, that "a lot in the World to Come," which is the nearest approximation in rabbinic Judaism to the Pauline and Christian idea of salvation, or eternal life, is ultimately assured to every Israelite on the ground of the original election of the people by the free grace of God, prompted not by its merits, collective or individual, but solely by God's love, a love that began with the Fathers.[97]

Sanders approaches the problem of comparing Judaism and Paul by insisting on understanding both in terms of a holistic focus on the overall pattern of religion reflected in the sources. He focused on three corpora of ancient Palestinian Jewish literature generally dated between 200 BCE and 200 CE: the Tannaitic literature (the Mishnah, the Tosephta, and the Tannaitic midrashim), the Dead Sea Scrolls, and the Apocrypha and Pseudepigrapha.[98] Sanders proposed that rabbinic religion be described as "covenantal nomism," that is, an individual Jew's place in the plan of God is established on the basis of the covenant, the central feature of which was that God had made a special covenant with the Patriarchs involving his choice of Israel to be a special people. In the covenant, God required obedience to its provisions while providing a sacrificial means of atonement for transgressions.[99] Obedience to the covenant is nowhere regarded as a burden in Tannaitic literature, which referred rather to "the joy of the law"[100] (though human nature being what it is, some Jews must have regarded the demands of the Torah as onerous), nor does the notion of perfect obedience concern the rabbis.[101] The rabbinic emphasis on obedience finds a correlative in the twin notions of repentance and forgiveness. The central concern of the rabbis was not how a person could earn salvation, but rather how one could best be faithful. Sanders also emphasizes that, for the rabbis, God's grace was not contradictory to human endeavor. Grace and works were never considered alternate roads to salvation. Sanders summarizes his conception of covenantal nomism as follows:

97. Moore, *Judaism*, 2:94–95. Moore's view on this subject was articulated several years earlier in "Christian Writers on Judaism."

98. Since the main corpora of Tannaitic literature were codified *after* 200 CE, the extent to which traditions in these texts date back to the first century CE is exceedingly problematic.

99. Sanders has devoted two articles to this subject: "Patterns of Religion in Paul and Rabbinic Judaism," *HTR* 66 (1973): 455–78, and "The Covenant as a Soteriological Category and the Nature of Salvation in Palestinian and Hellenistic Judaism," in *Jews, Greeks, and Christians: Studies in Honor of W. D. Davies*, ed. Robert Hamerton-Kelly and Robin Scroggs (Leiden: Brill, 1976), 11–44.

100. Solomon Schechter, "The Joy of the Law," in idem, *Aspects of Rabbinic Theology* (London: Macmillan, 1909), 148–69.

101. Alexander, "Torah and Salvation in Tannaitic Literature," 284.

The "pattern" or "structure" of covenantal nomism is this: (1) God has chosen Israel and (2) given the law. The law implies both (3) God's promise to maintain the election and (4) the requirement to obey. (5) God rewards obedience and punishes transgression. (6) The law provides for means of atonement, and atonement results in (7) maintenance or re-establishment of the covenantal relationship. (8) All those who are maintained in the covenant by obedience, atonement and God's mercy belong to the group which will be saved. An important interpretation of the first and last points is that election and ultimately salvation are considered to be by God's mercy rather than human achievement.[102]

One of the conundrums facing modern scholars is why Paul appears to portray Judaism as a religion of salvation based on works and nowhere alludes to Jewish notions of repentance and forgiveness. Sanders's answer is that Paul did not begin with the problem of man's plight and work from there to the solution of salvation in Christ. Rather, he began with the *solution* (salvation is available only "in Christ"), from which he deduced man's *plight* (all other ways to salvation are therefore both ineffective and wrong).[103] What Paul found wrong with Judaism was that it was not Christianity.[104] Paul did not misunderstand the law, nor was he disillusioned by it prior to his conversion; Romans 7 cannot be interpreted autobiographically. Rather, he gained a wholly new perspective through his conversion that led him to regard the law negatively in comparison with Christ.[105] According to Sanders, Paul transformed Jewish covenantal nomism in the following ways: (1) An individual enters the covenant through baptism; (2) membership in the covenant provides salvation; and (3) obedience to a set of commandments—or repentance when these commandments are transgressed—allows the individual to maintain the covenant relationship.[106] Unlike Judaism, however, Paul tended not to give concrete rules for living but regarded Christian behavior as flowing from the Spirit and not from commandments.[107] In short, "it is through faith in Christ, not by accepting the law, that one enters the people of God."[108] Sanders concludes that the religious pattern in Paul's thought is

102. Sanders, *Paul and Palestinian Judaism*, 422.

103. W. Gutbrod seems to agree, when he says: "Paul's negation of the Law derives from his affirmation of what has taken place in Jesus Christ, not from rational criticism or missionary tactics" ("*Nomos, ktl*," *TDNT* 4:1075).

104. Sanders, *Paul and Palestinian Judaism*, 552.

105. Sanders, *Paul, the Law, and the Jewish People*, 70–72.

106. Sanders, *Paul and Palestinian Judaism*, 513–14.

107. Sanders, *Paul, the Law, and the Jewish People*, 208.

108. Ibid., 207.

markedly different from anything reflected in Palestinian Jewish literature. What then is the source of Paul's distinctive pattern of religion? Since Sanders maintains that Paul's thought was not dependent on any one scheme of thought, he cautiously ascribes a degree of uniqueness to Paul, whose pattern of religious thought was determined by the fundamental conviction that Jesus is Lord and that in him God has provided salvation for all who believe.

J. D. G. Dunn, a second important representative of the New Perspective, agreed with Sanders that the conception of Judaism as a system whereby salvation was earned through the merit of good works, a coldly legalistic religion with no room for the free forgiveness and grace of God, was a gross caricature.[109] Dunn argues that Sanders was impressed with the difference between Paul and contemporary Judaism but failed to explore the extent to which Paul's theology could be explained in relation to Judaism's "covenantal nomism."[110] Sanders argued that Paul had jumped from one system to another, that is, that he broke with the law for the simple reason that it was not Christ. According to Dunn:

> The Lutheran Paul has been replaced by an idiosyncratic Paul who in arbitrary and irrational manner turns his face against the glory and greatness of Judaism's covenant theology and abandons Judaism simply because it is not Christianity.[111]

Dunn focused on the phrase "the works of the law" (*erga nomou*) in Galatians 2:16 (the phrase is used once in Romans [3:20] and repeatedly in Galatians [2:16; 3:2, 5, 10]), arguing that it referred not to the ethical commands of the law but to the social identification markers of Judaism, that is, such ritual practices as circumcision, kosher food regulations, and Sabbath observance.[112] Neither Paul nor his Judaizing competitors understood "works of the law" to mean works that earn God's favor or "good works" in general.

---

109. Dunn, "The New Perspective on Paul," 185. Dunn's many articles on the subject are collected in J. D. G. Dunn, *The New Perspective on Paul: Collected Essays*, WUNT 185 (Tübingen: Mohr Siebeck, 2005).

110. Dunn, *Jesus, Paul, and the Law*, 186–87.

111. Dunn, "The New Perspective on Paul," 187.

112. Ibid., 188–200. Dunn's views were anticipated 1,600 years earlier by the author of the first Latin commentary on the Pauline letters (late fourth century). This anonymous commentary, attributed to Ambrose during the Middle Ages, was attributed to Ambrosiaster by Erasmus. The author of this commentary based the exposition of justification by faith in Paul on the contrast between Christianity and Judaism, interpreting justification by faith to mean freedom from Jewish ceremonial law. See H. J. Vogel, ed., *Commentaria in XIII Epistulas Paulinas*, 3 vols., CSEL 81 (Vienna: Geroldi, 1966–1969); A. Souter, *The Earliest Latin Commentaries on the Epistles of Saint Paul* (Oxford: Clarendon Press, 1927).

They were simply badges of membership in the Jewish people.[113] For Paul, the covenant was no longer to be identified with such distinctively Jewish observances as circumcision, food laws, and Sabbath observance, but with the more fundamental identity marker of faith in Christ, which corresponded to Abraham's faith.[114]

Dunn has been widely criticized for restricting the meaning of "works of the law" to markers of Jewish identity.[115] Some of his critics (e.g., Douglas Moo) have proposed that "works of the law" rather means "deeds done in obedience to the law of Moses,"[116] implicitly rejecting Dunn's distinction. Dunn's earlier restriction of "works of the law" to mean markers of Jewish identity (Sabbath observance, food laws, circumcision) was subsequently broadened to mean "what the law required *of Israel as God's people*,"[117] that is, "the 'deeds' that the law makes obligatory."[118] Dunn continues to insist that Paul uses "works of the law" only in connection with the relationship between Jews and Gentiles, not in terms of the justification of the individual Jew or Gentile; the phrase refers to that practice of the law that distinguishes "us" from "them," that is, Jews from Gentiles.[119] "Justification by faith," argues Dunn, "is Paul's fundamental objection to the idea that God has limited his saving goodness to a particular people."[120] In a later article, Dunn deals with the phrase *ma'ase hatorah* (works of the law), which occurs in 4QMMT C26–27,[121] comparing the phrase *ma'ase hatorah* in 4QMMT

---

113. Dunn, "The New Perspective on Paul," 194–95. Dunn has discussed the phrase "works of the law" in several articles: "Works of the Law and the Curse of the Law (Gal 3.10–14)," *NTS* 31 (1985): 523–42; "Yet Once More—'The Works of the Law': A Response," *JSNT* 46 (1992): 99–117.

114. Dunn, "The New Perspective on Paul," 197–98.

115. Michael Bachmann, *Sünder oder Übertreter: Studien zur Argumentation in Gal 2.15ff.*, WUNT 59 (Tübingen: Mohr Siebeck, 1992), 91–92; Thomas R. Schreiner, *The Law and Its Fulfillment: A Pauline Theology of Law* (Grand Rapids: Baker Academic, 1993), 51–59; Moisés Silva, "Faith versus Works of the Law in Galatians," in *Justification and Variegated Nomism*, vol. 2: *The Paradoxes of Paul*, ed. D. A. Carson, Peter T. O'Brien, and Mark A. Seifrid (Tübingen: Mohr Siebeck; Grand Rapids: Baker Academic, 2004), 217–48, esp. 221–26.

116. Douglas J. Moo, *The Epistle to the Romans*, NICNT (Grand Rapids: Eerdmans, 1996) 90–99; idem, "'Law,' 'Works of the Law,' and Legalism in Paul," *WTJ* 45 (1983): 73–100, esp. 90–99.

117. James D. G. Dunn, *The Theology of Paul the Apostle* (Grand Rapids: Eerdmans, 1998), 355; italics in original.

118. Dunn, *Theology of Paul the Apostle*, 354–55.

119. James D. G. Dunn and Alan M. Suggate, *The Justice of God: A Fresh Look at the Old Doctrine of Justification by Faith* (Grand Rapids: Eerdmans, 1994), 27. This same position is held by Seifrid, *Christ, Our Righteousness*, 99–105.

120. Dunn and Suggate, *The Justice of God*, 28.

121. James D. G. Dunn, "4QMMT and Galatians," *New Testament Studies* 43 (1997): 147–53, and more recently, idem, "Noch Einmal 'Works of the Law'; the Dialogue Continues," in *Fair Play: Diversity and Conflicts in Early Christianity; Essays in Honour of Heikki Räisänen*, ed. Ismo Dunderberg, Christopher Tuckett, and Kari Syreeni (Leiden: E. J. Brill, 2002), 273–90.

and *erga nomou* (works of the law) in Paul, concluding that "both seem to refer to 'works of the law' understood as defining a boundary which marks out those of faith/faithfulness from others."[122]

The third influential representative of the New Perspective is N. T. Wright (Bishop of Durham, England), whose 1978 article on "The Paul of History and the Apostle of Faith," based on studies carried out in connection with his 1980 Oxford dissertation, reflects a rejection of the traditional Protestant conception of Judaism as a religion of works-righteousness, in full agreement with Sanders and Dunn.[123] Wright argued that real Judaism was based on a clear understanding of grace, with good works functioning primarily as an expression of gratitude that demonstrates faithfulness to the covenant.[124] Pauline interpretation, argues Wright, "has manufactured a false Paul by manufacturing a false Judaism for him to oppose."[125] The central importance of the covenant in Wright's scheme corresponds to similar concerns on the part of both Sanders and Dunn. God entered into a covenant with Israel (intended as a divine tool to free the cosmos from the effects of sin), according to Wright, to undo the sin of Adam and bring the blessings of God to the Gentiles.[126] Israel "recapitulated" the sin of Adam by disobeying the commands of Torah but nonetheless boasted of her special place in the plan of God, regarding the distinctive ritual practices of circumcision, dietary laws, and Sabbath observance as badges of superiority (or boundary markers or signs of Jewish ethnic identity).[127] Israel's violation of the covenant incurred the punishment of exile (cf. Deut. 27–28), and in the view of ancient Jews, Israel remained in exile into the first century (the continuing state of exile represents a critical part of the "story" of Israel that Wright sees as the basic narrative for his projected six-volume theology of the New Testament, *Christian Origins*

122. Dunn, "4QMMT and Galatians," 151.

123. N. T. Wright, "The Paul of History and the Apostle of Faith," *TynBul* 29 (1978): 61–88. Other contributions of Wright in line with the New Perspective on Paul include "Justification: The Biblical Basis and Its Relevance for Contemporary Evangelicalism," in *The Great Acquittal: Justification by Faith and Current Christian Thought*, ed. Gavin Reid (London: Collins, 1980), 13–37; *The Climax of the Covenant: Christ and the Law in Pauline Theology* (Minneapolis: Fortress, 1991); "Romans and the Theology of Paul," in *Pauline Theology*, vol. 3, *Romans*, ed. D. M. Hay and E. E. Johnson (Minneapolis: Fortress, 1992), 30–67; *The New Testament and the People of God* (Minneapolis: Fortress, 1992); *What Saint Paul Really Said: Was Paul of Tarsus the Real Founder of Christianity?* (Grand Rapids: Eerdmans, 1997).

124. Wright, "The Paul of History," 79–80.

125. Ibid., 78.

126. Wright, "Romans and the Theology of Paul," 33; idem, *The New Testament and the People of God*, 265–67.

127. Wright, *The Climax of the Covenant*, 197, 243.

and the Question of God).[128] However, the covenant curse that resulted in the exile of Israel reached its culmination in the representative death of Jesus the Messiah, the means by which the punishment of Israel was finally satisfied.[129] With the resurrection of Jesus, Israel's exile came to an end and her covenant was fulfilled. This fulfillment entailed the redefinition of Israel as the people God determined by grace, not race, or faith and not works (i.e., the "badges of superiority" mentioned above). The Israel destined for salvation is the single family of humankind drawn from all nations and marked by faith.[130]

Wright, like Dunn, defines the "righteousness of God" as his "covenant faithfulness" toward Israel.[131] For Wright, Paul's conception of justification does not represent individual or personal salvation.[132] Rather, justification is the means whereby one is identified as a member of the true people of God. More specifically, "justification" in Paul refers to the final vindication of God's people, not individuals, when God pronounces in their favor, declaring that they belong to the covenant.[133] For Wright, the "righteousness of God" is his covenant faithfulness.[134]

The New Perspective on Paul has had an enormous impact on Pauline studies, a fact made abundantly clear in Stephen Westerholm's silver anniversary review of the publication of Sanders's book in 2004.[135] Predictably, reactions to Sanders's work have ranged from blanket rejection to

128. For a critique and reformulation of Wright's conception of the "Exile narrative," see Brant Pitre, *Jesus, the Tribulation, and the End of the Exile: Restoration Eschatology and the Origin of the Atonement*, WUNT 2. Reihe, 204 (Tübingen: Mohr Siebeck, 2005).

129. Wright, *The Climax of the Covenant*, 141.

130. Ibid., 249–50; Wright, *What Saint Paul Really Said*, 103, 118.

131. Wright, *What Saint Paul Really Said*, 118–33; Dunn holds the same view: "God's righteousness is precisely God's covenant faithfulness, his saving power and love for his people Israel. God's justification is God's recognition of Israel as his people, his verdict in favour of Israel on the grounds of his covenant with Israel" ("The New Perspective on Paul," 190). Westerholm (*Perspectives Old and New on Paul*, 292) argues that while there is no antecedent reason why "God's righteousness should not mean his 'covenant faithfulness,' the fact is that in Paul 'righteousness' does not *mean* 'covenant faithfulness,'" a view also held by Schreiner, *Paul*, 197–99. Seifrid also argues against this equation, since "all 'covenant-keeping' is righteous behavior, but not all righteous behavior is 'covenant-keeping.' It is misleading, therefore, to speak of 'God's righteousness' as his 'covenant faithfulness.'" See Mark A. Seifrid, "Righteous Language in the Hebrew Scriptures and Early Judaism," in Carson, O'Brien, and Seifrid, eds., *Justification and Variegated Nomism*, 1:415–42, at 424. However, Seifrid later appears to give the game away by admitting that "the Qumran writings frequently associate *bryt* with righteousness terminology" (ibid., 434). Part of the problem is that being "in the covenant" can be construed in a number of ways because it is inherently a generative concept.

132. Wright, *What Saint Paul Really Said*, 60, 116.

133. Wright, "Romans and the Theology of Paul," 32–33.

134. Wright, *What Saint Paul Really Said*, 103.

135. Stephen Westerholm, "The 'New Perspective' at Twenty-Five," in Carson, O'Brien, and Seifrid, eds., *Justification and Variegated Nomism*, 2:1–38.

general acceptance to attempts to outdo Sanders with the accusation that the New Perspective has not gone far enough in liberating New Testament scholarship from the vestiges of anti-Semitism and smug supersessionism.[136] A. Andrew Das calls for a "new starting point" or a "newer perspective" on Paul, by which he means that "Paul's critique of the Law as based on works is a consequence of the transition in his thinking from one conception of grace to another."[137] Das bases this perspective on Paul's Damascus Road experience, when it dawned on Paul that Judaism did not offer a viable path to salvation, since the gracious elements in Judaism were never efficacious for salvation apart from the suffering, death, and resurrection of Jesus.[138] He argues this because he thinks that the law did produce salvation according to Second Temple Judaism and did enjoin perfect obedience.[139] Brendan Byrne, S.J., has judged that the New Perspective is essentially negative in terms of theological interpretation, arguing for a post-New Perspective perspective.[140] Given the work of Dunn and Wright under the aegis of the New Perspective, this critique strikes me as wrongheaded.

One incisive critique has been leveled by Philip Alexander, who associates Sanders with a line of interpreters of Tannaitic Judaism who have tended to stress its more "liberal" side, including liberal Protestants and liberal Jews influenced by them, such as George Foote Moore, Claude Montefiore, and Solomon Schechter.[141] Alexander suggests that just as Weber distorted classic Judaism by overemphasizing law, Sanders and his liberal predecessors have overemphasized grace.[142]

One important issue is Sanders's contention that "covenantal nomism" characterized most Palestinian Jewish literature from the second century BCE to the second century CE. Sanders considers 4 *Ezra*, written in the aftermath of the fall of Jerusalem, a striking exception.[143] Sanders also al-

---

136. Neil Elliott, *Liberating Paul: The Justice of God and the Politics of the Apostle* (Maryknoll, NY: Orbis Books, 1994).

137. A. Andrew Das, *Paul and the Jews* (Peabody, MA: Hendrickson, 2003), 13; see also his *Paul, the Law, and the Covenant* (Peabody, MA: Hendrickson, 2001), 268–71.

138. Das, *Paul and the Jews*, 12.

139. Das, *Paul, the Law, and the Covenant*, 7; idem, *Paul and the Jews*, 189. See also Das, "Paul, Judaism and Perfect Obedience," *Concordia Journal* 27 (2001): 234–52.

140. Brendan Byrne, S.J., "Interpreting Romans Theologically in a Post-'New Perspective' Perspective," *HTR* 94 (2001): 227–41.

141. Alexander, "Torah and Salvation in Tannaitic Judaism," 261–301, esp. 271–72.

142. Ibid., 272.

143. Sanders, *Paul and Palestinian Judaism*, 418, describes 4 *Ezra* as "the closest approach to a legalistic works-righteousness which can be found in the Jewish literature of the period." Richard Bauckham extends this judgment to claim that 2 *Enoch* is also characterized by a legalistic works-righteousness, in

lows that Hellenistic Jewish texts, like the *Testament of Abraham*, envision a final judgment on the basis of weighing good and evil works.[144] This, of course, indicates that Sanders does not relentlessly press his "covenantal nomism" model on texts resistant to it. A number of scholars have essentially accepted Sanders's model of covenantal nomism as a useful way for understanding the basic religious features of both Judaism and Paul. Morna Hooker, though recognizing that covenantal nomism does not apply to Paul himself because of his quarrel with the law, observes that there are significant parallels between the covenantal nomism of Judaism and Paulinism.[145] "Just as Palestinian Judaism understood obedience to the Law to be the proper response of Israel to the covenant on Sinai," argues Hooker, "so Paul assumes that there is an appropriate response for Christians who have experienced God's saving activity in Christ," that is, the "law of Christ," which Paul spells out in series of imperatives.[146]

In an early review (1979), the late Tony Saldarini thought that covenantal nomism was not an accurate way of categorizing all pre-70 CE Jewish literature.[147] C. K. Barrett disputes Sanders's conception of covenantal nomism, maintaining that Paul argued against works-righteousness in Galatians and elsewhere.[148] Hans Hübner criticized Sanders for failing to recognize that Paul's attack on legalistic works-righteousness was central to Pauline thought.[149] Jacob Neusner suggested that Sanders's soteriological conception of early Judaism, in terms of "getting in" and "staying in" the covenant, was based on largely Christian and Protestant theological presuppositions.[150]

"Apocalypses," in Carson, O'Brien, and Seifrid, eds., *Justification and Variegated Nomism*, 1:135–87, at 156. Bauckham (174) is rather more positive about covenantal nomism in *4 Ezra* than is Sanders: "But *4 Ezra* does rather importantly illustrate how the basic and very flexible pattern of covenantal nomism could take forms in which the emphasis is overwhelmingly on meriting salvation by works of obedience to the Law, with the result that human achievement takes center-stage and God's grace, *while presupposed* [my emphasis], is effectively marginalized." Comparing *2 Baruch* to *4 Ezra*, Bauckham observes (182): "As we have seen in discussion of *4 Ezra*, the idea of salvation as reward for righteousness need not be alternative to the idea of salvation as God's covenantal grace. It is in his grace that God makes the covenantal promises and lays down the requirement of obedience to the Law as the condition for receiving them."

144. E. P. Sanders, "The Testament of Abraham," in *The Old Testament Pseudepigrapha*, ed. James H. Charlesworth, 2 vols. (Garden City, NY: Doubleday, 1983–1985), 1:877.

145. Morna D. Hooker, "Paul and 'Covenantal Nomism,'" in *Paul and Paulinism: Essays in Honour of C. K. Barrett*, ed. M. D. Hooker and S. G. Wilson (London: SPCK, 1982), 52, esp. 47–56.

146. Hooker, "Paul and 'Covenantal Nomism,'" 48–49.

147. Anthony J. Saldarini, review of E. P. Sanders, *Paul and Rabbinic Judaism*, JBL 98 (1979): 299–303.

148. C. K. Barrett, *Paul: An Introduction to His Thought* (London: Chapman, 1994).

149. Hans Hübner, "Pauli Theologiae Proprium," NTS 26 (1979–1980): 445–73.

150. Jacob Neusner, "The Use of Later Rabbinic Evidence for the Study of Paul," in *Approaches to Ancient Judaism*, ed. W. S. Green (Chico, CA: Scholars Press, 1980), 2.43–63.

Notwithstanding Neusner's criticisms of Sanders's methodology, Neusner has accepted Sanders's understanding of Judaism in terms of "covenantal nomism" as valid.[151]

More recently a comprehensive examination led by a team of scholars dominated by Evangelicals (who, as a whole, have been highly critical of Sanders) investigated the problem of whether or not covenantal nomism should be regarded as an appropriate label for the overarching pattern of religion in Second Temple Judaism. The results were published in two substantial volumes with the title *Justification and Variegated Nomism*.[152] In the conclusion to the first volume, D. A. Carson, one of the editors, determines that covenantal nomism "is too doctrinaire, too unsupported by the sources themselves, too reductionistic, too monopolistic."[153] Dunn has correctly criticized this judgment as "unjustifiably harsh and unduly dismissive."[154] In another, shorter summary of the first volume of *Justification and Variegated Nomism*, dependent on the summary of Carson, Peter O'Brien, another project editor, maintains that (1) covenantal nomism was found in some but not all of the texts from Second Temple Judaism examined (and even where it does fit, he maintains, it doesn't fit very well); (2) the covenantal nomism model is reductionistic as well as misleading; (3) the categories of covenantal nomism are mistaken; and (4) there are difficulties in identifying God's righteousness with his covenantal faithfulness as well as defining human righteousness in terms of being in the covenant.[155] O'Brien has basically put his stamp of approval on the largely negative conclusions of Carson, and somewhat later in his essay criticizes Sanders's analysis of covenant nomism in the literature from Qumran.[156]

151. Jacob Neusner, "Comparing Judaisms," *History of Religions* 18 (1978–1979): 177–91.

152. D. A. Carson, Peter T. O'Brien, and Mark A. Seifrid, eds., *Justification and Variegated Nomism*, vol. 1, *The Complexities of Second Temple Judaism* (Tübingen: Mohr Siebeck; Grand Rapids: Baker Academic, 2001); and D. A. Carson, Peter T. O'Brien, and Mark A. Seifrid, eds., *Justification and Variegated Nomism*, vol. 2: *The Paradoxes of Paul* (Tübingen: Mohr-Siebeck; Grand Rapids: Baker, 2004). In fact, several contributors to the first volume show no particular interest in whether covenantal nomism is an appropriate model for the segments of Second Temple Judaism that they discuss (e.g., Craig Evans, Philip R. Davies, Roland Deines, Mark A. Seifrid). David M. Hay ("Philo of Alexandria," 1:357–79) does not mention the issue of covenantal nomism in his conclusion, but slips in a summary paragraph in the middle of his study that has no obvious organic connection with its context, but in which he observes that it is not very useful to regard Philo as representative of covenantal nomism (370).

153. D. A. Carson, "Summaries and Conclusions," in Carson, O'Brien, and Seifrid, eds., *Justification and Variegated Nomism*, 1:548.

154. James D. G. Dunn, "The New Perspective: Whence, What and Whither?" in *The New Perspective on Paul*, WUNT 185 (Tübingen: Mohr Siebeck, 2005), 57.

155. Peter T. O'Brien, "Was Paul a Covenantal Nomist?" in Carson, O'Brien, and Seifrid, eds., *Justification and Variegated Nomism*, 2:249–96, esp. 252–55.

156. Ibid., 2:256.

A number of contributors to the volumes do not see covenantal nomism in as negative a light as do Carson and O'Brien.[157] According to Seifrid, another project editor, "a number of essays in the previous volume on 'variegated nomism' found the various corpora of Jewish writings fit nicely into the scheme of 'covenantal nomism.'"[158] Seifrid refers specifically to the essays by Falk, Evans, Enns, Bauckham, and Bockmuehl. Bockmuehl's generally positive conclusions following his examination of the question of salvation in 1QS in the first volume of *Justification and Variegated Nomism* were obviously ignored in the summary assessment by both Carson and O'Brien:

> Overall, our findings are not fundamentally incompatible with those reached in E. P. Sanders's famous study of 1977. Qumran manifests an eschatological faith in which salvation and atonement for sins are not humanly earned but divinely granted by predestined election and membership in the life of the observant covenant community.[159]

Daniel Falk, too, in an examination of Jewish psalms and prayers, including some from Qumran, comes to a relatively positive conclusion:

> If the aim [of Sanders's covenantal nomism model] was to define a sort of "lowest common denominator" soteriology that would be recognized by most of the divergent expressions of Judaisms, Sanders's covenantal nomism would serve fairly well, given his generous allowances of flexibility.[160]

To be sure, he is not fully satisfied with the model, for he continues:

> To do so would be akin to grouping apples, oranges and bananas together as "fruit." For comparative purposes, such a harmonizing approach is of limited value. It masks very different conceptions of the problem of sin, the balance of focus on nationalism and individualism, and most significantly the boundaries of the covenant.

Falk is objecting to the high level of abstraction of the covenantal nomism model and in my view clearly expects more than one can rightfully ask any such general model to accomplish. Further, he (and the editors of the project)

157. See the comments of Das, *Paul and the Jews*, 11–12 n. 22.

158. Mark A. Seifrid, "Unrighteousness by Faith: Apostolic Proclamation in Romans 1:18–3:20," in Carson, O'Brien, and Seifrid, eds., *Justification and Variegated Nomism*, 2:144.

159. Markus Bockmuehl, "1QS and Salvation at Qumran," in Carson, O'Brien, and Seifrid, eds., *Justification and Variegated Nomism*, 2:381–414, at 412.

160. Daniel Falk, "Psalms and Prayers," in Carson, O'Brien, and Seifrid, eds., *Justification and Variegated Nomism*, 1:7–56, at 56.

shows little positive appreciation for the utility of the phrase "covenantal nomism," placing two poles of Jewish thought in tension—divine grace or election and observance of the Torah—without rigidly defining either term or their interrelationship.[161] Martin McNamara, the eminent Targum scholar, doubts whether covenantal nomism is an appropriate description of any form of the Jewish religion because "nomism" is static ("conformity to a set of rules") while "covenantal" reflects the dynamism of the living God.[162] Unfortunately, this criticism has little organic relation to the rest of an otherwise excellent essay, and by construing the term "nomism" pejoratively, McNamara does not appear to take seriously the central role of the Torah in Judaism, particularly in contexts where works-righteousness seems to predominate.

Despite the fact that the first volume of *Justification and Variegated Nomism* is intended to be the Evangelical equivalent of Gustav Krupp's *die dicke Bertha* (Big Bertha),[163] it misses some possible weaknesses in Sanders's covenant nomism model. Simon Gathercole has drawn attention to the absence of an eschatological dimension in Sanders's model. Since eschatology plays an obviously important role in the literature of Second Temple Judaism, Gathercole suggests that, in addition to the categories of "getting in" (past) and "staying in" (present), there should be the eschatological category of "getting into the world to come," or "getting into the life of the future age," or "getting *there*."[164] The additional category is needed because "there is very good reason to distinguish in the Jewish literature between entry into the covenant, which of course is based on God's election, and *final* justification, salvation in the end."

Rabbinic literature is an enormous body of literature. It lacks consistency, resists harmonization, and represents just one of several major strands of early Judaism. Friedrich Avemarie concludes that the classical Jewish texts can be read as supporting the notion that salvation can be achieved either through law or through grace.[165] One or another of these means of salvation

161. Dunn, "The New Perspective: Whence, What and Whither?" 62.

162. Martin McNamara, "Some Targum Themes," in Carson, O'Brien, and Seifrid, eds., *Justification and Variegated Nomism*, 1:303–56, at 355.

163. In 1914, the Alfred Krupp armament company in Essen, Germany, produced a mobile howitzer called Big Bertha (named after Gustav Krupp's wife). This 43-ton howitzer could fire a 2,200-pound shell over nine miles. Transported by Daimler-Benz tractors, it took a 200-man crew over six hours to reassemble it on site.

164. Gathercole, *Where Is Boasting?*, 24, 110–11.

165. Avemarie, *Tora und Leben*, 575–84; idem, "Bund als Gabe und Recht: Zum Gebrauch von *berît* in rabbinischen Literatur," in *Bund und Tora: Zur theologischen Begriffsgeschichte in alttestamenlicher, frühjüdischer und urchristlicher Tradition*, ed. F. Avemarie and H. Lichtenberger, WUNT 92 (Tübingen: Mohr Siebeck, 1996), 176–224; idem, "Erwählung und Vergeltung: Zur optionalen Struktur rabbinischer Soteriologie," *NTS* 45 (1999): 108–26.

was emphasized depending on the particular situation they happened to address at the moment. Avemarie has argued convincingly that Sanders's model of rabbinic soteriology is inadequate because it excludes the paradigm of judgment according to the majority of deeds.[166] Sanders's procedure in Tannaitic literature is to underinterpret texts that are problematic for his thesis, while texts that might support it are overinterpreted. Why the inconsistent juxtaposition of law and grace in rabbinic literature? Alexander makes the following proposal:

> I suspect what lies behind it [i.e., varied emphasis upon one or another contradictory means of salvation] is simply fidelity to Scripture, which is just as inconsistent as the rabbis are on this point. The rabbis were perfectly capable of accepting two contradictory statements as equally "words of the living God," if both were derived by correct method from Scripture.[167]

The tension between divine judgment and divine mercy, for example, is already found in the Hebrew Bible (e.g., Ps. 89:14).

Thomas Schreiner (1993) rejects the New Perspective, maintaining that Paul was arguing against a Judaism that maintained works-righteousness, and he is unwilling to accept the possibility that Paul, a former Pharisee, was not correct in his understanding.[168] Frank Thielman (1994) stakes out a position somewhere between the traditional understanding of the Reformation view of the law and the New Perspective.[169] While Sanders was concerned with the role of the law in rabbinic literature, Thielman rather reads Paul against the background of God's grace and God's demand in the Old Testament, arguing that "in those Scriptures obedience is not the means of earning God's favor, but the proper response to God's redemptive work."[170] While he does not think that Judaism was legalistic by nature[171]—though from my point of view there would be nothing inherently wrong with that—he does maintain that some but not all Jews in Paul's day tried to combine God's grace with keeping the law. Thielman maintains that Paul himself believed this and that it was the position of the Judaizers whom Paul opposed as well.[172] Paul regarded the

---

166. Avemarie, *Tora und Leben*, 39.
167. Alexander, "Torah and Salvation in Tannaitic Literature," 273.
168. Schreiner, *The Law and Its Fulfilment*.
169. Frank Thielman, *Paul and the Law: A Contextual Approach* (Downers Grove, IL: InterVarsity, 1994).
170. Ibid., 240.
171. Ibid., 239.
172. Ibid., 238.

Mosaic law as obsolete with the coming of Christ. Where Paul seems to be arguing for a legalistic Judaism, Paul is really rejecting the possibility of achieving righteousness through works, something never sanctioned by Judaism.

One common feature of the New Perspective is an attack on the Lutheran interpretation of Paul.[173] The New Perspective asserts that the Lutheran interpretation of Paul constitutes a caricature of Judaism as a legalistic and external religion in which good works automatically earn salvation. Luther in particular had a negative attitude toward his Jewish contemporaries, convinced that for ancient and medieval Judaism, like Roman Catholicism, salvation was based on works-righteousness. Another widespread feature of the New Perspective on Paul is the rejection of the attempt to profile the Judaism contemporaneous with Paul based exclusively on inferences from the Pauline letters.[174] The popularity of the New Perspective is in part the consequence of a social and political setting of the post-Holocaust period in which dialogue between Christians and Jews has, for many Christians, become increasingly urgent.

The "New View" of Paul

Two years after E. P. Sanders published his influential book *Paul and Palestinian Judaism* (1979), Lloyd Gaston published an article on "Paul and Torah," in which he argued against the traditional reading of Paul in quite a different way.[175] Gaston's article and several other related essays published in

173. Stephen Westerholm has argued in detail that Luther basically got much of his interpretation of Paul "right." Westerholm has contextualized the New Perspective on Paul through an insightful review of the portraits of Paul by Augustine, Luther, Calvin, and Wesley, followed by a review and critique of twentieth-century "responses to the 'Lutheran' Paul," and concluding with an investigation of several key themes in the Pauline letters (righteousness, law, and justification by faith), in *Perspectives Old and New on Paul*. This is a revision and expansion of an earlier book, *Israel's Law and the Church's Faith: Paul and His Recent Interpreters* (Grand Rapids: Eerdmans, 1998).

174. Analogously, Luther cannot be regarded as a reliable guide to the spectrum of soteriological positions maintained in the late medieval church; see Alister McGrath, *Iustitia Dei: A History of the Christian Doctrine of Justification* (Cambridge: Cambridge University Press, 1986; 2nd ed., 1998), 197. I hasten to add, however, that since Paul is a Pharisaic Jew of the first century CE, the only Pharisee from the pre-70 CE period whose writings have survived, his writings cannot be ignored as evidence for the history of early Judaism. In one problematic passage (*Vita* 12), Josephus seems to claim to be a Pharisee; see Steve Mason, *Life of Josephus: Translation and Commentary* (Leiden: Brill, 2003), 21. While that remains the majority view, there are weighty reasons for not accepting it; see Steve Mason, *Flavius Josephus on the Pharisees* (Leiden: Brill, 1991), 342–56.

175. Lloyd Gaston, "Paul and the Torah," in *Antisemitism and the Foundations of Christianity*, ed. A. T. Davies (New York: Paulist Press, 1979), 48–71.

1987[176] influenced the work of such scholars as Stanley Stowers,[177] John G. Lodge,[178] and John G. Gager.[179] The independent work of Mark D. Nanos, a Jewish New Testament scholar, on both Romans and Galatians can also be associated with this "new view," since he, too, advocates a similar perspective in Pauline thought.[180] Gager has referred to this more radical reading of Paul as "the new view" and traces its origins back to Krister Stendahl's articles published in the 1960s.[181] In a nutshell, the "new view," particularly in the form presented by Gager, resurrects the "two-covenant" model of salvation, that is, that Paul held that there were two separate paths to "salvation": the law for Judaism and faith in Christ for Gentiles. Thus faith in Christ was not necessary for Jews,[182] and "justification by faith" was intended for Gentiles only. Building on the work of Gaston, Stowers, and Lodge, Gager argues that the New Perspective on Paul promoted by Sanders and Dunn is really still mired in the traditional reading of Paul, that is, the view that Paul is critical of Judaism.[183] According to Gager, Sanders "comes so close to a radical break with the traditional view, yet misses it by a mile," and Dunn's work "represents a step backward from Sanders."[184] It is both remarkable and lamentable that few scholars have engaged in dialogue with this "new view," particularly in view of the fact that Gager claims that the "new view" introduced by Gaston is a "paradigm shift." In Dunn's recent collection of essays, introduced by an eighty-eight page review of the New

176. Lloyd Gaston, *Paul and the Torah* (Vancouver: University of British Columbia, 1987), a collection of essays published earlier, the most relevant of which for our purposes are "Paul and the Torah" (15–34), "Israel's Enemies in Pauline Theology" (80–99), and "Israel's Misstep in the Eyes of Paul" (135–50).

177. Stanley K. Stowers, *A Rereading of Romans: Justice, Jews, and Gentiles* (New Haven and London: Yale University Press, 1994).

178. John G. Lodge, *Romans 9–11: A Reader-Response Analysis* (Atlanta: Scholars Press, 1996).

179. John G. Gager, *The Origins of Antisemitism: Attitudes toward Judaism in Pagan and Christian Antiquity* (New York: Oxford University Press, 1983), and *Reinventing Paul* (New York: Oxford University Press, 2000).

180. Mark D. Nanos, *The Mystery of Romans: The Jewish Context of Paul's Letter* (Minneapolis: Fortress, 1996); idem, *The Irony of Galatians: Paul's Letter in First-Century Context* (Minneapolis: Fortress, 2002).

181. Gager, *Reinventing Paul*, 50. Stendahl has denied that he advocated a two-covenant model in his earlier reading of Paul: Krister Stendahl, *Final Account, or, Paul's Letter to the Romans* (Minneapolis: Fortress, 1995), x, 7.

182. Recognition of the continuing validity of the first covenant is an important issue for Jewish-Christian relations and is discussed by J. T. Pawlikowski, "Judentum und Christentum," *Theologische Realenzyklopädie* 17 (1988): 390–402; and idem, "Ein oder zwei Bünde?" *Theologische Quartalschrift* 176 (1996): 325–40. The two-covenant model for understanding Judaism and Christianity was proposed by the Jewish thinker Franz Rosenzweig, *The Star of Redemption*, trans. Barbara E. Galli (German 1930; Madison: University of Wisconsin Press, 2005).

183. Gager, *Reinventing Paul*, 47–49.

184. Ibid., 49.

Perspective, Stowers's *A Rereading of Romans* and Gager's *The Origins of Antisemitism* and *Reinventing Paul* are not listed in the bibliography, while he makes only desultory comments on Gaston's 1979 article, "Paul and the Torah." On the other hand, Frank Thielman offers as an appendix, "Paul's View of the Law according to Lloyd Gaston and John G. Gager."[185] In the following few paragraphs I will survey this "new view" by summarizing the views of Gaston, Stowers, Lodge, and Gager, prescinding from any criticism of this position.

Gaston argued that Paul was concerned with Gentiles, not Jews, and while the resurrection of Jesus was the fulfillment of God's promises for Gentiles, that did not nullify God's promise to the Jews.[186] In other words, the Gentiles, not the Jews, need Jesus. Modern interpreters should assume that Paul stands in continuity with Jewish traditions, not in opposition to them, and that Paul obviously knew enough about the Judaism of his day to know that it was not a religion of works-righteousness. Since Paul was the apostle to the Gentiles, one must assume that he is addressing Gentile problems, not Jewish problems. Gaston's view is salutary in that it pulls the rug out from under Christian supersessionism, at least with regard to Judaism, grounding Jewish and Christian coexistence as equals in his new way of reading Paul.

In *A Rereading of Romans*, Stowers rejects what he calls the "traditional reading" of Paul: "Romans has come to be read in ways that differ fundamentally from ways that readers in Paul's own time could have read it."[187] Arguing that 1,500 years of Augustinian interpretation have obscured Paul's original meaning, Stowers intends to read Romans as a first-century reader who would have been familiar with the rhetorical and generic conventions used by Paul. He assumes that the implied audience (which Stowers calls the "encoded explicit readers") of Romans consisted of Gentiles centrally concerned with the ethical concern of self-mastery of the passions.[188] The Gentile addressees of Romans had come to think that such self-mastery was possible through observing certain select precepts of the law. The phrase "works of the law" in Romans 2:20 was not a Jewish term used of Judaism, but rather means "the adoption of selected Jewish practices on the part of gentiles."[189] Like the Judaism of his day, Paul was not concerned with

---

185. Frank Thielman, *From Plight to Solution: A Jewish Framework for Understanding Paul's View of the Law in Galatians and Romans*, NovTSup 61 (Leiden: E. J. Brill, 1989), 123–32.

186. Gaston, *Paul and the Torah*, 66.

187. Stowers, *A Rereading of Romans*, 1.

188. Ibid., 42–82.

189. Ibid., 187 (quoting Gaston, "Paul and the Torah").

such issues as human sinfulness and salvation, a way of understanding Paul imposed by Augustine and Luther. Romans 2:17–29 begins a "speech in character" (*prosōpopoiia*) of a Jewish teacher who argues that Gentiles can be made right, that is, can master the passions, by observing certain select precepts of the law. Paul does not assume that all Jews are sinners or that God's covenant with them has been nullified. In passages that seem to support these views, Stowers offers interpretations strikingly different from the traditional understanding. When Paul says that both Jews and Greeks alike are under the domination of sin (Rom. 3:9), he may be using "rhetorical hyperbole" or may mean "Jews and Greeks as a whole."[190] When Paul says that no one (*pasa sarx*, "all flesh") is made right by the works of the law (Rom. 3:20), he refers to Gentiles who are outside of a positive relationship with God.[191] In Romans 7, where the rhetorical technique of *prosōpopoiia* or "speech in character" is used, Paul depicts the plight of the Gentile trying to overcome desire through the law. Jews and Gentiles, for Paul, have separate but related ways within the plan of God; Paul assumes that Israel continues to live by the law.[192]

In his book, *Romans 9–11*, John G. Lodge uses reader-response criticism to interpret Romans 9–11 in such a way as to discard the view that God has rejected the Jews; he also absolves Paul of the supersessionism and anti-Semitism with which he is sometimes charged. Paul, choosing the strategy of the unreliable implied author, has used a "strategy of indirection" to challenge the readers' views about the present and future status of Israel in the divine plan. Paul misleads both pro-Israel and anti-Israel implied readers into thinking that he supports their views in Romans 9–10. Beginning with Romans 11:11–12, however, when the true implied reader begins to emerge, he challenges the beliefs of both types of implied reader in an attempt to change their understanding of Israel. Paul argues that God is at work behind the responses of both Jews and Gentiles to the gospel; both responses serve the purpose of God.

In *The Origins of Antisemitism*, Gager demonstrates the falsity of the view that Gentile Christians were anti-Jewish because non-Christian Gentiles already were. He demonstrates that Jews were not universally despised in the ancient world, as many had thought. In the fourth part of *The Origins of Antisemitism*, Gager argues that Christian anti-Semitism arose not because Jews were generally despised in the ancient world but because Christians

190. Stowers, *A Rereading of Romans*, 181.
191. Ibid., 189–91.
192. Ibid., 205.

misinterpreted Paul. Modern scholars have wrongly understood Paul as maintaining that the Torah was invalid, whereas in fact he regarded the Torah as valid for Jews but invalid for Gentiles. Gager follows Gaston's interpretation of Paul and the law, which he regards as a "paradigm shift" in New Testament studies.[193] The canonization of the Pauline letters carried with it an anti-Jewish way of reading them.[194]

In *Reinventing Paul*, Gager argues for the view proposed by Gaston (now fortified by Stowers) in much greater detail, arguing that Christians have misread Paul's statements about the law for two thousand years by subordinating the pro-Israel passages in Paul to the anti-Israel passages. While Stowers focused on Romans, Gager engages much of the entire undisputed Pauline corpus. The anti-Israel passages have generally been interpreted in rejection/replacement categories, that is, God has rejected both the Jews and the Torah, replacing them with a new people of God for whom faith in Christ rather than obedience to the Torah is the path leading to salvation. Gager proposed to focus rather on the pro-Israel passages in Paul, absolving him of the charges made against him by his critics:[195] (1) Paul is not the father of Christian anti-Judaism. (2) Paul did not invent the rejection/replacement theory. (3) Paul did not repudiate the law of Moses. (4) Paul did not argue that God had rejected Israel. (5) Paul's enemies were not Jews outside "Christianity" but apostolic competitors within. (6) Paul did not expect Jews to find their salvation through Jesus Christ. When Paul speaks of the law, he speaks only of the relationship of Gentiles to the law and never discusses the law in Jewish life. Paul's negative statements about the law were forged in the context of opposition to Paul's law-free gospel for the Gentiles. For Paul, there were two paths to salvation, through the Torah for Israel and through Christ for Gentiles.

Justification by Faith

During the last forty years, various understandings of the doctrine of justification by faith have been debated within world Lutheranism,[196] as

193. Gager, *Antisemitism*, 198–99.
194. Ibid., 191.
195. Gager, *Reinventing Paul*, 9–10.
196. Mark C. Mattes, *The Role of Justification in Contemporary Theology* (Grand Rapids: Eerdmans, 2004), 3–20. The title would be more accurate if the adjective "Lutheran" were inserted before "Theology" since the author is Lutheran, as are the five theologians he critiques (Eberhard Jüngel, Wolfhart Pan-

well as in ongoing ecumenical dialogue between Lutherans and Roman Catholics. The same time frame saw the rise of the New Perspective on Paul that challenged the ways in which justification by faith had previously been understood (or misunderstood), fueled in part by the growing perception of the urgency of Jewish-Christian dialogue in a post-Holocaust world. Then too, Evangelicals, particularly in the United States, have had their own intramural debate about aspects of the doctrine of justification[197] and have also responded forcefully to aspects of the New Perspective that they think are harmful to the theological health of orthodox Christianity. The backdrop for many aspects of these debates has been the continued work throughout the last century by numbers of Pauline scholars, both Protestant and Catholic, seeking to make sense of Pauline soteriology within the overall context of his thought as well as within the framework of their own theological presuppositions. In 1986 the ongoing discussion of justification by faith was set in detailed historical perspective for both theological and biblical scholars by historical theologian Alister McGrath, author of a magisterial study of the history of the doctrine of justification in the Western church from Augustine to the Lutheran–Roman Catholic and Anglican–Roman Catholic discussions of justification during the last quarter of the twentieth century.[198]

One important feature of the inner-Lutheran debate on justification by faith is the Finnish Lutheran approach to Luther's soteriology in which justification is understood in an ontological sense as *deification* (thus opening ecumenical dialogue with Orthodoxy, for whom justification by faith has never been a theological issue).[199] This view, which is now being attributed to Luther, has a broader Reformation pedigree. After Luther's death, the

nenberg, Jürgen Moltmann, Robert Jenson, and Oswald Bayer); Robert Kolb, "Contemporary Lutheran Understandings of the Doctrine of Justification," in *Justification: What's at Stake in the Current Debates?*, ed. Mark Husbands and Daniel J. Treier (Downers Grove, IL: InterVarsity; Leicester: Apollos, 2004), 153–76.

197. See particularly Carson, O'Brien, and Seifrid, eds., *Justification and Variegated Nomism*; this work is presented as a "competent evaluation" of the new perspective on Paul. See also Thomas C. Oden, *The Justification Reader* (Grand Rapids: Eerdmans, 2002), and Husbands and Treier, eds., *Justification: What's at Stake in the Current Debates?* The contributors are largely Evangelicals but include one Roman Catholic: Paul D. Molnar.

198. McGrath, *Iustitia Dei*. A shorter discussion of the topic is available in idem, *Justification by Faith* (Grand Rapids: Eerdmans, 1988).

199. Tuomo Mannermaa, *Christ Present in Faith: Luther's View of Justification* (Minneapolis: Fortress, 2005); Carl E. Braaten and Robert W. Jenson, eds., *Union with Christ: The New Finnish Interpretation of Luther* (Grand Rapids: Eerdmans, 1998); Robert W. Jenson, "Theiosis," *Dialog* 32 (1993): 108–12; idem, *Systematic Theology*, vol. 2, *The Works of God* (New York and Oxford: Oxford University Press, 1999), 293–98, 340–46.

Augsburg Confession was translated into Greek by Melanchthon in 1559 (called the *Augustana Graeca*) for the patriarch of Constantinople. Melanchthon transformed Luther's teaching on justification by faith into the Orthodox concept of the deification of man through sacramental union with Christ.[200]

Aspects of the Lutheran-Catholic Debate

While the inner-Lutheran debates over the doctrine of justification by faith are primarily theological discussions often involving a close reading of the works of Luther and the Lutheran creeds collected in the *Book of Concord* (1580),[201] behind the joint Lutheran–Roman Catholic publications on justification by faith lies a great deal of biblical, particularly Pauline, exegesis, though strikingly little influence of the New Perspective on Paul is in evidence. This ongoing ecumenical discussion has recently culminated in the Joint Declaration on the Doctrine of Justification, agreed to by the Lutheran World Federation and the Roman Catholic Church at Augsburg, Germany, on October 31, 1999.[202] Earlier (1983), the United States Lutheran–Roman Catholic dialogue group produced a joint document titled *Justification by Faith*. This document reflects a great deal of exegetical work by both Lutheran and Roman Catholic biblical scholars. Several publications have appeared in response, typically containing both Lutheran and Roman Catholic contributions.[203] In this section I would like to discuss one work by this group of scholars: *Righteousness in the New Testament: "Justification" in Lutheran-Catholic Dialogue*, edited by John Reumann (1982).[204]

---

200. Ernst Benz, *Wittenberg und Byzanz: Zur Begegnung und Auseinandersetzung der Reformation und der östlich-orthodoxen Kirche* (Marburg: Elwert-Gräfe und Unzer, 1949), 108–22.

201. Some Lutheran groups accept only the *Augsburg Confession* and Luther's *Small Catechism* as confessionally binding.

202. The Lutheran World Federation and the Roman Catholic Church, *Joint Declaration on the Doctrine of Justification* (Grand Rapids: Eerdmans, 2000). Some but not all Lutheran objections to this document were satisfied by the formulation of the Annex to the Official Common Statement appended to the document. This document is the culmination of a great deal of earlier discussion, resulting in several important publications, such as the "Malta Report," i.e., "The Gospel and the Church," published in *Lutheran World* 19 (1972): 259–73, and *Worship* 46 (1972): 326–51.

203. Thomas Söding, ed., *Worum geht es in der Rechtfertigungslehre? Das biblische Fundament der "Gemeinsamen Erklärung" von katholischer Kirche und lutherischem Weltbund* (Freiburg, Basel, and Vienna: Herder, 1999); Paweł Holc, ed., *Un ampio consenso sulla dottrina della giustificazione: Studio sul dialogo teologico cattolico-luterano*, Tesi Gregoriana, Serie Teologia 53 (Rome: Pontifical Gregorian University, 1999); Theodor Schneider and Gunther Wenz, eds., *Gerecht und Sünder zugleich? Ökumenische Klärungen* (Freiburg im Breisgau; Göttingen: Vandenhoeck & Ruprecht, 2001).

204. John Reumann, ed., *Righteousness in the New Testament: "Justification" in Lutheran-Catholic Dialogue* (Philadelphia: Fortress, 1982).

The main essay by Reumann, virtually a monograph, is 192 pages long and titled "'Justification by Grace through Faith' as Expression of the Gospel: The Biblical Witness to the Reformation Emphasis." The rest of the volume consists of two responses by Roman Catholic scholars Joseph A. Fitzmyer and Jerome D. Quinn. Fitzmyer responds to Reumann's essay point-by-point and more often than not finds himself in agreement with Reumann or else makes slight qualifications of his positions. Quinn provides a short discussion of righteousness in the Pastoral Epistles, which tends to support and extend Reumann's comments on these texts.[205]

Reumann first presents the perspectives on justification by grace through faith expressed in the major Lutheran confessions formulated by 1580. He then surveys the biblical material relevant for a word study on the Hebrew and Greek words translated "righteousness" and "justification," and cognates. Beginning with the Old Testament, he proceeds to consider Jesus, earliest Christianity, Paul and the Pauline school, and various other relevant New Testament documents, particularly Matthew and Luke-Acts, Johannine literature, and James. In the New Testament, Reumann comments on each significant passage in which *dikaio-* terms occur. Reumann argues that justification is a pre-Pauline *theologoumenon* (and so, with Käsemann, not a Pauline invention), and is a more widespread theme in the non-Pauline portions of the New Testament than might otherwise be evident.

Like other Lutheran biblical scholars, Reumann is not satisfied with maintaining the centrality of justification in Pauline thought alone. The major area of disagreement between Reumann and Fitzmyer is whether justification by faith can be regarded as the center of Pauline thought. For both scholars, the gospel itself is the center of Paul's theology and justification is one among many ways of expressing or applying it. There the similarity ends, because for Fitzmyer, justification is one among many ways of expressing or applying the gospel, no one of which has any theological superiority over another, while for Reumann justification is the prime expression of the gospel in Paul and, in view of the breadth of its usage, a central theme in Scripture. This volume demonstrates that historical-critical exegesis has come a long way, for there are really very few points of disagreement between Reumann and Fitzmyer on the interpretation of specific texts. The point at issue is not the understanding of individual texts, but the understanding of the theological

205. Quinn's commentary on 1 and 2 Timothy was published posthumously (he died in 1988) by William Wacker, as Jerome D. Quinn and William C. Wacker, *The First and Second Letters to Timothy* (Grand Rapids: Eerdmans, 2000).

structures of which the texts are part and into which they must somehow be integrated. A problem for the Lutheran-Catholic dialogue generally is the fact that the biblical evidence is theologically contextualized in very different ways by Roman Catholics and Protestants.

Justification and the New Perspective

In the sketches of the views of several scholars who have contributed the most to launching the New Perspective (Stendahl, Sanders, Dunn, and Wright) made above, aspects of their understanding of the Pauline notion of justification by faith were placed in the context of each of their projects. None of the major proponents of the New Perspective regards the doctrine of justification as the center of Pauline thought, though each has a distinctive understanding of how it relates to other Pauline soteriological concepts.

As already noted, some aspects of the New Perspective were anticipated in the work of Krister Stendahl. According to him, Paul's doctrine of justification did not emerge from his supposed introspective struggles with the Jewish interpretation of the law but was specifically hammered out in defense of the rights of Gentile converts to be considered legitimate heirs of the promises of God to Israel.[206] When Paul uses the argument of justification by faith in Galatians, he does so to protect Gentile converts against the practice of Judaizing, that is, of Gentiles submitting to circumcision and food laws.[207] For Stendahl, Paul's doctrine of justification by faith should not be understood as an explanation of the individual's relationship to God, but of how Jews and Gentiles relate to each other within the covenant purpose of God now achieved in Jesus Christ. Stendahl is concerned with the social implications of the Pauline doctrine of justification, a concern that characterizes Stendahl's seminal article, "Paul and the Introspective Conscience of the West," first published in Swedish in 1960,[208] then in a revised English translation in 1963.[209]

E. P. Sanders identifies two main soteriological categories in Paul: the "juridical" and the "participationist," the former clearly subordinate to the latter. With regard to the terms "righteousness" or "justification" (the

---

206. Stendahl, *Paul among Jews and Gentiles*, 2; idem, "The Apostle Paul and the Introspective Conscience of the West," 84.

207. Stendahl, "Sources and Critiques," in *Paul among Jews and Gentiles*, 130.

208. Krister Stendahl, "Paulus och Samvete" (Paul and the Conscience), *Svensk Exegetisk Årsbok* 25 (1960): 62–77.

209. Stendahl, "The Apostle Paul and the Introspective Conscience of the West," 199–215.

dikaio- terminology), Sanders claims that these are "transfer" terms for Paul, though not for Judaism.[210] By this he means that this language is used to describe the transfer of those who are not God's people (i.e., Gentiles), but who become members of the people of God (i.e., members of the covenant). Paul's term "righteousness" or "justification" is used for the "extraordinary acquittal of sinners"[211] but applies only to Gentiles, since Judaism has no concept of original sin or lostness. For Wright, on the other hand, justification is not used as a transfer term signaling *"how someone enters the community of the true people of God, but of how you tell who belongs to that community."*[212]

For J. D. G. Dunn, when Paul speaks of "being justified" in a Jewish context (Gal. 2:15–16), he does not have a distinctively *initiatory* act of God in view (in inaugurating his covenant with Israel), but rather refers to God's acknowledgment that a person is in the covenant, either as an initial acknowledgment or a repeated action of God (i.e., his saving acts), or God's final vindication of his people.[213] This Jewish conception of justification finds a close correspondence to Paul's conception of Gentile justification:

> As the whole conception of God's righteousness has indicated, justification is not a once-for-all act of God. It is rather the initial acceptance by God into restored relationship. But thereafter the relationship could not be sustained without God continuing to exercise his justifying righteousness with a view to the final act of judgment and acquittal.[214]

Furthermore, "Paul is ready to insist that a doing of the law is necessary for final acquittal before God; but that doing is neither synonymous with nor dependent upon maintaining a loyal membership of the covenant people."[215] For Dunn, Paul's language of justification is an acknowledgment that a person is already in the community of the saved. Criticizing both the dichotomous formulations of the Reformation and Counter Reformation conceptions

---

210. Sanders, *Paul and Palestinian Judaism*, 544–45; idem., *Paul, the Law, and the Jewish People*, 45.

211. Westerholm, *Perspectives Old and New on Paul*, 294.

212. Wright, *What Saint Paul Really Said*, 119 (author's emphasis).

213. Dunn, "The New Perspective in Paul," 190.

214. Dunn, *The Theology of Paul*, 386. Though Evangelicals would disagree with this interpretation (see Seifrid, *Christ, Our Righteousness*, 147–50), even conservative Roman Catholics find this interpretation satisfactory: see Robert A. Sungenis, *Not by Faith Alone: The Biblical Evidence for the Catholic Doctrine of Justification* (Santa Barbara, CA: Queenship, 1997), 221–98 (the chapter is titled, "Is Justification a One-Time Event or an Ongoing Process?"). The author is one of a group of Catholic biblical scholars who have converted from Reformed churches. Their intense theological focus on Scripture is more typical of Protestant than Catholic presuppositions.

215. J. D. G. Dunn, *Romans*, 2 vols., WBC (Waco: Word, 1988), 1:97–98.

of justification, Dunn maintains that justification means neither "make righteous" (the traditional Catholic view) nor "reckon as righteous" (the traditional Lutheran view), but rather means both.[216]

N. T. Wright provides a clear description of his conception of what Paul means by justification:

> The verdict of the last day has been brought forward into the present in Jesus the Messiah; in raising him from the dead, God declared that in him had been constituted the true, forgiven worldwide family. Justification in Paul is not the process or event whereby someone becomes, or grows, as a Christian; it is the declaration that someone is, in the present, a member of the people of God.[217]

"Faith," according to Wright (following the general Reformation view), "is not an achievement which earns salvation, but the evidence of saving grace already at work."[218] Wright has been criticized for interpreting justification in Paul in terms of ecclesiology rather than soteriology.[219] This critique represents a thoroughly Protestant perspective, however, since Wright is an Anglican, and for Anglicans (as for Roman Catholics and Lutherans), "justification involves being incorporated into the community of the church, rather than a solitary life of faith."[220] In a less ecumenical age, Cyprian observed: *extra ecclesiam nulla salus* (apart from the church there is no salvation). Dunn essentially agrees with Wright and maintains that for Paul justification is the declaration that a person belongs to the people of God.[221]

An important issue in interpreting both Galatians and Romans is whether Paul is referring to the justification of individual Jews and Gentiles (what is understood, perhaps incorrectly, to be the traditional Reformation view),

216. J. D. G. Dunn, "Paul and Justification by Faith," in *The Road from Damascus: The Impact of Paul's Conversion on His Life, Thought, and Ministry*, ed. R. N. Longenecker (Grand Rapids: Eerdmans, 1997), 85–101, at 88; the parenthetical phrases are my comments. It is striking that in the *Apology* to the Augsburg Confession, Philip Melanchthon observed, "And 'to be justified' means to make unrighteous men righteous or to regenerate them, as well as to be pronounced or accounted righteous. For Scripture speaks both ways" (4.72).

217. Wright, "Romans," in *New Interpreter's Bible*, vol. 10, *Acts–First Corinthians*, ed. Leander Keck (Nashville: Abingdon, 2002), 10:468.

218. Wright, "Justification: The Biblical Basis," 16.

219. O'Brien, "Was Paul a Covenantal Nomist?" 288–89; Guy Prentiss Waters, *Justification and the New Perspective* (Phillipsburg, NJ: P&R, 2004), 129; Robert S. Smith, *Justification and Eschatology: A Dialogue with "the New Perspective on Paul"* (Doncaster: Reformed Theological Review, 2001), 92.

220. McGrath, *Iustitia Dei*, 394. See *Salvation and the Church: An Agreed Statement by the Second Anglican–Roman Catholic International Commission* (London: Published for the Anglican Consultative Council and the Secretariat for Promoting Christian Unity by Church House Publishing, 1987).

221. Dunn, "Paul and Justification by Faith," 85–101.

or dealing with the relationship between Jews and Gentiles as two groups (the view of Stendahl, Dunn, and Wright, as just discussed). In an article originally published in German in 1969, responding to Krister Stendahl's influential article, "The Apostle Paul and the Introspective Conscience of the West," Ernst Käsemann argues that justification was directed by Paul against Judaism, reflecting a common pre-New Perspective view no longer considered "politically correct."[222] He maintains, however, that justification is Paul's interpretation of his Christology and cannot be understood in terms of the individual.[223] "The Pauline doctrine of justification," he asserts, "never took its bearings from the individual, although hardly anyone now realizes this."[224] Here, Käsemann is reacting to Rudolf Bultmann, who conceptualized justification in Paul in a radically individual and existential way.[225] A few years before the New Perspective took shape, Markus Barth emphasized the social implications of Pauline soteriology, decrying the crass individualism that he thought had obscured the social and ethical character of justification within the Reformation traditions.[226] Thomas Tobin, whose recent book is not particularly concerned with the pros and cons of the New Perspective, has argued that in Romans, Paul and his audience are primarily concerned with the relationship between two groups, Jews and Gentiles, and not with individual Jews and Gentiles:

> This is crucial to keep in mind lest we fall back into the trap of thinking that Romans is primarily about the sin, guilt, justification, and salvation of the individual. To do so inevitably leads once again to the misinterpretation of Romans in the categories of the Reformation debates.[227]

Wright takes a similar line with regard to Galatians, maintaining that Paul is not concerned there with how an individual becomes a Christian or attains a relationship with God, but rather the issue is how one defines the people of God—by the ritual markers of Judaism or some other way.[228] Justification is in effect a two-stage process: primary for Paul is the future

222. Käsemann, "Justification and Salvation History," 70–72.
223. Ibid., 73–75.
224. Ibid., 74.
225. Bultmann, *Theology of the New Testament*, 1:270–84. Bultmann regards justification as both forensic and eschatological, i.e., as a present reality but also belonging to the future.
226. Markus Barth, "Jews and Gentiles: The Social Character of Justification in Paul," *Journal of Ecumenical Studies* 5 (1968): 241–67.
227. Thomas H. Tobin, *Paul's Rhetoric in Its Contexts: The Argument of Romans* (Peabody, MA: Hendrickson, 2004), 8.
228. Wright, *What Saint Paul Really Said*, 120.

justification of the believer, in view of which act the believer experiences present justification. Obedience is a necessary part of the eschatological vindication, and "justification, at the last, will be on the basis of performance, not possession."[229] Justification, rooted in the cross and anticipating the verdict of the last day, gives people a new status prior to the performance of appropriate deeds.

The Evangelical Debate on Imputation

In recent years there has been a lively debate among American Evangelicals centering on the late magisterial Reformation doctrine of the imputation of Christ's righteousness to the believer,[230] which some regard as the crucial touchstone for the orthodox Protestant doctrine of justification.[231] This debate has been characterized by close readings of the Pauline letters. N. T. Wright, an Evangelical Anglican, has argued that since Paul's term "righteousness" is the forensic language of the law court:

> If we use the language of the law court, it makes no sense whatever to say that the judge imputes, imparts, bequeaths, conveys or otherwise transfers his righteousness to either the plaintiff or the defendant. Righteousness is not an object, a substance or a gas which can be passed out in the courtroom. . . . To imagine the defendant somehow receiving the judge's righteousness is simply a category mistake. That is not how language works.[232]

Wright clearly rejects the late Reformation notion of the imputation of the righteousness of Christ.

Robert Gundry has provocatively argued that the imputation of Christ's righteousness is absent from the Pauline letters, playing no part in the Pau-

229. Wright, "Romans and the Theology of Paul," 440.

230. Melanchthon was primarily responsible for developing the *forensic* conception of justification that became normative in Protestantism, and was similarly responsible for developing the concept of imputation (in the sense that the believer is reckoned as righteous on account of the alien merit of Christ) in the *Apologia* (21:19) to the *Augsburg Confession* (see McGrath, *Iustitia Dei*, 210–12). Melanchthon's position was endorsed in the *Formula of Concord* (3:17, 1577 CE), indicating general agreement among Lutherans, and later was fully accepted by the Reformed churches. It should be noted that Luther, followed by Calvin, held the personal union of Christ and the believer in justification (i.e., the *unio mystica*), a position forsaken by Melanchthon (McGrath, *Iustitia Dei*, 224). The imputation of Christ's righteousness is mentioned in the Lutheran paragraphs of the Joint Declaration (§§22, 29).

231. One of the recent Evangelical defenders of this position is John Piper, *Righteousness in Christ: Should We Abandon the Imputation of Christ's Righteousness?* (Wheaton: Crossway, 2002), who presents his case through the detailed exegesis of the relevant Pauline texts.

232. Wright, *What Saint Paul Really Said*, 98.

line doctrine of justification.[233] In Paul, he argues, faith is counted in an unqualified way as *righteousness* (Gal. 3:6; Rom. 4:3, 5, 6, 9, 11, 22–24); no Pauline texts say explicitly that faith was counted as *Christ's* righteousness.[234] He concludes:

> In summary, where can sinners find righteousness? In Christ. Whose righteousness can they find there? God's. What does it consist in? God's counting faith as righteousness. How does he do so without contravening his wrath against our unrighteousness? By setting forth Christ as a propitiatory sacrifice.[235]

D. A. Carson, in his response to Gundry, agrees that, "Strictly speaking, there is no passage in the New Testament that says that our sins are imputed to Christ,"[236] yet nonetheless he maintains that the imputation of Christ's righteousness to the believing sinner is a legitimate reading of Paul, arguing that the phrase "his faith was imputed to him as righteousness" is "necessarily a kind of shorthand for the larger exposition," that is, that "righteousness" here means "the righteousness of Christ."[237] In the same volume, Mark Seifrid argues that Luther himself does not refer to the imputation of Christ's righteousness to the believer (presumably because Luther believes that Christ himself is present in faith),[238] and he essentially agrees with Gundry that the notion of the imputation of Christ's righteousness to the believer is not found in Paul.[239] Seifrid draws the following conclusion:

> The Protestant definition of justification in terms of imputation is no mere description of biblical teaching for which terminology is lacking in Scripture [the position of D. A. Carson], as is the case, for example, with the doctrine

233. Robert H. Gundry, "The Nonimputation of Christ's Righteousness," in Husbands and Treier, eds., *Justification: What's at Stake in the Current Debates?*, 17–45.

234. Ibid., 18.

235. Ibid., 43.

236. D. A. Carson, "The Vindication of Imputation: On Fields of Discourse and Semantic Fields," in Husbands and Treier, eds., *Justification: What's at Stake in the Current Debates?*, 46–78, at 78.

237. Carson, "The Vindication of Imputation," 67. Henri Blocher agrees with Carson's position; see Henri Blocher, "Justification of the Ungodly (Sola Fide): Theological Reflections," in Carson, O'Brien, and Seifrid, eds., *Justification and Variegated Nomism*, 2:465–500, at 498.

238. Mark A. Seifrid, "Luther, Melanchthon and Paul in the Question of Imputation: Recommendations on a Current Debate," in Husbands and Treier, eds., *Justification: What's at Stake in the Current Debates?*, 137–52, at 144.

239. Seifrid, "Luther, Melanchthon and Paul," 146; idem, "Paul's Use of Righteousness Language against Its Hellenistic Background," in Carson, O'Brien, and Seifrid, eds., *Justification and Variegated Nomism*, 2:39–74, at 71; idem, *Christ, Our Righteousness*, 173–75.

of the Trinity. Here we are dealing in some measure with the replacement of the biblical categories with other ways of speaking.[240]

One approach to the problem of the doctrine of justification in Paul in recent New Testament scholarship is that of Karl Donfried.[241] Retaining the distinctively Reformation differentiation between justification and sanctification,[242] Donfried proposes that the Pauline notions of justification, sanctification, and salvation should be arranged in a history of salvation schema, with justification regarded as a past event with present implications, sanctification as a present event dependent on the past event of justification and with future implications (salvation), and salvation as a future event, partially experienced in the past event of justification and the present event of sanctification. This arrangement is somewhat artificial, since in Paul justification has a future as well as a past reference (Rom. 2:13; 8:30–34; Gal. 5:4–5), sanctification can refer to a past event (1 Cor. 6:11) or a future event (1 Thess. 5:23), and salvation is too complex a conception in Paul to be restricted to the future.

The apparent contradiction or inconsistency in Pauline thought between judgment according to deeds and justification by faith (see 1 Cor. 4:4–5 and 6:9–11) was taken up by Kent Yinger.[243] With Sanders, Yinger accepts covenantal nomism and rejects legalism in Judaism. He also shares with Dunn an understanding of "works of the law" to mean Jewish ritual markers (circumcision, kashrut, Sabbath observance). He reports an impressive pre-Pauline Jewish tradition in which a salvation deriving from the grace of God is found side by side with the view that the righteous will be judged for what they do or do not do. The author demonstrates a strong continuity between Paul and Judaism in holding both judgment according to works and salvation by God's gracious election (buttressing the conclusions of E. P. Sanders). Paul, according to Yinger, adopts the covenantal nomism of Judaism, yet differs from Judaism in that Christ rather than the Torah is the means whereby a person becomes a member of the people of God.

240. Seifrid, "Luther, Melanchthon and Paul," 151.
241. Karl Donfried, "Justification and Last Judgment in Paul," ZNW 67 (1976): 90–110.
242. McGrath, Iustitia Dei, 182.
243. Kent L. Yinger, Paul, Judaism, and Judgment according to Deeds, SNTSMS 105 (Cambridge: Cambridge University Press, 1999). Mark A. Seifrid, review of Yinger, Paul, Judaism and Judgment according to Deeds, JBL 120 (2001): 174–75, criticizes Yinger for treating only part of the material available from Second Temple Judaism. Thomas R. Schreiner, review of Yinger, Paul, Judaism and Judgment according to Deeds, JETS 43 (2000): 552–53, chides Yinger for generally ignoring the role of faith in Paul. O'Brien has a lengthy critique of Yinger's book but many of his points are wide of the mark, like his theological criticism that, by rejecting legalism in Judaism, Yinger "has taken a positive view of human beings and failed to account for the radical nature of evil" ("Was Paul a Covenantal Nomist?" 268).

Justification and the Center of Pauline Thought

For Lutherans, the doctrine of justification was the *articulus stantis et cadentis ecclesiae* (the article by which the church stands or falls), that is, the heart of all Christian theology and spirituality.[244] This view is argued in detail by John Reumann, as we have seen above. N. T. Wright, on the other hand, explicitly warns against the temptation "to make the Pauline doctrine of justification the article by which the church stands or falls."[245] The issue of the theological center of Pauline thought has become important in Pauline scholarship, particularly since World War II.[246]

At the beginning of the twentieth century, William Wrede was one of the first Protestant New Testament scholars to argue that justification by faith was not only *not* at the center of Pauline thought but originated as a polemical doctrine (*Kampfeslehre*) intended to counteract the theological threat posed by Judaism.[247] For Wrede, Paul's thought centered rather in the idea of redemption through Christ. Werner Georg Kümmel asserted that if Paul hammered out the doctrine of justification in a polemical context, then justification was a "mere polemical doctrine" and could not be the center of Paul's theological thought, since the Pauline proclamation of salvation in Christ runs counter to the "Jewish doctrine of salvation."[248]

Albert Schweitzer, Paul Wernle, and other German New Testament scholars at the turn of the last century agreed that the Pauline doctrine of justification was the product of polemic and not the heart of Pauline theology. In a now famous phrase, Schweitzer called the Pauline doctrine of justification "a subsidiary crater, which has formed within the rim of the main crater—the mystical doctrine of redemption through the being-in-Christ."[249] This Pauline mysticism was linked to sacramental union with Christ and with apocalyptic presuppositions. Following Schweitzer, some modern New Testament scholars, including J. Christiaan Beker and Louis

244. Actually, it was not Luther but Valentin Löscher (1673–1749), an orthodox Lutheran theologian, who first used this phrase, though it was based on a statement in Luther's *Smalcald Articles* (1537); see Friedrich Loofs, "Der articulus stantis et cadentis ecclesiae," *Theologische Studien und Kritiken* 90 (1917): 323–40.

245. N. T. Wright, "Gospel and Theology in Galatians," in *Gospel in Paul: Studies on Corinthians, Galatians and Romans for Richard N. Longenecker*, ed. L. Ann Jervis and Peter Richardson (Sheffield: Sheffield Academic Press, 1994), 222–39, at 232.

246. Hans Hübner, "Paulusforschung seit 1945: Ein kritischer Literaturbericht," *ANRW* 2.25.4, ed. Wolfgang Hase (Berlin and New York: Walter de Gruyter, 1987), 2721–29 ("Rechtfertigung als Mitte paulinischer Theologie").

247. Wrede, *Paulus*.

248. Kümmel, *Theology of the New Testament*, 195.

249. Albert Schweitzer, *The Mysticism of Paul the Apostle* (New York: Macmillan, 1953), 225.

Martyn, have identified apocalypticism as the center of Paul's thought, but they express this insight in distinctive forms. Beker's emphasis on the dialectic between contingency and coherence understands the Pauline letters as responses to contingent situations that are expressions of a theological coherence. This coherence is grounded in Paul's apocalyptic worldview, understood in positive terms as the coming triumph of God.[250] In theological circles, justification (with its assumption of the sinfulness of humankind) was similarly marginalized in the dialectical theology of Karl Barth, who centered his theology rather in the revelation of God.[251]

More recently, major representatives of the New Perspective have argued that justification by faith is not the center of Pauline thought. This is certainly true for Stendahl, for whom that role is played by salvation history.[252] Ernst Käsemann responded to Stendahl's article "The Apostle Paul and the Introspective Conscience of the West" with a robust rebuttal.[253] While Käsemann agrees that salvation history forms the horizon of Pauline theology, for him justification is the center of Pauline theology (just as it was for his teacher, Rudolf Bultmann) and is "the key to salvation history, just as, conversely, salvation history forms the historical depth and cosmic breadth of justification."[254] More specifically for Käsemann, "justification remains the centre, the beginning and the end of salvation history."[255]

On the theological role of justification in Paul, Sanders observed that "the catch-word 'righteousness by faith' must be given up as the clue to Paul's thought."[256] For Sanders, the real problem of Pauline interpretation is determining the relation among various soteriological terms in Paul, which fall under the two major categories of the "forensic" or "juridical" (e.g., justification) and the "participatory" (e.g., "in Christ"). Sanders, as we have already observed, regards Paul's juristic soteriological category as subordinate to the participatory category.[257] According to Sanders, Paul's

250. J. Christiaan Beker, *Paul the Apostle: The Triumph of God in Life and Thought* (Philadelphia: Fortress, 1980); idem, *Paul's Apocalyptic Gospel: The Coming Triumph of God* (Philadelphia: Fortress, 1982).

251. McGrath, *Iustitia Dei*, 357–71.

252. Stendahl, "The Apostle Paul and the Introspective Conscience of the West," 84 n. 10, and 95.

253. Käsemann, "Justification and Salvation History," 60–78.

254. Ibid., 75.

255. Ibid., 76.

256. Sanders, *Paul and Palestinian Judaism*, 438.

257. Ibid., 503 (further on this topic, see 453–72 and 502–8). Timo Laato argues that, contrary to Sanders, Paul makes no distinction between the juridical and participatory categories of his soteriology, since both are complimentary and not in competition; see his "Paul's Anthropological Considerations," in Carson, O'Brien, and Seifrid, eds., *Justification and Variegated Nomism*, 2:343–59, esp. 345–50.

"participationist transfer terms" are completely different from the covenantal nomism conception characteristic of Judaism:

> The heart of Paul's thought is not that one ratifies and agrees to a covenant relation with God and remains in it on the condition of proper behaviour; but that one dies with Christ, obtaining new life and the initial transformation which leads to the resurrection and ultimate transformation, that one is a member of the body of Christ and one Spirit with him, and that one remains so unless one breaks the participatory union by forming another.[258]

If I understand Sanders correctly, the phrase "participationist transfer terms" links two types of language. On the one hand, he discusses Paul's participatory union language, consisting of: (1) members of Christ's body, the body of Christ; (2) one Spirit; (3) in Christ; and (4) Christ's, servants of the Lord.[259] Sanders puts all these participatory terms together in a concluding paragraph:

> God has appointed Christ as Lord and saviour of the world. All who believe in him have the Spirit as the guarantee of future full salvation and are at present considered to participate in Christ's body, to be one Spirit with him. As such, they are to act in accordance with the Spirit, which is also to serve Christ as the Lord to whom they belong.[260]

Sanders then discusses, on the other hand, the various metaphors of Paul's "juristic" or "transfer terminology":[261] (1) participation in the death of Christ; (2) freedom; (3) transformation, new creation; (4) reconciliation; and (5) justification and righteousness. Sanders insists that Paul himself did not distinguish between "mystical" or "participatory" conceptions and "juristic" conceptions.[262] Sanders later argued that he never maintained that participationist rather than juridical categories form the *center* of Pauline theology, since he is interested only in the terminology that is most revealing for "understanding Paul's conception of how one *enters* the body of Christ."[263] In due course Sanders admits that "righteousness by faith and participation in Christ ultimately amount to the same thing."[264] Though Sanders does

---

258. Sanders, *Paul and Palestinian Judaism*, 514.
259. Ibid., 453–63.
260. Ibid., 463.
261. Ibid., 463–72.
262. Ibid., 472.
263. Sanders, *Paul, the Law, and the Jewish People*, 5–6, 12–13 n. 15.
264. Sanders, *Paul and Palestinian Judaism*, 506.

not refer to the work of Gerd Theissen, the latter analyzes Paul's soteriological statements in terms of two symbolic groups that generally parallel Sanders's taxonomy:[265] (1) the symbolism of social interaction (freedom from an enslaving power through elevation and redemption, acquittal of guilt through the accursed death of the redeemer, and reconciliation from enmity through the loving gift of the redeemer); and (2) the symbolism of transformation of nature (salvation overcomes human finitude through dying and rising with the redeemer and overcoming the enclosed self through unity in the body of Christ).

Wright admits that justification cannot be put at the center of Paul's thought, since that center is already occupied by "the person of Jesus himself, and the gospel announcement of his sovereign kingship." Nevertheless, he insists that justification is not a secondary or inessential matter.[266] Wright essentially agrees with Wrede, Schweitzer, Wernle, and Kümmel, however, that "we must see justification by faith as a polemical doctrine, whose target is not the usual Lutheran one of 'nomism' or '*Menschenwerke*,' but the Pauline one of Jewish national pride."[267] Most recently Douglas A. Campbell has argued in some detail that the "pneumatologically participatory martyrological eschatology" model (often referred to as the "participatory," "apocalyptic," or "eschatological model") constitutes the heart of Paul's gospel (which dominates Rom. 5–8), and that the justification by faith and salvation historical models (which dominate Rom. 1–4 and 9–11 respectively) ought to be subordinated to the first model.[268]

A different way of looking at the structure of Paul's soteriology is exemplified by Adolf Deissmann, who argued that there were five important metaphorical expressions for salvation in Christ found in Pauline thought: (1) justification, (2) reconciliation, (3) forgiveness, (4) redemption, and (5) adoption (or sonship).[269] These metaphors, he argues, correspond to the fact that the human person stands before God as an accused person, an enemy, a debtor, and (in the fourth and fifth metaphors), as a slave.[270] Further, for Deissmann, justified persons are not completely righteous but still have the goal of righteousness before them.[271] Yet Deissmann agreed

---

265. Gerd Theissen, "Soteriologische Symbolik in den paulinischen Schriften: Einer strukturalistischer Beitrag," *Kerygma und Dogma* 20 (1974): 282–304.

266. Wright, *What Saint Paul Really Said*, 114.

267. Wright, "The Paul of History," 78.

268. Douglas A. Campbell, *The Quest for Paul's Gospel: A Suggested Strategy*, JSNTSup 274 (London and New York: T & T Clark International, 2005); see esp. 17–28 and 29–55.

269. Deissmann, *Paul*, 167.

270. Ibid., 168.

271. Ibid., 170. This is, of course, the Lutheran doctrine of *simul iustus et peccator*.

with Schweitzer that the center of Paul's thought is to be found in the phrase "in Christ" (or one of its variants), which permeates the Pauline corpus and which is synonymous with phrases like "the faith of Jesus Christ," which is an example of the "mystical genitive" or the "genitive of fellowship."[272] This experience of Christ is for Deissmann the center of Paul's thought, with the five metaphors mentioned above as ways of conceptualizing that experience.[273]

In line with Deissmann, Joseph Fitzmyer calls attention to the ten images Paul used to summarize the effects of the Christ-event: justification, salvation, reconciliation, expiation, redemption, freedom, sanctification, transformation, new creation, and glorification. He regards these ten images as simply different ways of understanding the basic mystery of Christ and his role. The Christ-event, he suggests, is conceived of as a decahedron, a ten-sided figure, each panel of which expresses only one aspect of the whole.[274]

More recently, J. D. G. Dunn, one of the three foremost proponents of the New Perspective, has sided with Deissmann and Fitzmyer in insisting that justification is a legal metaphor and that Paul uses other metaphors for the experience of the "new beginning," such as redemption, liberation, freedom, reconciliation, citizenship, kingdom-transfer, salvation, and inheritance.[275] No single one of these metaphors should be emphasized over the others, for many of Paul's readers undoubtedly "experienced the gospel as acceptance, liberation, or rescue, as cleansing and new dedication, as a dying to an old life and beginning of a new."[276] Though Protestant theology has taken the metaphor of justification and given it primary or normative status, Dunn considers this inappropriate.[277] The three metaphors that Dunn believes captures the central features of the new beginning are: justification by faith, participation in Christ, and the gift of the Spirit.[278] However, Dunn can speak of "the centrality . . . for Paul" of righteousness/justification language,[279] though by "centrality" he clearly does not mean "center."

272. Ibid., 161–66.

273. Deissmann suggests a number of diagrams to capture this relationship in an appendix (293–99).

274. Joseph A. Fitzmyer, S.J., "The Biblical Basis of Justification by Faith: Comments on the Essay of Professor Reumann," in Reumann, ed., Righteousness in the New Testament, 216; idem, Paul and His Theology, 2nd ed. (Englewood Cliffs, NJ: Prentice Hall, 1989), 59.

275. Dunn, Theology of Paul the Apostle, 328–29.

276. Ibid., 332.

277. Ibid., 332.

278. Ibid., 333.

279. Ibid., 341.

The *Pistis [Iesou] Christou* Debate

The Pauline phrase *pistis [Iesou] Christou* (faith of Christ) is as ambiguous in English as it is in Greek, for *[Iesou] Christou* can be construed as either an objective genitive or a subjective genitive. The phrase occurs six times in the authentic letters (Gal. 2:16 [*bis*]; 3:22; Rom. 3:22, 26; Phil. 3:9).[280] The traditional way of translating the phrase construes *Christou* as an objective genitive meaning "faith in Christ," faith in the atoning death of Jesus, which makes the believer righteous. More recently, a number of scholars (predominantly American) have insisted that *Christou* is a subjective genitive and should be understood to mean "the faith [or faithfulness] of Christ," that is, the personal faith or faithfulness of Christ, his obedience that led to his death on the cross.[281] The relevance of this issue for the modern discussion of justification by faith in Paul is clearly expressed by J. D. G. Dunn (who argues for the objective genitive) against Richard Hays (who argues for the subjective genitive):

> More to the point, on Hays's thesis we have no clear reference to the "faith" of believers. There are two such references using the equivalent verb (2:16 and 3:22). But Hays leaves us with no noun counterpart, no noun to denote the Galatians' act of believing. Hays's thesis vacuums up every relevant reference to "faith" in Galatians in order to defend the subjective genitive reading of 2:16, 20 and 3:22. This is nothing short of astonishing. It now appears that a text (Galatians), which has provided such a powerful charter of "justifying faith" for Christian self-understanding, *nowhere* clearly speaks of that "faith."[282]

280. Karl Kertelge catalogs five ways in which the genitive of *[Iesou] Christou* can be construed, of which the first two are the objective and subjective genitive (the latter is itself understood in several ways); see *"Rechtfertigung" bei Paulus: Studien zur Struktur und zum Bedeutungsgehalt des paulinischen Recht-fertigungsbegriffs*, NA, neue Folge 3 (Münster: Verlag Aschendorff, 1967), 162–66. A brief history of these competing views is found in Richard B. Hays, *The Faith of Jesus Christ: The Narrative Substructure of Galatians 3:1–4:11* (Chico, CA: Scholars Press, 1983; 2nd ed., Grand Rapids: Eerdmans; Dearborn, MI: Dove, 2002), 142–48. In a later article, Hays provides a partial bibliographical survey of the *pistis [Iesou] Christou* debate in Richard B. Hays, *"Pistis Christou* and Pauline Christology: What Is at Stake?" in *Pauline Theology*, vol. 4, *Looking Back, Pressing On*, ed. E. Elizabeth Johnson and David M. Hay (Atlanta: Scholars Press, 1997), 35–60, at 35–37 nn. 2–4. The linguistic and exegetical arguments for interpreting the phrase as either an objective or subjective genitive are reviewed by R. B. Matlock (who favors the objective genitive), "'Even the Demons Believe': Paul and *Pistis Christou*," *CBQ* 64 (2002): 300–18, and "Detheologizing the *Pistis Christou* Debate: Cautionary Remarks from a Lexical Semantic Perspective," *NovT* 42 (2000): 1–23.

281. Richard N. Longenecker, "The Obedience of Christ in the Theology of the Early Church," in *Reconciliation and Hope*, ed. R. Banks (Exeter: Paternoster, 1974), 142–52.

282. J. D. G. Dunn, "Once More, *Pistis Christou*," in Johnson and Hay, eds., *Pauline Theology*, vol. 4, 61–81, at 69.

Since the grammar of the phrase is ambiguous,[283] scholars have had to provide various types of contextual arguments. Kertelge interprets the phrase as an objective genitive meaning "the believing confession of Jesus Christ as the new Lord,"[284] based on what he regards as the parallel use of the verb *pisteuō* in Romans 10:14, Galatians 2:16, and Philippians 1:29. The verbs in Romans 10:14 make it clear that Christ is the object of belief:

> And how are they to believe in one of whom they have never heard? But how are they to call on one in whom they have not believed?

In Galatians 2:16, the phrase *pistis Iesou Christou* is juxtaposed with the verb *pisteuō*, which serves to interpret the noun phrase:

> Yet we know that a person is justified not by the works of the law but through faith in Jesus Christ [the NRSV construes *pistis Iesou Christou* as an objective genitive]. And we have come to believe in Christ Jesus, so that we might be justified by faith in Christ [*pistis Christou* is also construed as an objective genitive].

The verb *pisteuō* similarly occurs in Philippians 1:29: "For he has graciously granted you the privilege not only of believing in Christ, but of suffering for him as well." In two important articles, Douglas A. Campbell has argued in part that reading *pistis Iesou Christou* and analogous uses of *pistis* as a subjective genitive fits a participationist rather than a justification-by-faith model of the theological center of Paul's theology.[285]

One of the striking features of the *pistis Christou* debate is how a new way of reading a Pauline text can have important ramifications for understanding Pauline theology. While the *pistis Christou* debate continues, proponents of the subjective genitive interpretation remain in a vocal minority, while proponents of the objective genitive construal have weighty arguments on their side.

Conclusions

Despite the length of this review of recent readings of Paul relating to justification, I have only been able to scratch the surface of the enormous,

---

283. Paul J. Achtemeier, "Apropos the Faith of/in Christ: A Response to Hays and Dunn," in Johnson and Hay, eds., *Pauline Theology*, vol. 4, *Looking Back, Pressing On*, 82–92, at 82–84.

284. Kertelge, *"Rechtfertigung" bei Paulus*, 176.

285. Douglas A. Campbell, "The Meaning of 'Faith' in Paul's Gospel," and "The Coming of Faith in Paul's Gospel: Galatians 3," in idem, *The Quest for Paul's Gospel*, 178–207 and 208–32.

complex, and diverse range of twentieth- (and some twenty-first-) century scholarship on these issues. In the context of Protestant-Catholic dialogue on the Pauline doctrine of justification by faith, a few concluding observations or reflections are in order.

First, when it comes to the exegesis of individual passages in the Pauline letters, there is remarkably little disagreement among Protestant and Catholic biblical scholars. This view is expressed in one of the Roman Catholic curial documents produced by the Pontifical Biblical Commission in 1993, "The Interpretation of the Bible in the Church":

> Although it cannot claim to resolve all these issues [eschatology, the structure of the Church, primacy and collegiality, marriage and divorce, etc.] by itself, biblical exegesis is called upon to make an important contribution in the ecumenical area. A remarkable degree of progress has already been achieved. Through the adoption of the same methods and analogous hermeneutical points of view, exegetes of various Christian confessions have arrived at a remarkable level of agreement in the interpretation of Scripture, as is shown by the text and notes of a number of ecumenical translations of the Bible, as well as by other publications.[286]

A few years earlier, Raymond E. Brown emphasized how historical biblical criticism had made important contributions to ecumenical dialogue.[287]

Two sterling examples of this kind of exegetical scholarship based on an historical-critical approach to Scripture can be found in the work of the Lutheran New Testament scholar John Reumann and Roman Catholic New Testament scholar Joseph Fitzmyer, S.J., showcased in the book edited by Reumann discussed above, *Righteousness in the New Testament: "Justification" in Lutheran-Catholic Dialogue* (1982). The main area of disagreement between Reumann and Fitzmyer is not the interpretation of particular texts, but rather whether justification by faith can in any sense be regarded as the center of Pauline thought—although just what "center" means remains vague. The point at issue is both the theological structure of which the texts are part (the

286. Dean P. Béchard, ed. and trans., *The Scripture Documents: An Anthology of Official Catholic Teachings* (Collegeville, MN: Liturgical Press, 2002), 312–13; a helpful discussion, "The Interpretation of the Bible in the Church," is found in Joseph Fitzmyer, S.J., *The Biblical Commission's Document "The Interpretation of the Bible in the Church": Text and Commentary* (Rome: Pontifical Biblical Institute, 1995); and Peter S. Williamson, *Catholic Principles for Interpreting Scripture: A Study of the Pontifical Biblical Commission's "The Interpretation of the Bible in the Church"* (Rome: Editrice Pontificio Istituto Biblico, 2001), 322–23.

287. Raymond E. Brown, "The Contribution of Historical Biblical Criticism to Ecumenical Church Discussion," in *Biblical Interpretation in Crisis: The Ratzinger Conference on Bible and Church*, ed. R. J. Neuhaus (Grand Rapids: Eerdmans, 1989), 24–49.

disputed synthesis of Pauline theology) as well as the modern theological systems into which they must somehow be integrated. A general problem for the Lutheran-Catholic dialogue generally is the structural differentia in the theologies of these two major forms of Christianity, which makes it inevitable that the New Testament perspectives on various theological issues will be both understood in different ways and utilized in different ways. This is made clear by Fitzmyer's concluding call for a consideration of the theological conceptions of reward and merit and their relationship to justification. While the center of Pauline thought is itself a moot point—in part because of the unsystematic character of Pauline thought and in part because the evidence is seen through the prism of differing confessional perspectives—it is even more difficult to determine the place of justification in the thought of New Testament authors other than Paul, not to mention pre-Pauline evidence. Thus if justification is more or less a central concern of one author (e.g., Paul, for the sake of argument) and more marginal to another (e.g., Matthew), how can they be meaningfully compared? The New Testament itself offers a paradigm for theological diversity under the overarching unity provided by the gospel. We are left with the problem that exegetical agreement does not mean theological agreement.

Second, the New Perspective on Paul with its distinctive approach to understanding the role of justification in Pauline thought has had little impact on the Joint Declaration on the Doctrine of Justification, an issue addressed by John Reumann in this volume. There are several reasons for this. First, the New Perspective originated as and has continued to remain a largely Anglo-American approach to Paul. This is due at least in part to the perception that the New Perspective is critical of the traditional Lutheran interpretation of Paul.[288] Westerholm, in response, has argued that Luther generally "got it right" and that the insights of Luther can be maintained as a valid interpretation of Paul while avoiding a negative caricature of Judaism.[289] Second, the fields of systematic theology and biblical scholarship are separated by a rather wide gulf; systematic theologians are rarely acquainted with recent trends in biblical scholarship, and many biblical scholars are functionally illiterate when it comes to systematic theology. Third, the Lutheran-Catholic dialogue predates the advent of the New Perspective by more than a decade and it is still being debated and tested in the academy.

288. Dunn bends over backward to deny this and has argued that for him the New Perspective is not opposed to the classic Reformation doctrine of justification; see "The New Perspective: Whence and Whither?" 17–22, 33. Dunn even agrees that it is *articulus stantis et cadentis ecclesiae* (ibid., 21).

289. Westerholm, *Perspectives Old and New on Paul*.

Of course, both Reumann and Fitzmyer have discussed the work of E. P. Sanders in the context of Lutheran-Catholic dialogue, though they have not been impressed. Reumann is troubled by Sanders's assertion that "righteousness/ justification by faith" is not an adequate term to indicate the center of Pauline theology. He questions Sanders's distinction between juridical and participationist categories and is not satisfied with his focal emphasis on eschatological participation.[290] While Fitzmyer agrees with this last criticism by Reumann, he goes further and takes Sanders to task for using Tannaitic rabbinic literature to represent the Palestinian Judaism that was known to Paul.[291] The publication of the Reumann book on *Righteousness in the New Testament* (1984), of course, predates much of the development of the New Perspective.

Third, one aspect of the New Perspective that might prove fruitful in future discussions on the doctrine of justification is the renewed importance of the social or ecclesial significance of the Pauline doctrine of justification by faith that, though not new, was proposed by Krister Stendahl in the 1960s.[292] A few years later, Nils Alstrup Dahl published "The Doctrine of Justification: Its Social Function and Implications," originally in Norwegian (1964),[293] then in an English translation (1977).[294] The title of the essay indicates that Dahl shares Stendahl's emphasis on the sociological significance of the doctrine of justification. In this essay, Dahl argues that "this doctrine not only concerns the individual and his relation to God but is also of importance for the common life of Christians."[295] Dahl suggests that the social implications of the doctrine of justification that were assumed by both Paul and (in a different context) by Luther were subject to a narrowing during the period of Lutheran orthodoxy in the seventeenth century, when the focus of justification by faith became the individual's relationship to God, an important step in the *ordo salutis*, and so lost its comprehensive character.[296] The connection between justification and its social implications was also discussed by Joachim Heubach,[297] and the same emphasis was reported by

290. Reumann, *"Righteousness" in the New Testament*, 120–23.

291. Fitzmyer, "The Biblical Basis of Justification by Faith," 217.

292. Krister Stendahl, "Rechtfertigung und Endgericht," *Lutherische Rundschau* 11 (1961): 3–10.

293. Nils Alstrup Dahl, "Rettferdiggjørelseslaerens sosiologiske funksjon og konsekvenser," *Nordisk Theologisk Tidsskrift* 65 (1965): 284–310.

294. Nils Alstrup Dahl, "The Doctrine of Justification: Its Social Function and Implication," in idem, *Studies in Paul* (Minneapolis: Augsburg, 1977): 95–120.

295. Dahl, "The Doctrine of Justification," 95.

296. Ibid., 118.

297. Joachim Heubach, "Rechtfertigung und Kirche," in *De fundamentis ecclesiae: Gedenkschrift für Pastor Dr. theol. Hellmut Lieberg*, ed. Eckhard Wagner (Braunschweig: Herausgegeben im Namen des ev. Luth. Konvents um Brüdern-St. Ulrici in Braunschweig, 1963), 132–35.

Gottfried Martens in his exhaustive study of justification in Martin Luther and modern ecumenical discussion.[298] This link between justification and ecclesiology, again outside the New Perspective, has been emphasized by Walter Klaiber, a German Methodist bishop and student of Ernst Käsemann, in a 1982 book titled *Rechtfertigung und Gemeinde*.[299] In Klaiber's view, the basic principle of Paul's ecclesiology was his Christology. While he shared with the early church the view that Christ was the foundation of the community and through him one shares in eschatological salvation, Paul took another step by emphasizing the link between the righteousness of God and the church. Through the justification of sinners, God creates a new people, the church. Since it is through Christ that this justification occurs, the connection between Christ and community becomes clear. Thus in its corporate life, the church is God's righteousness incarnate.

This social emphasis on justification was incorporated into the New Perspective on Paul by Wright and Dunn. According to Wright, Paul's conception of justification does not represent individual or personal salvation[300] but is the means whereby the one who believes and is baptized is identified as a member of God's people. Justification therefore is oriented toward the future, to the final vindication of God's people, not individuals, when God pronounces in their favor, declaring that they belong to the covenant.[301] Dunn is careful to maintain that justification by faith includes both individual and social dimensions:

This I say once again is what the "new perspective" is all about for me. It does *not* set this understanding of justification by faith in antithesis to the justification of the individual by faith. It is *not* opposed to the classic Reformed doctrine of justification. It simply observes that a social and ethnic dimension was part of the doctrine from its first formulation, was indeed integral to the first recorded exposition and defense of the doctrine—"Jew first but also Greek."[302]

He reiterates this point in the conclusion to "The New Perspective: Whence and Whither?": "Justification by faith was never simply about individuals as

298. Gottfried Martens, *Die Rechtfertigung des Sünders—Rettungshandeln Gottes oder historisches Interpretament?* (Göttingen: Vandenhoeck & Ruprecht, 1992), 164–65.

299. Walter Klaiber, *Rechtfertigung und Gemeinde: Eine Untersuchung zum paulinischen Kirchenverständnis*, FRLANT 127 (Göttingen: Vandenhoeck & Ruprecht, 1982). The same emphasis occurs in a later and more popular book by Klaiber on justification: *Gerecht vor Gott: Rechtfertigung in der Bibel und Heute* (Göttingen: Vandenhoeck & Ruprecht, 2000), 146–54.

300. Wright, *What Saint Paul Really Said*, 60, 116.

301. Wright, "Romans and the Theology of Paul," 32–33.

302. Dunn, "The New Perspective: Whence and Whither?" 33.

such. Paul's theology of justification had a social and corporate dimension that was integral to it."[303]

∽✧∽

What are the future prospects of Pauline interpretation for ecumenical discussion given the fact that Protestants and Catholics are now able not only to reread Paul together, but also to come to general agreement on how specific passages in the Pauline corpus ought to be understood? That this important achievement is possible at all is due primarily to the widespread acceptance and use of the historical-critical method by progressive scholars from major Christian denominations as a shared perspective from which to interpret and understand the Pauline letters as well as the New Testament as a whole. Critical biblical scholarship is essentially an ecumenical enterprise. The two largest biblical societies in the United States, the Society of Biblical Literature (founded in 1880) and the Catholic Biblical Association of America (founded in 1936), today have Protestant, Catholic, Orthodox, and Jewish members. Further, major biblical reference works published in the United States, such as Bible dictionaries (e.g., the six-volume *Anchor Bible Dictionary*, published in 1992, and the forthcoming five-volume *New Interpreter's Dictionary of the Bible*) and commentary series (e.g., the *Anchor Bible*) all have Protestant, Catholic, and Jewish contributors as part of stated policies. These ecumenical projects emphasize the shared heritage of Scripture and bode well for the future of biblical studies and Pauline studies in particular.

303. Ibid., 87.

Select Bibliography

Alexander, Philip S. "Torah and Salvation in Tannaitic Judaism." In Carson et al., eds., *Justification and Variegated Nomism*, 1:261–301.

Anderson, H. George, T. Austin Murphy, and Joseph A. Burgess, eds. *Justification by Faith*. Lutherans and Catholics in Dialogue 7. Minneapolis: Augsburg, 1985.

Avemarie, Friedrich. *Tora und Leben: Untersuchungen zur Heilsbeduntung der Tora in der frühen rabbinischen Literatur*. Tübingen: Mohr Siebeck, 1996.

Babcock, William S., ed. *Paul and the Legacies of Paul*. Dallas: Southern Methodist University Press, 1990.

Bassler, Jouette M., ed. *Pauline Theology*, vol. 1, *Thessalonians, Philippians, Galatians, Philemon*. Minneapolis: Fortress, 1991.

Becker, Jürgen. *Paul: Apostle to the Gentiles*. Translated by O. C. Dean Jr. Louisville: Westminster John Knox, 1993.

Beker, Johan Christiaan. *Paul the Apostle: The Triumph of God in Life and Thought*. Philadelphia: Fortress, 1980.

———. *Paul's Apocalyptic Gospel: The Coming Triumph of God*. Philadelphia: Fortress, 1982.

Boer, Martinus de. "Comment: Which Paul?" In *Paul and the Legacies of Paul*, ed. William S. Babcock. Dallas: Southern Methodist University Press, 1990.

Boyarin, Daniel. *A Radical Jew: Paul and the Politics of Identity*. Berkeley: University of California Press, 1994.

Braaten, Carl E., and Robert W. Jenson, eds. *Union with Christ: The New Finnish Interpretation of Luther.* Grand Rapids: Eerdmans, 1998.

Bultmann, Rudolf. *Theology of the New Testament.* Translated by Kendrick Grobel. 2 vols. New York: Scribner, 1951–1955.

Carson, D. A. "The Vindication of Imputation: On Fields of Discourse and Semantic Fields." In ed. Husbands and Treier, *Justification: What's at Stake in the Current Debates?*, 46–78.

Carson, D. A., Peter T. O'Brien, and Mark A. Seifrid, eds. *Justification and Variegated Nomism.* 2 vols. Tübingen: Mohr Siebeck; Grand Rapids: Baker Academic, 2001, 2004.

Conzelmann, Hans. *An Outline of the Theology of the New Testament.* Translated by John Bowden. New York and Evanston: Harper & Row, 1969.

Dahl, Nils Alstrup. "The Doctrine of Justification: Its Social Function and Implication." In *Studies in Paul: Theology for the Early Christian Mission,* 95–120. Minneapolis: Augsburg, 1977.

Das, A. Andrew. *Paul and the Jews.* Peabody, MA: Hendrickson, 2003.

———. *Paul, the Law, and the Covenant.* Peabody, MA: Hendrickson, 2001.

Davies, W. D. *Paul and Rabbinic Judaism: Some Rabbinic Elements in Pauline Theology.* 1948. Rev. ed., London: SPCK, 1955.

Deissmann, Adolf. *Paul: A Study in Social and Religious History.* Rev. and enlarged ed. New York: Harper & Row, 1957.

Dietzfelbinger, Christian. *Die Berufung des Paulus als Ursprung seiner Theologie.* Wissenschaftliche Monographien zum Alten und Neuen Testament 58. Neukirchen-Vluyn: Neukirchener Verlag, 1985.

Dodd, Brian J. *Paul's Paradigmatic "I": Personal Example as Literary Strategy.* Journal for the Study of the New Testament: Supplement Series 177. Sheffield: Sheffield Academic Press, 1999.

Dunn, James D. G. "4QMMT and Galatians." *New Testament Studies* 43 (1997): 147–53.

———. *Jesus, Paul, and the Law: Studies in Mark and Galatians.* Louisville: Westminster John Knox, 1990.

———. "The New Perspective on Paul," *Bulletin of the John Rylands University Library of Manchester* 65 (1983): 95–122. Repr. with an additional note in Dunn, *Jesus, Paul, and the Law: Studies in Mark and Galatians,* 183–214.

————. "The New Perspective: Whence, What and Whither?" In *The New Perspective on Paul*, 17–22. Wissenschaftliche Untersuchungen zum Alten und Neuen Testament 185. Tübingen: Mohr Siebeck, 2005.

————. *The Theology of Paul the Apostle*. Grand Rapids: Eerdmans, 1998.

Elliott, Neil. *Liberating Paul: The Justice of God and the Politics of the Apostle*. The Bible and Liberation Series. Maryknoll, NY: Orbis, 1994.

Ferguson, E., ed. *Studies in Early Christianity*, vol. 10, *Doctrines of Human Nature, Sin, and Salvation in the Early Church*. New York: Garland, 1993.

Fitzmyer, Joseph A., S.J. *Paul and His Theology: A Brief Sketch*. 2nd ed. Englewood Cliffs, NJ: Prentice Hall, 1989.

————. *Romans*. Anchor Bible 33. New York: Doubleday, 1993.

Froehlich, Karlfried. "Which Paul? Observations on the Image of the Apostle in the History of Biblical Exegesis." In *New Perspectives on Historical Theology: Essays in Memory of John Meyendorff*, edited by Bradley Nassif, 279–99. Grand Rapids: Eerdmans, 1996.

Gager, John G. *Reinventing Paul*. Oxford and New York: Oxford University Press, 2000.

Gaston, Lloyd. *Paul and the Torah*. Vancouver: University of British Columbia, 1987.

Gaventa, B. Roberts. *From Darkness to Light: Aspects of Conversion in the New Testament*. Overtures to Biblical Theology 20. Philadelphia: Fortress, 1986.

Gorday, Peter. *Principles of Patristic Exegesis: Romans 9–11 in Origen, John Chrysostom, and Augustine*. Studies in the Bible and Early Christianity 4. New York: Edwin Mellen, 1983.

Greer, Rowan. *The Captain of Our Salvation: A Study in the Patristic Exegesis of Hebrews*. Tübingen: J. C. B. Mohr, 1973.

Hay, David M., ed. *Pauline Theology*, vol. 2, *1 and 2 Corinthians*. Minneapolis: Fortress, 1993.

Hay, David M., and E. Elizabeth Johnson, eds. *Pauline Theology*, vol. 3, *Romans*. Minneapolis: Fortress, 1993.

Hays, Richard. *The Faith of Jesus Christ: The Narrative Substructure of Galatians 3:1–4:11*. Chico, CA: Scholars Press, 1983. 2nd ed., Grand Rapids: Eerdmans; Dearborn, MI: Dove, 2002.

Horsley, Richard A., ed. *Paul and Empire: Religion and Power in Roman Imperial Society*. Harrisburg, PA: Trinity Press International, 1997.

————, ed. *Paul and Politics: Ekklesia, Israel, Imperium, Interpretation: Essays in Honor of Krister Stendahl*. Harrisburg, PA: Trinity Press International, 2000.

Husbands, Mark, and Daniel J. Treier, eds. *Justification: What's at Stake in the Current Debates?* Downers Grove, IL: InterVarsity; Leicester: Apollos, 2004.

Jenson, Robert W. *Systematic Theology*. New York: Oxford University Press, 1997.

Johnson, E. Elizabeth, and David M. Hay, eds. *Pauline Theology*, vol. 4, *Looking Back, Pressing On*. Society of Biblical Literature Symposium Series 4. Atlanta: Scholars Press, 1997.

Johnson, Luke Timothy, and William Kurz. *The Future of Catholic Biblical Scholarship: A Constructive Conversation*. Grand Rapids: Eerdmans, 2002.

Jüngel, Eberhard. *Justification: The Heart of the Christian Faith: A Theological Study with an Ecumenical Purpose*. Translated by Jeffrey F. Cayzer. Edinburgh: T & T Clark, 2001.

————. "Um Gottes willen—Klarheit!" *ZTK* 94 (1997): 394–406.

Käsemann, Ernst. *Perspectives on Paul*. Philadelphia: Fortress, 1971.

Kertelge, Karl. "Paulus zur Rechtfertigung allein aus Glauben." In T. Söding, ed., *Worum Geht es in der Rechtfertigungslehre?*, 64–75.

————. *"Rechtfertigung" bei Paulus: Studien zur Struktur und zum Bedeutungsgehalt des paulinischen Rechtfertigungsbegriffs*. Neutestamentliche Abhandlungen 3. Münster: Aschendorff, 1967.

Kim, Seyoon. *The Origin of Paul's Gospel*. Grand Rapids: Eerdmans, 1981.

————. *Paul and the New Perspective: Second Thoughts on the Origin of Paul's Gospel*. Grand Rapids: Eerdmans, 2002.

Klaiber, Walter. *Gerecht vor Gott: Rechtfertigung in der Bibel und heute*. Biblisch-theologische Schwerpunkte 20. Göttingen: Vandenhoeck & Ruprecht, 2000.

Koester, Helmut. *Introduction to the New Testament*, vol. 2, *History and Literature of Early Christianity*. New York: Walter de Gruyter, 2000.

Kolb, Robert, and Timothy J. Wengert, eds. *The Book of Concord: The Confessions of the Evangelical Lutheran Church*. Minneapolis: Fortress, 2000.

Koperski, Veronica. *What Are They Saying about Paul and the Law?* New York: Paulist, 2001.

Lehmann, Karl, ed. *Justification by Faith: Do the Sixteenth-Century Condemnations Still Apply?* Translated by Michael Root and William G. Rusch. New York: Continuum, 1997.

Lehmann, Karl, and Wolfhart Pannenberg, eds. *The Condemnations of the Reformation Era: Do They Still Divide?* Translated by Margaret Kohl. Minneapolis: Fortress, 1989.

Lindemann, Andreas. *Paulus im ältesten Christentum: Das Bild des Apostels und die Rezeption der paulinischen Theologie in der frühchristlichen Literatur bis Marcion.* Beiträge zur historischen Theologie 58. Tübingen: J. C. B. Mohr (Paul Siebeck), 1979.

Luther, Martin. *Luther's Works.* American ed. St. Louis: Concordia; Philadelphia: Fortress, 1955.

Lutheran–Roman Catholic Joint Commission. *The Church and Justification: The Understanding of the Church in Light of the Doctrine of Justification.* Geneva: Lutheran World Federation, 1994.

The Lutheran World Federation and the Roman Catholic Church. *Joint Declaration on the Doctrine of Justification.* Grand Rapids: Eerdmans, 2000.

Malina, Bruce J., and Jerome H. Neyrey. *Portraits of Paul: An Archaeology of Ancient Personality.* Louisville: Westminster John Knox, 1996.

Marshall, Bruce D. "Justification as Declaration and Deification." *International Journal of Systematic Theology* 4 (2002): 3–28.

Martens, Gottfried. "Agreement and Disagreement on Justification by Faith Alone." *Concordia Theological Quarterly* 65:3 (July 2001): 195–223.

McGrath, Alister. *Iustitia Dei: A History of the Christian Doctrine of Justification.* 2nd ed. Cambridge: Cambridge University Press, 1998.

Meyer, Louis. *Saint Jean Chrysostome: Maître de perfection chrétienne.* Paris: G. Beauchesne et ses fils, 1933.

Mitchell, Margaret M. "The Archetypal Image: John Chrysostom's Portraits of Paul." *Journal of Religion* 75 (1995): 15–43.

———. *The Heavenly Trumpet: John Chrysostom and the Art of Pauline Interpretation.* Tübingen: Mohr Siebeck, 2000.

———. "Rhetorical Shorthand in Pauline Argumentation: The Functions of 'The Gospel' in the Corinthian Correspondence." In *Gospel in Paul: Studies on Corinthians, Galatians, and Romans for Richard N. Longenecker,* edited by L. Ann Jervis and Peter Richardson, 63–88. Journal for the Study of the New Testament Supplement Series 108. Sheffield: Sheffield Academic Press, 1994.

Moore, George Foote. *Judaism in the First Centuries of the Christian Era: The Age of the Tannaim*. 3 vols. Cambridge, MA: Harvard University Press, 1927–1930.

Neuhaus, Richard John. *Biblical Interpretation in Crisis: The Ratzinger Conference on Bible and Church*. Encounter Series 9. Grand Rapids: Eerdmans, 1989.

Oakman, Douglas E. "The Promise of Lutheran Biblical Studies." *Currents in Theology and Mission* 31/1 (February 2004): 40–52.

Plevnik, Joseph. *What Are They Saying about Paul?* New York: Paulist, 1986.

Reid, Gavin, ed. *The Great Acquittal: Justification by Faith and Current Christian Thought*. London: Collins, 1980.

Reumann, John. *"Righteousness" in the New Testament: "Justification" in the United States Lutheran–Roman Catholic Dialogue*. With responses by Joseph A. Fitzmyer and Jerome D. Quinn. Philadelphia: Fortress; New York: Paulist, 1982.

Root, Michael. "The Jubilee Indulgence and the *Joint Declaration on the Doctrine of Justification*." *Pro Ecclesia* 9 (Fall 2000): 460–75.

Sanders, E. P. *Paul*. Past Masters. Oxford: Oxford University Press, 1991.

———. *Paul and Palestinian Judaism: A Comparison of Patterns of Religion*. Philadelphia: Fortress, 1977.

———. *Paul, the Law, and the Jewish People*. Minneapolis: Fortress, 1983.

Schoeps, H. J. *Paul: The Theology of the Apostle in the Light of Jewish Religious History*. Translated by Harold Knight. Philadelphia: Westminster, 1961.

Schreiner, Thomas R. "Did Paul Believe in Justification by Works? Another Look at Romans 2." *Bulletin for Biblical Research* 3 (1993): 131–55.

———. *The Law and Its Fulfilment: A Pauline Theology of Law*. Grand Rapids: Baker, 1993.

———. *Paul, Apostle of God's Glory in Christ*. Downers Grove, IL: InterVarsity; Leicester: Apollos, 2001.

Segal, Alan F. *Paul the Convert: The Apostolate and Apostasy of Saul the Pharisee*. New Haven and London: Yale University Press, 1990.

Seifrid, Mark A. *Christ, Our Righteousness: Paul's Theology of Justification*. Downers Grove, IL: InterVarsity; Leicester: Apollos, 2000.

Smith, Jonathan Z. *Drudgery Divine: On the Comparison of Early Christianities and the Religions of Late Antiquity*. Chicago: University of Chicago Press, 1990.

Söding, Thomas, ed. *Worum geht es in der Rechtfertigungslehre? Das biblische Fundament der "Gemeinsamen Erklärung" von Katholischer Kirche und Lutherischem Weltbund*. Quaestiones Disputatae 180. Freiburg: Herder, 1999.

Stendahl, Krister. "The Apostle Paul and the Introspective Conscience of the West." *Harvard Theological Review* 56 (1963): 199–215. Repr. in *The Writings of Paul: Annotated Text and Criticism*, edited by W. A. Meeks, 422–34. Norton Critical Editions in the History of Ideas. New York: W. W. Norton, 1972.

―――. *Paul among Jews and Gentiles*. Philadelphia: Fortress, 1976.

Stowers, Stanley K. *A Rereading of Romans: Justice, Jews, and Gentiles*. New Haven and London: Yale University Press, 1994.

Strecker, Christian. *Die liminale Theologie des Paulus: Zugänge zur paulinischen Theologie aus kulturanthropologischer Perspektive*. Forschungen zur Religion und Literatur des Alten und Neuen Testaments 185. Göttingen: Vandenhoeck & Ruprecht, 1999.

Tappert, Theodore G., ed. and trans. *The Book of Concord: The Confessions of the Lutheran Church*. Philadelphia: Fortress, 1959.

Thielman, Frank. *Paul and the Law: A Contextual Approach*. Downers Grove, IL: InterVarsity, 1994.

Westerholm, Stephen. *Perspectives Old and New on Paul: The "Lutheran" Paul and His Critics*. Grand Rapids: Eerdmans, 2004.

Wiles, Maurice. *The Divine Apostle: The Interpretation of St Paul's Epistles in the Early Church*. Cambridge: Cambridge University Press, 1967.

Williamson, Peter S. "Catholic Principles for Interpreting Scripture." *Catholic Biblical Quarterly* 65 (2003): 327–49.

―――. *Catholic Principles for Interpreting Scripture: A Study of the Pontifical Biblical Commission's "The Interpretation of the Bible in the Church."* Subsidia Biblica 22. Rome: Pontifical Biblical Institute, 2001.

Wrede, William. *Paulus*. 2nd ed. Tübingen: Mohr Siebeck, 1907.

Wright, N. T. *The Climax of the Covenant: Christ and the Law in Pauline Theology*. Minneapolis: Fortress, 1992.

―――. "The Paul of History and the Apostle of Faith." *Tyn Bul* 29 (1978): 61–88.

————. "Paul's Gospel and Caesar's Empire." In Horsley, ed., *Paul and Politics: Ekklesia, Israel, Imperium, Interpretation: Essays in Honor of Krister Stendahl*, 160–83. Harrisburg, PA: Trinity Press International, 2000.

————. *What Saint Paul Really Said: Was Paul of Tarsus the Real Founder of Christianity?* Grand Rapids: Eerdmans, 1997.

Yeago, David. "Lutheran–Roman Catholic Consensus on Justification: The Theological Achievement of the 'Joint Declaration.'" *Pro Ecclesia* 7 (1998): 449–70.

Yinger, K. L. *Paul, Judaism, and Judgment according to Deeds*. SNTSMS 105. Cambridge: Cambridge University Press, 1999.

Subject Index

255

Index of Ancient Sources

Index of Modern Authors